CW01301055

THE SECRET LIFE OF LEGO® BRICKS

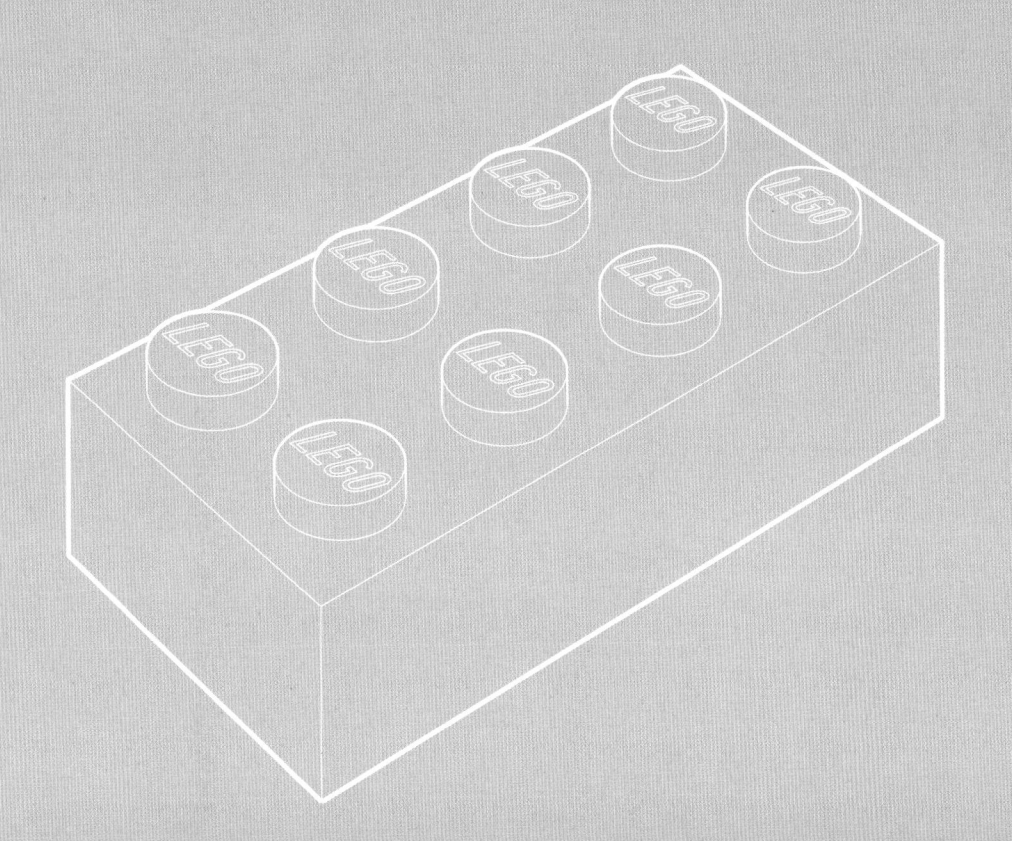

THE SECRET LIFE OF LEGO® BRICKS

Daniel Konstanski

unbound

LEGO, the LEGO logo, the Minifigure, the Knob and Brick configurations, DUPLO and the DUPLO logo, BELVILLE and the BELVILLE logo, FRIENDS and the FRIENDS logo, NINJAGO and the NINJAGO logo, HIDDEN SIDE and the HIDDEN SIDE logo, LEGENDS OF CHIMA and the LEGENDS OF CHIMA logo, NEXO KNIGHTS and the NEXO KNIGHTS logo, BIONICLE and the BIONICLE logo, MINDSTORMS and the MINDSTORMS logo and LEGOLAND are trademarks of the LEGO Group. ©2024 The LEGO Group.

Manufactured by AMEET Sp. z o.o. under licence from the LEGO Group.

AMEET Sp. z o.o.
Nowe Sady 6, 94-102, Łódź – Poland
ameet@ameet.eu
www.ameet.eu

First published in 2022 by Unbound

The edition published in 2024 by Unbound
Level 1, Devonshire House, One Mayfair Place, London W1J 8AJ
www.unbound.com
All rights reserved

No part of this publication may be copied, reproduced, stored in a retrieval system, or transmitted, in any form or by any means without the prior permission of the publisher, nor be otherwise circulated in any form of binding or cover other than that in which it is published and without a similar condition being imposed on the subsequent purchaser.

BATMAN and all related characters and elements © & ™ DC. (s24)

WIZARDING WORLD characters, names and related indicia are © & ™ Warner Bros. Entertainment Inc. WB SHIELD: © & ™ WBEI. Publishing Rights © JKR. (s24)

FANTASTIC BEASTS characters, names and related indicia are © & ™ Warner Bros. Entertainment Inc. WB SHIELD: ™ & © WBEI. WIZARDING WORLD trademark and logo © & ™ Warner Bros. Entertainment Inc. Publishing Rights © JKR. (s24)

© New Line Productions, Inc. All rights reserved. THE LORD OF THE RINGS: THE FELLOWSHIP OF THE RING, THE LORD OF THE RINGS: THE TWO TOWERS and THE LORD OF THE RINGS: THE RETURN OF THE KING and the names of the characters, items, events and places therein are ™ of The Saul Zaentz Company d/b/a Middle-earth Enterprises under license to New Line Productions, Inc. (s24)

© Warner Bros. Entertainment Inc. All rights reserved. THE HOBBIT: AN UNEXPECTED JOURNEY, THE HOBBIT: THE DESOLATION OF SMAUG and THE HOBBIT: BATTLE OF FIVE ARMIES and the names of the characters, items, events and places therein are TM of The Saul Zaentz Company d/b/a Middle-earth Enterprises under license to New Line Productions, Inc. (s24)

THE LEGO® MOVIE™ and THE LEGO® MOVIE 2™ © & ™, Warner Bros. Entertainment Inc. & The LEGO Group. LEGO, the LEGO logo, DUPLO, the Minifigure and the Brick and Knob configurations are trademarks and/or copyrights of the LEGO Group. ©2022 The LEGO Group. All rights reserved. WB SHIELD: ™ & © WBEI. (s24)

© & ™ 2024 LUCASFILM LTD.

Nickelodeon's SpongeBob SquarePants and Avatar used with permission by ©2024 ViacomCBS Media Networks. All rights reserved. Nickelodeon, all related titles, characters, and logos are trademarks owned by ViacomCBS Media Networks, a division of Viacom International Inc.

TM & © 2021 Columbia Pictures Industries, Inc. All Rights Reserved.

"Mercedes-Benz" and the design of the enclosed product are subject to intellectual property protection owned by Daimler AG. They are used by The LEGO Group under license.

The Volvo trademarks (word and device) are registered trademarks of Volvo Trademark Holding AB and are used pursuant to a license.

Other trademarks and trade names are those of their respective owners.

The trademarks CLAAS, XERION and the corresponding colour trademarks are owned by CLAAS KGaA mbH. They are used by LEGO System A/S under license.

Under license of Porsche AG.

The Bugatti logo and Bugatti wordmark are trademarks of Bugatti International S.A. and are used under license.

© A.P. Moller – Maersk

Text design by Amazing15

ISBN 978-1-800-18350-6

Printed at Hung Hing ShenZhen, China

1 3 5 7 9 8 6 4 2

**To adult fans of the
LEGO® brick everywhere**

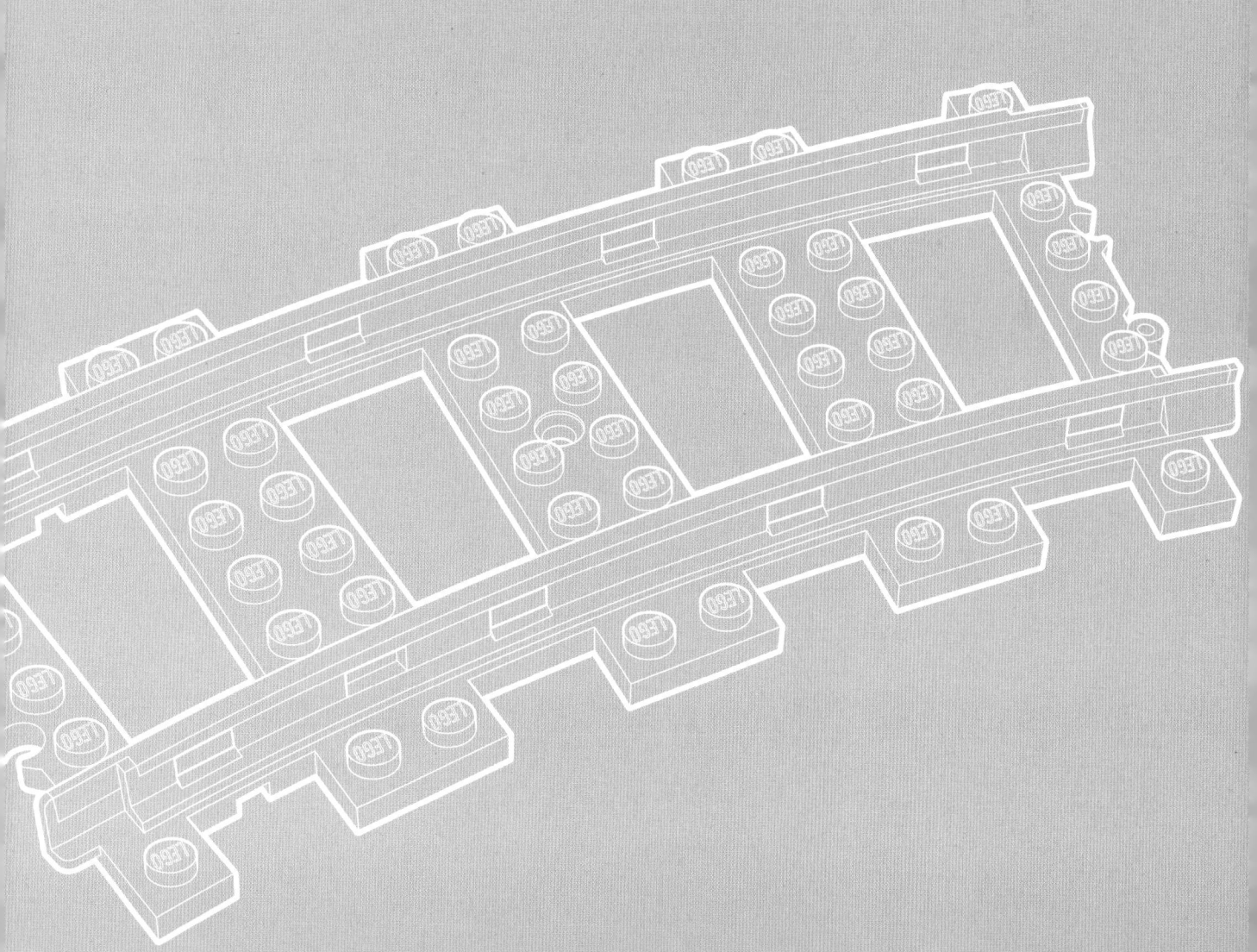

Contents

	Introduction	1
1	Seeing the System	4
2	Rolling Along	26
3	Populating the LEGO® World	58
4	Past, Present and Future	84
5	Monorails and Rollercoasters	114
6	Everyday Life	132
7	Building at the Highest Level	166
8	New Worlds	198
9	Playing with Story	220
10	Big Bangs	250
11	Everything is Awesome	284
	Epilogue	314
	A Note on Colour	317
	A Note on Sources	319
	Acknowledgements	321
	Index	323

Fig. 1

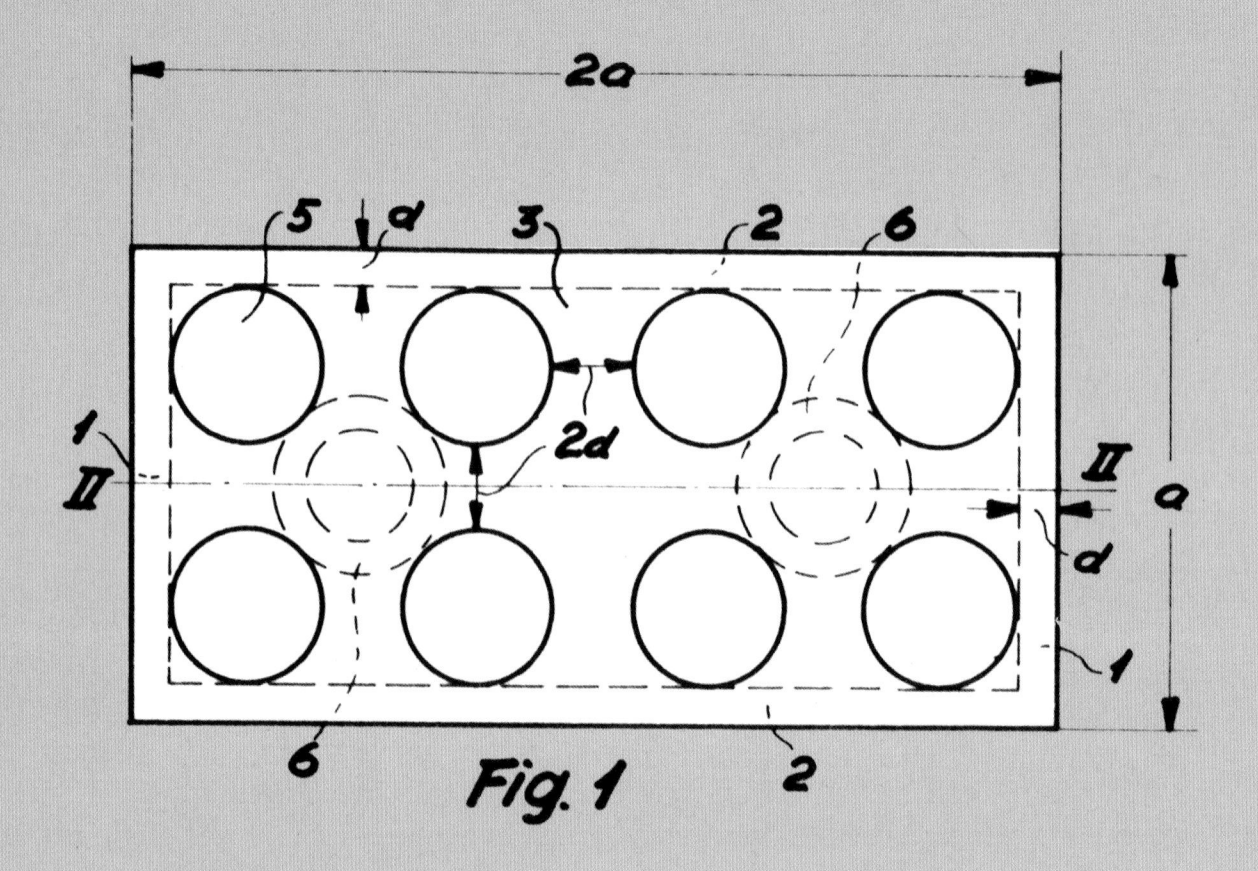

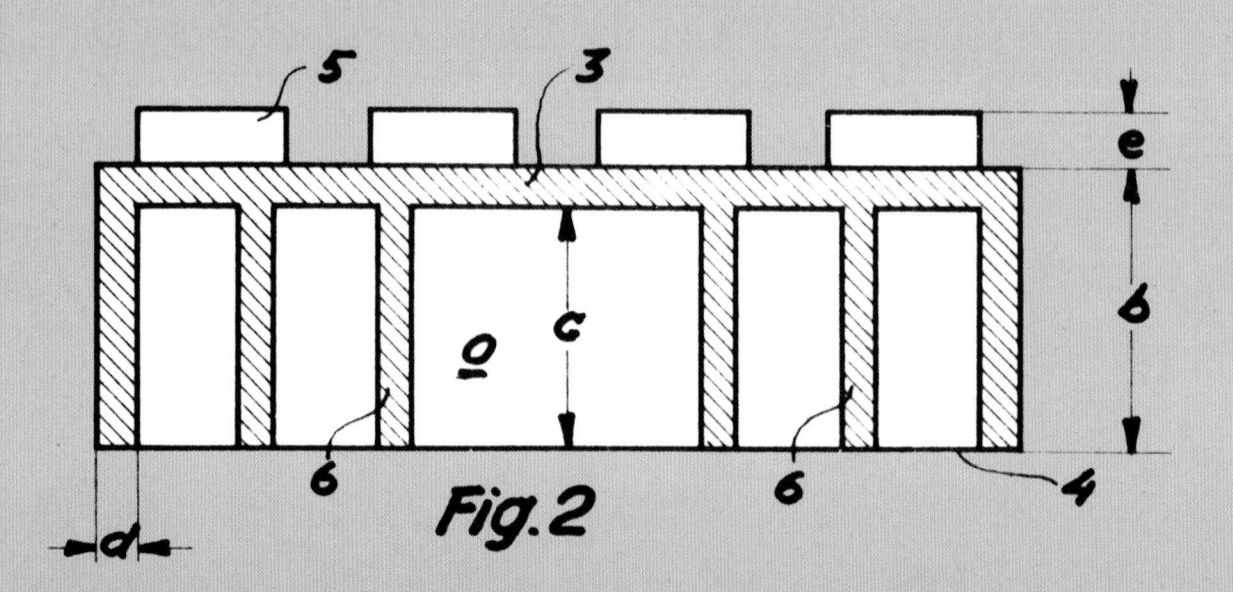

Fig. 2

Introduction

I thought it would be a simple question. I was wrong. Over the course of nearly fifty interviews – some with employees who had worked for the LEGO Group all the way back in the 1960s – I asked one question in particular over and over again. My mission was to discover for myself the stories behind LEGO® bricks and this particular one was becoming my holy grail.

I remember distinctly when the question first arose. This book, *The Secret Life of* LEGO® *Bricks*, was selected by fans via an online vote from three different options. It was a week after I had learned the result and my mind had not stopped racing: there were so many exciting possibilities. Much like the many designers and company insiders I would soon get to speak with, I had been given my own open-ended brief from the Publishing team at the LEGO Group and its fans. I had been entrusted with the responsibility of picking which tantalising stories and secrets I should try to uncover from a host of options. That evening I sat mulling over different ideas with a small pile of random bricks on the table in front of me. Amid the contemplation, it occurred to me to do something that, despite having written professionally about LEGO bricks for more than half a decade, on top of collecting and building continuously for over 30 years, I had never done before: I examined a brick.

From the table I picked up the most basic and iconic of all LEGO elements, a red 2×4. Almost immediately attributes and questions began figuratively leaping off the page at me. How did these plastic bricks stick together? I knew it had to do with the proprietary studs on top and tubes beneath, but how did they actually work? Where did this design and its dimensions come from? Picking up a second 2×4 brick, I noticed differences in wall thickness. Why was that the case? LEGO bricks work so well that I had never needed to stop and think about how they actually functioned, but as I sat there really looking at one for the first time, it occurred to me how little I knew about these toys I loved so much.

In the days and weeks that followed I got an education, and a team. Simon Beecroft, who served as editorial director and my 'handler', as I came to think of him, worked with me to develop the book plan, which was vetted and approved by the Publishing team at the LEGO Group. Next came one of this project's greatest joys. I was granted access to the very heart of the LEGO Group history: the digital archive. In this inner sanctum resides tens of thousands of documents and images going all the way back to the 1800s. Signe Wiese, one of the LEGO Group corporate historians, and a friend from many previous collaborations on projects, graciously

OPPOSITE Images like this one, from the LEGO brick's Danish patent, helped me to understand more than ever before exactly how elements work.

approved my hundreds of requests for numerous files to examine.

Concurrent with constant deep dives into the archives came a frenzy of networking. Randi Sørensen, a Senior Editor in the Publishing team at the LEGO Group, came alongside to be my champion and guide through the maze that is the company's inner workings. I came with a list of key elements and questions. Randi took them and began asking anyone and everyone to connect us with people who could provide answers.

Over the weeks and months that followed, names came pouring in, each of whom I interviewed. I spoke with machine technicians, set designers, marketers, element masters, outside vendors and many more. Revelations came pouring in, and many interviews yielded even more names to track down. It was an awe-inspiring experience.

At the beginning I thought that each brick or theme examined would have, more or less, a stand-alone story. What emerged instead was a lineage. Ideas built, refined, sometimes discarded and then brought back for consideration again and again to see if they could meet the needs of a new era. Each successive generation had been inspired by and built upon the solutions and ideas that came before; an unbroken creative line that reached all the way back to Ole Kirk Kristiansen, the LEGO Group founder. Nothing had been developed in a vacuum, and the tapestry of stories turned out to be far richer and more vibrant than I could have imagined. The harvest was plentiful, but one answer eluded me, and getting to the bottom of that question became my own personal mission.

After my moment of contemplation with the 2×4 brick, I had subsequently dug deeply into its dimensions. I wanted to know why its creators selected those particular measurements, specifically its length, width and height. Length and width quickly revealed their logic. They were nice, even intervals. Height, on the other hand, proved frustratingly elusive. When the other two dimensions had been so clean, the height – a fractional number – seemed an odd selection. What was so magical about this value? As the interview circuit started, I thought it would be an easy question to answer; after all, someone in the company would know – but who?

After talking to the LEGO Group foremost element master, a man who had worked at the company for over forty years, I began to think I would never find an answer. According to him, that knowledge was buried deeply in LEGO history. Reluctantly, I set aside my quest, only to have a discovery rekindle it three weeks later.

During one of my dives into the digital archive I came across a file labelled 'Original LEGO Brick Patent'. I took no notice at first. After all, this patent has been available for years; prints of it can be found on LEGO.com. But then I noticed something. The file had a lot more pages

ABOVE LEFT Some images from the archive were just bizarre and others humorous, like this minifigure knight, who was surfing on a shield long before Legolas in *The Lord of the Rings: The Two Towers!*

ABOVE RIGHT Finding images like this one, which shows multiple unreleased sets and parts, most notably the gorgeous road plates, were some of the greatest delights as I plumbed the LEGO Group archive.

that I would have expected. My instincts tingled as I opened the file to be greeted by scans of a document completely in Danish.

After scrolling through a few pages, something became apparent in spite of the language barrier: this was not the same patent emblazoned on prints and t-shirts. I would later determine that those motifs come from excerpts of the American patent, which was filed over a decade after the document that now stared back at me from the computer screen. This was the original.

I scrolled down, not realising I was holding my breath, until it came rushing out as an involuntary shout. Several pages in, something leapt from the screen. After many lines of text in Danish, which I could not read, I saw numbers arranged in two mathematical equations. I could work with equations, even if the wording around them remained elusive. Perhaps these equations would help me to understand the reasons for the specific height of a LEGO brick. In fact, at first, they made the whole picture far muddier, but after several weeks of returning to them over and over again, I finally began to comprehend the two foundational relationships from which every LEGO brick ever created has been derived. Finally, I knew why the basic LEGO brick is the height it is... and very soon you will too.

ABOVE From childhood, I had always wondered how the old LEGO® Aquazone backgrounds were made. Thanks to thousands of behind-the-scenes images from promotional photoshoots across every theme in the archives, I got my answer.

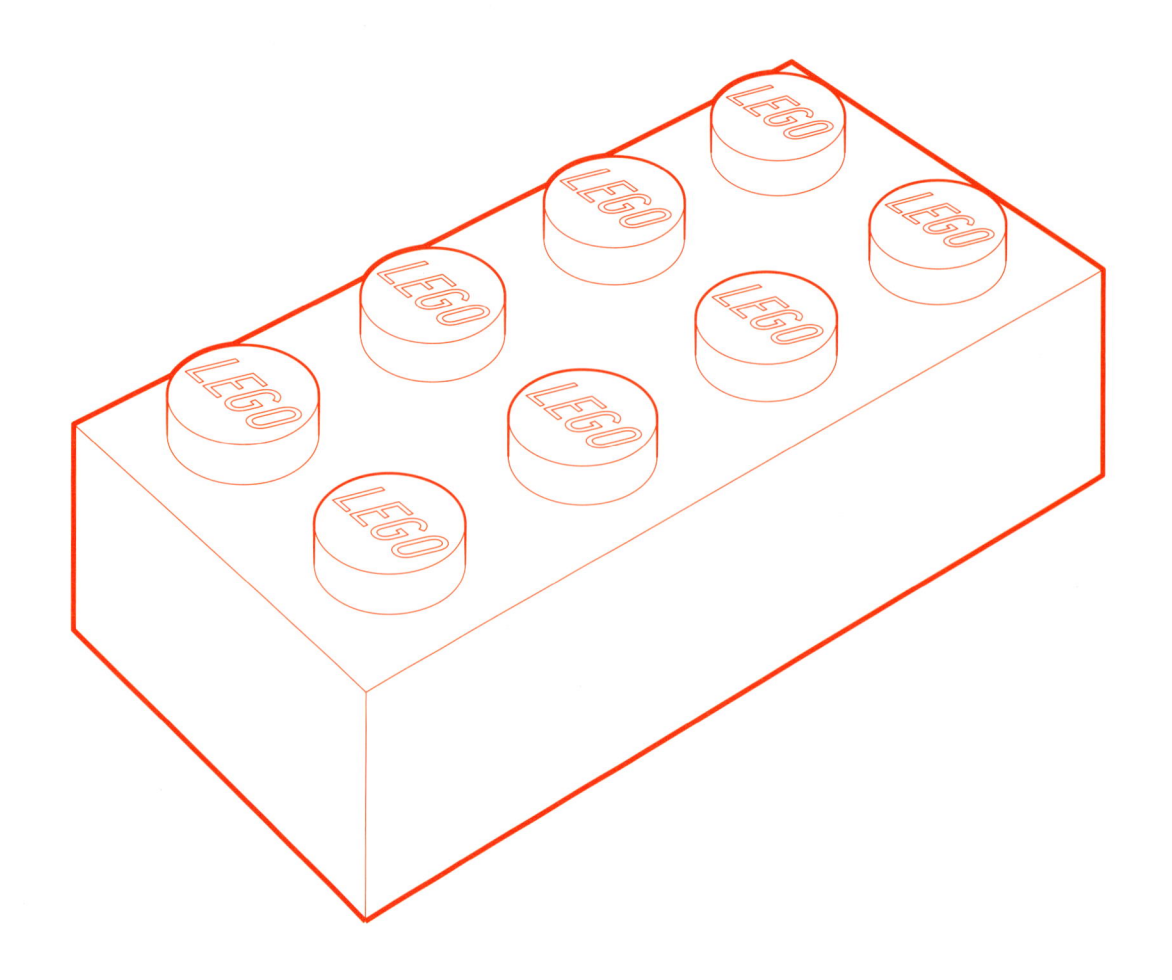

> On January 28, at 1:58 p.m., the patent was handed in and the LEGO brick as we know it today was born.

Jetta Orduna, Head of LEGO® Idea House

1

Seeing the System

The invention of LEGO® bricks and the science of how they work

TOP The first LEGO® trees stood on small, integrated stands at their base.

BOTTOM The classic 2×4 stud brick has been the foundational element of the LEGO® System in Play since the very beginning.

The dark workshop sat empty. LEGO® models of all shapes and sizes dotted every flat surface. Work desks, tops of cabinets and shelves along the walls were filled with castles, aeroplanes and Moon bases. Some would go on to be approved for production, becoming the stuff of legend and defining childhood play for untold numbers of children

BELOW LEGO designer Jan Ryaa working on a LEGO® Technic model in LEGO Futura in 1979.

BOTTOM LEGO Futura office in the early 1980s.

Godtfred Kirk Christiansen, the LEGO Group second-generation owner, referred to throughout the company as 'GKC', would often make after-hours visits to the design workshop known during the 1970s and 1980s as LEGO Futura. These visits were a touchstone with the springs from which all his company's products flowed. For decades Godtfred Kirk Christiansen would peruse the various worktables to admire the models on which his designers, all of whom he knew by name, were working. Employees remember returning to their desks in the morning and seeing faint traces of cigar ash, a sign that the owner had inspected a detail on their model. During the working day, Godtfred Kirk Christiansen would often also offer thoughts on specific designs to their creators. Such lines of communication worked both ways. Futura employees would sometimes attempt to seek approval for a new model or element from the owner himself.

Godtfred Kirk Christiansen had a passion for design that kept him coming back to Futura after hours. He was also the inventor, years before, of the LEGO® System in Play. One of the reasons that children love LEGO bricks is because they are reliable. It wouldn't matter how appealing a set looked if the bricks didn't snap and click together securely in that distinctive, satisfying way, not budging until pulled apart. Godtfred Kirk Christiansen had created the LEGO System in Play to ensure this perfect reliability, on which his company depended. He had perfected it through years of experimentation and protected it far and wide with patents across the world. Finally, in his later years, he stood guard as a sentinel, watching to make sure that the traits of excellence, reliability and versatility, which were the foundation of the LEGO® System, remained his designers' guiding stars.

Inventing a System

The 2×4 brick was the brick on which the LEGO System was built, and its story begins on a frigid ferry ride in January 1954 somewhere between the UK and Denmark. Godtfred Kirk Christiansen and the head of the toy department from one of Copenhagen's most distinguished department stores were returning from a toy fair in Brighton, England, by ferry and struck up a conversation.

ABOVE Godtfred Kirk Christiansen was the LEGO Group second-generation owner.

It turned into a lengthy discourse and eventually the buyer, a man named Troels Petersen, offered a perceptive critique of the toy industry. Years later, after the LEGO brick became popular, Troels Petersen was sought out and interviewed about this insight and he recalled the story as follows: 'We had a long discussion until well after midnight. Of course, we talked about toys. During our discussion, Godtfred Kirk Christiansen asked me what I thought about the toy industry. I said it all seemed very muddled, as though there was no system.'

Godtfred realised his fellow passenger was right and his father Ole Kirk Kristiansen's company was no exception. Since 1932 they had made individual toys. Each toy was a one-off. No two products were intentionally designed to work together, let alone be underlain by a system which informed their design. Craftspeople worked on products that they thought would appeal to children, end of story.

Upon returning home, Godtfred cast a critical eye over all of the LEGO Group toys to see if any might be able to support such a system. No product was left unscrutinised, whether it was made of wood or plastic. Despite having so many options, only one ended up meeting the criteria Godtfred created for an ideal product that might satisfy the demand for a system outlined by his fellow ferry-goer. The winner was the small, stacking, plastic bricks that his father had begun

ABOVE Ole Kirk Kristiansen, founder and original owner of the LEGO Group.

RIGHT In 1957, Town Plan layouts were one of the first incarnations of the LEGO System in Play.

BELOW Early bricks were hollow on the inside and had slits on the side.

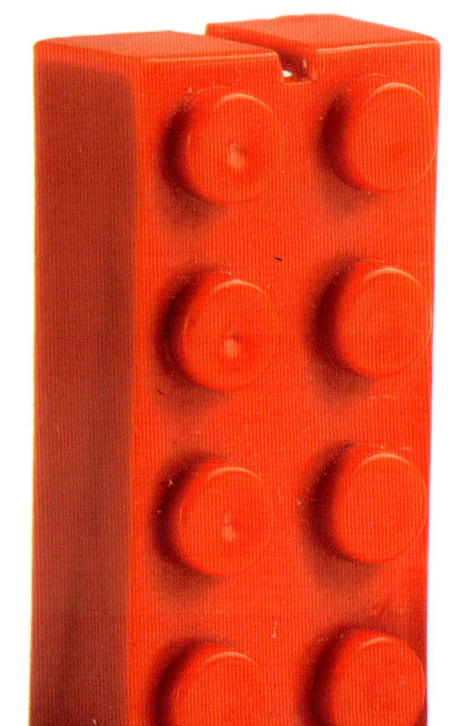

producing in 1949. At the time, the family saw plastic bricks as a sideline and wooden toys as the company's core business. In a newspaper interview of the time, Godtfred had said, 'You can make nice, cute things in plastic, but wood is a stronger material.' Although those plastic bricks had enjoyed only minimal success to date, they were going to transform the company.

Godtfred Kirk Christiansen's vision was an entirely new approach to toys, which he called 'the LEGO System in Play'. His idea was to use the plastic bricks to create different categories of models, all to the same scale, and sell them as sets. Together, these sets could create a town with buildings, vehicles and foliage. All the sets were designed to work together year after year, built of the same selection of compatible elements, but sold separately. While this approach would become widespread throughout the toy industry later, it was revolutionary at the time.

The first incarnation of Godtfred Kirk Christiansen's LEGO System evolved into a line of products known as Town Plan, which consisted of different playmats on which buildings made of bricks could be placed, intermixed with vehicles, pedestrians and trees. Town Plan sets would last into the 1970s before morphing into the LEGOLAND® Town theme after the introduction of the minifigure in 1978.

There was, however, a challenge. As of 1953, just before the fortuitous ferry ride, the LEGO Group produced fewer than two dozen elements, not nearly enough to realise Godtfred Kirk

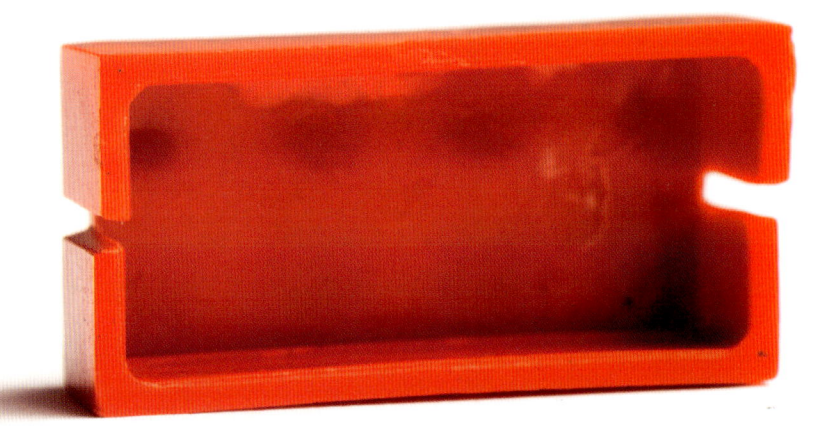

> It took a year and a half to develop the concepts and elements for the System in Play before its launch in October 1955. When Godtfred Kirk Christiansen got an idea, it was all hands on deck. He was very good at inspiring his team to do their best and to come up with new ideas themselves. The idea was to create a realistic urban setting in a Danish style. In the mid 1950s, many more people could now afford a house and a car. Then, of course, you needed gas stations, and so it went on.

Jetta Orduna, Head of LEGO Idea House

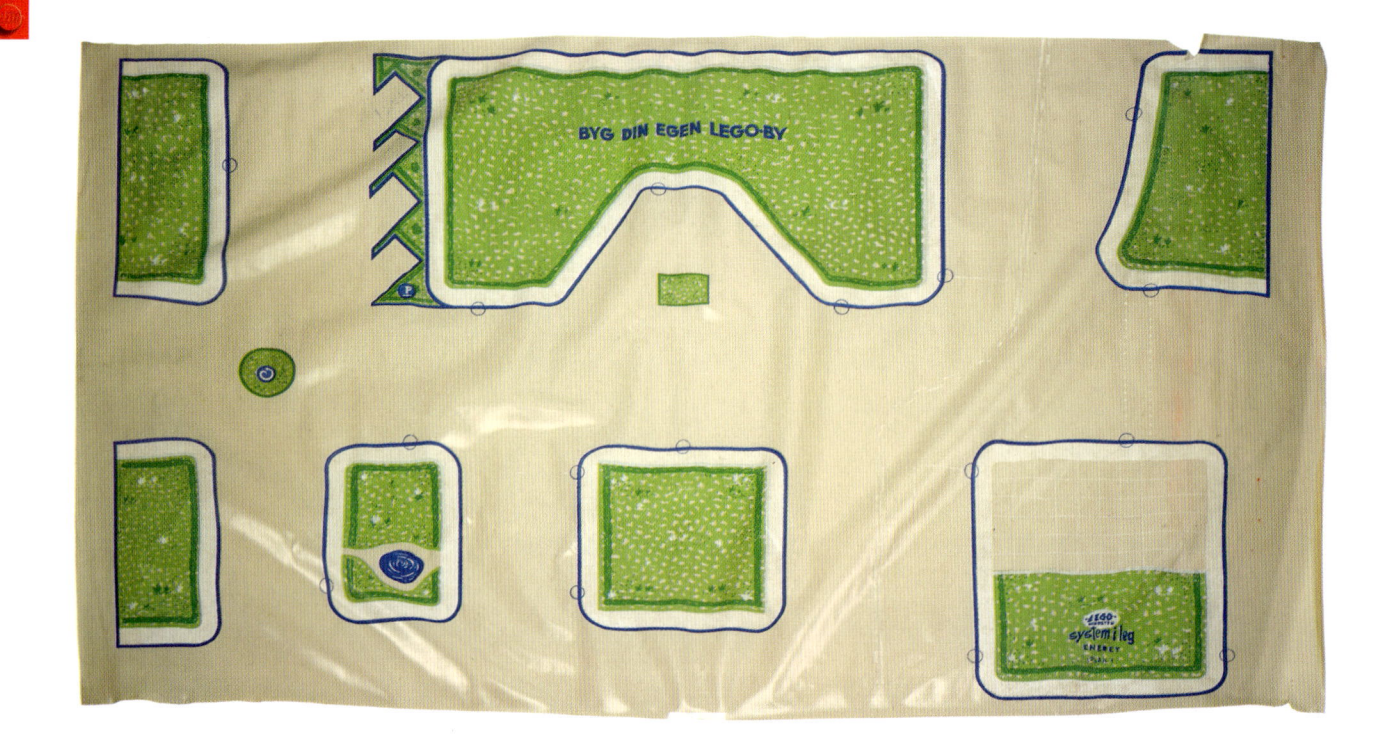

ABOVE Playmats were released with the first Town Plan sets.

Christiansen's grand vision. Furthermore, all of those elements were basic, consisting of bricks with 2×2 and 2×4 studs respectively, as well as a few types of windows and doors.

Realising that more types of bricks would be needed, Godtfred and his team began observing the architecture and shapes around them as Denmark modernised. At some point, they started making sketches of new elements on special pieces of paper printed with a grid of circles to represent brick studs, referred to in the LEGO Group as 'knobs'. By 1956 the LEGO Group had grown its assortment to more than sixty distinct elements in support of Godtfred Kirk Christiansen's vision. Curved elements, early plates and a large baseplate, among others, added versatility.

A second major change was to consolidate colours. Early building bricks had been produced in an array of hues. This was not an issue when selling individual boxes of assorted elements intended only for free building, but it became more challenging as the goal turned towards uniform aesthetics across a range of official model sets. The rainbow of brick colours was reduced so that the majority of elements appeared in two main pigments, white and red, with one major, clever exception.

Early moulding machines produced an amount of wastage during normal operation. Throughout the day employees would collect the various moulding sprues, products that didn't meet quality standards, and random bits that had been clipped off finished items. Bricks were not the only plastic toys made by the company at this time, so there were a host of sources to draw from. All of this, in its many colours, would go into a machine which ground the bits back into granules so they could be reused. Rather than try to sort and colour match, the mixed batch from the grinder would be supplemented with new granules and re-moulded, creating a random yet beautiful mix of colours unique to each and every batch.

This recycled plastic was used for a variety of toys, called 'marbled products', in which the mismatched colours would not matter, such as baby rattles and some early bricks. In order to preserve this efficient practice, marbled plastic also was used for elements that were ultimately painted, most notably the first LEGO trees. This clever solution preserved the waste-saving practice of using marbled plastic even after other colours were eliminated.

Seeing the System   13

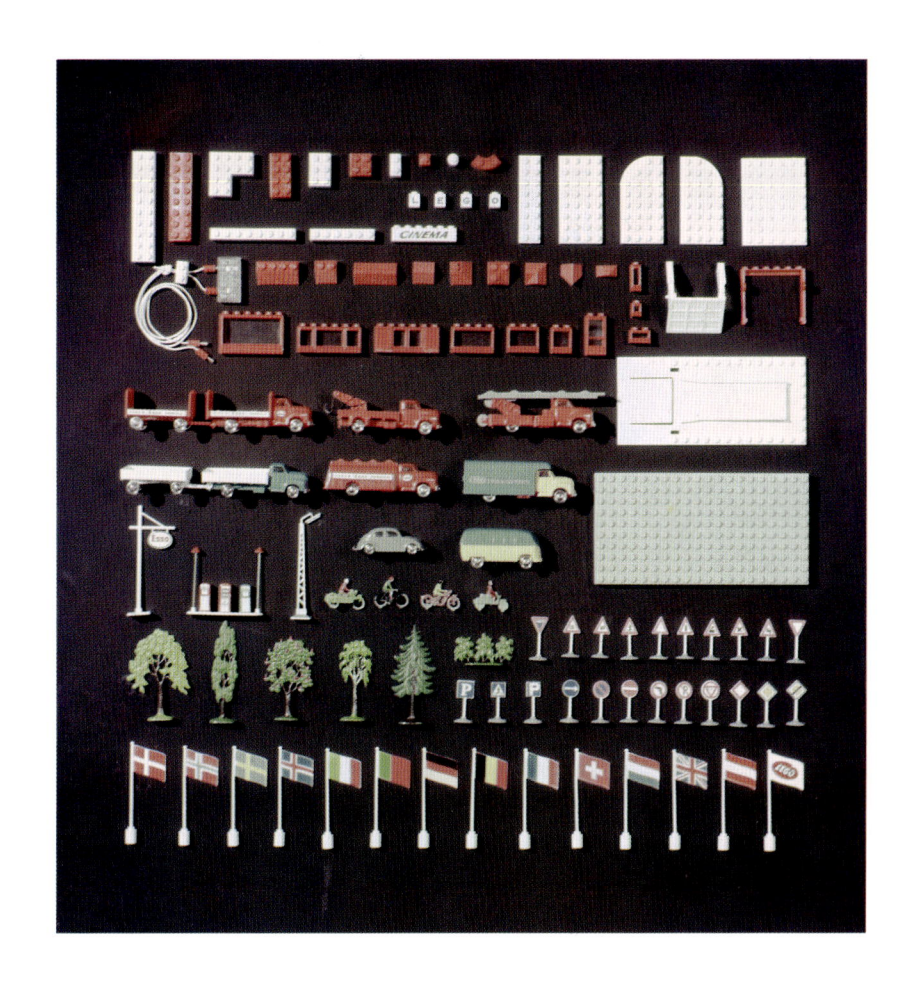

LEFT Many new elements were developed for Town Plan sets, including trees, flags, street furniture and vehicles, all of which were not made of bricks.

BELOW Early LEGO trees were created without studs or tubes.

Upon its debut in 1955, the LEGO System in Play Town Plan line was a success at none other than Troels Petersen's department store in Copenhagen, and quickly solidified itself in Godtfred Kirk Christiansen's mind as the future of the company. The influx of new elements had done its job and fortunately there was still at least one piece of the special gridded paper left after the flurry of design work. Godtfred Kirk Christiansen would soon need it, because the LEGO System, and the 2×4 brick especially, were about to be further improved.

The search for stability

In the middle of a cold January in 1958, Axel Thomsen, head of the LEGO sales company in Germany, travelled to Billund. After thawing from his trip, Axel sat down with Godtfred Kirk Christiansen and explained a challenge he was facing, one he had become aware of through many letters sent by purchasers of LEGO products

LEGO bricks were selling well in Germany, but children and parents were finding that models were not always stable. Up to that time, all bricks produced by the company were completely hollow on their undersides. In theory, when two of them were pressed together, the walls of the brick above would contact the studs, or knobs, of the brick below. That contact was meant to force the upper brick's walls out slightly while at the same time the elastic properties of plastic would try to force the brick back into its original shape, squeezing the knobs and creating grip.

However, the points of contact – already quite small – were weakened by minor inconsistencies in brick sizes thanks to plastic injection-moulding technology still being in its infancy. The end result was that elements did not always stick together reliably. When children tried to move their models, they would often see them fall apart.

When Axel Thomsen consulted with Godtfred Kirk Christiansen, the LEGO owner took a piece of the special gridded paper. He and Axel huddled together and over the next few hours produced an array of options to achieve what Godtfred called 'clutch power', a gripping force that would allow elements to firmly and reliably cleave together.

Without testing, Godtfred Kirk Christiansen had no idea how much surface area needed to be in contact between two bricks in order for them to stick together satisfactorily, so he sketched every option possible within a 2×4 brick's underside that he could contrive. Two variants of the now famous hollow tube approach were ultimately joined by seven other possibilities, including crosses and several other shapes. Godtfred was pretty sure tubes were the answer, but he decided to be exhaustive nevertheless. It is significant, however, that while all options were sketched, only one got its own special piece of paper, which, despite not being nearly so neat as even grids of knobs, was just as important. It would go on to eventually supplement the official patent in the LEGO Group archives.

Brick proportions

On that piece of paper, two foundational proportions were defined, from which all LEGO bricks are derived. One has a formal name within the patent: 'modules'. The other will be referred to in this book as 'sections', as no official designation has been found.

The attribute that was causing the reliability problems was the wall thickness. The right dimension was not known. It would need to be determined later through experimentation, but whatever thickness was found to achieve an acceptable clutch power would need to be used. Therefore, every other dimension was based around this as-of-yet-unknown wall thickness value which, from this point forward, will be called a section.

Next, the distance was defined from one interior wall to the other beneath a brick with only one row of studs – a distance of three sections. Therefore, a single-width brick would be five sections across: two wall thicknesses (one on each side) plus the open space in between. This dimension was given its own name: a module, equal to five sections (see diagram 1 on page 18).

Once a brick's width was defined, it dictated each stud's diameter, which must be three

OPPOSITE Godtfred Kirk Christiansen sketched his designs for achieving clutch power on a piece of paper printed with a grid of knobs, or studs.

Seeing the System 15

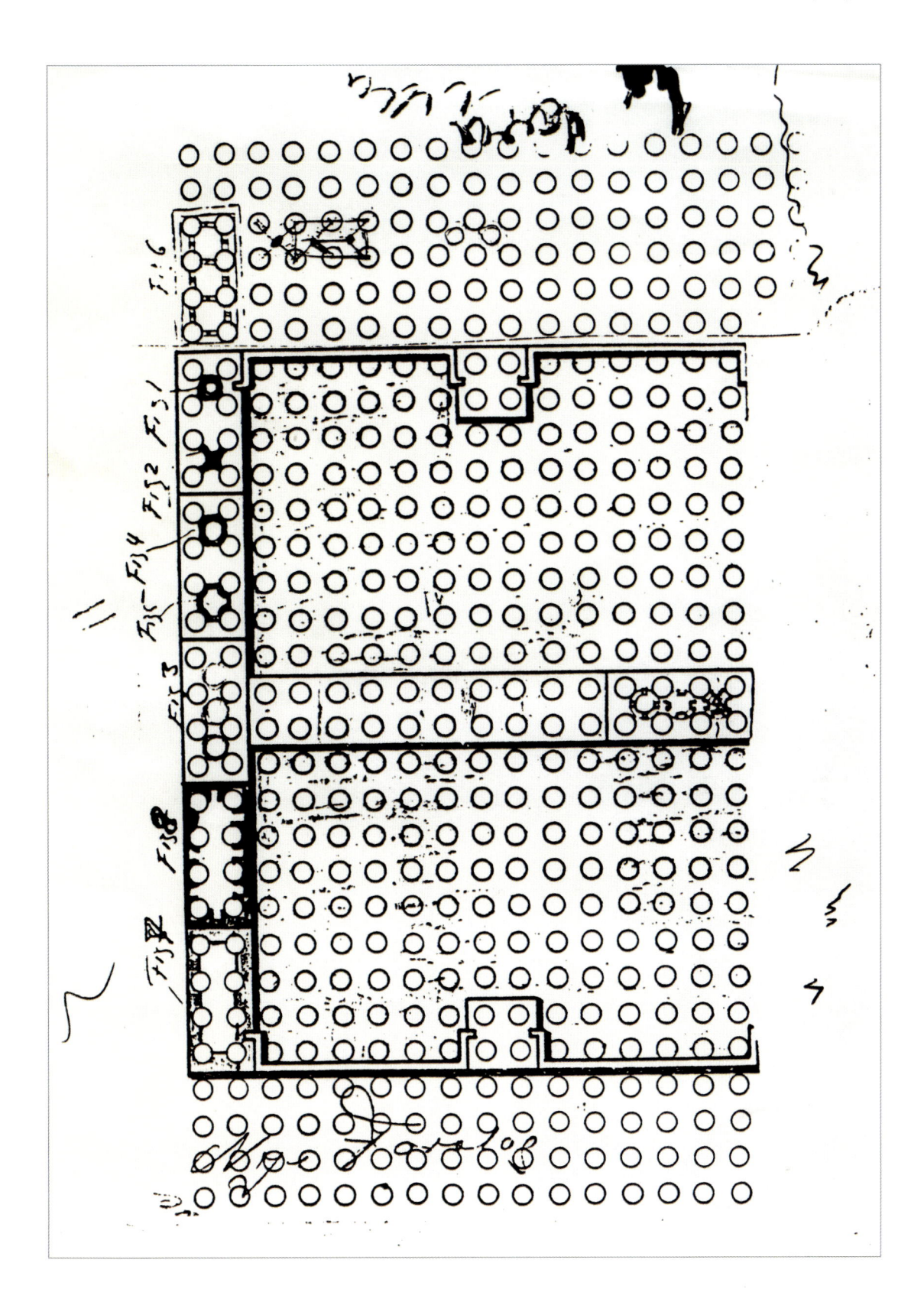

"

Godtfred Kirk Christiansen and Axel Thomsen met on January 23, 1958. During their meeting that afternoon they discussed the issue of lack of clutch power in the bricks and Godtfred made some drawings [of the stud and tube principle] on a piece of paper. The next day, Godtfred went to Copenhagen with the drawings and some samples of bricks with two tubes. He asked the patent agency to help prepare the drawings for the patent application, while an engineer at the LEGO Group started working on the actual bricks with the different solutions, to be added to the patent application. At first, Godtfred Kirk Christiansen believed that two tubes were sufficient, which is why there are only two tubes to be found in the drawings for the patent application. However, on January 25, he decided that three tubes would be better, so the physical model that became part of the application has three tubes. A week later, on January 28, at 1:58 p.m., the patent was handed in and the LEGO brick as we know it today, with the perfect clutch power, was born.

"

Jetta Orduna, Head of LEGO Idea House

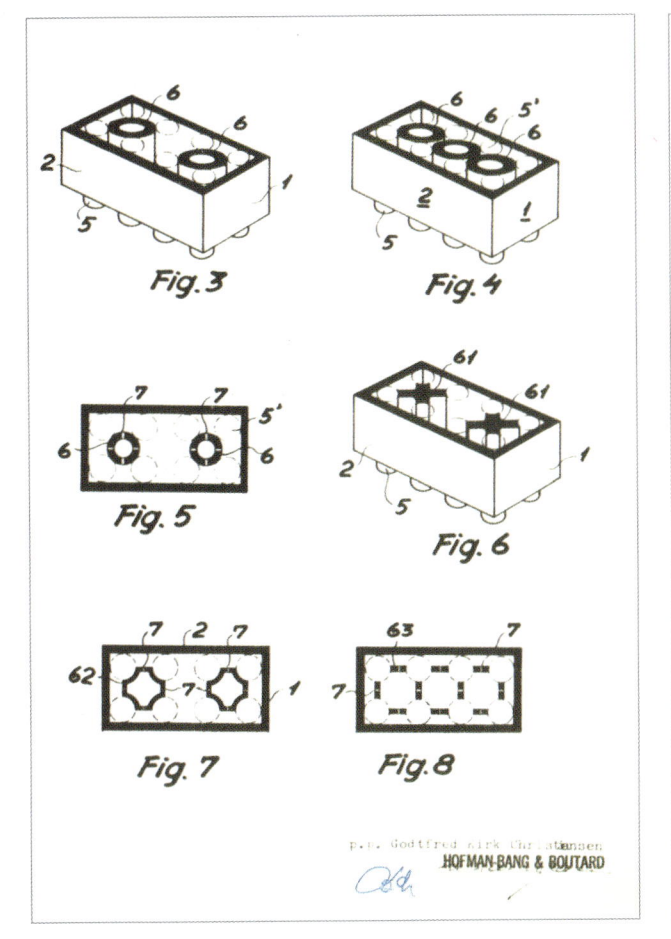

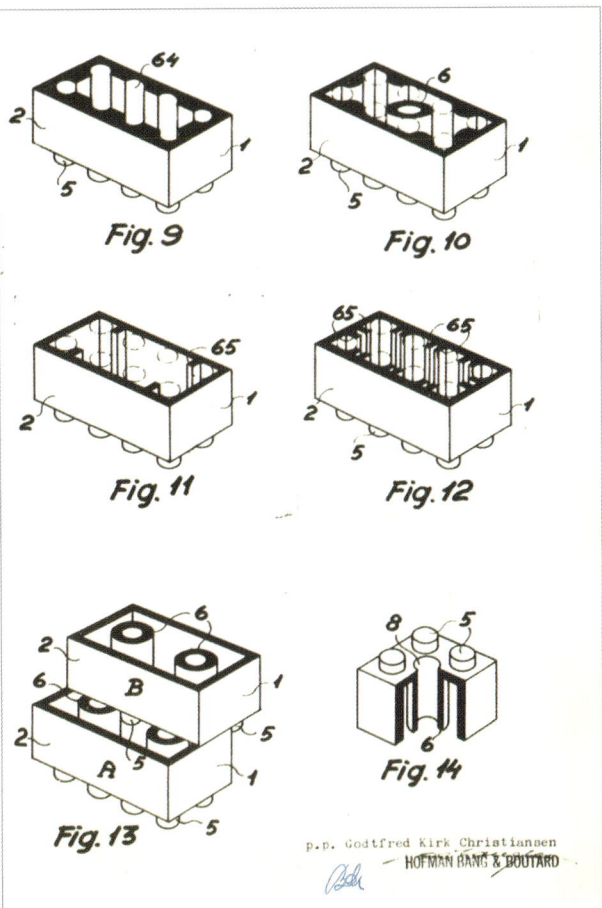

sections across. Two bricks side by side would then have one module between their studs: Two sections for each wall, and one and a half sections for half the stud on each brick; five sections in total. Thus, a module also became the distance between studs (see diagram 2 on page 18).

Based on the assumption that what was strong enough for the walls would also work for the ceiling, the brick's top thickness was defined as one section – the same as its walls. This resulted in a height of six sections – equivalent to a fractional number – for a standard LEGO brick.

Many LEGO element dimensions can initially seem random until viewed as multiples of modules and sections. When broken down this way, almost everything comes out as nice, even, whole numbers. LEGO Technic beams are a module in every dimension. Plates are two sections thick. Lightsaber handles, developed almost half a century later, are composed of two clean sections. Minifigure hands are just slightly smaller than two sections, so they quite literally clutch most standard elements. The LEGO System is built on these two foundational dimensions. However, all those actual numerical delineations came later. Initially the LEGO brick was defined purely in terms of proportion with the all-important wall thickness, or section, serving as the cornerstone.

Seeing the System

The morning following the brainstorm with Axel Thomsen, 24 January 1958, Godtfred Kirk Christiansen packed up the sketches and headed off to Copenhagen, Denmark's capital city and main industrial hub. Up to this point, LEGO building bricks had been unpatented and Godtfred

ABOVE Pages from the original Danish patent showing the various options for tubes that Godtfred Kirk Christiansen developed.

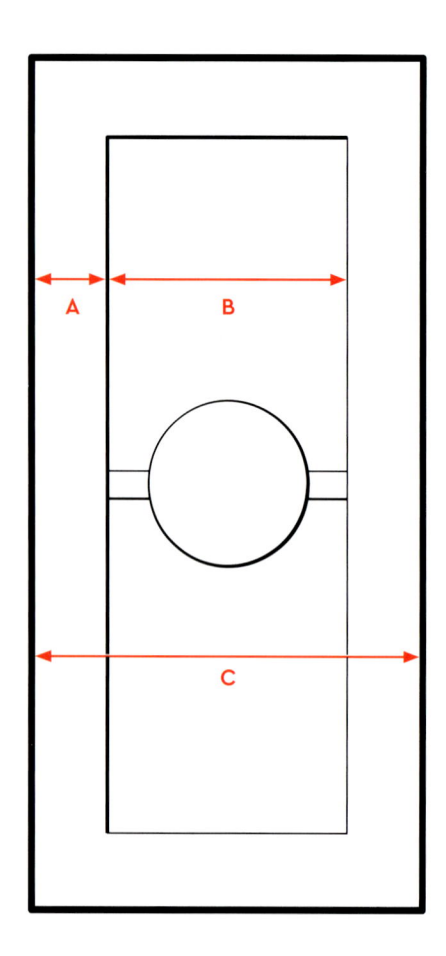

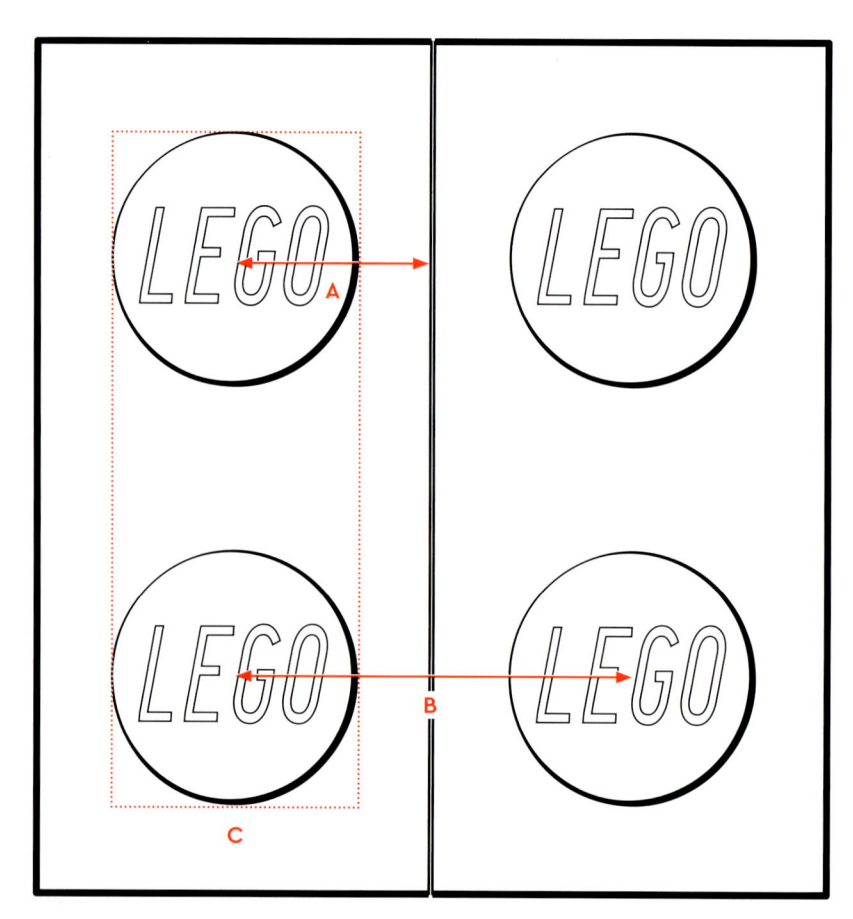

was aware that copying ran rampant in the industrial free-for-all that was Europe's post-World War II toy industry. At that time, toy companies rarely patented product designs outside their home country, if at all. Because designing and fine-tuning new moulds was expensive, a toy maker could save lots of money and effort by getting one of the few companies that produced plastic-injection tooling to simply make another few copies of mould designs already on hand.

Counterintuitively, this was not necessarily always illicit. During the years both before and immediately after World War II, toy makers from different regions, including the LEGO Group, would sometimes write to each other requesting ideas and even finished designs. Sometimes this would lead to official authorisation for mould-making companies to produce copies as a favour to toy makers from distant markets. Examples are plentiful from the 1950s of identical products showing up in adjoining countries distinguishable only by a stamp identifying which company made them.

Such copying was, however, not always authorised. Mould producers could make a quick sale by churning out a few extra moulds and selling them to other toy makers when no patent was involved. This was made doubly easy by the fact that it was often the mould-making companies themselves who applied for patents on behalf of toy makers, so they knew when a design wasn't protected and could be reused with no legal consequence.

Different types of stackable plastic bricks had appeared in many countries long before the invention of the LEGO brick and continued to do so during the 1950s and 1960s as well, sometimes authorised, other times not. Nevertheless, Godtfred Kirk Christiansen was keen to patent his new invention in as many countries as possible, starting with Denmark. He had grand ambitions to sell the redesigned bricks all over Europe. He had seen the System.

ABOVE LEFT
Underside of a standard 1×2 brick
A: wall thickness = 1 section
B: inner cavity = 3 sections
C: full width = 5 sections = 1 module

ABOVE RIGHT
Topside of two standard 1×2 bricks side by side
A: centre of one stud to outside edge = 5 half sections = 2.5 sections
B: centre of one stud to another = 10 half sections = 5 sections = 1 module
C: inside edge of wall on brick underside

Once the patent was filed, the real work began. Over several years, workable dimensions were calculated that were fed into the patented formulas and proportions. This work created the iconic 2×4 brick's final design, along with other fundamental elements such as the 2×2 brick and roof slopes.

Over the following decades Godtfred Kirk Christiansen remained the LEGO System guardian, personally approving most new parts to ensure they remained compatible with each other. In order to manage production costs, he also carefully controlled the expansion of the element library. Designer Bjarne Tveskov recalls, 'I heard GKC would give a prize to designers who could do a full year of new models without any new elements.'

ABOVE Moulds are protected carefully to prevent them from being copied, even after they have become no longer usable. This mould had been buried in the foundation of a new building and was recovered years later. Originally, multiple types of parts were cast in the same mould, as can be seen here.

> An element could be quite rough when it came before the Element Committee. Often, it had been made at a worktable from existing elements that had been cut and glued together. Sometimes plasticine clay would be added to an existing element to try and show in 3D what you were proposing. Those who could draw would bring handmade sketches along with physical prototypes. If an element made it through the committee, it would go to management for approval. Finally, the technical department at LEGO Futura would make a precise prototype, which would connect with standard LEGO bricks. That detailed design would then go to the mould team, who developed the injection mould to make the new brick.

Carsten Michaelsen, former Designer, the LEGO Group

The Element Committee

As the LEGO patriarch aged, Godtfred Kirk Christiansen's role as guardian of the LEGO System shifted away from him and entered its own process of evolution, beginning with the formation of a body known as the Element Committee, whose job it became to protect and grow the System.

It is not now known exactly when this body was created, though it seems likely that it was something informal that eventually became codified. In its earliest days, serving on the Element Committee was an unofficial part of a product designer's job description. When a designer developed a new type of LEGO brick, it had to be brought before the Element Committee, which consisted of fellow designers acting as a peer review, complete with critiques and suggestions. Their mission was to ensure that any new piece that went into production was as compatible as possible with every other element already in the LEGO System. By the 1980s the Element Committee had grown even more formal, with a representative from each LEGO theme, including LEGO® Town, LEGO® Space, LEGO® Castle and LEGO Technic, selected to serve for a period of time.

Such a committee existed in this format throughout the 1990s and 2000s until company growth made such an approach unwieldy. As the number of sets and themes released each year began to increase almost exponentially in the early 2010s, asking designers to not only generate all those products but also take time to thoroughly peer review each other's proposed new elements became too great a burden.

In 2004 a new role was created in the LEGO Group, called Element Coach. The department of element coaches carries Godtfred Kirk Christiansen's legacy as keepers and guardians of the LEGO System. Initially this department was populated with some of the LEGO Group most senior

BELOW Godtfred Kirk Christiansen and his team relied on physical testing. They experimented with different approaches to moulds and noted which ones didn't work, sometimes as a result of not enough plastic being inserted. The results of several such tests are shown here.

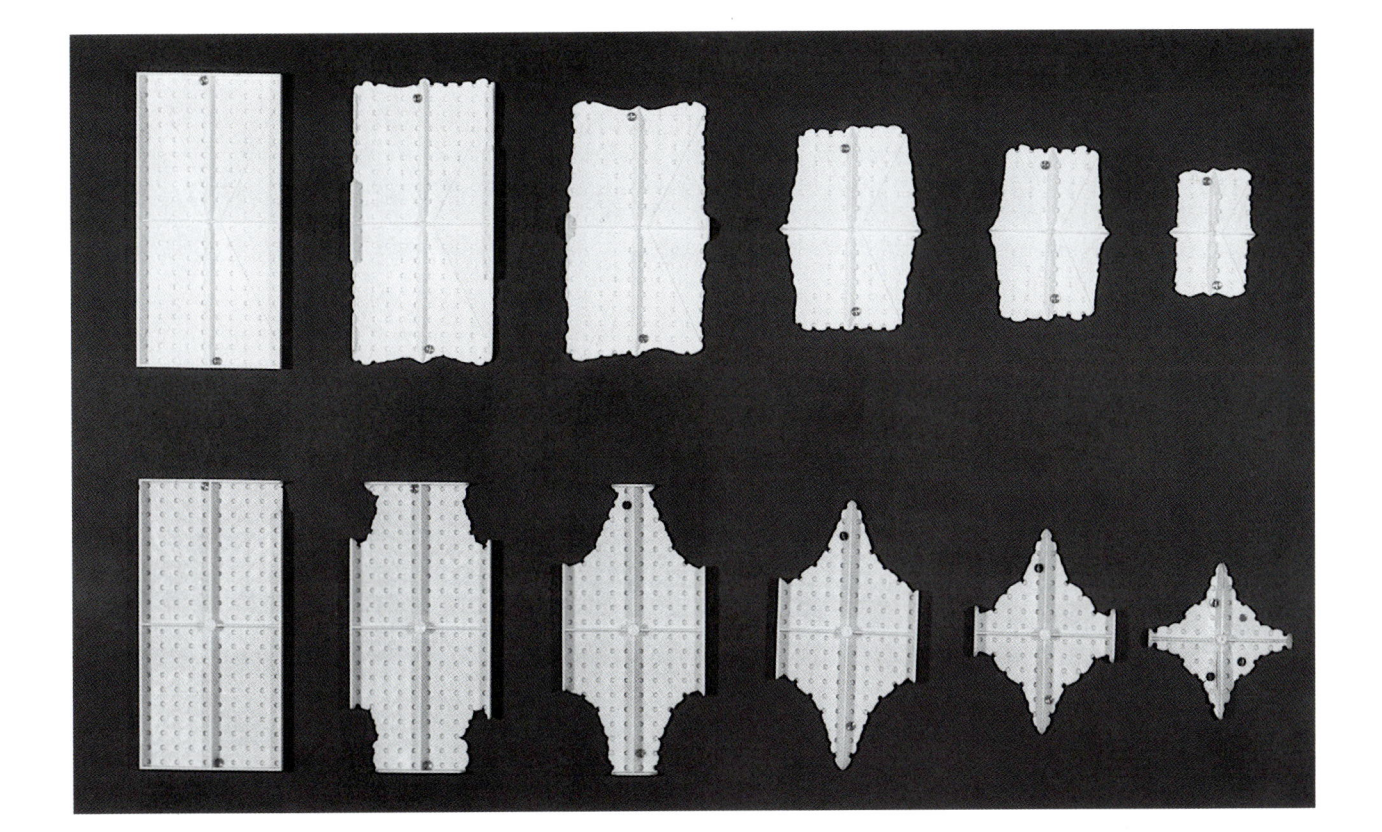

designers and experts, legends within the company, some of whom had worked there since before minifigures were developed in the late 1970s and who carried with them decades of knowledge. It was this team which consolidated and formalised the variety of guides, test results and rules of thumb that had floated around the company in various states of formality for years. Together with another group of specialists within the company who are responsible for measuring bricks at unbelievably tight tolerances, element coaches have been able to use modern material science and magnification tools to supplement generations of in-house experience. This has allowed them to quantify and manage, more accurately than Godtfred Kirk Christiansen could have dreamed, exactly how the LEGO System works. The key is connector pairs.

Clutch power

Clutch power in LEGO elements derives from deflection and is managed by connector pairs that define how to achieve just the right amount of strength between two individual connectors for the bricks' all-important reliability. When the first 2×4 bricks were created, the first connector pair, composed of studs and tubes, was also invented. It worked like this: studs on top of the lower 2×4 pressed into contact with the upper brick's tubes and walls. Because studs are round, the point of contact was very small, so all of the force was concentrated. Force distributed over a small area is stronger than when dispersed over a large one. This is why tubes work so well, as they concentrate pressure.

Studs push at their points of contact, forcing the receiving brick's walls and tubes to deflect. Walls pop out ever so slightly, while tubes simultaneously get compressed in on themselves. Run a finger along two joined bricks and the slight bump out of walls can be felt, though it is very subtle.

Since 1963, LEGO elements have primarily been made of acrylonitrile butadiene styrene, or ABS, a plastic which is naturally elastic, meaning parts want to return to their original shape when deformed, just like a rubber band. Clutch power is created by the opposing forces of studs pushing out and walls trying to pull back in. While the ideal strength's value must remain secret, it is a defined number measured in newtons.

To accommodate the slight expansion of a brick's footprint when its walls pop out, LEGO elements are never quite full modules in either length or width. Each edge is shorted by ~0.1 millimetre to create a small air gap between joined elements. The distance from a brick's terminal studs to those of its adjacent neighbour remains a full module, but the tiny space created between

RIGHT An internal schematic of LEGO bricks shows how studs make contact with tubes and brick walls when connected.

> The role of element coach is different from element designer. Element designers work with model designers on a specific model. They concentrate on creating the perfect element needed in that model. Whereas element coaches think about the whole LEGO System and how new elements might be used across different themes. We encourage teams to work together to avoid too many similar elements being made. We also coach the model designers to make sure models are appropriate for their age group. For example, if a model is for younger children, we might avoid having left and right elements, as these elements can be difficult to identify correctly. Sometimes a new element looks cool but doesn't have a lot of other applications. But changing it to make it more widely usable can make it more difficult for younger children to understand. In that case we might say it's better to make a super-specialised element that only comes in a few boxes. We also keep an eye on moulding requirements; we have a deep collaboration between the whole value chain, from designer to engineering and production. Ultimately though, our main task is to guide designers to make sure that new elements adhere to the rules of the LEGO System. We want consumers to see a new element and instantly know how to use it. That's our most important task.

Jan Hatting, Master Element Coach, the LEGO Group

walls gives enough wiggle room for bricks to be added and removed without grinding against one another and creating unwanted points of contact that would negate the force or make it hard to insert a brick into a space surrounded by other elements.

Such an air gap is not, however, incorporated into vertical stacking. All standard bricks are exactly six sections tall. Wall thickness, the original section, has also been altered and now varies from brick to brick, including in the original 2×4. Despite the depiction in the patent, the walls of a 2×4 brick are no longer exactly a section wide. Several years after developing the 2×4, Godtfred Kirk Christiansen and his engineers realised that, in lieu of a uniform wall thickness across its whole length, they could narrow the wall's width and add small ridges where studs needed to make contact. Reducing the amount of plastic used for the LEGO Group most produced element netted substantial benefits to both the company and the environment. The thinner variant with ridges has been used exclusively for decades, but collectors of older bricks can usually find examples of 2×4s with full wall thicknesses. The alteration did, however, change the connector pair. Managing and cataloguing such alterations, as well as new types of connectors, is another job for the element coaches.

Making connections

Reliable connections are the LEGO System lifeblood, and through the years many different types of connectors have been added. Studs and tubes are the oldest and most basic, but they have been joined by clips, bars, snaps, cross holes, and many, many more. When two elements can be joined, the portions of each which facilitate attachment form a connector pair. Minifigures holding goblets in their claw hands create a connector pair between the hand and cup stem.

A good connector pair causes deformation, which results in an overall gripping force equal to the ideal clutch power value. When the classic pair of 2×4 bricks are connected, a corner stud will be in contact with two walls and a tube. The three points of contact create a force that is right at the target clutch power when added together, which in turn creates just the right amount of grip and therefore reliability in terms of components staying together. Three points of contact was, in fact, the longstanding rule of thumb within the LEGO Group for element design before science caught up and explained why.

While simple in concept, the number of possible connector-pair combinations quickly becomes

RIGHT Vertical air gaps can be seen between the bricks in this construct.

dizzying. Take, for example, the stud atop a simple 1×1 brick. This could form a connector pair with the walls of another 1×1, the circular base of a round element, or a minifigure's foot, and that is before considering numerous ways it could be inserted into various other basic bricks.

There are lots of ways connector pairs can potentially go wrong. Some may be too weak, leading to stability issues. Others can be too strong, making models frustratingly hard to pull apart. They can introduce stresses which are too great, resulting in permanent deformation and damage to one or both bricks.

Beyond physical considerations, some connections may be possible but too confusing for children, or so specific that they limit a brick's wider usefulness. Astonishingly, the LEGO Group has catalogued and analysed nearly every possible connector pair. Much discussion is made among LEGO fans concerning 'illegal connections'. When a LEGO designer refers to an illegal connection, what they mean is that a connection has gone wrong in one of the ways listed above. How they make that determination stems from analysing a connector pair's most important attribute: function.

Form follows function

Not to be confused with 'play functions', connector-pair functions have a different and very specific internal meaning. Hearkening back all the way to the beginning, they refer to the clutch power achieved when two elements are joined. Internally, LEGO designers use the term 'clutch power' primarily in reference to an element's tubes, whereas connector-pair functions describe every type of connection. Today, thanks to advancements in technology, ideal clutch power is a precise value quantified by the element coaches, who are responsible for steering designers toward creating new bricks that achieve it.

The element coaching process sometimes pushes back on new prototypes created by designers, however potentially exciting they seem, simply because they would modify connector pairs in ways that would hinder the overall building system. Therefore formal guidelines have been created – the spiritual successor to Godtfred Kirk Christiansen's watchful eye. These guides remove the complexity of having to think about material properties by consisting almost entirely of key dimensions along with a few forbidden connections. Those dimensions have been derived from hard science and, if followed, ensure that all connections meet their function.

Godtfred Kirk Christiansen could, of course, not see this amazing future back when he sketched with Axel Thomsen on a cold January afternoon. However, the relationship between modules and sections that he defined still serves as the foundation for all the rich complexity that now exists within the LEGO System. As the new stud and tube elements slowly displaced their hollow predecessors, even more new and exciting bricks were about to be imagined.

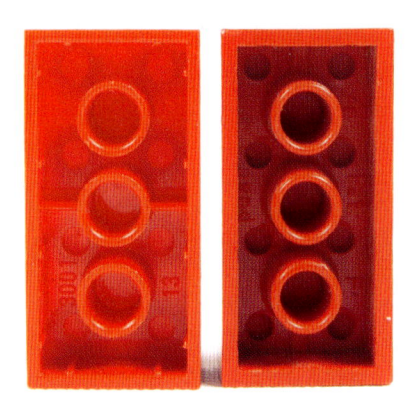

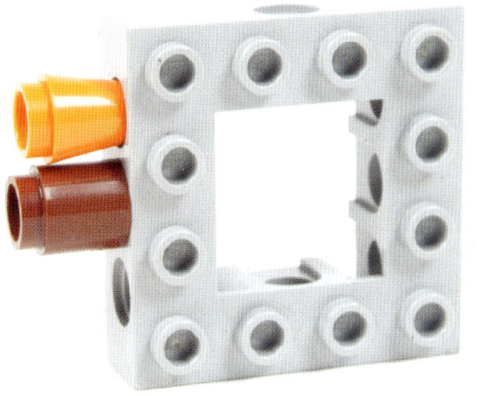

FAR LEFT Older 2×4 bricks, seen on the right, have slightly thicker walls than newer variants, seen on the left.

LEFT The brown 1×1 round brick makes a good connection with the grey brick because it has a stop in the top that anchors it. However, the orange cone has no stop at the top, so it could be pushed in too far. This would result in unacceptable stress on the pin and inner walls of the grey brick. This is considered an 'illegal connection'.

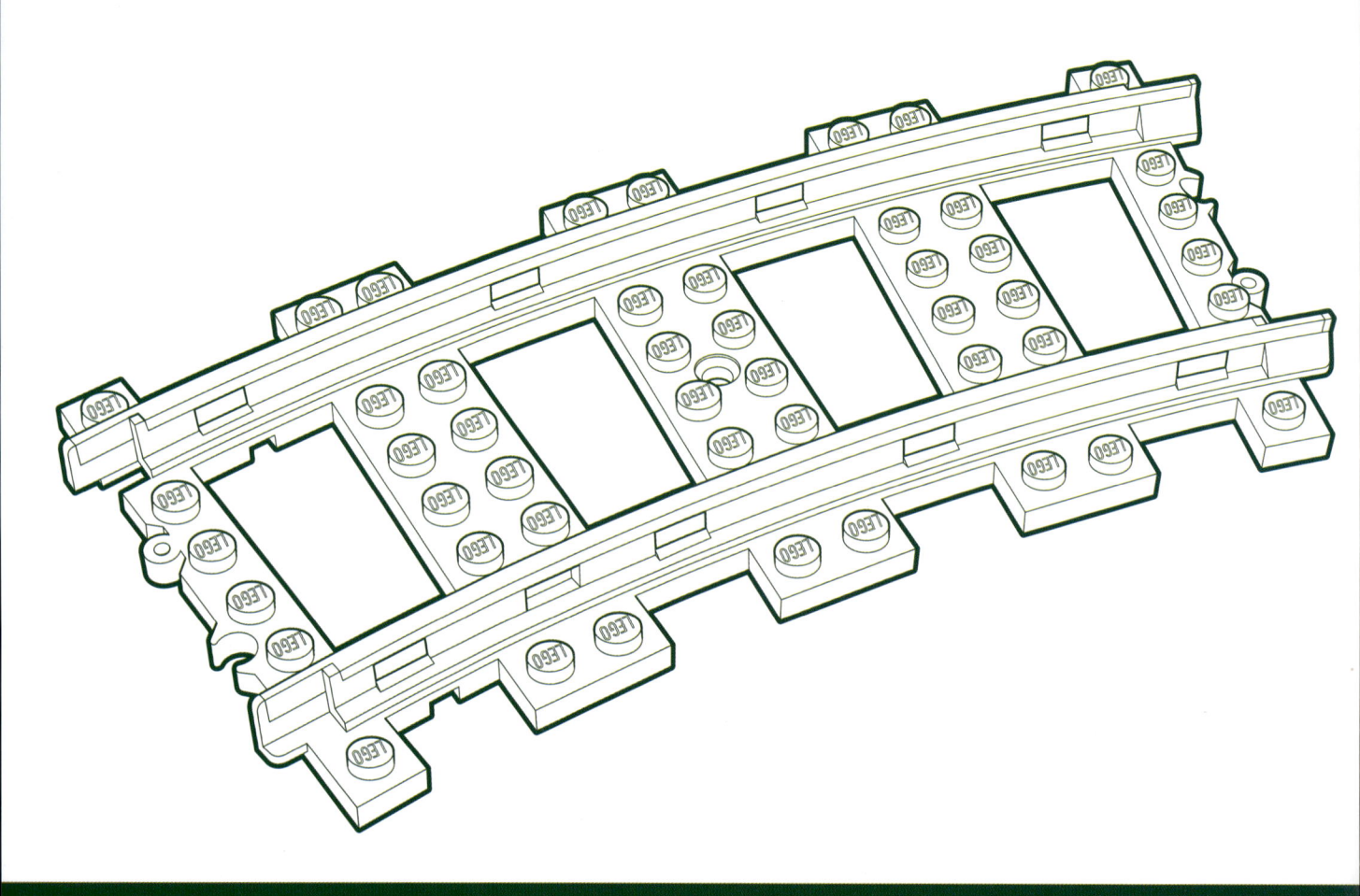

> Trains were always popular with adults, and the more detailed and realistic we made them, the more popular they were.

Henrik Andersen, Design Master, the LEGO Group

2

Rolling Along

How the dynamic LEGO® wheel created a world of movement, got LEGO trains on track and paved the way for sets aimed at adults

TOP Metallic inlays on the plastic track elements allowed for a current to be conducted along the rails in order to power LEGO® trains.

MIDDLE Set 10194 The Emerald Night, released in 2009, included multiple copies of both large train wheel variants.

BOTTOM The first LEGO wheel element was the end result of a long design process.

Some LEGO® products enjoy a privileged position as front-runners for release every couple of years, thanks to demand never being in doubt. Young children, after all, will always want police stations. Other products must constantly fend off younger, flashier rivals to hold their precious spots on production lines. Champion among these survivors is LEGO® Train, which has strung together an unparalleled string of reinventions and has lived an ever-threatened and improbable existence stretching over half a century. Along the way it has served as an incubator for innovation, generated amazing elements, been fashioned into awe-inspiring sets and, perhaps most importantly, shown that adults formed a sizeable fanbase for LEGO products. All of that drama and struggle, however, would have seemed unimaginable back at the beginning. Upon their release, trains were the LEGO Group darling, thanks to a new, foundational element.

As the 1950s drew to a close, the Town Plan series of products was still going strong. Up until then, toys under that banner almost exclusively used LEGO bricks to build structures that depicted urban or village life. Petrol stations, houses, office buildings and churches were all regular favourites, along with small-scale LEGO vehicles that populated children's cityscapes. Within the LEGO Group, however, there was a growing desire to make models even more dynamic.

An initial effort to introduce variety involved prompting children to use bricks already owned in new ways. Designers created inspiration models whose pictures were reproduced on leaflets, in boxes and across special ideas booklets, all intended to give young builders a sense of what was possible. Ships were immediately popular, with concepts for all manner of seagoing vessels gracing printed materials, along with a few official sets. The company wanted to do more, though, and set about inventing an element that didn't yet exist: a LEGO brick with movement.

There was a clear, natural choice for the first dynamic element due to the sheer number of possibilities it would open up: a LEGO wheel. In fact, lack of wheels was a primary driver behind the popularity of ships among designers. Brick-built boat hulls, simple though they were, due to the limited number of parts available during the 1950s, were paragons of realism when compared to a vehicle that should have wheels. Square elements stood in as best they could, but came off looking somewhat like a caveman's first prototype. With beautiful wooden trucks, trains and tractors in the company's recent past, the contrast was even more stark. Something needed to be done!

ABOVE Many different types of small-scale vehicle were produced for Town Plan sets.

ABOVE A display shows some of the ships that could be built from LEGO bricks in 1960.

Initially there was no formal project to develop a wheel. Instead, several employees began experimenting independently. Eventually Christian Lasgaard, who had been hired in 1954 and risen to head the development department, responsible for creating new products, was officially charged with creating a wheel that would be compatible with existing bricks. Several prototypes were developed but none were quite right. Staying true to the LEGO® System turned out to be a foundational issue. Whichever final design emerged would need to be removable and interchangeable, just like any other brick. Normal toy cars have their wheels and axles cast together then affixed securely to a chassis, but such permanence wasn't right for LEGO toys. Prototype wheels that could satisfactorily be popped on and off vacillated between what felt like two mutually exclusive extremes. If the axles were held snugly enough to prevent wobble, they inevitably cracked any brick serving as a chassis or anchor point when being pulled out or inserted. Conversely, designs that didn't crack held on so loosely that models wobbled in a way that everyone knew would frustrate children.

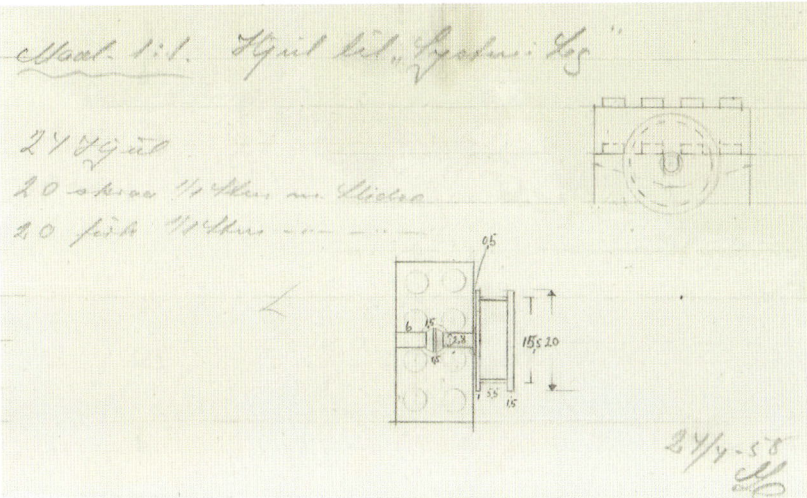

Observing the development and rejection of all these prototypes was a long-serving employee named Knud Møller. Having come onboard back during the 1930s, working in the woodshop, he transitioned to the design department in 1951. Knud Møller began developing his own wheel solution, which involved a new variant of the 2×4 brick. His idea was to cast a channel from the outside edge of a 2×4 brick's long side all the way to its centre tube, creating an open 'valley' from one side to the other. This U-shaped channel would fit in between the studs at a depth of about one third the brick's height. An axle could then lie within it and be secured by placing another brick on top.

However, Knud's design had another attribute which made it even more appealing. Because the centre of his valley was a standard LEGO tube, that area was wider than the rest of the channel. This allowed him to propose axles that could flare at their ends, meaning they would rotate within the channel but still be kept from slipping out. Unfortunately, this first design failed when Knud produced a prototype and tested it. Rolling caused the wheels and axles to rock, popping apart the bricks between which they were secured.

TOP Before LEGO wheels were invented, regular bricks had to stand in, which greatly limited functionality.

ABOVE Knud Møller's first wheel design was held in place by two bricks. It ultimately proved unstable.

Fortunately, Knud Møller realised that the concept of independent wheels and axles held in place by a modified 2×4 brick was sound. Through several more prototypes, Knud honed his design, eventually solving the original cracking problem that had plagued his co-workers by developing a special double-walled 2×4 brick with holes bisecting it through both its long and short dimensions. A wheel with a short metal axle cast into its centre could be inserted into these holes. Eventually his design was brought to Godtfred Kirk Christiansen's attention. A couple of modifications and additions were made, including the first-ever LEGO tyre, and the design was scaled up so that two sizes were produced using Knud Møller's special 2×4 brick as their attachment. The pair of LEGO wheels were unleashed upon the market in 1962 at the Nuremberg Toy Fair, where they were heavily showcased.

One special young LEGO fan in particular was absolutely delighted with the new elements. Kjeld Kirk Kristiansen, Godtfred Kirk Christiansen's son and future owner of the company, was already a car enthusiast by this point in his life. During the 1960s, he often sat next to one of the company's handful of full-time designers, watching them work, and built his own models at home. Kjeld had fully embraced the late 1950s ship boom, constructing every seagoing vessel in Denmark's Royal Navy, but cars remained his favourite subject matter. Using the new wheel element, he built his own large garage filled with all manner of sports cars, limousines and off-roaders. Kjeld Kirk Kristiansen dubbed his creation 'LECA', an amalgam of the LEGO word + 'CAR', and would put prices on each vehicle, noting if they were for sale, before showing them to his father.

BELOW The final design for the first two LEGO wheels.

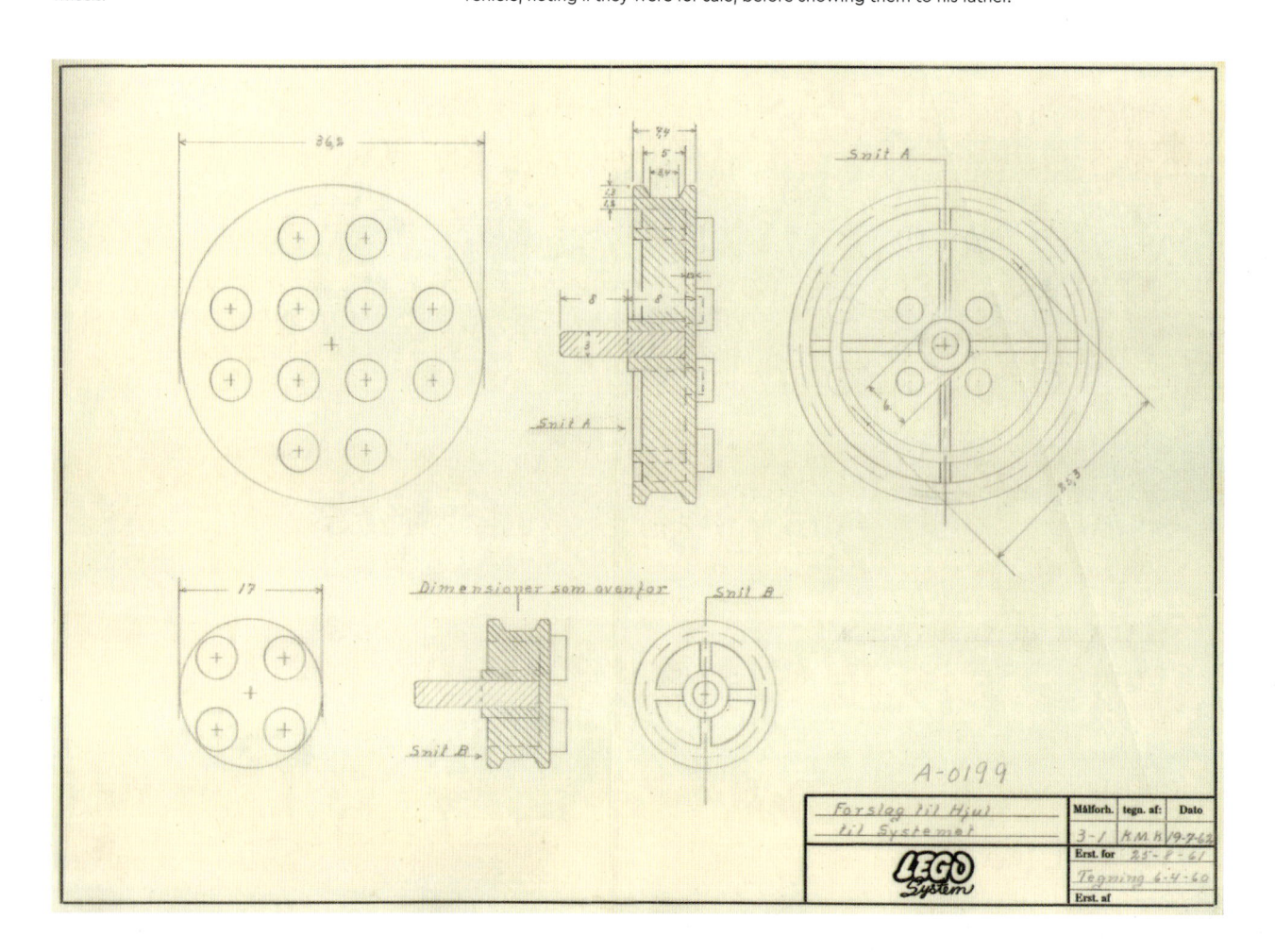

One model was apparently good enough to close the deal as, in 1968, Kjeld Kirk Kristiansen's rendition of a four-wheel-drive-style vehicle became set 330. Many of Kjeld's models survive to this day. Upon seeing them years later, during the early 2000s, a designer, Henrik Andersen, asked if he could recreate one of them with some modern touches and Kjeld happily assented. Henrik discovered that some of the youthful Kjeld's building techniques were not a simple matter of replicating: for instance, current rules didn't allow a plate to be pressed on its side into the studs of a brick beneath. However, the LEGO Group owner gave the designer special permission to be as flexible as possible in this instance!

TOP The 1962 Nuremberg Toy Fair, where the LEGO wheel was unveiled.

ABOVE LEFT Godtfred Kirk Christiansen inspects the selection of vehicles in Kjeld's LECA showroom.

ABOVE RIGHT A slightly modernised version of Kjeld Kirk Kristiansen's childhood jeep design became set 330, released in 1968. In the background is a modern car inspired by another of Kjeld's childhood designs.

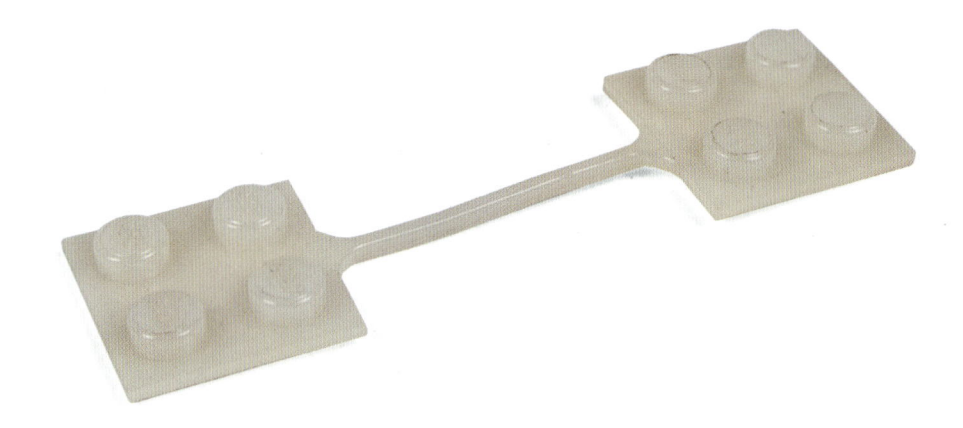

Making trains possible

Over the next year after their release, LEGO wheels spread like wildfire, unleashing a torrent of creativity from designers that previously would have been impossible. Wheeled vehicles of every size, shape and type rose ever higher on worktables; production could barely keep up with the number of possible options. Many designs appeared as sets, while the alternates were used in promotional material or as inspirational pictures in company literature. Along with the wheel, another element was produced, known as the nylon hinge coupling. One of the LEGO Group first soft elements, it consisted of a pair of 2×2 plates joined with a short run of flexible plastic and was developed so that multiple wheeled vehicles could be joined together. The first application was a tractor and wagon. Taken together, the nylon connector and wheel meant a train was inevitable. Images in the LEGO Group archive show at least ten different prototype models, each vying for the title of first-ever functioning brick-built train. The winner came to market in 1964 as set 323 Train.

Godtfred Kirk Christiansen's heart and passion were in product design, but he also took his responsibility as the LEGO Group financial steward very seriously. Accordingly, as the company matured, a budget-management strategy was put in place that is still used to this day: frames. Frames evolved from looking at a target release date and projecting backwards to when work on the toys needed to start, and calculating costs accordingly. Eventually, frames became the designation for each category of a new toy's cost and, by the 1970s, it had become a formal system which has only grown more granular and complex since. Today, it is inexorably interwoven into element design and product development.

Product lines will receive a number of new element frames, colour-change frames and decoration frames. Each of those categories can be broken down even further. Decorations are divided into more expensive printed element frames versus more economical sticker frames. Some types of moulds are more expensive to make, so not all new part frames are created equal, either.

Once the allocations are made, teams will sometimes trade frames both within their own groups and across departments. If an idea is especially good, a special case can be made for an extra frame or two. By far a theme's easiest year is its first, when the need for novelty and to distinguish itself from what has come before usually leads to a windfall of frames. In the mid-1960s, the formal frame system was still some years away, but LEGO Train was nevertheless about to experience that first-year phenomenon.

A new category

With the wheel established and the Town Plan line nearing its tenth birthday, a single product was about to receive the largest volume of new elements since the first development of the LEGO® System in Play. Rather than simply make models of trains, a whole new category of

ABOVE Early trains were joined with a flexible plastic element known as a nylon hinge coupling, rather than with magnets.

OPPOSITE TOP Set 323, released in 1964, is the first-ever LEGO train.

OPPOSITE BOTTOM This early LEGO train design dates from the 1960s.

Rolling Along

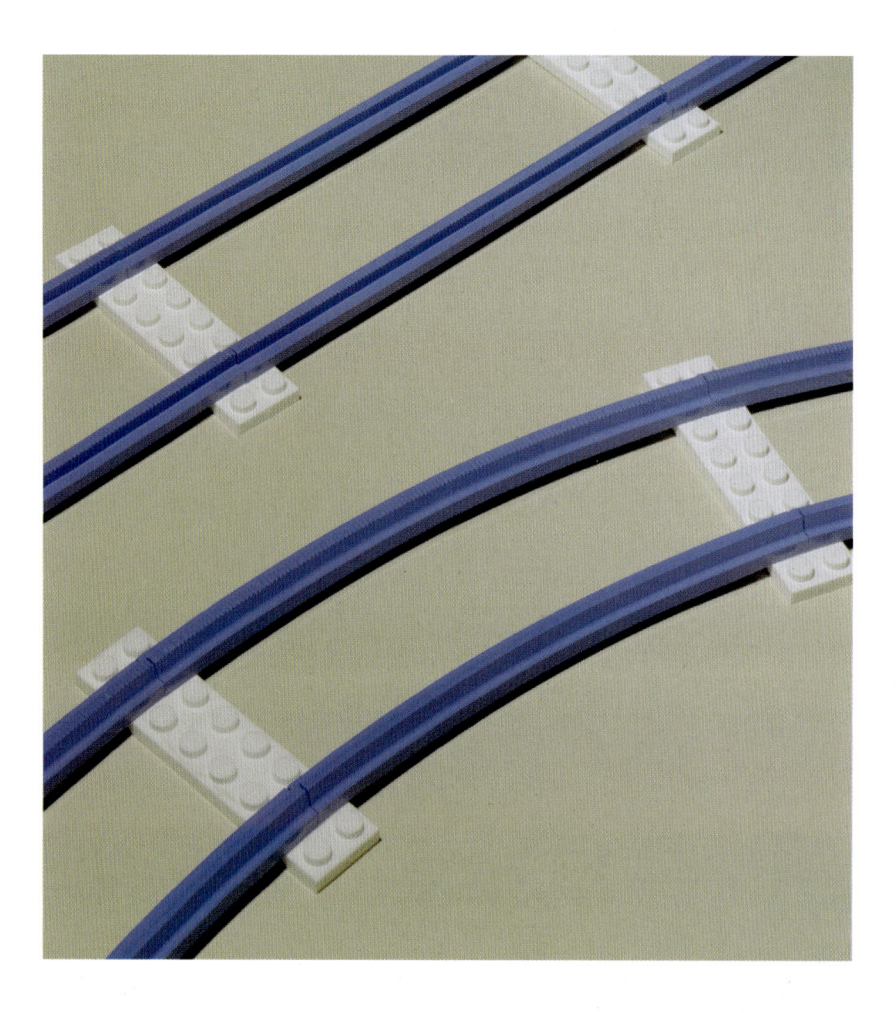

toy was being developed. First came multiple track elements in a distinctive blue hue, a train-specific wheel that could grip that track, and coupling components for joining wagons, soon followed by 4.5-volt electric motors and battery boxes.

By the end of 1966, LEGO Train became its own subgenre of the LEGO System, with both push-along and powered options. Ever-greater realism and detail had become possible thanks to an element invented in 1962. During the 1960s many Danes sought to build or modify their homes, sometimes using LEGO bricks to plan and build 3D models of their dream houses. To improve the realism of the builds, LEGO plates were developed and released in 1962 as part of the Scale Model line. At two sections tall, or exactly one third of a standard brick's height, plates allowed for far more subtle shapes and angles, and were perfect for depicting a slightly tapered roof or a change in texture on walls. They also worked well for vehicles and were incorporated into both locomotives and wagons.

Trains saw healthy success and a truly astonishing toy was developed for the 1968 line: a motorised engine controlled by a whistle. Blowing the whistle once started the engine, blowing it again made it stop, and a third blast made it reverse direction. Trains were officially the LEGO Group new blockbuster. To make it even easier for children, the entire line was revamped in 1969 with a 12-volt electric system that incorporated metallic rails set into the track. This meant that a transformer element could be used to power motors with no need for an onboard battery pack, making LEGO sets function in the same manner as mainstream

ABOVE The original blue track elements were joined by a shared 2×8 plate at either end.

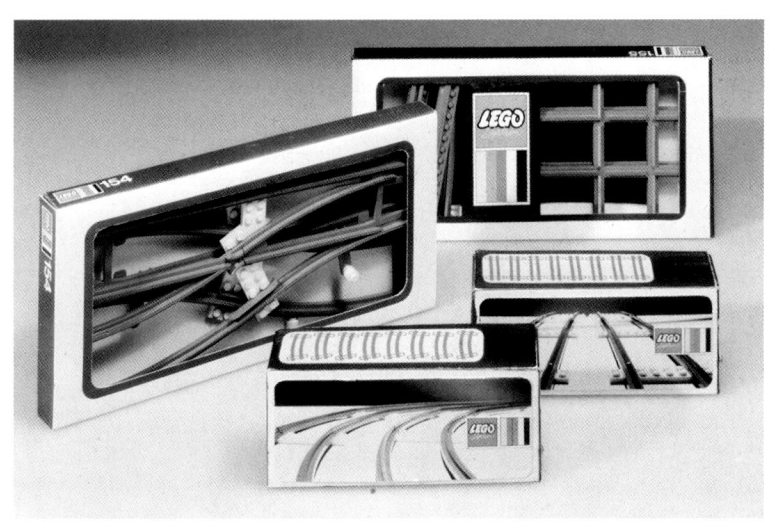

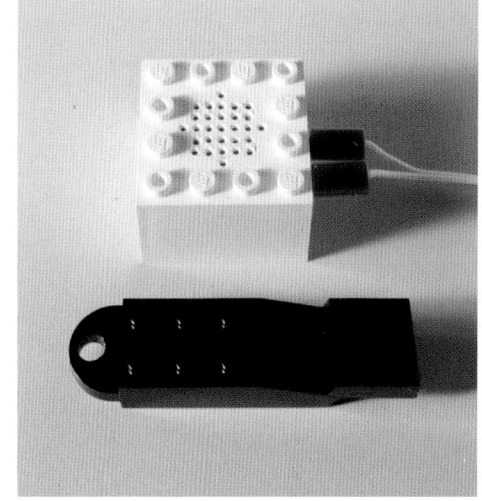

model-train layouts. Never forgetting younger children, over many years the company continued to release push variants that shared ever more detailed and realistic pieces with their powered big brothers.

Trains became a staple of larger Town Plan sets, providing another dimension to layouts, which children could make as big as they wanted, thanks to track accessories sold in boxes. However, LEGO Train's first fight for survival was on the horizon. Through the 1970s, other themes like the precursor to LEGO® Technic began introducing exciting and complex movement to their models. Trains started to get less attention as excited designers moved to innovate in new places. At that time, with so many ideas and limited production slots, sets needed champions to help push them through and LEGO Train was losing out. Models continued to be released, but in smaller numbers. Then came the minifigure and with it, a reckoning.

TOP Twelve-volt trains were powered by a separate rail element that ran in the centre of the tracks.

ABOVE LEFT Boxes of train parts were available during the 1960s.

ABOVE RIGHT Set 118 Electronic Train, released in 1968, featured a black train whistle and white receiver brick that stopped and started the train remotely.

OVERLEAF Town Plans like this would have been the stuff of childhood legend in the 1960s.

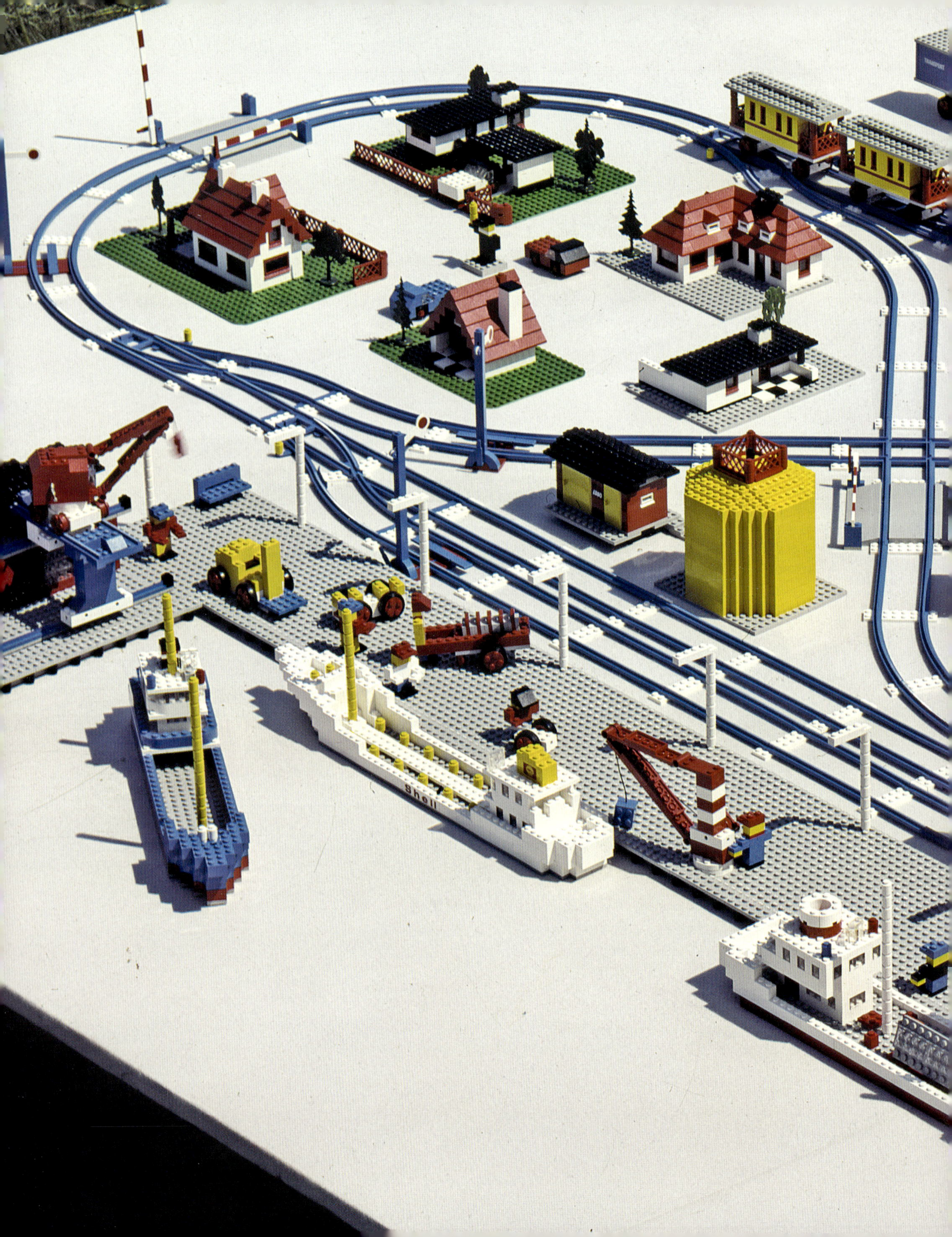
Shell

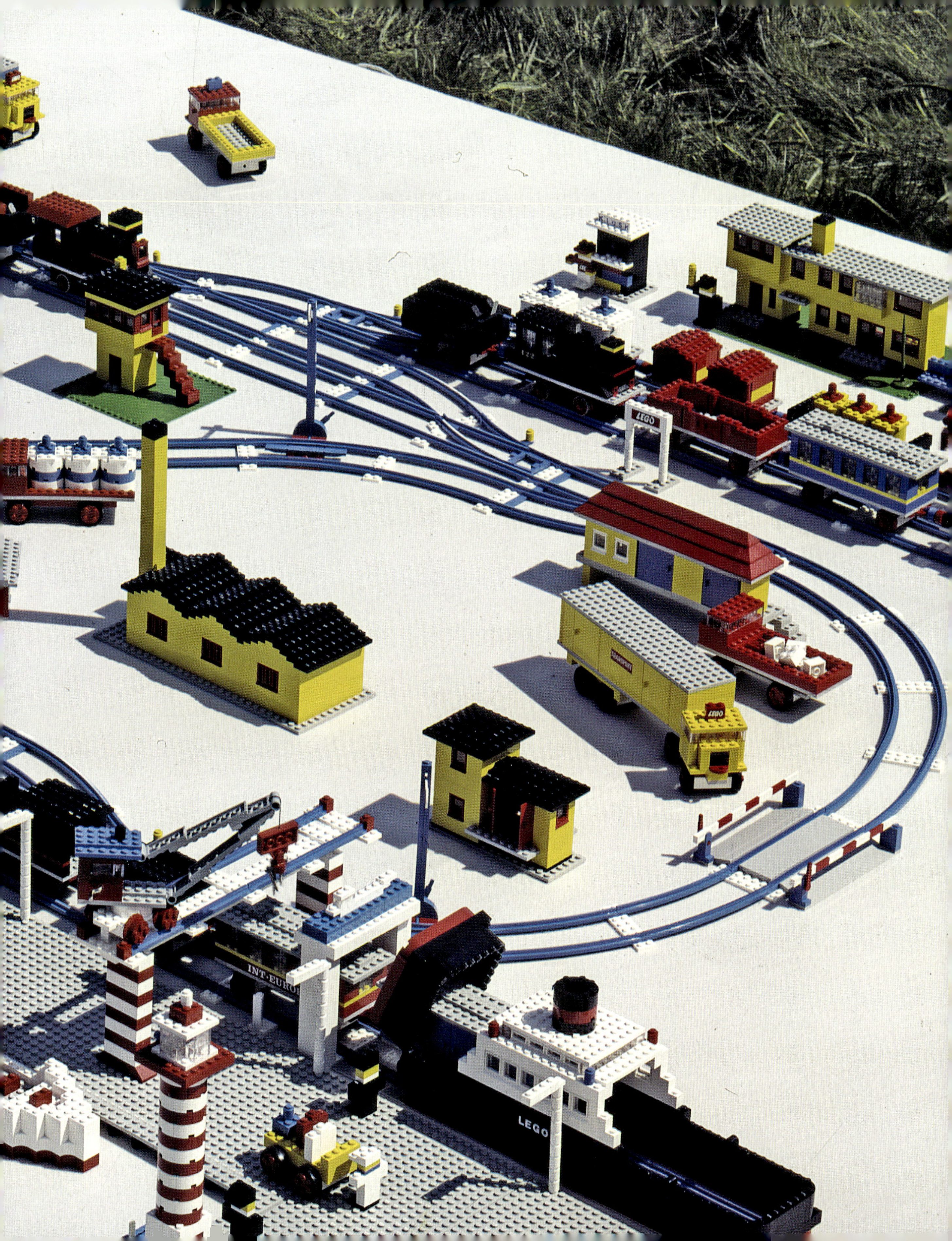
LEGO
LEGO

As one of the only legacy themes to predate minifigures, the entire portfolio of elements for LEGO Train had been designed without the LEGO Group minifigure populace in mind. Contemporaries in 1978 such as LEGO® Space and LEGO® Castle were developed and released concurrently with the minifigure and all of their new components were scaled to fit. Four LEGO Train sets were released that year, but the trains were not sized to accommodate minifigures. Train elements would need an overhaul to survive in the new minifigure-centric world the LEGO Group was chugging into. Fortunately, at just the right moment, both frames and a veteran designer briefly became available.

Minifigure-scale trains

Jan Ryaa, best known as one of the founding fathers of LEGO Technic, shows up as a key character in the stories of multiple LEGO products. Having wrapped up the initial release of LEGO Technic precursor (the theme would not be officially called LEGO Technic until the 1980s), he and his team took up the challenge for LEGO Train. Town Plan had already been transitioned over to LEGO® Town, with a host of updated elements scaled to the minifigure. It, along with the brand-new LEGO Castle and LEGO Space themes, was still permeating markets both in Europe and America as the 1970s closed. Jan and his team realised that they had a unique opportunity. None of those themes needed major element updates: sets using existing parts would be more than sufficient to keep them fresh. In a bold gambit, they prevailed upon their colleagues to allocate almost every frame of the 1980 product cycle to an overhaul of LEGO Train, setting an ambitious goal of establishing it as a minifigure-scale theme in its own right, with twenty-eight new sets.

RIGHT Set 7750 Steam Engine with Tender, from 1980, included multiple new parts, including the train doors and larger train wheels.

BELOW Set 7740 Inter-City Passenger Train, from 1980, sported new train buffers and wheels.

Rolling Along 41

For the next six months designers created concept after concept, literally filling their team's workspace such that there was barely room to walk. They didn't want to just do *some* of their ideas, they wanted to do *all* of them. Sets, parts, types of trains, crossings, accessories – all of it. One designer built an antique steam engine pulling a pair of classic coaches with new windows and doors. Another developed a fully realised cargo train with new tenders, couplings and wheels. Yet another crafted a flashy, yellow, modern-looking passenger train set with even more new elements. Ideas for new bricks were swapped, refined and spread across as many trains as possible to stretch the allotment of frames, generous though it was, as far as possible. Creative energy and excitement buzzed in the room despite the inconvenience of having to nearly hop on one foot to reach the bathroom.

Jan Ryaa himself tackled the upgrading of the blue track, which had remained virtually unchanged since its release in 1969. He had personal experience with the track's main drawback: stability. Jan Ryaa's son loved LEGO trains and at weekends he would set up a board on his bed, then spend the day constructing a layout. At night, when it was time to sleep, Jan would try to move the track for his boy. No matter how careful he was, the layout inevitably broke. Blue track consisted of independent rail elements that were joined by a single 2×8 plate, each rail clinging for dear life to a single stud on each end. Jan realised what was needed: a special railroad tie element that could more firmly attach to the track. Ultimately this led to new rails as well, with small slots that clipped into this tie component. Jan's personal challenge was to make the connections so secure that train layouts could be hung on a wall. Were it not for the heavier metallic rail elements needed to power the new 12-volt engines that also had to be attached to his rail tie, Jan would have succeeded.

The demanding pace required to meet their ambitious target led to Jan and his team working hard – and finding the occasional unorthodox approach for meeting deadlines. One designer tasked with creating 7822 Railway Station fell ill a week before his due date. While the build itself was complete, he had yet to finish the alternate models that were always shown on the back of a set's packaging. In a move that would never happen today, he got permission to take the unreleased model home, where his wife developed the alternate builds while he lay sick in bed with pneumonia.

BELOW In addition to studs, the new grey track system's cross members had clips that locked into the rails in order to provide extra strength.

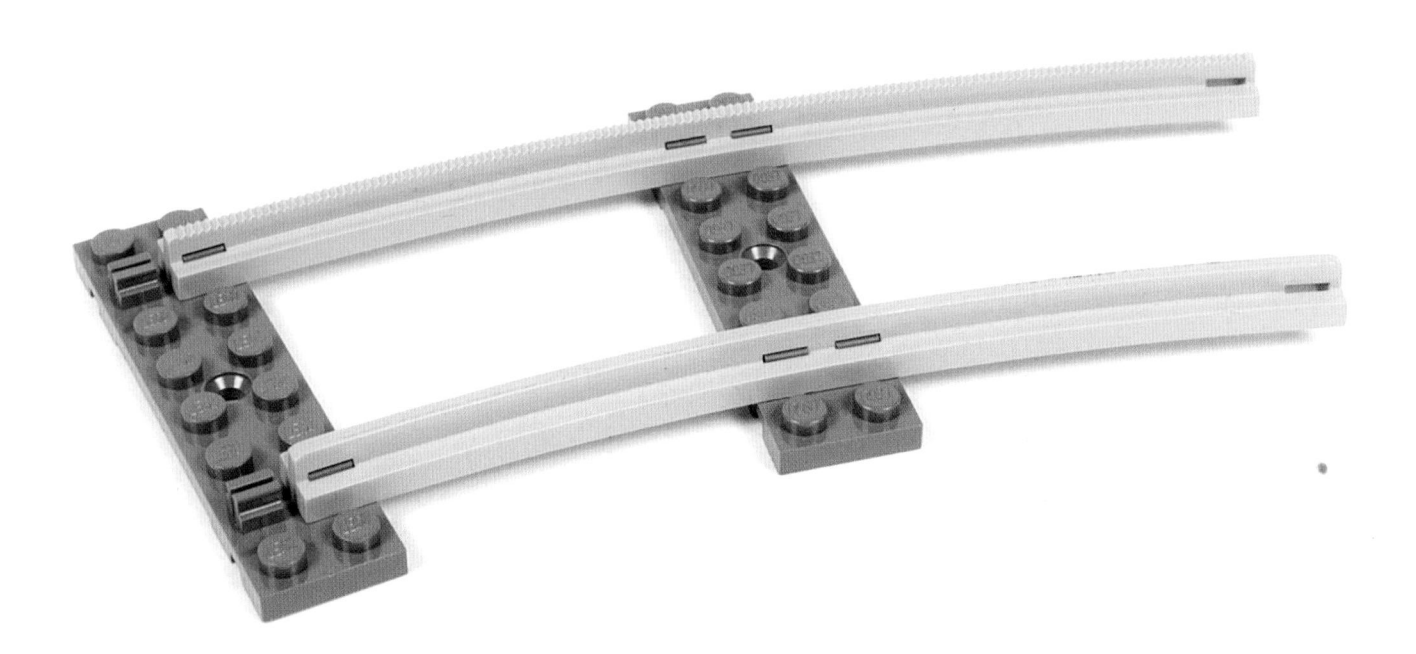

> I actually made a mistake on the train station. At that time, in the beginning of the new trains, I made a little extra money doing the decorations for some of the models. I made them at home at night after my regular hours were over. When we made the first train station, we decided to make an arrivals and departures board. And actually, I made a mistake on one of those stickers because there was a time schedule of 24:07, which doesn't exist. I didn't notice that. Maybe I was a little tired at that time.

Jan Ryaa, former Design Master, the LEGO Group

NOTE: Fortunately for Jan, someone must have later caught his error, because the finished set, 7922 Railway Station, did not include his mistake on its departures/arrivals sticker.

ABOVE 7720 Diesel Freight Train Set, with track and platform, was one of the four complete train starter sets released in 1980.

BELOW Set 7727 Freight Steam Train Set from 1983 was the next generation of cargo train during the 1980s.

After a two-year hiatus, LEGO Train was reborn in 1980 with an unprecedented launch of twenty-eight products, including an astonishing four complete starter sets with full trains and enough track to get them running. These mega-sets were supplement by seven individual engine and coach models, a train station and a host of electrical accessories – all of which would have allowed Jan Ryaa's son to create layouts beyond his wildest dreams. The entire portfolio of train parts had been updated in a single year and modernised so thoroughly that the theme ran for another decade. Much of the 1980s saw a steady stream of new models chugging onto those grey tracks until, once again, elements became a new challenge.

A new system

As the decade waned, LEGO designers were developing new ways to create novelty in what were now the established primary product lines of LEGO Space, LEGO Castle and LEGO Town. One of several cross-theme elements developed was a family of electrical pieces that used a 9-volt power supply to create lights and sounds. The collection of components was dubbed the 9V system and at its core was a battery box that incorporated electrical plates to which conducting elements could be attached. The first two accessories were a light brick and a small speaker that produced a sound that was shrill to a degree utterly disproportionate to its size. Thanks to housing only a single battery, the power box could be incorporated into smaller models than ever before. It was, however, not powerful enough to motorise trains, but was capable of a propelling a pair of monorail sets. In 1990, LEGO Technic adopted the new system, which meant that LEGO Train was now the only product line still using the old 12-volt components. Once again, all the motors and electrical components were updated, this time to incorporate the 9V system so that parts could share internals with elements from the new family.

Visually, the biggest update was once again the track, which was completely overhauled into single moulded elements with brand new connectors. Jan Ryaa's original dream was realised, as this new system was so secure it could be hung from a wall. Between 1991 and 1994, some of the most detailed and beautiful LEGO trains ever were brought to market, including the legendary 4558 Metroliner, which introduced a new windshield element.

BELOW Set 4558 Metroliner included brand-new windows and fronts for its train engine.

By merging rails and ties into a single, moulded element, designers had succeeded in both simplifying and beatifying track components. But the update also meant that the metallic rails, which up until this point had been their own separate parts, had to also be incorporated into the new track element. While undoubtedly more realistic and aesthetically pleasing, there was now no way to produce inexpensive track for push-along trains which, until this point, had always existed alongside their more expensive powered counterparts.

Electrical components can enable novelty and a type of play unattainable through any other means. Conversely, they are in direct conflict with one of the central tenets of the LEGO System in Play: backwards compatibility. Electrical systems, like computer technology, become obsolete. They also degrade much faster than basic LEGO bricks and, once a battery box or wire from an older system fails, it cannot be replaced or easily substituted, unlike almost every other LEGO element. LEGO Train has long been in the unenviable position of being the theme most inexorably tied to electrical components; only LEGO® MINDSTORMS® could even compete for that title. When the 1990s waned, obsolescence reared its head once again. Light and sound had fallen out of favour and every other theme was moving away from electrical elements. With each passing year, the number of other product lines with applications for 9V fell until LEGO Train stood alone. It seemed as if LEGO Train might be reaching the end of the track.

Rise of the adult fan

Innovation has long been the LEGO Group lifeblood. Often this takes the form of an inspired new piece or product line. Sometimes, however, it is more subtle. A pivot, or slight change in strategy; thinking about something in a different way. It was such an innovation that saved LEGO Train. At the close of the twentieth century, the LEGO Group discovered something surprising. A small but growing and passionate community of adults were enjoying large numbers of LEGO sets, including trains. The company created an official liaison position. A dialogue ensued and the liaison brought back a clear message: massive cooperative train layouts were the backbone of this emerging community. Ending the theme would, at a minimum, frustrate these passionate customers and might put an end to the movement all together.

An experiment was proposed. The 9V transformer and other expensive electrical parts would be placed on hiatus, but train-specific elements like doors and windows would continue to be manufactured. Those would be maintained for a line of products targeted towards what adults were saying they wanted: individual train cars not sold as part of a starter set so they could easily buy multiples. That experiment became the My Own Train line, which ran from 2001 through 2002 and consisted of both finished models and bags of bricks geared towards trains. These were also sold briefly as a collection along with a rerelease of the legendary Metroliner, originally from 1991.

As the liaison for the adult fan community had expected, grown-up fans, who began referring to themselves as AFOLs (Adult Fans of LEGO products), loved the line. Unfortunately, it didn't have the same appeal for the general public or new adopters, who had no easy or obvious way to purchase components that would power their trains, but still had to buy costly metal-lined train track. However, a certain boy wizard was about to intervene and put his magical hand on the scale.

LEGO® Harry Potter™ sets launched to huge success in 2001, and 4708 Hogwarts Express in particular was a favourite. After all, every child at that time wanted to ride off to the magical school for witches and wizards themselves! Overnight, the situation changed for 9V and the train elements. Instead of those specialised components having a home in only one theme, there was now the possibility for three. In the wake of My Own Train, it became clear that modern children had simply viewed LEGO Train as not for them; it had been separated off into its own theme and even appeared in the back of most brand catalogues along with LEGO Technic and LEGO® Model Team, lines both targeted at older children.

Such placement was understandable: after all, the sets were complicated both to build and

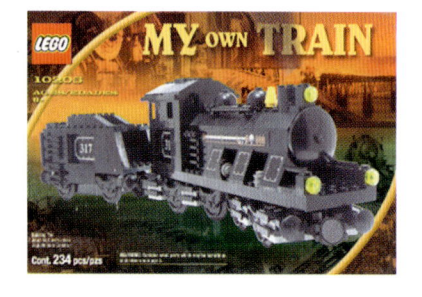

ABOVE My Own Train was the first theme targeted at the adult market.

operate. Unfortunately, this created a market mismatch. Trains were and are extremely popular with younger children, but by the time most children were developmentally capable of owning a LEGO variant, they had outgrown the interest. To solve this dilemma, a plan was hatched to fold trains back into the mainstream family of LEGO® City products, which generally target a younger demographic. Concurrently, the latest AFOL liaison continued to push for more products in the vein of My Own Train: highly detailed products targeted at the emerging adult market. In the end all three approaches were realised. The results, released between 2002 and 2004, were an expansive theme within LEGO City, the only motorised Hogwarts Express ever made, and a legendary set for adult collectors.

Creating collectibles

Most of the first LEGO models targeted at adults in the first half of the 2000s began as LEGO designers' passion projects. Designers speak of this time as if the LEGO Group were a tech startup, with many employees having the freedom to initiate and develop their own ideas. Many amazing sets and product lines were incubated and birthed from this extraordinary period, including 3451 Sopwith Camel, 10189 Taj Mahal, 10124 Wright Flyer, 10181 Eiffel Tower, 3723 LEGO® Minifigure, 3450 Statue of Liberty, as well as Modular Buildings, some LEGO® *Star Wars*™ Ultimate Collectors Series ships, and many others. They were true passion projects. It was within this special atmosphere that a new vein of trains emerged – collectibles, starting with the legendary 10020 Santa Fe Super Chief from 2002.

Collectability was the AFOL liaison's pitch. Children would play with the new LEGO City trains, fans of Harry Potter would enter the fantasy with LEGO® Harry Potter™ Hogwarts Express™, and adults would have limited-edition, ultra-realistic models to include with their expansive layouts. The project was authorised with a caveat: it needed to be a real-world train made with no new element frames.

The designers of 10020 Santa Fe Super Chief met that challenge through clever use of the available moulds catalogue and by advocating for an allocation of colour-change frames. A one-off train window from 1994's set 4564 Freight Rail Runner was found to be a perfect windshield when

BELOW Set 10020 Santa Fe, released in 2002, achieved its iconic look through colour changes and clever parts usage.

switched to red. The designers' biggest battle was wheel bearings, which had to be in grey or the Santa Fe wouldn't look right. Fortunately, LEGO® World City, the theme that was replacing LEGO Town at that time, was slated to have two trains as well as individual wagon sets. Designers from that team agreed to use grey wheel bearings on set 4511 High Speed Train and 10158 High Speed Train Car, donating one of their colour-change frames to the cause.

Upon release in 2002, all 9,999 of the collectible Santa Fe Super Chiefs sold out quickly, resulting in a second, unexpected production run that omitted the specially numbered bricks included in the first wave. Several other successful collectible trains, produced primarily for adults, followed in the next few years, as well as an independent pair of sets within the new LEGO City theme that replaced LEGO World City in 2005.

Power functions

By this point, 9-volt motors, special components just for the first LEGO City trains in 2006, and a variety of other electrical systems used by LEGO Technic were all being manufactured and then warehoused. Production space in the factories is precious and switching between moulds takes time. Something new was needed and, in the late 2000s, a team was commissioned to begin working on a single electrical system that could be adapted to meet the needs of every theme and which contained powered elements. Once it was ready, all the other different elements would be retired. Painstakingly designed over several years as a family of elements, this effort culminated in Power Functions, a system of interchangeable and fully compatible battery boxes, motors, controllers and more.

By the late 2000s, the LEGO Group had hired several designers from the growing AFOL community. They and the AFOL liaison of that time knew that retiring 9V was going to hit the fans hard. New generations of children getting a LEGO train for the first time would not even notice the change but, for adults who had invested heavily in 9V trains for nearly twenty years, it could be cataclysmic. Power Functions returned to battery boxes, which meant that all the new train track, while compatible with the previous version from a connector standpoint, would not need metal rails. This had the advantage of making track less expensive to produce, thereby lowering the bar of entry, but it meant that new track would be incompatible with 9V train motors that relied on electrified rails. Furthermore, the element managers, predecessors of today's element coaches, working in collaboration with designers, had earmarked all of the train-specific elements for deletion. From now on, trains would have to utilise windows and doors shared by other product themes.

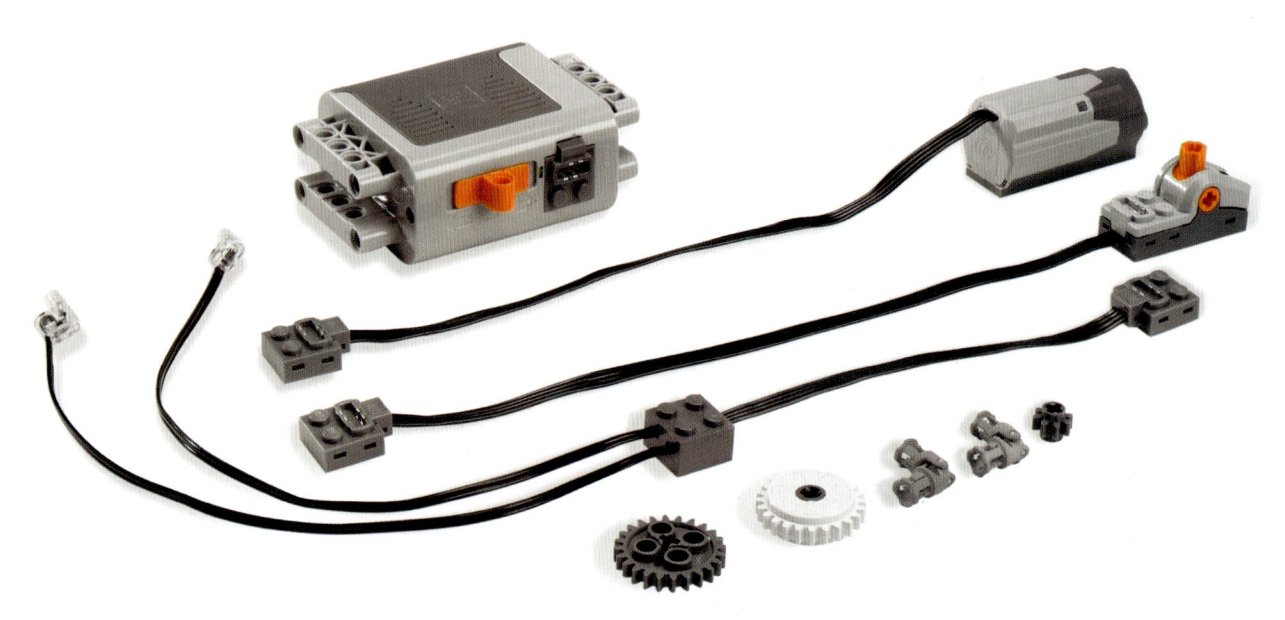

BELOW A selection of Power Functions elements.

The LEGO Group has thousands of moulds in active use every year with even more on standby. Every one of them must be regularly calibrated, maintained, polished and stored in a massive climate-controlled environment. Prior to the mid-1990s, when computers began making it possible to store information in databases, designers relied on an analogue element archive, personal lists and their own memories to know which parts were available and which were not. Retiring elements and destroying moulds occurred rarely; normally only when a new or better element came along and replaced it, such as what was about to happen with 9V. However, around the year 2000, a host of new moulds were created in a very short time for a number of themes that struggled in the marketplace. Many of the elements were highly specialised for a particular theme and were unusable when that theme ended. Over just a couple of years, storing such a large number of moulds, elements and colour variants had become a challenge.

It was time to simplify the element library. Several veteran designers were asked to join a team to use their extensive knowledge of parts and colours to reduce the number of elements. They managed to reduce the number of moulds and parts needing storage by thousands. One example was the humble wheel. Over many years since its introduction, the number produced had ballooned to over a hundred different types, many with equal diameters and only slight differences between them. Such scenarios were commonplace across many element families.

It took a whole decade, from 2000 to 2010, but by the end designers had assigned ID numbers to every element, created a company-wide database to manage its parts catalogue, called Easy Builder System (EBT), and began establishing standards for existing families of components that defined rules for when they could be added to. Wheels were a primary area of focus during this

ABOVE Moulds are stored on shelves inside a special warehouse in Billund.

> In order to keep a healthy balance of available building elements, we regularly have to decide which shapes are exited in order to make room for all the new elements that are created each year. When it came to train parts, barely anyone was using them for quite a while, so it became harder and harder to justify keeping them over other new elements that everyone was using. Some designers have been quite creative at keeping elements active, such as by using cow-catcher train elements as Samurai mech shoulder decorations. It's not only showing off the versatility of our elements, but it also sometimes helps keep good elements active for future projects.

Jamie Berard, Design Lead, the LEGO Group

effort. After cutting over 50 per cent of the variants, only forty-five wheels remained, along with a fresh new guide for developing tyres and rims only when needed. After completing their task, the responsibility for managing the parts library was rolled into the newly created role of element coach, with several of the veterans who completed the initial effort transitioning into that position.

Today, element coaches lead a yearly parts catalogue review effort. Thanks to the digital EBT database, they can tell exactly how many products a given part has been included with in recent years. Design teams each select an element ambassador from their ranks to join this review effort and make their case for parts that should be preserved for one reason or another. An element that may not currently be in use could be working its way through the approval process as a key piece in new products. Their argument must be robust, however. This team 'polices' the element library, keeping it trim and agile.

When an element does not make the cut, it is marked as retired and its mould is destroyed. This practice stems from a study that was conducted during the initial reduction in elements and which yielded surprising results. The LEGO Group found that for most moulds the cost of remaking them was less expensive than five years of storage. That finding became part of the calculus during yearly evaluations. If a strong case can't be made for an element in the next five years, retirement is more economical than storing its mould. Unfortunately for trains, the transition from 9V came at the reduction effort's height.

Nearly every unique train piece, with the exception of fenders and couplings, was marked for retirement soon after the introduction of Power Functions in 2006. In a move that was both practical and a parting gift to the AFOLs, several generous product collections of the metallic 9V track were bundled together and sold in order to quickly clear stock from shelves, but no new collectible trains appeared.

BELOW Set 7938 Passenger Train was the first LEGO City train to fully integrate the new Power Functions elements.

The plan was to continue integrating train sets into LEGO City using the remaining train-specific elements but adding no new ones. This, however, is when those designers who used to be fans re-enter the story. Several of them were working for the LEGO® Creator Expert theme, the team that was at the epicentre of the culture of designer-originated projects. A couple of them banded together and championed the idea of resurrecting a collectible train for adults. Their clever angle was to pitch it as a means of getting the fan community to embrace Power Functions.

Secretly, a small, handpicked selection of the most well-known LEGO train builders were contacted and invited to a clandestine, week-long workshop at LEGO headquarters in Billund, Denmark. Once there, these superfans were presented with Power Function elements as well as the few surviving train pieces and challenged to see what they could do with them. The group looked at what was spread on the table before them and immediately responded by asking: 'What have you guys done with all your train parts? You are missing stuff!'

Despite that initial hesitancy, over the next several days they provided valuable but challenging feedback to designers. Two omissions stood out. First, a large wheel whose greater surface area would allow for trains with many wagons, something which wasn't a concern for children but was vital for large-scale convention layouts. Secondly, train-specific windows, which had given many past legendary sets their distinctive aesthetic. At this point, however, no new element frames had been granted to the project.

Designers sprang into action. After talking with colleagues across the company, LEGO Education, a department that creates products to be used in classrooms, generously offered up one of their frames so a large train wheel could be made. A further challenge presented itself. It was quickly discovered that in order to do the train at the size they wanted – a gorgeous dark green engine with gold-lined accents – another wheel was needed. This was due to length: their prototype was so large that the number of wheels needed for support impeded its ability to go through turns and switches. A wheel with no flanges would fix the problem.

Ingenuity once again came to the rescue when manufacturing came up a clever solution: cast both wheels together and immediately bag them right at the machine. While this still required two new moulds, the elements could be stored together from the onset, saving space in the warehouse. Because frames are a function of both cost and space, that unorthodox solution, which only worked because the parts were both so unique and would always be needed together, reduced costs enough that LEGO Education single donated frame could support two new elements.

Another frantic call went down to the warehouse. To the team's delight, while all train windows were retired in EBT, their moulds had not yet been destroyed. The warehouse supervisor agreed to hold off while they made their case. After several rounds of cajoling, designers managed to gain approval to reactivate the necessary parts.

While their prototype was just an engine in keeping with previous adult-oriented train sets, the AFOL group had been adamant that there should be a wagon as well. Designers obliged and, in 2009, set 10194 Emerald Night became LEGO Creator Expert's first train set. The base model did not include Power Functions, but instructions were included for motorising it using separately purchased packs of the new electrical elements.

BELOW Set 10194 Emerald Night with its large train wheels.

A positive reception by the adult collectors implied that their objective to win over some fans to the new system succeeded, but wider sales were surprisingly sluggish. Unfortunately, appeal seemed to be fairly limited for this type of product now that children could get fully powered trains, complete with some track, to cruise around their LEGO City layouts for roughly the same price. But then a unique opportunity arose concerning the shipping mega-company Maersk.

The LEGO Group had partnered with Maersk several times before, going all the way back to 1974 for limited-release promotional items. Because of this, a special colour, Maersk blue, had been developed and maintained until the 2000s, when the overall number of elements was reduced. The largest promotional set, 10152 Maersk Sealand Container Ship, had been issued in 2004, after which the colour was retired. Now, however, the LEGO Group and Maersk planned to update the model and release it again, this time as a regular set available everywhere.

Maersk blue was back on the menu and the LEGO Creator Expert team decided to take full advantage, both to make a special product and to give hardcore fans a little gift, though there was a complication along the way. The design team did research and found the perfect subject matter: a Maersk train painted with the distinctive blue based in the US. A few months later the team visited Maersk to seek approval for its prototypes, taking an early model and those pictures with them. The odd thing was that Maersk's records seemed to show that the train did not exist.

After some digging, it was found that the train had been specially painted with the distinctive Maersk livery for a photoshoot, but it had never been expected that it would be left that way. Declaring it providential, the design team received the go-ahead to produce their model and, with Maersk's blessing, slipped in a little treat for fans. Some of the earlier Maersk sets from the 1980s had included minifigure helmets in their distinctive blue. These had long been discontinued and, due to only ever being included in promotional sets, were rare to begin with. Designers noted that they were selling for extremely high prices on the aftermarket and decided, since that element mould was still active, to give all the minifigures helmets in the distinctive blue, in what eventually became set 10219 Maersk Train.

TOP RIGHT One of the rare promotional Maersk sets with the unique blue colouring.

BELOW Set 10219 Maersk Train featured minifigures with the special blue helmets.

Rolling Along 55

> We knew that trains were always popular with adults and the more detailed and realistic we made them, the more popular they were. So initially we investigated making the Santa Fe in silver just like the real train. We got a special run of bricks all in silver, but that simply didn't look nice, so it was decided not to go that way. You get all these flow lines in the bricks that look weird. As soon as you get them, it looks like poor quality. It's because of the pigments in the plastic. The same with gold and all metal colours. It's very hard to get them to look right. That is why those colours are usually used as accents or something like that, because of the difficulty in maintaining the quality. So we had to find a different way to do it. We ended up doing everything in grey, which meant we had to get permission to do the wheel bearings in grey, which was hard. Then I had to challenge the decorations department on the side windows. They needed to be round, almost like a ship's window, which meant the deco had to go as far to the edges as possible. They didn't really want to do that. I remember I had to refer them to all the decorations they did in the 1980s, which are close to the edge, to show them it could be done. The other designer, Jørn Thomsen, and I were working and doing different versions of the Santa Fe and then taking pieces from one version and joining them with pieces from the other version. My final version was a little more detailed than the one that ended up in the box. We were also investigating this new idea of collectability, that LEGO sets could be collectibles. So the Santa Fe came with these numbered bricks at first; the first 9,999 sets had a number printed on an element inside. You didn't know which number you would get, so it was definitely intended for the adult market and the train fans.

Henrik Andersen, Design Master, the LEGO Group

Such awareness and intentionality on the part of model makers is, actually, a frequent occurrence. Element colour changes are often used as a way to both add novelty and sometimes give little treats to fans. In an instance of the latter, when designers were working on set 10235 Winter Village Market, which came out in 2013, they noted a similar spike on a different aftermarket element. They needed to use a 1×8 arch element for several small stalls for selling winter treats. The set itself included a vibrant array of colours so there were multiple options for the arch, all of which would look good. Thanks to following fan sites, the designers knew that this arch in dark blue had recently spiked in price on the aftermarket due to being an integral part of two early Modular Buildings. The last set to include it had been retired six years prior and people looking to collect all the parts for making either 10812 Café Corner or 10190 Market Street were having to pay a king's ransom for their dark blue arches. As it was all the same to them from a design perspective, the LEGO Creator Expert team selected dark blue solely to refill the aftermarket supply for fans.

Both applications of trains – affordable starter sets under the LEGO City banner and collectible adult-oriented sets – have continued right up to the present day and appear to be in no danger of retirement. Freight and passenger variants have become part of the regular LEGO City rotation, though they appear less frequently than police stations. Collectible models targeted at adults have been sparser, having to compete with other subject matter for one of the coveted and far fewer AFOL product slots. Likewise, wheels have continued as well, with every new iteration having to prove its need against the guidelines laid down in the mid-2000s. If Knud Møller could see how far his little invention has gone, he would surely be delighted.

BELOW 60051 High Speed Passenger Train is one of many produced for the LEGO City theme.

> **We went on an exciting design journey to develop a high-quality buildable figure. It was quite a challenge!**

Rosario Costa, Creative Lead, Design Director, the LEGO Group

3
Populating the LEGO® World

Brick-built people evolve into minifigures, setting the stage for collectible LEGO® Minifigures and the mini doll for LEGO® Friends three decades later.

TOP Buildable figure arm elements were joined by interlocking teeth.

ABOVE RIGHT Minifigure arms bend to allow interaction with the LEGO® System standard measurements in different positions.

ABOVE LEFT Mini doll arms have a different profile from those of a standard minifigure.

The origin story of the LEGO® minifigure may well have begun in 1968 – though an exact date has been lost to history. A trio of female designers had been hired to design sets that would bring more girls into the LEGO experience. During a brainstorming session, the idea of doll's house accessories was discussed. Doll's houses were extremely popular, but filling them required a host of accessories, mostly made of wood. In an inspired moment, the three designers realised that LEGO bricks would be perfect in such a setting. Children could use them to construct whichever customised accessories they desired. Chairs, tables, countertops, beds: the opportunities were limitless. Another factor further recommended the concept: just a few new elements, namely cabinets and drawers, could be used across kitchen, bathroom and bedroom-themed sets, thereby greatly increasing their value. Finally, an element that was still quite new when these initial discussions occurred could take the concept even further.

In 1965 element designers released the first LEGO® tile: a plate with no studs on its top. This new class of part enabled smooth, polished surfaces, making models look sleek and clean. Recalling the days when varnish was used to make wooden toys shine, these tiles covered the surfaces of brick-built furniture with a sort of 'topcoat', which helped them to avoid looking alien in a third-party doll's house. Their smoothness was like a canvas – ready and waiting for printing. No need for a new cooking-top element: black circles on a white tile would do the trick just as well.

In 1971, the first Homemaker product – as this line came to be known – hit shelves with a kitchen-themed set. All the elements of the set were compatible with existing bricks, meaning that if a child were lucky enough to have lots of spare parts, they could construct a LEGO brick-built doll's house. Set 261 Dolls Kitchen was followed by 262 Children's Bedroom, along with several small accessory sets featuring desks, sinks, bureaus, clocks and more. Before long, an obvious question emerged: why rely on outside entities to populate these playscapes? Why couldn't the LEGO Group make dolls itself?

Immediately, several challenges presented themselves. Dolls of this era were articulated, incorporating a type of movement that had no parallel in the LEGO® System. Furthermore, the type of moulding required for dolls was a different skill set from the one the LEGO Group technicians possessed at that time. It did not make sense to retool moulding machines for an

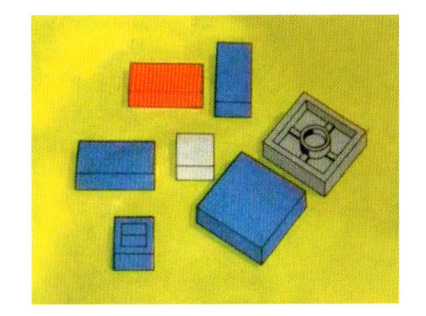

ABOVE The first LEGO tile elements were released in 1965.

ABOVE One of the first Homemaker sets, with tiles used on the table's surface. The set is staged in a brick-built environment with generic dolls. The final sets did not include the walls, but promotional images like this showed children what was possible.

unproven experiment centred around a small product line. There was only one conclusion: this would need to be a uniquely LEGO figure that worked within the LEGO System itself.

Ultimately, a clever and distinctive solution emerged. Around a dozen new elements were developed. A few of these were specific to building people, but most were generic and could be used in a variety of applications. One of the elements that would be exclusive to constructing people was the head, which was printed with one of three different face designs, while the top of the head could be adorned with a choice of five different hairstyles. Heads were designed to fit onto a special 2×2 brick that had a single hole through its centre to receive the head as well as holes on the sides for joining arms. Below this brick, a body could be built using standard LEGO elements. There would be no specialised torsos for individual figures, nor would there be parts specifically meant to mimic legs or feet. However, design team members recognised that completely static people would not facilitate enough action to make them desirable, so, in keeping with the approach of making bricks as widely usable as possible, they developed a group of generic parts that could meet multiple needs. A trio of rounded, articulating hinge pieces could be joined together via interlacing protrusions to form arms. The base hinge was attached to the special 2×2 torso brick that also held the head. The hinge's other end had two protrusions. To these protrusions could be attached either an intermediate hinge comprised of three protrusions on one end and two on the opposite, or a terminal hinge with three protrusions and a socket respectively. Each intermediate hinge boasted both odd and even numbers of protrusions, allowing as many of these as were desired to be strung together to create articulating arms of various lengths. It was possible to make extremely short arms by omitting intermediate hinges altogether, joining base and terminal hinges directly. The receiving 2×2 torso brick allowed the base hinge to rotate and the two parts were permanently joined during manufacture.

TOP LEFT For buildable figures, the torso/shoulder, two arm pieces and hands were new elements, used interchangeably across all the figures. Heads were printed with unique face prints and each featured unique hair elements.

BOTTOM LEFT The arm elements created for buildable figures proved so versatile that they were still in use two decades later in LEGO® Aquazone sets.

ABOVE Buildable figures were static from the waist down, but their heads and arms could move.

Finishing off the arm system was a part whose impact would prove completely disproportionate to its size. A tiny hand with a ball-shaped wrist could be inserted into the terminal hinge's socket, twisting freely once in place. While a clever mechanism, it was the hand's other end that would prove far more important, with a reach stretching to this day.

Buildable figures

Early on in the process, designers could see that, due to bodies and legs being made of bricks, their LEGO figures might not be able to compete with regular dolls on realism but they could win on the field of functionality. Most dolls at that time couldn't hold things, and even fewer could do it well. However, it seemed possible that, with the right design thinking, a LEGO figure might be able to hold just about anything. Nobody now knows who came up with the final proposal, but it stands as another testament to how well designed the basic LEGO brick is.

Years earlier, after developing the stud-and-tube principle for the 2×4 brick and other widely used pieces, Godtfred Kirk Christiansen and his team had turned their attention to elements with only a single row of studs. Tubes sit in the centre of four studs, making contact with each stud when joined to another brick. But that isn't possible when there is only one row of studs in a line – tubes are simply too big. Enter the bar.

A bar is another fundamental LEGO construct. Generally, in elements with widths of only one stud, bars play the same role as tubes do in components with widths of two studs or more. At exactly two sections in diameter, bars are compressed slightly by studs when pieces join, creating that all-important clutch power.

As the first LEGO figures came together, someone proposed an inspired solution for the hand. It would be round, one module in diameter and the same thickness as a LEGO plate element, which would allow it to grip a single stud. The breakthrough, however, was making the stud hollow, leaving an opening equal in size to a brick's bar. Modern element designers are always

TOP A special machine was purchased in order to print faces onto the new people heads. Figure development was done in stages with lots of experimentation in order to prove the concept worked before large-scale adoption.

ABOVE Bars grant clutch power in bricks whose geometry precludes the inclusion of full tubes.

keen to use dimensions over and over so that as many types of bricks as possible can work with a new element, and clearly their predecessors were too. Suddenly, accessories didn't need to have studs and could be much more realistically sized. Furthermore, a bar inserted into the hand was an incredibly strong connection, creating a grip far superior to any doll. This design would inform that of LEGO minifigure hands a few years later and give them many of the distinct qualities that make them so versatile and useful to this day.

The LEGO Group new buildable figure made its debut in 1974 as part of several Homemaker products and a dedicated people set that included five brick-built characters sporting all the new elements. They were a huge success, especially set 200 LEGO® Family with the five figures.

In parallel with the effort to create residents for the Homemaker line, some scattered experimentation had been done towards creating a smaller figure that could be used in conjunction with Town Plan-scale products. Thus far, these had all involved cutting and gluing existing elements, then using clay to stand in where new elements would be needed. The results had been fair but somewhat crude. However, when Homemaker proved that figures could send sales through the roof, creating a smaller version became an overnight priority in 1974, and a passionate young designer was challenged to take it on.

ABOVE The hands on buildable figures can hold objects both by attaching to studs and by passing objects through the holes in them. The legs on these figures were constructed of bricks.

BELOW Set 200 LEGO Family featured five buildable figures and was released in 1974.

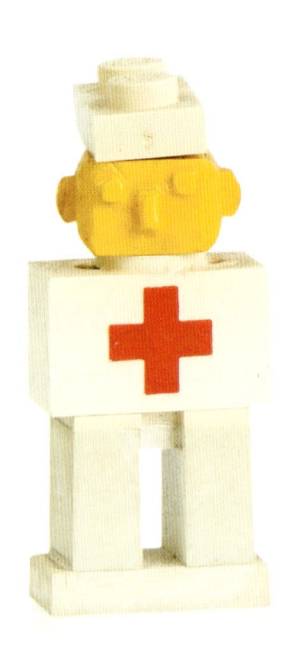

The road to minifigures

Jens Nygaard Knudsen wasted no time in assembling a small team of those who, along with himself, had been tinkering with smaller figures. Collectively they began their official effort by taking stock of everything created so far and developing some parameters based on what they knew would not work. At the top of that list was 'moulded facial features'. Heads at this scale were just too small for 3D facial features to look good. Closely following in second place was 'brick-based torsos'. To date, figures had been made of existing brick elements, giving them a boxy look.

While ultimately rejected, the need for heads to sit in the centre of a 1×2 brick, as was the case in many of those early experiments, was the inspiration for jumper plates, where a single stud is placed in the center of a 1×2. Jumper plates would make their debut a few years later in 1978 as a happy accidental byproduct of creating minifigures. Not every lesson was about what the team wanted to avoid in the new figure: a key positive observation emerged from those early experiments. Heads, whatever their final incarnations, should have studs on the top so that different accessories could be placed there.

Jens and his team broke down the problem by correlating sub-teams with a minifigure's key divisions – head, torso and legs – and tackling each of them separately. Before long, though, they ran headlong into a problem: their scale was too small for articulation to be assembled at home. Homemaker, with its much larger size, could incorporate loose hinge elements for a figure's arms. Nothing like that would be possible here: any rotation would have to be factory assembled, which meant expensive new tooling and machinery to mount the parts. Making that a reality would require betting on an unproven concept and the risk was too great, so the road to minifigures took an experimental detour known as the salt pillar.

Jens Nygaard Knudsen's team had fairly quickly homed in on two features that they felt were correct: overall dimensions and head design. Dimensionally, their prototype retained one aspect of the earliest prototypes: to maintain established measurements whenever possible. Heads would be six sections tall, torsos were eight sections, and legs would be an even ten sections,

ABOVE RIGHT Some of the earliest figure designs for minifigures were hand-carved from existing elements.

ABOVE LEFT Jumper plates allow a stud to be placed between two others on the element beneath.

for a grand total of twenty-four sections, equaling exactly four regular bricks – the minifigure's height to this day.

As with Homemaker, it was decided to conduct an experiment. Taking those dimensions, they developed the 'salt pillar', or 'stage extra', as it was sometimes called internally. Although these names initially seem strange, they actually describe the creation perfectly. Salt pillar references the story of Lot's wife being turned into a lifeless, immobile statue made of salt. Stage extras are placards or mannequins, which are similarly human-like in appearance, but immobile. Their finished product was a sort of proto-minifigure consisting of the three main components but with a few key differences. In lieu of moving legs and arms, static elements stood in, with only a little contouring that gave the crude appearance of appendages. The salt pillar's leg piece was two sections shorter than the piece that would ultimately be incorporated into minifigures, so that a 1×2 plate could be inserted between it and the torso. This was intended as another means of decoration, since the plate would resemble belts in a variety of colours. Taken all together, these three elements could be assembled into something akin to a colourful statue that was just the right size. Since nothing moved, each piece could be moulded using existing technology without the requirement for expensive new machines. Despite a lack of movement, some novelty was possible thanks to a head that could join with a small group of hat accessories that were developed concurrently. On the head, however, they broke some rules. At least, some modern ones. And that would lead to interesting challenges many years later for another team of minifigure designers.

Collectible minifigures

In 2008 Matthew Ashton, now Vice President of Design at the LEGO Group, returned to LEGO headquarters in Billund from a trip abroad with three inspiration boards. He had been fleshing out an idea: could minifigures be collectible? On the boards were his sketches for more than fifty designs of various characters and costumes. In the decades since its debut, minifigures had become almost as iconic as the brick, but they had never been packaged individually, devoid of any larger model to build. Making minifigures collectible would also require packaging in blind bags, which was without precedent in the LEGO world.

In the early 2000s, the LEGO Group had experimented with a similar concept, creating special packs with a trio of minifigures for LEGO® Star Wars™ and the American National Basketball Association (NBA). Each had come with a card and a stand for display. However, since almost none of the minifigures within the LEGO Star Wars line were exclusive – all could be obtained in regular sets – fans were not incentivised to buy them individually. The NBA figures did well in the US where the league and its players were popular, but awareness was much lower in other markets. Both lines lasted just one year, though the special hinged leg elements, which allowed the basketball figures to bend over and pick up a ball, had several years of use in LEGO® Sports.

Nevertheless, Matthew Ashton and his team got the go-ahead on the basis that it only required a few frames and wouldn't tie up much production capacity, so the risk was deemed fairly low. Who knew, it might work.

An initial list of minifigure ideas was created, which has served as the backbone of the collectible LEGO® Minifigures line ever since. Initially, hundreds of characters populated it, not all of them appropriate, according to the designers in the brainstorming session, and since then ideas for even more minifigure characters have been added to it. Some are brought by other designers passionate about a certain niche interest. Children and fans even write in with ideas. Unlike almost every other LEGO theme, there is no formal testing of ideas for LEGO Minifigures. Since the minifigures are bought randomly in blind bags, the popularity of individual figures is tracked differently to other LEGO sets. Early waves included various subtle methods of identifying bag contents, but these were intended for safety reasons in the event that a recall was required. Later waves dispensed with these systems altogether.

ABOVE A 'salt pillar' figure of a cowboy.

BELOW LEFT Released in the first wave of LEGO Minifigures in 2010, Circus Clown came with a unique horn element and the first use of a new hair element.

BELOW RIGHT Released in 2010, the Cowboy has a unique print, but no unique parts, since his revolvers and hat are reused from previous themes. Every collectible minifigure in the line has at least one unique feature, which could be an element, a torso print, and/or a face print.

OPPOSITE A range of just some of the novelty parts created for various collectible LEGO Minifigures.

When selecting new figures for the line, the LEGO Minifigures team chooses characters that will appeal to a broad range of children, showcase the humour of the brand and wouldn't fit well into another play theme. As the first few series were followed by another and then another, those working on the line developed an approach. An essential aspect of the LEGO Minifigures theme is novelty parts; it relies on them more than any other product group. Despite that, even today, the theme is rarely able to give each figure a unique part. While cost is, of course, a consideration, there is also a purely logistical consideration. Every new element requires hundreds of hours' work by designers and mould engineers. There simply isn't enough time for them to create a special element for every figure. The balance is made up with colour change and graphic-design frames for torsos, legs or accessories, so that every character is unique in some way.

Each new series brings with it a dance. First comes the selection of characters, which are picked from the master list. While an official formula doesn't exist, choices generally fall into three categories: iconic characters such as bandits or space marines; figures that will synergise with an IP or other current/upcoming theme; and, finally, fun or wacky characters that will just make fans smile.

Populating the LEGO® World   69

> Early on, we realised we had a good approach. We want every series of collectible LEGO Minifigures to have a minifigure for everyone. Our core audience is children, but we are well aware that adults are fans too. So we include nods to older characters or themes and little storylines that tie characters together from different series. Overall, the feel of each wave is positive, lighthearted, silly and fun. But we also have a few everyday or more serious figures, but not so many that the feel switches to mundane or dark. We also try to include figures that will inspire interesting role play or building: for example, a warrior or a historic or futuristic figure. Then of course we love putting in totally silly figures: somehow Hot Dog Man has become an ambassador for our brand! Cactus Girl is also one of our favourites.

Tara Wike, Senior Design Manager, the LEGO Group

The next stage after character selection is the brainstorming of how to make each one interesting. Lists of potential accessories are developed and these are reviewed by mould engineers for both feasibility and complexity. That latter trait relates directly to distribution within the final boxes. While collectible minifigures are individually bagged, they are sold in boxes, each containing the same number of each figure. Designers push for more of those figures which they believe will be most popular, but sometimes their preferences are not possible. Logistically, more complex accessories can tie up production lines. If their moulding process takes more time, then sometimes fewer are produced and that character takes one of the lower-count slots in the final box.

Finally, after preliminary designs are complete, envoys get dispatched to interface with other product teams and find out where there could be overlap. To avoid wasteful duplication of resources, if a magician is on the menu for LEGO Minifigures and the LEGO® City team is thinking of doing a rabbit, only one variant should be made. Such synergy is, however, sometimes problematic for LEGO Minifigures. Novel parts truly are their main selling point, so they have been granted a privilege normally reserved for licensed themes or product lines in their first year: the ability to lock elements.

Exclusive elements

Some pieces are locked into a licensed theme because they are iconic to that theme, while others are part of a new product line and are integral for imparting the theme's distinctive look or appeal. LEGO Minifigures and other internal themes will normally be granted a six-month lock on new elements before designers can use them anywhere. This preserves novelty and focuses consumer attention on their products instead of immediately dispersing and diluting a new

TOP The Hazmat Guy minifigure is an example of intricate moulding.

ABOVE Unique elements such as those for the Rock Monsters in LEGO® Power Miners will be locked, at least initially, to preserve a new theme's novelty.

LEFT Some elements are so unique to their subject matter that they remain locked even after a licensed theme is discontinued, never to be used again. Many of the unique head pieces for dwarves in LEGO® The Hobbit™ fall into this category.

Fig.1

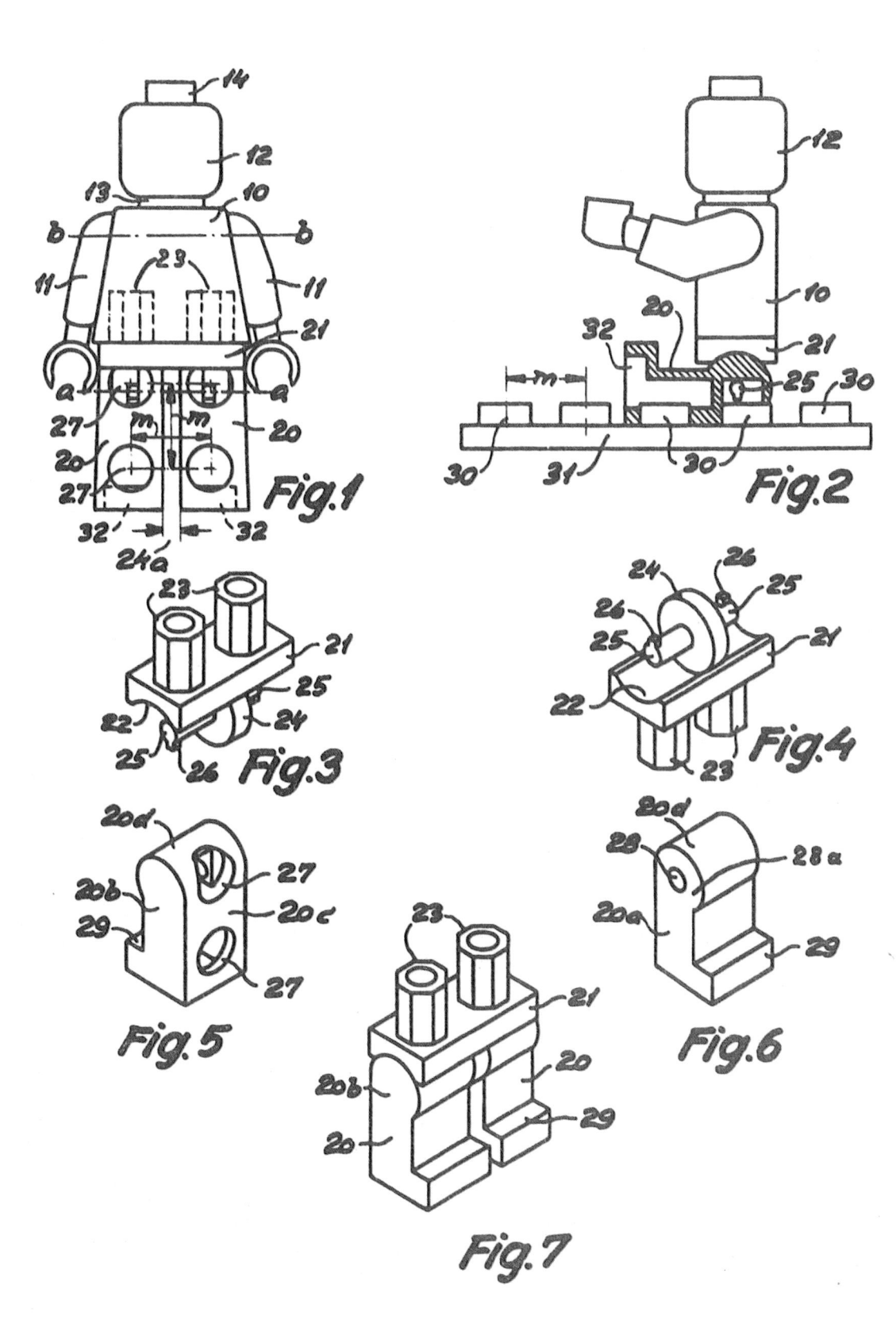

Fig.2

Fig.3

Fig.4

Fig.5

Fig.6

Fig.7

part across the company's whole portfolio. Such exclusivity is an absolute necessity for LEGO Minifigures.

The second great challenge for collectible LEGO Minifigures traces its roots all the way back to Jens Nygaard Knudsen and his team in the 1970s. Guided by a desire, first and foremost, to make their new figures appealing, choices were made along the way which did not cleanly fit into the LEGO System basic dimensions. While the key measurements of a minifigure's three primary components are even sections, several of its other key attributes are not. Some of these serve a practical purpose. For example, minifigure legs are slightly less than two modules in width. Normal two-module-wide elements, such as 2×2 brick, include a tiny air gap on each side, but minifigures allow for larger air gaps. This is to make it easier for children to slide their characters into and out of seats and other tight spaces.

Other deviations, though, are purely aesthetic. When the final head design was completed and placed atop the 'salt-pillar' body, it protruded out over the torso's back and front at a dimension which didn't match any established proportion or value. Making it stick out a full section, or even half a section, would have made minifigure heads unrealistically large. Sets that included salt-pillar figures went on sale in 1975 to test the concept of including miniature people in LEGO products. Sets with minifigures went on to sell extremely well in comparison to their non-populated counterparts. With their basic dimensions and a final head design finalised, Jens and his team received the go-ahead to begin phase two of their process: making the figure move.

Over the next three years, from 1975 to 1978, the minifigure's final form was created. Taking a cue from buildable figures, Jens Nygaard Knudsen and his team first tackled the arms, reasoning that, if need be, they could stop there, having attained similar mobility and play options as those earlier doll's-house residents. Thanks to the desire to improve on the earlier blocky

OPPOSITE A portion of the minifigure patent showing numbered parts. For each part shown here, Jens Nygaard Knudsen and his team had to work out exact dimensions.

ABOVE Salt pillar figures being used as cowboys.

figures, salt pillars had established a slight taper for torsos that imparted a visually correct human proportion when taking all the other dimensions into consideration. This would need to be maintained in the new minifigure, but two additional angles needed to be determined: those for the arms and hands.

The team experimented with many different combinations and options before settling on a design that considered arms outstretched the most likely orientation for play and therefore the base position. When a minifigure stands with its arms extended in front of it, the distance from centre to centre of its claw hands will be exactly two modules. Even so, the unique dimensional world in which minifigures exist became apparent. Half sections and half modules, or even quarter variants, are the domain of minifigures, necessitated by their need, first and foremost, to mirror human child proportions as much as possible. Raise a minifigure's hands all the way up, the centre-to-centre dimensions of its hands equals seven and a half sections. Fully lowered, twelve- and three-quarter sections. No other element in the LEGO System is so irregular with its connection points and measurements.

A key difference between minifigures and their predecessors are hands. While the clever dimensions of buildable figure hands allowed for all manner of accessories to be clutched, such a design would be too big for the much smaller minifigure. However, an important aspect of LEGO play was the ability to hold bars and one-module-width elements, so designers set out to maintain both capabilities. The answer ended up being a hand with two slightly curved

RIGHT A family tree in Billund depicts the early evolution of LEGO figures. The earliest buildable figures are shown at the trunk of the tree, with branches for (from left to right) the LEGO minifigure, LEGO® Fabuland figures, LEGO® Basic figures, the LEGO® Technic figure, and LEGO® DUPLO® figures.

sides extending out like claws. Their angles were set such that a single stud component could be clicked into place on the top while bars could be slid in between and held firmly by the protrusions. They were dubbed claw hands.

For many years, the irregular fit between minifigure dimensions and LEGO System dimensions was not a consideration. Minifigures retained their original, simple shape and facilitated role play when placed in vehicles or locations. The collectible LEGO Minifigures theme changed all that. Accessories often have connectors on them which designers strive to make compatible with standard measurements. If at all possible, accessories placed on a figure should bridge the gap between those respective dimensional frameworks. This is not always an easy task and determining whether designers have succeeded is accomplished through a surprisingly analogue method, considering all the sophisticated digital tools being used throughout the rest of the process. A sort of brick-built obstacle course has been constructed through which any potential minifigure in the LEGO Minifigures theme must pass. It has to be able to sit in a chair, go through various doorways, ride in cars and interface successfully with a variety of connectors. Accessories must work in the non-standard space of minifigures as well as the brick-built world of normal LEGO System parts, and bridging that gap is often extremely challenging for designers.

Legs were the final piece of the puzzle for Jens Nygaard Knudsen and his team. Thanks to the plate for belts that had been included in the salt-pillar figure, there was just enough room at ten sections tall when standing to find space for a 2×2 set of holes which could receive studs when minifigures were seated. When the figure was standing, the uppermost holes needed to be slightly recessed and hidden in the curve, which proved the trickiest design aspect. In a parallel effort, machinists and the purchasing department worked to acquire the equipment necessary for mounting arms on torsos and legs on hips.

ABOVE Some of the first minifigures ever made included a female medic and a policeman. Note how the torsos are not printed yet; instead, details were added via stickers.

Everything came together in 1978 when the minifigure was released alongside the first three play themes, LEGO® Space, LEGO® Castle, and LEGO® Town. The new themes were scaled for the new figure and took the world absolutely by storm. Just as impressive, if not more so, is how robust and versatile the minifigure's design proved to be. Minifigures have remained virtually unchanged since their inception and have been able to accommodate ever more advanced and complex sets. Billions of them have been produced since 1978 and thanks to collectible LEGO Minifigures, along with licensed themes, which have seen many popular figures from book and film immortalised as LEGO people, they have only grown in popularity. Just because the design was perfect from the outset, however, did not mean that the story of innovating with figures at the LEGO Group was finished. History would repeat itself several times over during the next few decades.

Developing a new figure

One of the original driving forces behind figure innovation was the motivation to develop products that would draw more girls into the LEGO experience. After unleashing minifigures upon the world, the LEGO Group assembled another team in the early 1980s and tasked it with the same charge as the trio that had come up with Homemaker years earlier. At that time, the doll market was dominated by fashion-doll franchises, so designers started there as they began to work out how to make a new LEGO figure. Articulation was their main takeaway; many popular dolls had multiple joints for movement. This was a difficult trait to emulate in LEGO figures, not because designers couldn't work out how to do it, but once again because LEGO production processes were different from those for fashion dolls.

Moulding parts and then transporting them for assembly takes time and resources. Other doll makers moulded and then assembled appendages like articulated arms and legs in the same machine, dramatically cutting down the number of parts that had to be moved and connected in a second machine. The LEGO Group equipment was not set up to work in this way.

During the early 1980s, therefore, a lot of experimentation was done to try and replicate such a process. None of the results seemed quite right, but a new marketable figure did come

BELOW LEFT One of the many machines purchased from equipment maker Poul Johansen for manufacturing and assembling minifigures. Tooling up for the new figures was a huge investment.

BELOW RIGHT The new machine for assembling LEGO Technic figures was eleven metres long and assembled each figure through sixty operations from a total of twenty-five feeding stations. Despite its size and cost, the machine could handle just thirty figures per minute.

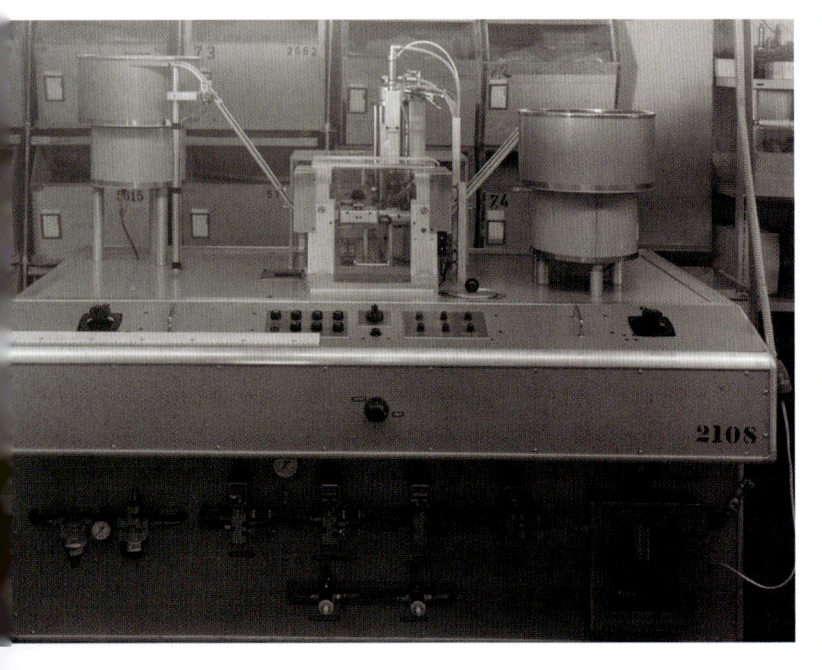

out of the experimentation – which was deemed perfect for infusing role play into one of the LEGO Group more cerebral themes: LEGO Technic. Designers utilised the new processes and parts created through experimentation to design a special LEGO Technic figure, which debuted in an Arctic-inspired subtheme. The theme was designed to accommodate the new figure in a manner similar to the way in which LEGO Space and LEGO Castle had been scaled to fit minifigures. This LEGO Technic figure would feature in many more sets until it was phased out in the great parts purge of the early 2000s. Experimentation to work out how to make a doll-like figure, however, did not stop.

Designers and mould-makers continued to work on the challenge and, as the 1980s drew to a close, they began homing in on a solution. During the early 1990s, confidence was strong enough that a new theme, named LEGO® Belville, began working its way through the approval process.

LEGO Belville introduced a new scale of larger, articulated figures, who lived in houses constructed of large, moulded elements that were compatible with regular LEGO bricks. While interaction was possible, the parts for this new theme were on average noticeably larger, and were intended for creating spacious, open air-style homes.

LEFT An early LEGO Technic figure.

ABOVE LEGO Belville elements and sets were generally larger than LEGO System models. The theme reused some parts, such as cabinets, from the earlier Homemaker theme.

Despite the success at making a figure, it came down to the wire as to whether LEGO Belville would get the green light. For much of the 1980s, the LEGO Group had produced a theme called LEGO Fabuland, which was intended to bridge the gap between LEGO DUPLO and LEGO System sets. The delightful theme featured a vibrant, imaginative world populated by charming, sentient animal-headed figures who walked on two legs and were about twice a minifigure's size.

LEGO Fabuland had been retired a few years earlier, but a revival targeted at girls was pitched as an alternative to LEGO Belville. There were some major advantages, since a plethora of moulds for Fabuland already existed. Designers experimented with revamped colour schemes that kept all the traditional colours but added pastels and new decorations to give them a different visual look. Eventually, the two options went head-to-head and ultimately LEGO Belville more detailed figure was chosen for release. By that time, engineers had gone beyond the technology which had enabled production of the LEGO Technic figure and could now mould articulated appendages whole, without any need for separate assembly at the machine or otherwise. That process would go on to be used in LEGO Belville replacement in the late 1990s: a new doll's house-style theme called LEGO® Scala.

These themes, as well as a minifigure-based subtheme of LEGO Town called Paradisa, ran for two to four years during the 1990s. Then, in 2008, a new team was tasked with the same challenge from all those years ago. This time, however, they did something different: research.

Rather than looking at other fashion dolls on the market and trying to add a LEGO twist, designers spoke directly to potential customers and their parents. What they discovered surprised them. For a whole subset of children, the minifigure was not an asset but an impediment. These children described the minifigure as lacking emotion, not being realistic enough, and not being able to facilitate the type of feelings-based role play they wanted. A LEGO Space set, for example, was great for action and play potential – it doesn't need to focus on how each of the astronauts relate to one another. Some children who sought to express themselves through their toys were not connecting with minifigures. In parallel, the team also learned that these same children did not want a separate building system. LEGO Belville and especially LEGO Scala distinctive universe of parts was anathema. They wanted to build with LEGO bricks – they just didn't want to play with minifigures. It was a revelation, but also a challenge.

It was clear that a new figure was needed, something wholly different from the minifigure but also not completely alien like the large, moulded dolls of years past. As the idea developed, parameters were laid down based on all the company's past experience with LEGO Belville, LEGO Technic, LEGO Scala and LEGO® Paradisa, as well as all the recently conducted research. The new figure, which ultimately became the mini doll, needed to be compatible with LEGO System elements. In other words, it had to fit in all the standard LEGO doorways, vehicles and other regular sets, even if it didn't attach to them in the same way as a minifigure. All hair and accessories needed to work with both types of figures. Lastly, the same three-part platform of legs, torso and head should be replicated.

Despite the fact that it was being developed for release in a single theme, eventually named LEGO® Friends, designers were aware that there would be a huge range of applications for the new figure including, potentially, in licensed product lines. Through testing, they had found that

ABOVE A LEGO Fabuland figure.

TOP LEGO Scala sets were some of the largest LEGO products ever created.

ABOVE LEGO Scala figures emulated other, more traditional fashion dolls on the market, instead of using the more stylised figures of previous LEGO themes.

the group of children that overlooked LEGO toys because they did not connect with minifigures was such a big group that it included subgroups. Initially, their focus was on the large contingent that responded during testing to product lines focused on everyday adventures among a group of co-equal friends. There was another group, especially on the upper end of the age bracket, that loved fantasy themes and heroes who went on daring missions. To service that niche group, LEGO® Elves appeared a few years later, in 2015.

Before long, the new mini doll's development began to intertwine with possible worlds for it to inhabit and the development of the key characteristics of those worlds. Designers homed in on three key traits that would help differentiate the worlds for their new figure: setting, characters and degree of tension. Each of those traits would eventually lead to new parts. Setting defined where the story would occur. Was it a world like ours or something fantastical? Was it on land, air, sea or something else? The category of characters was likewise expansive. Were the key heroes equals, giving children options for projecting themselves, or was there a primary protagonist? Past offerings had included both approaches, but they were usually in service to the nature of the theme, not the other way around. LEGO® Alpha Team, a secret-agent theme from the early 2000s, had included a team of equals fighting a singular bad guy with nameless drones. LEGO® Knights' Kingdom, a couple of years later, employed the same strategy.

Degree of tension proved one of the most difficult challenges. In most themes to date, tone

> LEGO Belville was a very different platform. It used some LEGO System bricks, but not exclusively. LEGO Friends is one of the most researched product lines in the company's history. Previously, we had made a lot of assumptions about how girls like to build. But children and their parents didn't want a separate system; they wanted a true LEGO experience based on the LEGO core values, inspiring children to build and rebuild, be creative and even develop three-dimensional motor skills. We realised we needed a new figure offering. Most children who were not playing with LEGO toys and were more into role-play themes wanted more realistic, detailed figures in order to feel more emotionally attached to the characters. These children want to project themselves into the characters so the figures need to look more real and have more personality. We then went on an exciting design journey to develop a high-quality buildable figure, which took several years. It is really hard to create something that can be used for many different purposes and themes for years to come. It was quite a challenge! However, the mini doll has become a crucial factor in the success of LEGO Friends.

Rosario Costa, Creative Lead, Design Director, the LEGO Group

of voice had been about action, resulting in a high degree of tension. The location changes, but characters are essentially avatars for different approaches to dealing with that tension. Do they plan, attack head on or try to think their way out of it? Children would identify their favourite approach to a problem, then pick the figure – usually with a corresponding colour – who shared it. The new mini doll needed to be something different; the platform should be able to support complex, emotional role play, where children saw themselves in the characters. Round after round of testing was conducted, mixing and matching colours, figure prototypes and more, trying to find the right balance of setting, character and degree of tension to connect with this underserved demographic.

After four years, in 2012, the mini doll – the end result of their efforts – appeared on shelves. Like Jens Nygaard Knudsen and his 1970s-era team that preceded them, the mini-doll team prioritised realistic proportions over LEGO System dimensions; when compared head-to-head, mini dolls are even more out of System than minifigures are. To achieve more human-like proportions, an extra three sections of height were added, for a total of twenty-seven. However, none of the three components – legs, torso or head – are whole sections. The distance between the connectors beneath feet are equal to that of a minifigure, but the depth of the feet (toe to heel) was increased to six sections, equal to the height of a brick, allowing a more realistic proportion. That tiny bit of extra space means that legs can curve slightly at the back and the overall shape of the whole body is more realistic.

While the biggest visual difference between a mini doll and a minifigure is the height, the biggest functional difference between the two figures lies in the arms. Because a minifigure's torso tapers slightly, the distance from one hand to the other changes depending on how high the arms are raised. Mini dolls maintain a consistent hand distance apart no matter where they are rotated; it is always the same as a minifigure's hands when they are fully down: from one hand to the other is twelve- and three-quarter sections. Tests with children found that these sacrifices in consistency with easy LEGO System dimensions, which allowed for smoother, more realistic shapes and less blocky appearances, helped test subjects relate to the figures to a degree they didn't with standard minifigures. Children who had never before connected with LEGO toys built and played with enthusiastic abandon.

RIGHT LEGO® Elves was the mini doll's second major theme. To help differentiate it from LEGO Friends, LEGO model makers consulted with a fashion designer to help develop more exciting clothing to fit with the theme's adventure story.

From their inception, figures have consistently revolutionised how consumers could interact with LEGO sets. The salt pillar and buildable figures proved that there was an appetite for role play within the LEGO brick's world. New play experiences were made possible by minifigures and, later, mini dolls, as well as to a lesser extent LEGO Belville and LEGO Scala. Back at the beginning, as Jens Nygaard Knudsen was working, big plans were afoot for some of the new worlds minifigures could inhabit – and designers were about to be briefed.

TOP LEGO Friends focuses on a group of equal friends in a world like ours, with low tension. From the very first wave, settings for roleplaying interactions between close friends and family have been a mainstay of the theme.

LEFT Another major minifigure evolution arrived with detailed faceprints and dual-sided head elements.

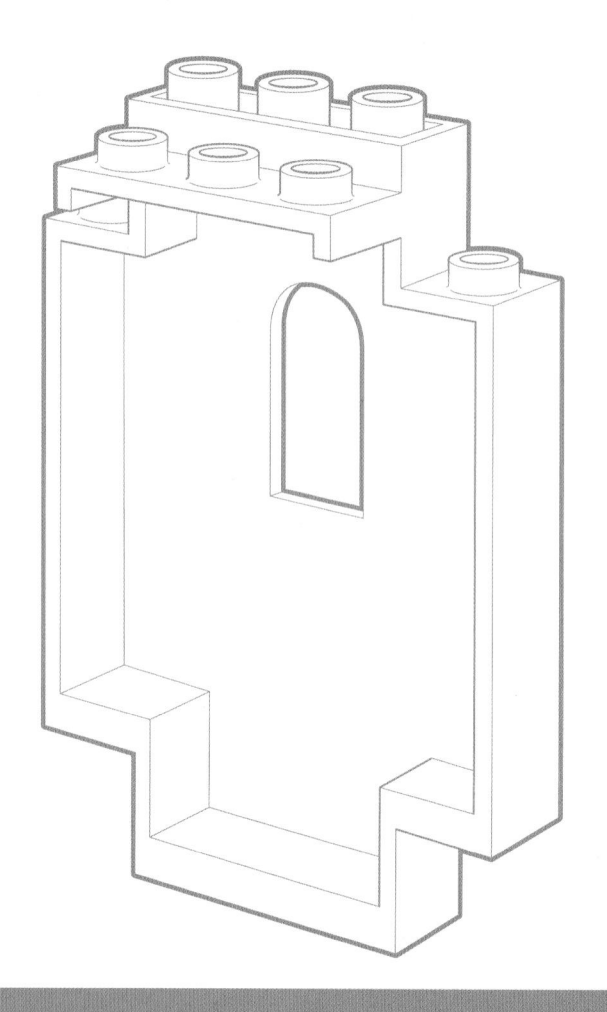

> ## We built the first grey castle prototypes from a stack of handmade elements!

Niels Milan Pedersen, Designer, the LEGO Group

4

Past, Present and Future

Kjeld Kirk Kristiansen's vision for a System within the System leads to the first LEGO® themes and a world of knights, pirates, bandits and adventurers

TOP LEFT The castle wall panel was an efficient means of covering a large amount of space.

TOP RIGHT The original horse, with its one smaller leg.

ABOVE Different versions of the canon, both firing and non-firing, were produced for different countries.

The iconic LEGO® minifigure was under development and these tiny figures had the potential to transform the company. Alone, however, they would not be enough; the missing ingredient was worlds. For many years, Town Plan and its selection of everyday-life-inspired products had defined the LEGO® System in Play. Single products like a Lunar Lander or sailing ship had hinted at other settings, but minifigures could go anywhere and be anything. Kjeld Kirk Kristiansen, the third-generation owner of the company, is credited with providing the concept of systems within the System based on three distinct time-period settings: past, present and future.

Along with perfecting the new figures, designers were tasked with developing three inaugural worlds, scaled to match a minifigure's size, for this miniscule populace to inhabit. Something from the past, something from the present day and something futuristic. Present day was simple: the Town Plan model would simply morph into an updated version of itself that integrated minifigures. As an enthusiast of space rockets almost as much as cars, Kjeld Kirk Kristiansen was also quickly sold on a space theme. Focusing on an Apollo-like aesthetic was also perfectly

LEFT One of the modern storage halls in Billund shows how much space LEGO elements take to store. While fewer elements existed in the 1980s, limits in technology for retrieval in some ways made the process more difficult.

timed, as many children aged between eight and twelve, who were the target demographic, had grown up watching those missions on TV; space was a natural choice.

Past proved briefly more challenging, as there were multiple viable options to choose from. LEGO® Vikings were under consideration, but then a prolific designer named Daniel August Krentz presented a fully conceptualised medieval theme, with catapults, multiple castles and jousting lists. While much liked, there were concerns: first, the LEGO Group took seriously its mandate to never make war into child's play. The second concern was practical. A major reason the company had not previously expanded much beyond everyday life sets was to limit the production of too many new elements and moulds. When the company decided to move ahead with Daniel August Krentz's castle models, designers were encouraged to use elements already cast in grey, rather than recasting a variety of existing bricks in realistic grey. This was to reduce the risk of the company having to store large assortments of elements in what was perceived as a speciality colour. Frames were, after all, functions of both cost and physical space. Storing a large number of grey pieces until uses could be found for them was not ideal. Only elements already cast in grey could be used, which amounted to plates alone.

Nevertheless, this venture into recreating history with bricks was going to require at least some new frames, starting with a challenge with Daniel August Krentz's initial castle designs. In order to make a castle big enough for children to be able to reach their hands inside to play, the fortress needed to be prohibitively large. Since every wall and tower was constructed of individual bricks, production costs kept rising beyond the realm of the manageable. This resulted in a novel solution: castles that could open.

Through cutting and gluing existing bricks, designers affixed LEGO® Technic pins and receiving holes to the sides of standard 1×2 bricks. Pins could slide down into holes but still rotate, creating a strong yet mobile hinge. Incorporating such elements into the castle's side walls allowed them to open, transforming tight interior courtyards into expansive play areas. It was a perfect solution. Siege scenarios could be enacted outside, with models closed, since any action would occur on the walls or in front of the fortress, while jousts or feasts could be played out in the opened configuration.

Those rough prototypes became the first swivel hinges, which went on to be used in nearly every major LEGO theme and in lots of minor ones too. Access problems had been solved but another hurdle remained. How could there be a medieval theme without conflict?

To keep conflict at a playful level, Daniel August Krentz had focused on jousting, which could be justified as contest. There was also a valid practical concern. Two children sitting down to play should not have to choose between who would be the hero versus the villain. Friendly

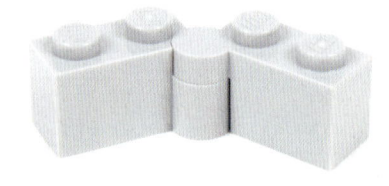

ABOVE Swivel hinges were originally created to facilitate the opening of castles.

RIGHT Set 375 Castle, released in 1978, opened wide to facilitate play, taking advantage of the new hinge elements.

competition at the jousting lists would mitigate such situations. To that end, these little knights would only carry lances and lance-like weapons, along with shields.

Daniel and his team, however, desired swords as well. Initially, they gave their blades the same name as a Danish utensil for cutting cakes: banquets in the castle would, after all, need cutlery. Several types of helmets rounded out the ensemble. The LEGO Group did not yet have the ability to print graphics onto minifigures, so a sticker sheet was included with the first castle set, allowing for application of crests onto both torsos and shields. While a necessity, it also meant that only one type of piece had to be stored instead of multiples with different icons on them. This would be the only time that approach was taken.

Production constraints meant that only a limited number of sets for each new theme could be manufactured in time to correspond with the launch of the LEGO minifigure in 1978. At this point, the present was the only era with a proven record. Accordingly, LEGO® Town received the lion's share of allocations, ultimately debuting with a whopping thirty-four sets to its name, including models for land, air and sea, as well as gorgeous new road baseplates. Both LEGO® Space and LEGO® Castle were considered experiments and therefore received a smaller percentage of available production capacity for their initial offerings. LEGO Space launched with four sets, two small vehicles and two medium-sized bases. LEGO Castle was a different story.

> "If you are a child and you are playing with a friend, who would want to be the bad guy? Nobody wants that. That was how we thought, anyway. So, when I designed the sword for the first castle, we called it in Danish a word that means 'big knife for cutting cakes'. That was the official name for the sword at first. We did that a lot back then, both in LEGO Space and LEGO Castle. We made a 'radio pole' or 'megaphone', knowing that they would give children a few different options for play."

Niels Milan Pedersen, Designer, the LEGO Group

Past, Present and Future 91

Even after having been shrunk down from Daniel August Krentz's initial prototype, thanks to those new hinges, the model which became set 375, called simply 'Castle', clocked in at 767 elements, one of the highest piece counts of any set produced by the LEGO Group to date by a wide margin. By comparison, all four products making up LEGO Space inaugural wave included 622 bricks combined, more than 200 fewer than what would become known as the 'Yellow Castle'. Sorting all those parts meant that no other set could be produced for the castle experiment: set 375 would have to be enough to prove that medieval should be the past's subject all on its own. Fortunately, it was up to the challenge.

Set 375 Castle was released in 1978, alongside the LEGO minifigure and both LEGO Town and LEGO Space themes. Set 383 Knight's Joust came out the following year with similar inclusions. Both sets sold so well that they were rereleased in 1981. The medieval era was clearly an appealing time period for a LEGO theme.

The next step was to create a full LEGO Castle product line demarcated by a formal relaunch, this time with a range of sets across multiple price points, an allocation of frames including colour changes, and the potential for multiple waves across successive years. Yellow Castle, however, had been constructed from walls and towers made of solid bricks, which were expensive to produce and store. Designers set about trying to find a new approach and, as is usually the case with LEGO products, the answer turned out to be elements.

After many discussions, designers realised that the ideal approach would be to invent a simpler way to construct walls. Individual bricks require a lot of raw material for creating the spaces in which studs and tubes interact; faces and wall thicknesses result in substantial surface area. Three designers – Daniel August Krentz, along with Jens Nygaard Knudsen and Niels Milan Pedersen – spent many hours working on the challenge.

Eventually, these designers concluded that the perfect solution would be a part that had tubes on the bottom and studs on the top, with those surfaces connected by a sheet of plastic just thick enough to be rigid. Thus, the castle panel was born. Initially, the designers intended for it to be six studs in width at the top and bottom. However, impatience got the better of them. At this time, it took a while to get new prototype elements, even when taking advantage of the less

ABOVE One of the knights from set 375 Castle, with armour sticker applied, wields the 'cake-cutting utensil'.

BELOW Set 383 Knight's Joust, released in 1979, made it clear that LEGO Castle was about friendly competition, not battles.

exacting process of pre-moulding, which produced moulds at lower quality and was therefore quicker. Anxious to start working on models for the relaunch of what would now be a fully-fledged LEGO Castle theme, the three designers began creating versions of their panel design with existing bricks. To add detail, each wall element was slated to have a small arched window cut out of its centre. Two existing arch pieces were already in the parts catalogue, one four studs long, the other three, which could be used to depict this window. Centering it within a six-stud-wide panel would require the use of the four-stud-long arch piece, meaning the opening would be about two studs wide. The designers, however, were avid history enthusiasts, and they knew that castle windows should leave little room beyond what was needed for archers. At the same time, they were not happy with creating mock-ups with the properly sized window, created using the three-stud-long arch element off-centre.

In order to get building while also satisfying their historical and aesthetic sensibilities, Daniel, Niels and Jens created brick-built prototype panels that were five studs wide so the three-stud-long arch could be properly centred. Those prototypes ultimately became the basis for the final designs, resulting in some of the only five-stud-wide elements ever created. In tandem, they developed a corner component allowing for walls to bend ninety degrees so that they could join seamlessly with the panels.

The first moulded LEGO horse

The next idea from designers was moulded horses. Considering that jousting was supposed to be this theme's focus, horses were a necessity and had dutifully been included with sets 375 and 383. But in both cases, they were brick-built and, while designers liked the size, each animal was inherently fragile and somewhat simplistic. If LEGO Castle was going to continue over the long haul, designers felt that something stronger and more realistic was needed. Until now, moulded animals had been resisted, since the company did not want to set a precedent and risk children not accepting future brick-built animals if they knew detailed, moulded versions could be made. The thinking was that such creatures would require more specialised parts, leading to a proliferation of elements.

ABOVE One of the early brick-built horses in a promotional shot.

BELOW Created for LEGO Castle, panels are an efficient way to build walls.

BOTTOM Early arch elements came in two sizes, which resulted in the width of the LEGO Castle wall panel.

RIGHT The original LEGO horse, with the thinner front leg visible (*left*), alongside its replacement from several decades later (*right*).

> The castle wall panel is five studs wide instead of six because we had the three-studs-long arch element with the window opening. That piece already existed, so we could build prototype panel elements out of existing bricks. We would actually sit in the evening and build all the elements we would need and glue them together. We would have a stack of handmade elements and we built the first grey castle prototypes with those because it would take such a long time before we got anything from the engineers and we couldn't wait for that. Many people have wondered why we made this odd five-stud width: it's because we could build it. We couldn't build the six-stud-long one because to do that we would have had to use the four-stud-wide arch with window opening and that was too big for a castle because, in an actual castle, the windows are more like slits. So that's why the castle wall panels ended up being five studs long instead of six. If it had been today, with computer programs and instant 3D printing of prototype elements, I am sure it would have been an even number of studs. In fact, when the piece was revised, they made the new castle panels four studs long. We were right about the window size though: they kept that the same!

Niels Milan Pedersen, Designer, the LEGO Group

> I had made several sculps of the horse, and some technical drawings, too. The horse prototype I had made was going to the engineers to make the mould. I had made two versions: one was OK and the other one was slightly wrong. Somehow, the incorrect version was delivered to the engineers. By this time, it was too late. Amazingly, nobody noticed it, even when they made the big brass sculpt at 3:1 scale, from which moulds are produced. Once you know, though, you can't unsee it. One of the front legs is a tiny bit thinner than the other. This was wrong on the second-to-last sculpt and it was why I made the final version, but it was never delivered. However, it was corrected when a new horse was made for LEGO® The Lord of the Rings™.

Niels Milan Pedersen, Designer, the LEGO Group

Crafting the new LEGO horse began with tracing an existing brick-built version. Then, a skeleton of bricks was constructed, with clay added on top, to form possible body designs. Designers had wanted it to be articulated, but this meant more parts and manufacturing time, so they incorporated only a single function to make the horse's neck move. All those designs led to a mix-up that resulted in a horse being produced for over twenty-five years that had one leg thinner than the other three.

LEGO Castle was officially relaunched as a proper theme in 1984 with an assortment of eight sets, including two castles facilitated by generous quantities of the designers' new wall panels cast, along with standard bricks, in more realistic grey. Horses also abounded, coming with all but two of the products. Like LEGO Space and LEGO Town, a range of sets in different sizes were included, from small pocket-money offerings to the castles that would require top billing at Christmas for most children. After six years of consistent sales for both the Yellow Castle and Knight's Joust, it seemed likely that children would love this new LEGO Castle theme, but even so, designers left nothing to chance.

Designers Daniel August Krentz, Jens Nygaard Knudsen and Niels Milan Pedersen began exploring other historical options. Daniel wanted to do Ancient Rome, going so far as to build a whole assortment's worth of buildings with classic columns, chariots and more. Ultimately, that idea was dropped due the popularity of an Asterix the Gaul TV show in Europe at the time. Multiple other options were considered alongside Romans. Niels suggested a Jules Verne-inspired theme which, while not so far back in the past, was still historical. Like Daniel, he built an entire theme's worth of models to prove the concept, including a large *Nautilus*-style submarine. In tests, however, children didn't know Jules Verne from a twelfth-century monarch. The only reaction from the clearly confused room was one boy who declared, 'The guy who made these things must be bonkers.'

Jules Verne was out. Vikings came up again and was developed for the second time, along with several other ideas: Western, Pirates and a Napoleonic Wars theme, eventually dubbed

ABOVE 6080 King's Castle from 1984 was one of the first sets to include the new castle panels and horse elements.

ABOVE When placed in a minifigure's hand, LEGO bows appear only to be held, not aimed.

Europa, which would combine aspects of LEGO Castle and LEGO® Pirates together. The challenge with all these latter ideas was how to avoid overt conflict, as had been achieved so far with LEGO Castle. The relaunch of LEGO Castle in 1990 had even managed to feature a bow-and-arrow. However, in both the LEGO Castle and LEGO Space teams, sometimes known within the company as the past and future groups respectively, designers did begin to hint at loose factions through the use of tones, colours and, especially in the case of LEGO Castle, insignia. Knights at the jousting lists were resplendent in different crests or livery, which, of course, made perfect sense. Designers would develop a graphic for printing on shields and torsos to distinguish each noble competitor. Early on, falcons, crossed axes, shield patterns and lions were used, later followed by dragons. Since these prints were already created, each was reused across multiple sets on numerous figures somewhat randomly to avoid any appearance of official factions or nations. Set 6061 Siege Tower from 1984, for example, includes a knight with a crossed-axe insignia emblazoned across his chest pushing a siege tower to attack a wall defended by... a knight with the same design on his torso.

Trusting again that children would know what to do, designers began to purposefully assign specific colour schemes to the minifigures tagged with each of the insignias and then used them consistently. Some, like those with the falcon insignia, for example, were given darker colours such as black and blue. Their lion-insignia-emblazoned counterparts received brighter, more vibrant hues. Children lucky enough to have multiple sets would be able to assemble small armies if they so wished.

Nevertheless, in later years, fans struggled to break these older LEGO Castle sets into nice, clean factions for categorising, a testament to how well designers succeeded in mixing all the pieces together. But similar strategies could not be employed with LEGO Pirates, where loyalties would be far more obvious and binary. Accordingly, designers opted for a different approach.

ABOVE 6061 Siege Tower included knights with the same crests both attacking and defending the walls.

Pirates on the horizon

Pirates would not be shown marauding, looting, pillaging and making prisoners walk the plank – though designers did include a plank as a means of boarding one ship from another! Instead, designers focused on a completely different popular conception of pirates, where they played the role of swashbuckling adventurers. There would have to be factions, but it didn't have to be 'good' versus 'bad'. Pirates could be daring rogues competing in a race for treasure against bumbling navy officers: jousting, but at sea, with treasure as the prize.

Designers knew that children got a lot of their inspiration from films, which would be how they would play with a pirate theme. Knowing their audience, designers also considered numerous possible synergies with other product lines. Romans was still a potential theme at this time, so it would be an option to use boat hulls across both themes for schooners and galleys respectively. In fact, this possibility made it all the way to production. Initial designs for pirate-ship hull elements were far more specific to classic sailing ships from colonial times. Realising that these would have limited use, they were made more generic over literally hundreds of sketches, which teased out specific attributes that would be needed for sailing ships in various historical contexts.

Not all of what designers deemed necessary got used as intended. Bow components were eventually finalised with twin openings on either side, which were included solely to facilitate a feature for those Roman galleys that never saw the light of day. Other potential parts also had multiple uses pitched. Cannons could be used in Western, Europa and pirate settings, along with pistols and rifles. Synergy related to weapons actually ended up counting against Western due to fear that rifles and six-shooters shared too many similarities with modern weapons. That fact, along with concern over a play theme that would inevitably be associated with storylines about shootouts and violence, eventually led to Western being scrapped. However, a rifle that resembled a flintlock musket, or blunderbuss, was eventually created for LEGO Pirates when it was launched in 1989, with designers arguing that they looked nothing like current armaments and were notoriously inaccurate anyway: pirates and soldiers were just as likely to miss as hit anything while racing each other for treasure in massive sailing ships!

As soon as everything was completed for the formal relaunch of LEGO Castle in 1984, designers began to develop Europa, Western and Pirates, with a winner to be decided later. Thus began one of the most intensive periods of element development in decades.

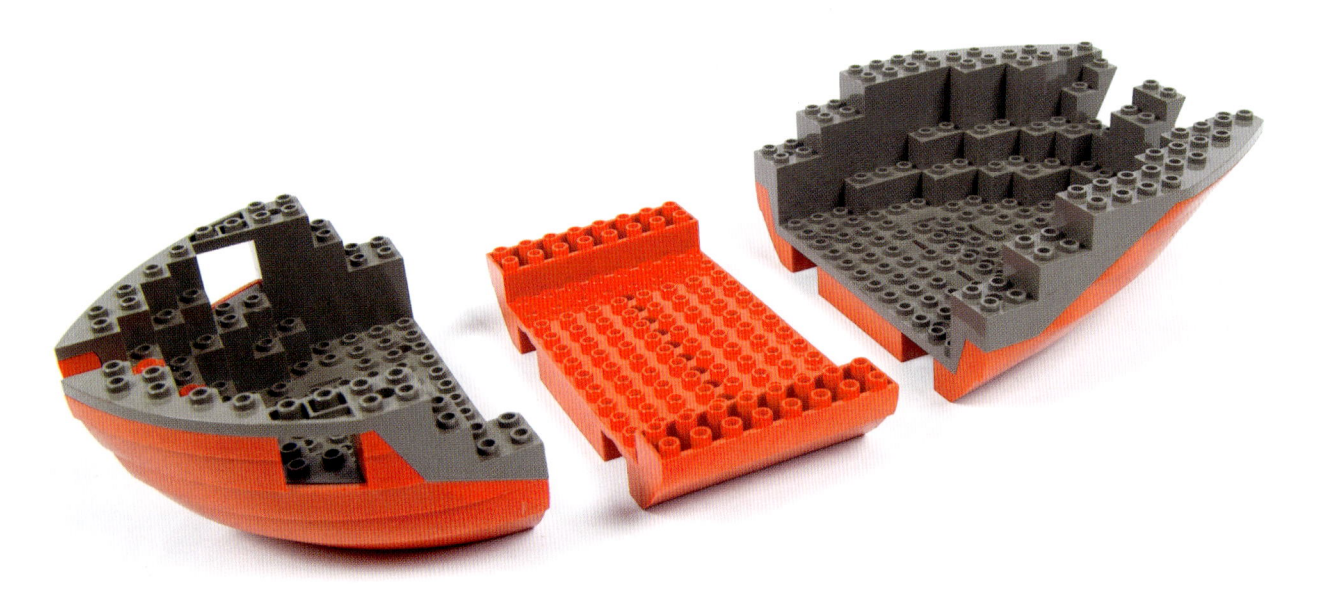

BELOW Pirate-ship hulls went through numerous iterations before the final design was settled upon.

Past, Present and Future   99

Everyone got to work. At this time there were no specialised departments, so the past team was responsible for creating everything they would need, including the full assortments of models, new elements, graphics and, beginning with LEGO Pirates, faceprints on minifigures. Until LEGO Pirates, minifigure heads had all featured simple smiley faces, to reduce the number of different heads that would need to be stored if different faces were used. From the time of the relaunch of LEGO Castle in 1984, designers had lobbied for a wider variety of facial expressions, but it took LEGO Pirates to make it happen: after all, pirates had to have eye patches and beards, otherwise children wouldn't find them believable.

Changes in facial prints would not be the only new elements. The three model options being explored would require palm trees, treasure chests, monkeys, anchors, cannons, teepees,

TOP RIGHT Captain Redbeard modelled one of several new faceprints and sported new elements including his hat, peg leg, hook and... shoulder ornament.

ABOVE Released in 1989 with the launch of LEGO Pirates, the small flintlock pistol and larger blunderbuss elements were the first official LEGO guns for minifigures.

LEFT LEGO Pirates, launched in 1989, featured the first minifigures with facial hair and eye patches, as well as many other new elements.

masts, rigging, minifigure accessories, log walls, rowing boats, boat hulls, peg legs, oars and more. With so much to do, it is little wonder that product development took an astonishing three years, a long time by toy-industry standards, even back then. Along with that already extensive list, there were two new components which proved especially challenging but were highly necessary: raised baseplates and sails.

Hoisting the baseplate!

Until this time, baseplates had always been flat pieces of plastic, but designers wanted to expand beyond, or more specifically above, these ground-level sheets. Initially, they began experimenting with brick-built terrain as foundations for future sets, but these were quickly deemed impractical due to the sheer number of elements required. Even so, raised structures built on those initial mounds of plastic were eye-catching; the concept seemed solid. Three-dimensional foundations would allow for such options as islands rising from the sea, Napoleonic forts atop bluffs, mesas for western vistas and castles built on mountains.

Eventually, designers decided to use a technology the LEGO Group had newly acquired: vacuum forming. First, designs and shapes were built with bricks, just like the specialised panels developed for LEGO Castle but on a much larger scale, followed by forms carved from wood that mimicked them. Long before the days of 3D computer modelling, designers had to use trial and error to work out what was possible and could be reliably produced. Raised baseplates began life as a flat sheet, which was then heated and pressed onto the wooden mock-up. Vacuum forming sucked out all the air, forcing the plastic sheet to take on the wooden form's shape, effectively extruding the 3D baseplate.

Each original flat sheet had to be a certain thickness and heated so as to still be pliable, but

BELOW In LEGO Pirates sets, raised baseplates gave the illusion of an island fortress rising from the sea.

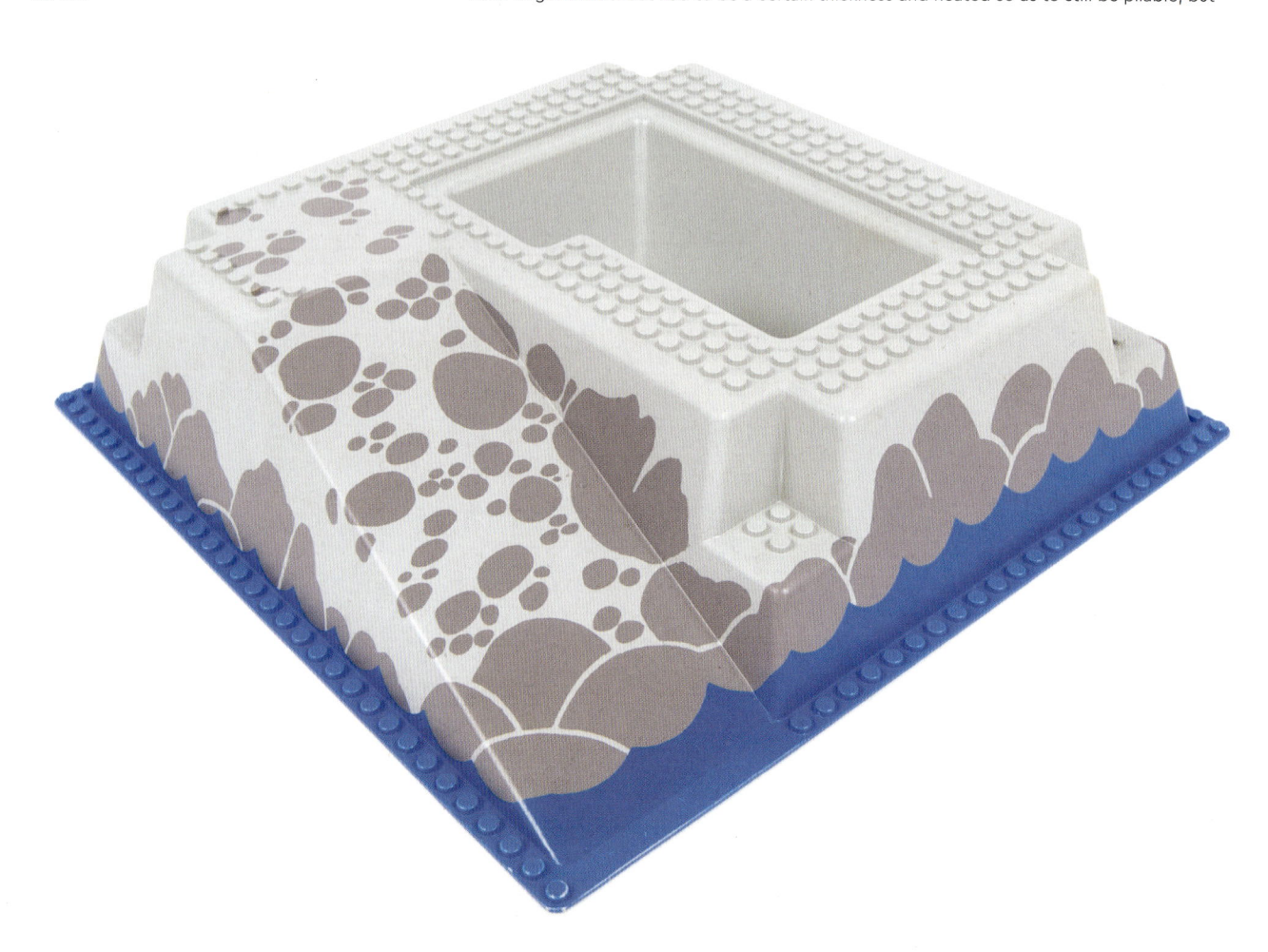

ABOVE 6276 El Dorado Fortress, released in 1989, was the first set constructed on top of the new ramp-and-pit baseplate.

not so hot that the paint would run. Contrary to common belief, 3D baseplates had their designs printed on them while still flat, not after being raised. Initially, progress was frustrating, as many early designs failed for the same reason. Trying to make the walls of any 3D shape as thin as possible meant that any open expanse on the top lacked support and bent easily when bricks were pushed down while building on it.

Rising to this challenge ultimately led to the inclusion of sections near the middle, which dropped back down to ground level as a pit providing support to raised sections around their perimeter. Such pits would become part of every variant of 3D baseplate ever produced. It took many different tries before what is now known as the legendary ramp-and-pit baseplate was finalised. While it was exactly what the designers wanted – and 3D baseplates would appear in sets for nearly two decades after their creation – the Achilles heel that would lead to its eventual discontinuation was present right from the start.

Despite their efficient use of plastic, 3D baseplates were so large there was often little left in the budget for the bricks needed to build a model on top of them. This led to a design technique that, while cleverly hidden thanks to different colours and genres, can be found in most sets that included a 3D baseplate: strategically placed towers. The new giant baseplate element made its debut in set 6276 LEGO Pirates El Dorado Fortress, released in 1989. A main gatehouse rises at the top of a ramp. A prison tower and a crane flank it on opposite corners. Although the walls were only two or three bricks high across the majority of the set, the raised baseplate allows an impressive sense of scale and height, with arches connecting the three towers – all shown to great effect on the image on the box, where the baseplate is situated diagonally to create a fluid sense of raised structures spread across the entirety of the model

Billowing sails

Sails proved almost as challenging as 3D baseplates. The LEGO Group had never before produced cloth elements, so designers were truly starting from scratch and they knew there was no room for error. Aesthetically, sails would become any ship's most dominant visual feature, whether Roman, Napoleonic or pirate. They would also feature dominantly by default on the large boxes that would eventually adorn store shelves.

The challenge for designers was lack of wind. Look at any book cover or movie poster featuring sailing ships and the vessels will be out to sea with their massive sheets billowing full of air. LEGO Pirates needed to look like that – but on living-room floors. Brick-built variants were quickly eliminated as an option because the piece counts required would make them too expensive.

Searching for an answer eventually led into the world of textiles, where designers encountered a term that finally put them on the right path: bending length. This piece of industry-speak is how cloth stiffness is measured, referring to the distance along its length that fabric can resist gravity before folding over. Designers learned that their ships needed sails with large bending lengths, closer to paper. This is because paper can hold its shape for a longer stretch than, for example, t-shirt fabric, which has virtually no bending length. Sails made with the right bending-length fabric would billow rather than droop. After searching long and hard, designers found a textile producer in Sweden that could provide material meeting all their requirements. Special hot-die machines were purchased in order to cut fabric while preventing its edges from unravelling – after all, cloth elements would likely be needed for not just pirate and Roman sails but Native American teepees and many future models as well.

ABOVE 6285 Black Seas Barracuda from 1989 was the largest set in the LEGO Pirates theme's inaugural wave. Its sails showcase the billowing look that designers were seeking.

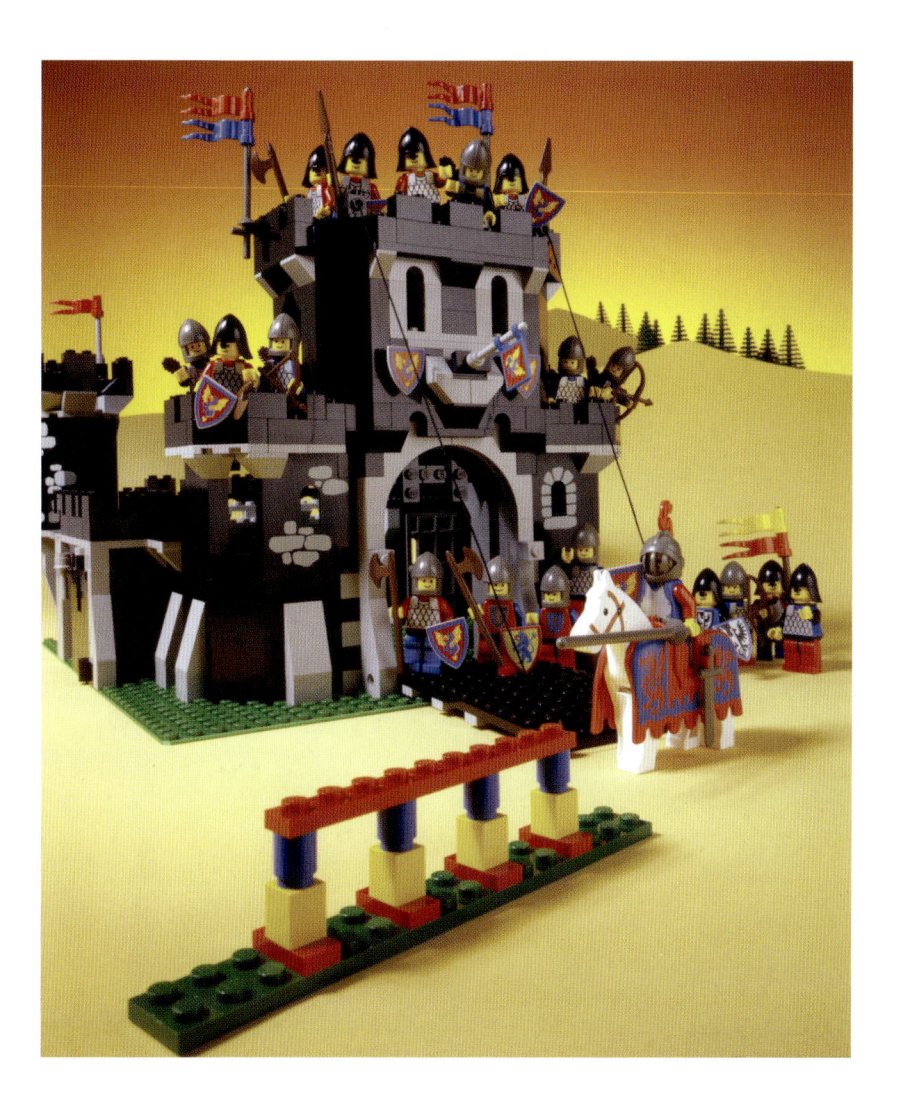

Several years after starting work, everything was ready. Along the way LEGO Pirates had been chosen as the new theme over Western and Europa. There was just one issue: partly thanks to the new elements developed for its relaunch, LEGO Castle was still hugely successful. If LEGO Pirates reproduced even some of LEGO Castle success, there would not be adequate manufacturing capacity. For toy makers, one of the worst-case scenarios is when customers are looking for a popular product that has sold out. Unlike adults, who will hold out for, for example, a top-rated vacuum cleaner, children are quickly distracted and move on. Despite LEGO Pirates being ready, it was delayed for several years while moulding, sorting and packing capacity were increased enough so that two successful themes could be supported. It was the right decision. Upon release, LEGO Pirates proved just as popular as LEGO Castle.

Forest pranksters

In 1988, a new flagship model for LEGO Castle was set 6085 Black Monarch's Castle. True to its name, many of the key elements released in 1984 were recast in jet black to create a highly distinctive look. Notably, the set also featured a dragon crest. While formal factions were still off limits, designers had taken to focusing each major fortress on one of their insignia designs with

ABOVE 6085 Black Monarch's Castle recast many castle elements in black, with the focus still on jousting in order to avoid warring conflict.

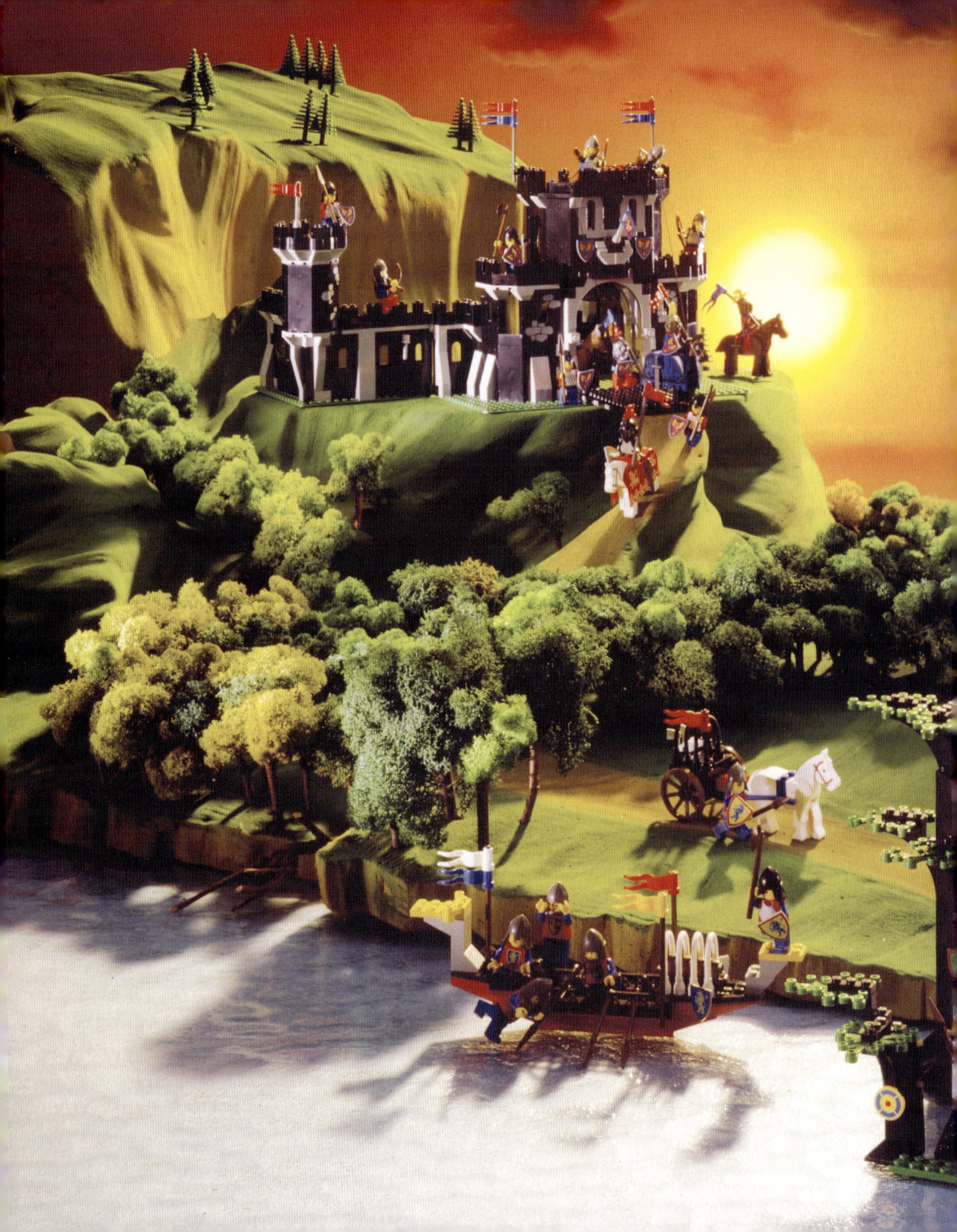

LEFT Crests and insignias were still mixed together during the late 1980s, but factions with distinctive colouring were beginning to emerge.

most, or all, of the included minifigures sporting that livery. In essence, castles were presented as functioning as a sort of home for a jousting knight and his support staff, but factions were emerging across multiple sets. As the 1980s went on, flags began to be printed to match factions.

Knowing 6085 Black Monarch's Castle was coming, in 1987 the past team had an idea: they would produce a couple of elements in the new colour early on in the process, specifically the castle panel corner piece and a large half-arch. Together, these could be fashioned into trunks and branches of trees that would serve as the foundation for a forest-based robber set in the vein of Robin Hood's merry band.

Conveniently, all that was needed to produce this massive infusion of novelty was to create some new torso prints and a single element. Using a combination of wood for the centre and lead for its brim, designers crafted a three-times-scale bycocket, known more commonly as a 'Robin Hood hat'. With that one piece, a band of robber minifigures in 'Sherwood green' livery could be printed and given a distinctive look. As with pirates, designers presented thieves as merry pranksters stirring up good-natured trouble at jousting tournaments. Furthermore, trees, caves and hideouts would bring another genre into LEGO Castle beyond stone fortresses. Set 6066 Camouflaged Outpost was released in 1987 and was a huge success, proving that a couple of well-placed colour changes and a single minifigure element could work wonders in terms of infusing freshness into a theme.

Once LEGO Pirates and LEGO Castle became established, designers were able to use the incredible repertoire of parts introduced in their launch waves for a long time, with most lasting

BELOW Trees and secret hideouts added novelty to the LEGO Castle theme.

until the great parts purge in the 2000s. Both themes would receive major new waves every three to five years or so, with different flagship models, usually a castle and ship respectively. Moulds and parts remained the same as those used in year one, refreshed only by new colours and building techniques. One of the only major exceptions was 3D baseplates. While the inaugural ramp and pit baseplate enjoyed near continual use throughout the 1990s, it was joined by several other variations that saw use in science-fiction themes as well as historical ones.

Official factions

Over time, cycles of defined factions emerged in almost every LEGO theme. LEGO Space was the first theme to really crack that wall with the introduction of formal federations, starting with Futuron in the late 1980s. Space Police, which hit shelves in 1989, naturally needed bad guys, shown to be Blacktron, which had come out two years earlier. Blacktron had followed the LEGO Castle theme's strategy of hinting at evil through dark colours and other aesthetic choices, but Space Police made it official: every set that included prison pods also came with a Blacktron minifigure to incarcerate.

LEGO Castle, too, began going dark with Wolfpack, a faction of bandits included in sets in 1992. Replacing the merry, treasure-hunting Forestmen, these rugged figures wore a villainous wolf insignia. It was hard to imagine the largest model, 6075 Wolfpack Tower, as anything but an evil lair. Jousting-based sets also disappeared from the line. Then, in 1993, the shift was fully completed with a new faction built on the back of an ambitious new element.

TOP New elements, like this jolly ghost (who will haunt you with his briefcase of eternal memos!), inject novelty into themes such as LEGO Castle and LEGO Pirates.

ABOVE With Wolfpack in 1992, designers included a villainous emblem on shields for the first time.

LEFT Set 6075 Wolfpack Tower is guarded by the rugged new bandit characters.

While the humble horse stood alone for a couple years, LEGO Pirates saw the introduction of new animals, including a monkey, shark and parrot elements. Taking that trend a step further, designers who were looking for ways to infuse fresh novelty into LEGO Castle took on their biggest creature yet: a dragon.

Effort was made to try and limit runaway numbers of new fauna through a rule being implemented. Every new animal had to have uses planned for it for at least ten years. Recognising that dragons would be in danger of having limited applications, as much versatility as possible was infused into its design, starting with repurposing an unapproved creature. A crocodile had been created for LEGO Pirates, but was deemed redundant and unnecessary, considering the theme's menagerie of other animals. When the launch of LEGO Pirates was delayed, the crocodile was officially dropped from the assortment. However, its design was complete, including all its parts.

Designers worked their new dragon body around the crocodile's existing tail and top jaw element. Striving to meet the rule about ten years' worth of uses, they also incorporated a feature which, in the end, was not used. Inside the dragon's body, a tube system was implemented that originated underneath the stomach and terminated in the mouth. Possible uses envisioned included a light element for making fire-breathing look real and – when paired with a hydraulic pump that the LEGO Technic team were experimenting with – spraying water. Unfortunately, mould engineers forgot to include the terminal mouth hole, so none of these uses were possible, despite the tube being incorporated within the body's bowels as intended. Thankfully, that miss did not impede final production and the first LEGO dragon was released as the cornerstone of a LEGO Castle subtheme called Dragon Masters in 1992.

ABOVE Monkeys in LEGO Pirates used minifigure arms on a new body torso.

BELOW The original LEGO dragon utilised the tail and top jaw from a crocodile originally created for LEGO Pirates.

Success with Dragon Masters, as well as Forestmen and Wolfpack, inspired the past team to brainstorm how they could branch out with LEGO Pirates as well. A variety of different approaches were prototyped and several whole subthemes were developed in detail. These were presented, and one inspired by exotic islanders was chosen. Becoming a new subtheme of LEGO Pirates, Islanders required new minifigure prints and ornate headpieces, while reusing multiple elements from both LEGO Castle and LEGO Pirates and taking advantage of a new canyon-shaped 3D baseplate that had been created for use across multiple themes.

Both LEGO Pirates and LEGO Castle continued to go from strength to strength, and still the past team kept on innovating. Two ideas in particular were working their way towards approval in the background during the early 1990s. Designers returned to Western with a new twist on the idea: the theme would feature villainous bandits. These bandits would be plaguing an innocent Western town made up of iconic buildings such as banks and general stores. Opposing the outlaws would be a heroic sheriff and traditional frontier soldiers. A Western-style theme had been in the works for well over a decade by this point, so several test moulds for palisade versions of 1×2 and 1×4 bricks already existed and were ready for fully fledged production.

ABOVE The LEGO Castle subtheme Dragon Masters introduced the first dragon – and the first wizard. The ramp-and-pit baseplate from LEGO Pirates was given a new print and appeared in the theme's largest set, 6082 Fire Breathing Fortress, released in 1993.

ABOVE LEFT Flatfoot Thomsen was one of the three bandits in LEGO Western. He sported the most detailed printing ever on a minifigure at that time. His name, printed on the poster tile, is a callout to one of the theme's designers.

ABOVE RIGHT A log textured version of the LEGO Castle wall panel was created for LEGO Western.

BELOW Iconic western buildings from several different LEGO Western sets.

Concurrently, designers pitched another idea that had been kicking around in various forms since the early 1980s, when Daniel August Krentz, Jens Nygaard Knudsen and Niels Milan Pedersen developed some prototype themes based on Tarzan and King Solomon's Mines. Those earlier forays had been shut down when the Indiana Jones films began to be released; as with Asterix, it was thought that children might mistakenly believe the sets were based on the movies. By the mid 1990s, Indiana Jones was far enough in the rearview mirror that a LEGO theme based on archaeology and tomb raiding would not be considered derivative.

Early iterations of both LEGO® Western and what would eventually become LEGO® Adventurers were presented to management during one of the annual designers' showcases. During these events, model makers would display their prototype sets and themes in a large room. Perused by management, winners were developed further and, if production capacity allowed, released. Both themes were selected, but LEGO Western had the advantage, since many of its key parts were already somewhat, if not fully, developed. Designers added time-period-accurate pistols, rifles, a large barrel element, calvary horns, and a palisade version of the castle wall, all used in the creation of its flagship model, 6769 Fort Legoredo, released in 1996.

Three individual bandits were printed with the most detailed graphics to date for minifigures: designers wanted to make sure children knew they were the bad guys. Graphics were utilised more than ever before, not just for figures but also on a variety of standard pieces to transform them into unique elements, which helped create the frontier setting. Both printed elements and stickers were employed for banks, forts, decks of cards, mines, the sign for the town of Legoredo, sticks of dynamite and – amusingly for one of the designers, whose name appeared on it! – 'wanted' posters. Many other themes would emulate this approach during the latter part of the 1990s and early 2000s.

Thanks to its jump start, LEGO Western beat LEGO Adventurers to the first available slot in the production lines, hitting shelves in 1996 to great success. It was so successful in Germany that the LEGO Group was inundated with requests from that country's children for Native Americans to go along with the theme. Here again, the fact that various versions of a Western theme had been considered for so long saved the day. Multiple elements for unique headdresses had already been designed, so a line of Native American sets could be produced quickly, reusing the Islander canoes alongside new cloth teepees, and a headpiece with feather combo included on every Native American minifigure.

Mindful of historical injustices, Native Americans were only ever shown communing with nature and each other; no box, magazine or promotional material ever placed them in conflict with either the calvary or frontier townsfolk. Interestingly, Western lasted only two years – the first historical theme to do so after the unanticipated long-lived success of LEGO Castle. Fort Legoredo remained extremely popular for several years, however, and would eventually be rereleased as part of the Legends line during the early 2000s.

Upon its release in 1998, LEGO Adventurers completed the four big historical themes. Designers had taken a little longer to ensure the theme's parts and feel were right, but that extra time paid

ABOVE Set 6769 Fort Legoredo, released in 1996, was the largest LEGO Western set, made almost entirely out of the new palisade bricks.

> To help make it feel like one of those iconic Western movies, we did a 'wanted' sign. We put it on a 1×2 tile. The guy making it asked me what name he should put on it. I said you can write my last name as it would not be able to be seen anyway because of the small letters. So it was made with the text: 'Wanted Flatfoot Thomsen Reward $500'. The text 'Flatfoot Thomsen' could only be seen with a magnifying glass. However, for the theme's launch we designed some cardboard figures and some placards showing key elements. These display pieces were enlarged a lot, and suddenly you could see the wanted sign with 'Flatfoot Thomsen'. So that was quite fun. And they kept the name: that bandit is named after me!

Jørn Thomsen, Designer, the LEGO Group

Note: In the US, although the name was changed to Flatfoot Thompson, the wanted poster still depicted the name as 'Thomsen'.

off. Led by dashing archaeologist Johnny Thunder, LEGO Adventurers would far surpass LEGO Western in both number of sets and longevity. First exploring Egypt, Johnny and his team would go on to face off against their arch-nemeses, Baron von Baron and Sam Sinister, in the Amazon, Dino Island – which saw production of the first LEGO dinosaurs – and India and China in Orient Expedition. Special parts including sarcophaguses, burial masks and jewels, along with historically inspired hats, weapons and accessories, all of which would help LEGO Adventurers endure for four distinct waves between 1998 and 2003, when it took its final bow just before the launch of the very franchise that had inspired it: a licensed Indiana Jones theme.

Outside licences was the coming wave. With the advent of LEGO® Harry Potter™ in 2001, LEGO Castle temporarily bowed out, but later experienced an incredible resurgence known as the Fantasy Era. The theme lives on with individual sets released every few years. LEGO Pirates temporarily dropped anchor after its third wave in the late 1990s. A planned reintroduction during the 2000s was temporarily postponed. A couple of standalone LEGO Pirate collections were released a few years later. LEGO Western was briefly resurrected alongside Disney's live-action *Lone Ranger* film, as well as for THE LEGO® MOVIE™, and LEGO Adventurers rose again as LEGO® Pharaoh's Quest™. During those two amazing decades in the 1980s and 1990s, LEGO Castle and LEGO Pirates, along with the other two counterparts created by the past team, helped drive incredible growth for the LEGO Group, as well as producing some amazing elements, many of which are still used to this day either exactly as first developed or with only slight alterations, a true testament to their quality. The past team was not alone in this feat, however. Kjeld Kirk Kristiansen had also said the company should look to the future. Doing that fell to another group of designers.

ABOVE LEFT In promotional materials, Native Americans never appeared in the same picture as bandits or cavalrymen.

ABOVE Designed wanted to give their archeological hero a distinctive hat, so they opted for an Australian style, which led to Johnny Thunder and his team hailing from down under.

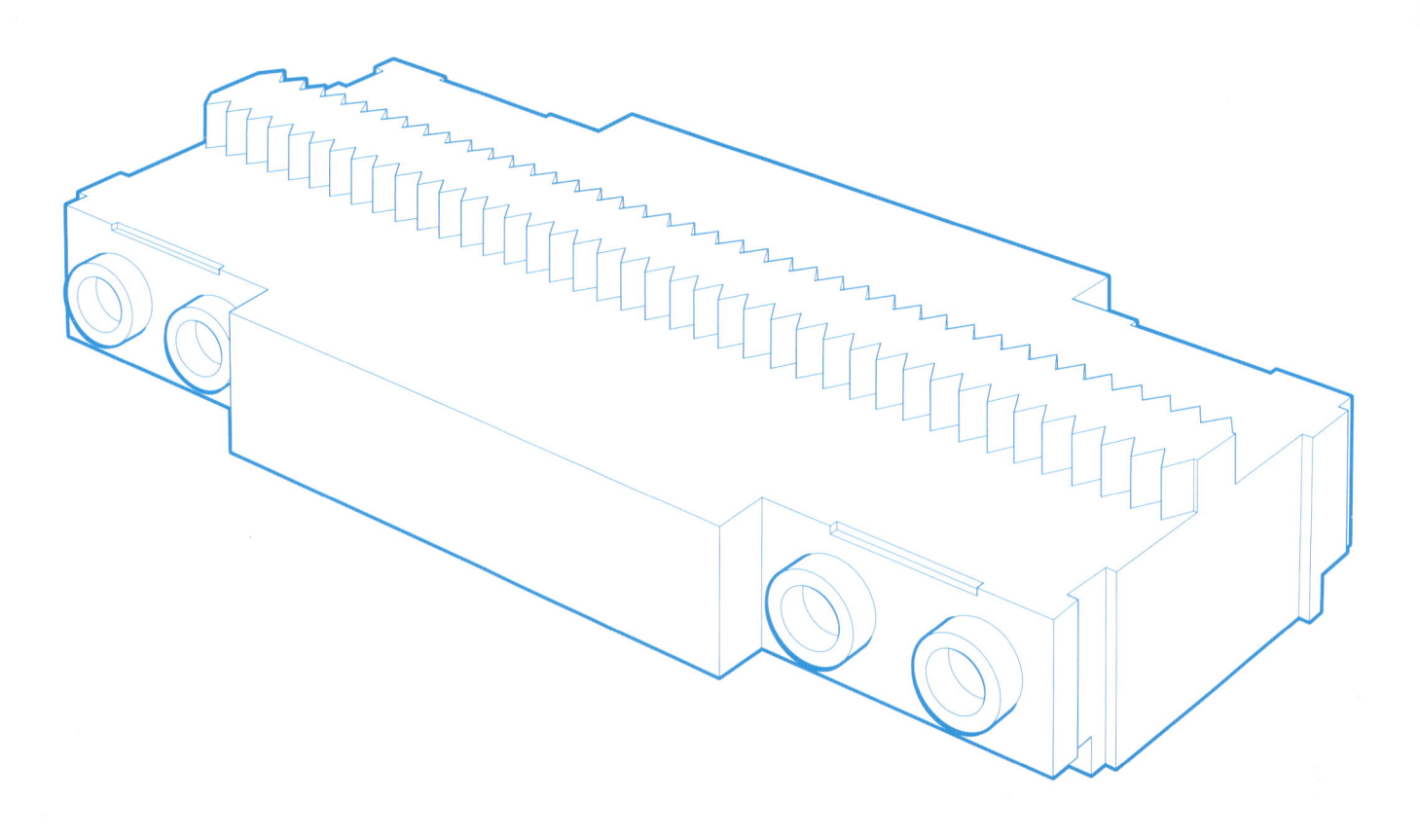

> **Unexpected things happen once you get really deep into designing with LEGO elements.**
>
> Bjarne Tveskov, former Concept Developer, the LEGO Group

5

Monorails and Rollercoasters

How the legendary LEGO® Space monorail raised the stakes on innovating new LEGO elements

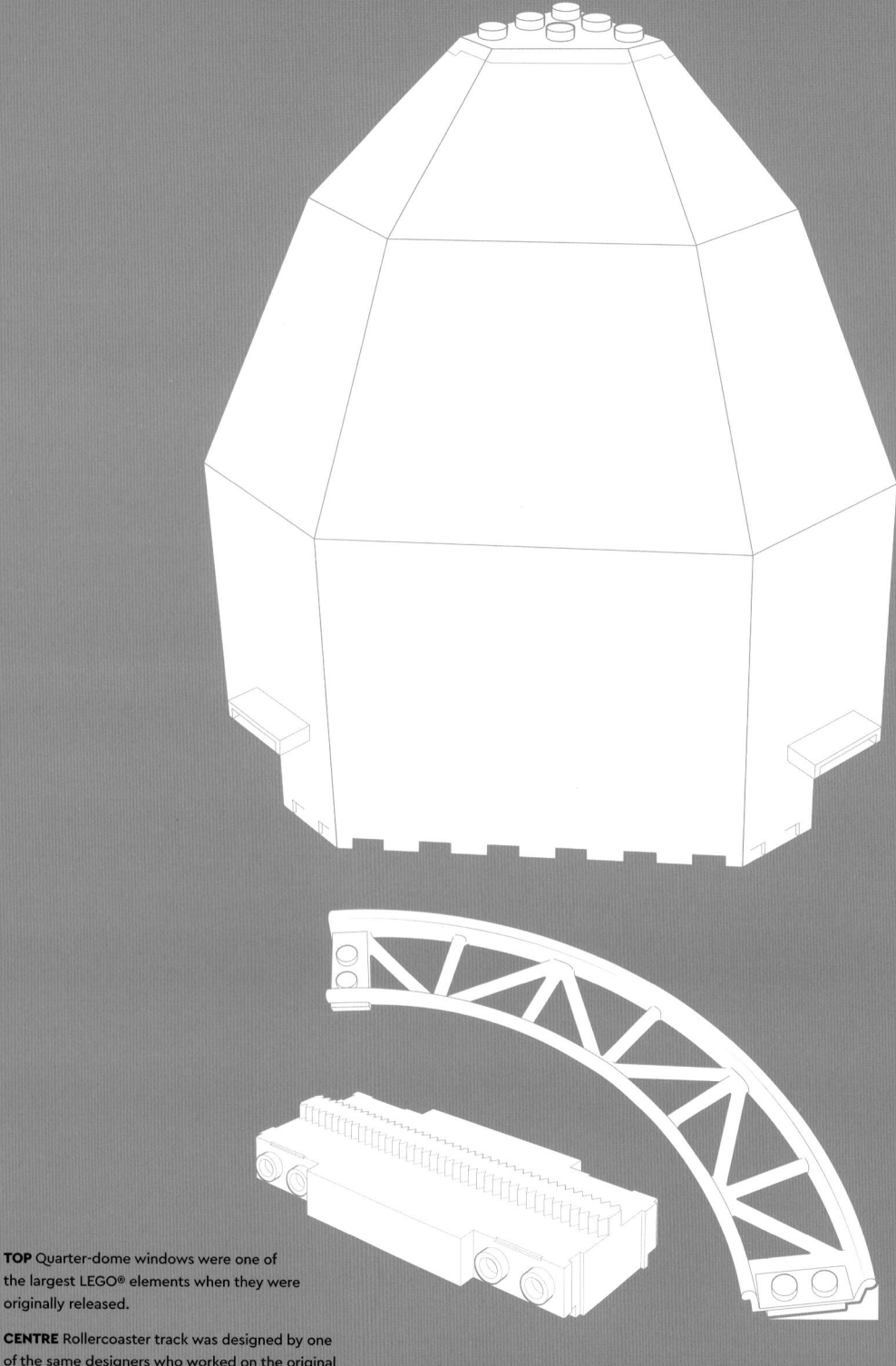

TOP Quarter-dome windows were one of the largest LEGO® elements when they were originally released.

CENTRE Rollercoaster track was designed by one of the same designers who worked on the original monorail.

BOTTOM The eight-stud-long monorail track element was a breakthrough for LEGO monorail designers when it was released in 1988. This small element opened up huge possibilities for exciting new track layouts.

'Let's do a monorail!' someone shouted. The excitement was almost palpable, as if crackling in the air like electricity. In 2016, a small gathering of designers was discussing a new initiative that had just come down from management. Their enthusiasm was warranted: it was not every day that management called for the creation of a whole new play experience.

The initiative was equal parts open-ended and specific. Its overall intent was laid out in a call to 'create a wow moment for children' by introducing 'a new type of movement to the LEGO® System'. After that almost limitless invitation, the initiative narrowed its focus by listing several specific options to explore.

It was one of these options, a 'new rail system', that excited the group of designers, many of whom had grown up coveting the trio of monorail sets from the LEGO Group in the late 1980s and early 1990s. Some of the most expansive sets of their time, monorail trains' strong onboard motors turned a gear that meshed with a special type of track that featured a single rail of teeth running down its centre. The designers knew that there was a chance to make their dream of a modern monorail set into reality. This realisation led to the almost immediate, excited suggestion that such a track system would perfectly meet the initiative's criteria.

Unknown to almost all the team members sitting around the table that day, history was repeating itself. The very first monorail track elements, released almost thirty years earlier, had also been conceived out of an effort to create a new and different play experience. Furthermore, its creation process had showcased the need and laid the foundation for an entirely new model of designing elements: the 'platform' model.

New frontiers

The LEGO® Space theme was one of the inaugural three play themes released concurrently with the introduction of the minifigure in 1978. All three themes, LEGO® Town, LEGO® Castle and LEGO Space, enjoyed incredibly successful launches. By the mid-1980s, the LEGO Town theme had established itself as an evergreen: a product line which is intended to be continued indefinitely, with new sets released every year. The LEGO Castle theme had enjoyed a successful relaunch and was well on its way to being deemed an evergreen theme as well, but its counterpart exploring the stars required updating. This was largely due to LEGO Space aesthetic. The theme's initial designers were all children of the 1950s and 1960s who had witnessed the Space Race first-hand. Childhoods steeped in Apollo missions had deeply informed the industrial aesthetic and focus on exploration reflected in LEGO Space first years of sets, which fans now lovingly refer to as Classic Space. Children of the 1980s, however, were growing up in a different time, a world apart from the Moon missions witnessed by their parents.

With many unreleased themes jostling in the wings and limited production capacity, there was an open discussion as to whether LEGO Space could or should be continued as an evergreen product line like LEGO Town. If it were deemed a novelty line instead and retired accordingly, plenty of new offerings were sitting fully developed in the design halls to take its place immediately. Fortunately for its many fans, LEGO Space had a champion who had seen this problem coming in advance and was already leading a charge to address it.

Jens Nygaard Knudsen is a legend within the LEGO Group. He is most widely known as the 'father of the minifigure' for his role as primary designer of the tiny LEGO populace. After guiding the minifigure's debut alongside LEGO Space, LEGO Castle and LEGO Town in 1978, he had moved on to, among other responsibilities, leading the designers of LEGO Space during the 1980s. Jens was a passionate element designer known for creating more prototypes than his team could build models to keep up with. He was so prolific that during the 1980s Jens kept on retainer an external craftsman who owned a small model shop in Billund to create quick and dirty prototypes for him; a necessary supplement to keep up with Jens' excitement and impatience for seeing new ideas realised as quickly as possible.

In around 1982, the first seed that would eventually lead to a new direction for LEGO Space, as well as a host of additional elements, was planted in Jens' mind when he learned of the newly opened, go-to family destination: EPCOT Center in the Walt Disney World Resort, Florida. Jens saw EPCOT, with its innovative Future World section, as emblematic of what this new generation

BELOW Set 6990 Monorail Transport System, released in 1987, included a host of new elements, including parts for the train and track, as well as transparent dome windows.

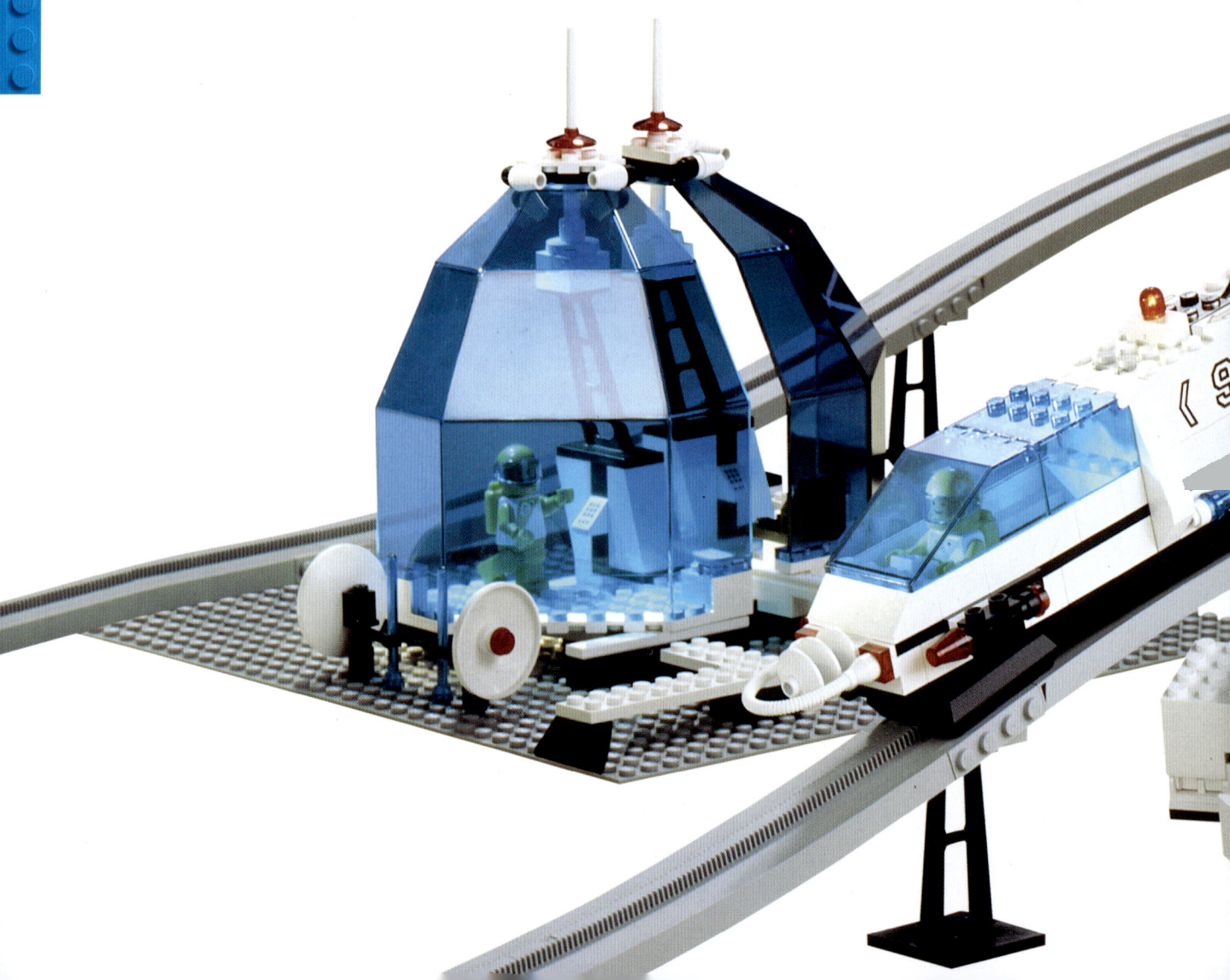

of children imagined space travel to look like. EPCOT's optimistic view of the future and sleek aesthetic became an early inspiration for what would become LEGO Space evolution. In addition, one of its major attractions planted an idea in Jens' mind for a new type of flagship set: a trainline in the sky, described as the 'public transport of the future' – the monorail!

Jens and his team got to work and, throughout the mid-1980s, facilitated two parallel efforts aimed at revamping both LEGO Space look along with its mission. First, the aesthetic of the theme was slowly altered organically from within over several years of releases. Industrial greys, blues and transparent yellows were slowly mixed with and then displaced by futuristic whites and transparent blues so that the eventual relaunch would be 'small steps' rather than 'giant leaps'.

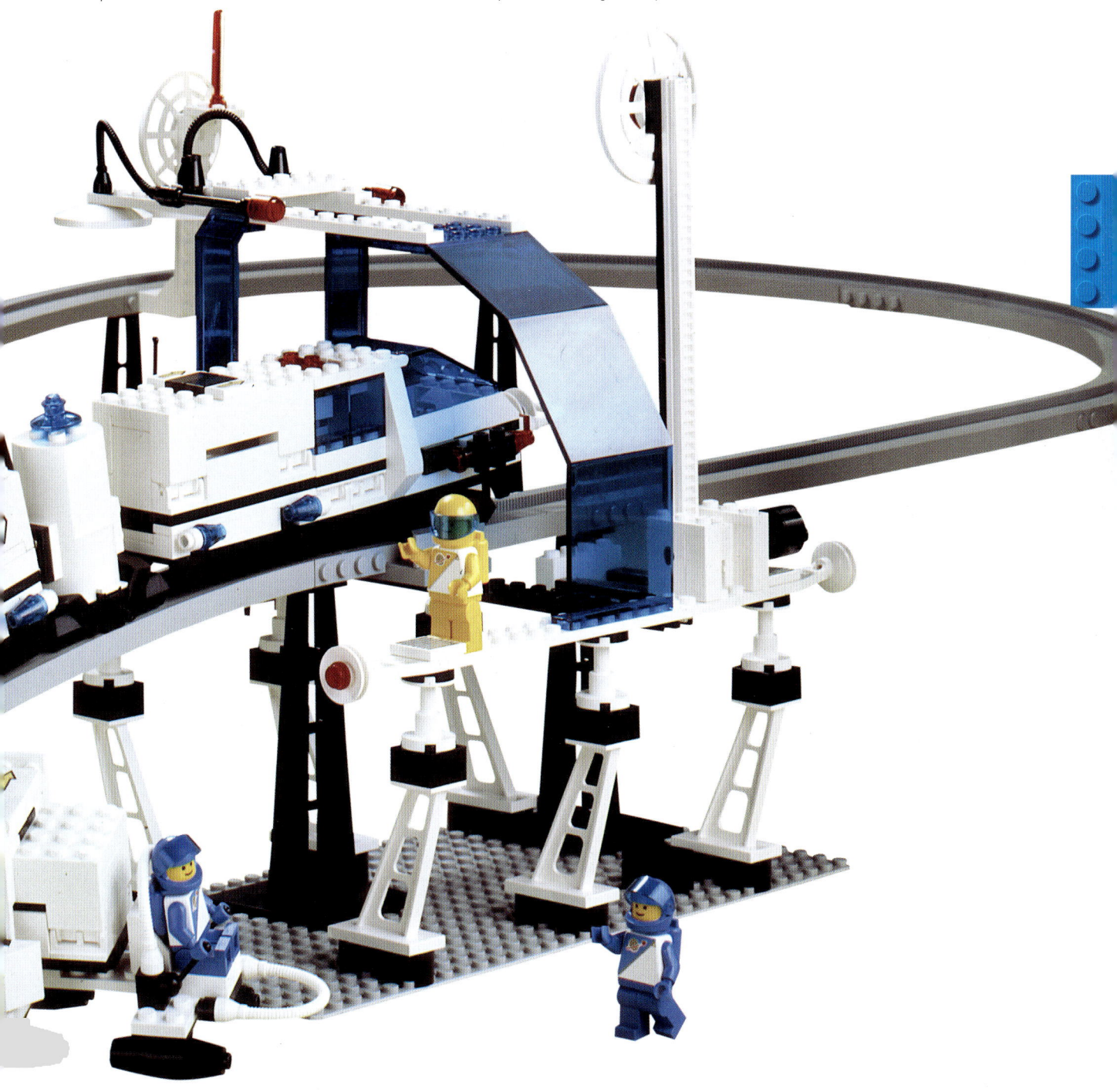

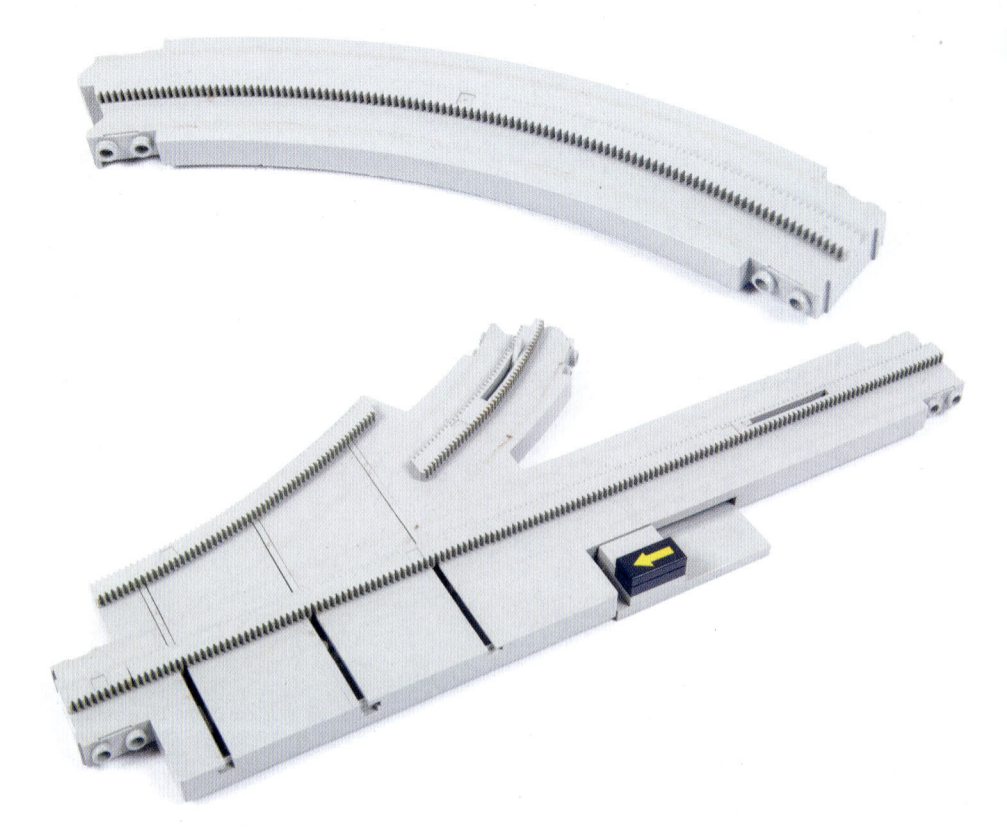

ABOVE Additional monorail track elements were added to the assortment for 6991 Monorail Transport Base and later models, most notably a short curve and a switch track. With a total of eight track types, more complex layouts than ever before were now possible.

At the same time, Jens and his team prototyped a trove of elements aimed at taking LEGO Space in a new direction, which they summed up in one word: landing. The designers asked themselves the question: what came next after the exploration depicted in those early LEGO Space sets? What happened when the explorers landed? Their answer: society and civilisation. Bases would switch from outposts for launching probes to hubs of commerce and trade. Furthermore, close proximity and competition for resources would inevitably lead to conflict and people taking sides, which fitted perfectly into a larger movement towards role play and factions that was concurrently sweeping through the company as a whole during this time. To date, LEGO Space had been open-ended, with alliances only hinted at. Having landed and established a civilisation, the tiny space-farers would henceforth be grouped into clearly defined factions, each pursuing its own roles and agendas. The challenge was how to communicate the change from exploration to civilisation visually.

One element soon emerged as a cornerstone of the new vision: a massive, faceted, transparent quarter-dome. Futuristic societies imagined in science fiction during this time almost always appeared beneath such protective barriers; visually, domes instantaneously suggested the idea of an advanced civilisation. Once identified, a lot of time and effort was put into designing the quarter-dome element so that, when placed together in groups of four, they created an enclosed space beneath a vibrant full dome. Designers prototyped many sizes, shapes and colours and then experimented to see which kinds of models they could facilitate, until a final design emerged. Many other types of elements followed a similar pattern throughout the mid-1980s, as Futuron, LEGO Space first official faction, took shape. Domes would go on to be used in LEGO Space sets throughout the 1990s before being retired at the decade's end.

Amid all the windows, engines and other components, a special sub-collection of elements was emerging under Jens Nygaard Knudsen's watchful eye. Designers created tracks of various shapes and sizes in pursuit of Jens' dream of a Disney-esque monorail in LEGO form. It would be an eye-popping flagship set for Futuron, unlike anything ever done before. There was a problem

> With new elements, there is always a way they are intended to be used. But we would also try to figure out unexpected ways to use them. A great example is the elevator element [known in the fan community as the rack winder]. It was intended for transporting people up and down in the new, bigger bases for LEGO Space. But I came up with an alternative way to use the part. I made these opening models where the top would split open when you turned the handle. Turning the wheel to make something happen added a magical touch. This is a good example of the unexpected things that happen once you get really deep into designing with LEGO elements.

Bjarne Tveskov, former Concept Developer, the LEGO Group

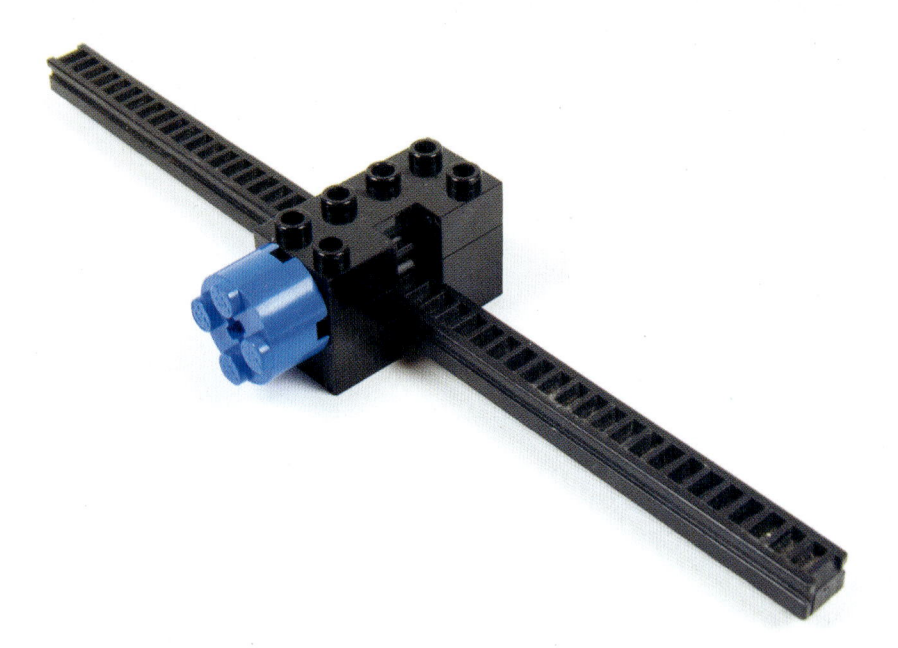

however: cost. So many new elements were already necessary for LEGO Space unofficial relaunch that the monorail components were pushing an already generous budget over the edge. The theme simply couldn't support all the new components needed to update its aesthetic as well as create an entirely new family of track and support elements for a monorail system.

A licence to innovate

This type of conundrum is what would eventually lead the LEGO Group to implement the new approach known as platforms. Most new elements are designed within the confines of a specific theme to meet its needs: different headpieces to distinguish one wave of ninja heroes from another or a distinctive aesthetic piece such as a log wall for a fort. Features to facilitate wider use are included when practical, but the needs of an element's theme of origin take precedence. The problem, as Jens Nygaard Knudsen and his designers discovered back in the 1980s, is that this disenfranchises a certain type of innovation. Sometimes a concept is developed that unlocks previously impossible build opportunities, but it requires more than just a new piece or two: a whole family of elements is needed. From both a time and budget perspective, the development of such a family is too great a burden for any solitary theme on its own. Overcoming that hurdle, however, would mean everyone would benefit, as often these big ideas would have wide application across multiple LEGO themes.

Back in the 1980s, if designers or managers wanted to get a new family of elements developed and produced, like all the track and supports for a monorail, they would go around advocating for the idea themselves in the hope that other design teams would back it with some of their own resources. Eventually the LEGO Group realised that this was both a waste of designers' time and a disincentive to innovate on grand scales, so they created platforms.

Platforms are families of elements developed above and apart from the normal set-design process by a dedicated team not associated with any specific theme. Their purpose is to create new types of construction opportunities, classes of pieces, or even whole building systems, which will have wide-ranging applications. Platforms are rare because of the huge upfront investment in both time and money, but such a high cost is justified because the new family will be useful across multiple product lines for years to come, and quite possibly forever.

Examples of long-running element categories which began as platforms can be found peppered throughout the LEGO Group parts catalogue. Even if all of a platform's parts are not immediately produced, they are designed, or, at the very least, have rules established which govern their geometry. Should a new, previously unconceived element be needed within the family later, the platform's rules ensure it will fit in seamlessly with what came before. A prime

ABOVE The rack winder was originally created to facilitate working elevators, but designers found many other uses for it over the years.

> The Platform Team develops totally new groups of elements. They interview different teams, starting with the ones they know might want to use the elements. They ask each team in turn: 'What do you see in this? What do you need from this? Which types of connectors would be most useful to you?' Once the interviews are complete, the team determines priorities for primary and secondary functions. Then they try to build with them and develop different solutions. They test the functions and stability. They also look into how the new portfolio of elements could evolve over time in an attempt to future-proof them. Finally, they come to a consensus on what the new group of elements is and how it could contribute to the building system.

Jan Hatting, Master Element Coach, the LEGO Group

illustration is the family of elements referred to within the company as bow slopes and known as sloped curves among fans. The first entrant was released in 2004 as part of a platform which prototyped and tested a variety of radiuses and tangents before selecting ones which the entire family would adhere to. New additions have come out regularly ever since, each matching the initial geometry and therefore fitting seamlessly with what came before.

A monorail for the city

Unfortunately for Jens Nygaard Knudsen, platforms didn't exist back in the 1980s, so he made a pitch to his long-time colleague Erling Dideriksen, who was running the successful LEGO Town team. Jens proposed a joint venture to develop the monorail for use in both LEGO Town and LEGO Space. There were a lot of potential synergies. Monorails had a single point of contact with the track, so they offered a more compact alternative to LEGO trains and could easily weave in and out of buildings, whether on Earth or a distant planet. An onboard motor meant no expensive transformers or metal being integrated onto the tracks. Freed from these necessities, a starter monorail set could offer more value than a similarly priced train set. Finally, thanks to a strong motor integrated into the drive module, monorails could do something regular LEGO train variants never could: go up inclines. Designers experimented with a plethora of different carriage designs and found that monorail trains could ascend far longer inclines with heavier loads than they had ever imagined.

Erling Dideriksen agreed to the partnership, and development proceeded in earnest, with the first major task being to finalise the basic track geometry on which everything else would depend. It was Erling and his team that ultimately made the final call, selecting a curve radius of thirty

BELOW : Set 6399 Airport Shuttle was envisaged as the first of multiple monorail sets for LEGO Town.

126   The Secret Life of LEGO® Bricks

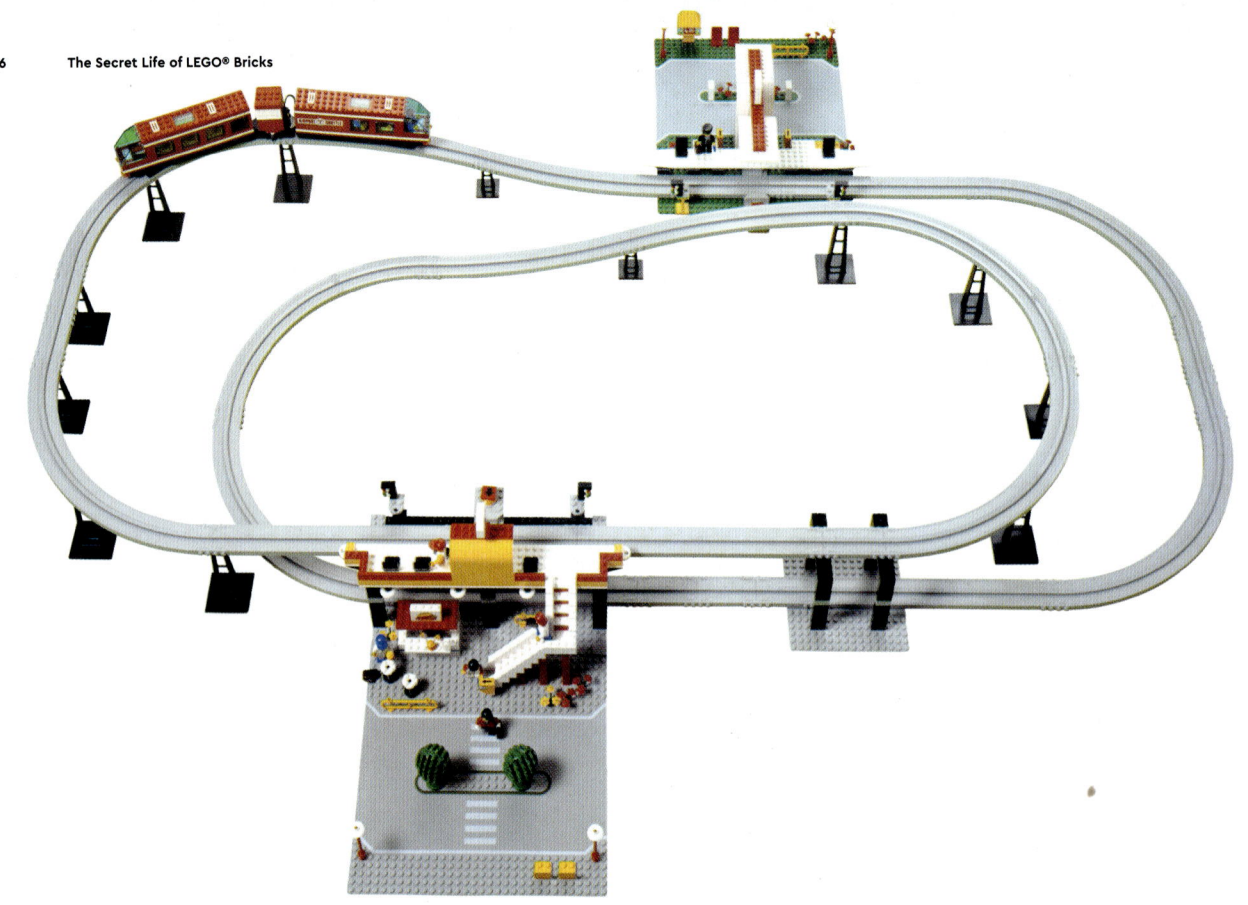

ABOVE The first and only monorail for LEGO Town incorporated a pair of 32×32 baseplates. Its unique geometry required the eventual eight-stud-long track element.

BELOW Many of the new and exciting elements for 6990 Monorail Transport System were showcased on the set's packaging, including its specialised motor, track pieces, train wheels and elevator lift.

BELOW RIGHT The final train design for 6990 Monorail Transport System featured cargo loading as well as personnel transport options.

studs. Their rationale: curved elements needed to fit on a 32×32 stud baseplate with at least one row of studs available on all sides for joining the baseplate to adjacent ones. It seemed a sensible idea at the time. Little did they know, however, that those dimensions would create a challenge for designers and ultimately delay the launch of LEGO Town monorail. But for the moment, that discovery was in the future.

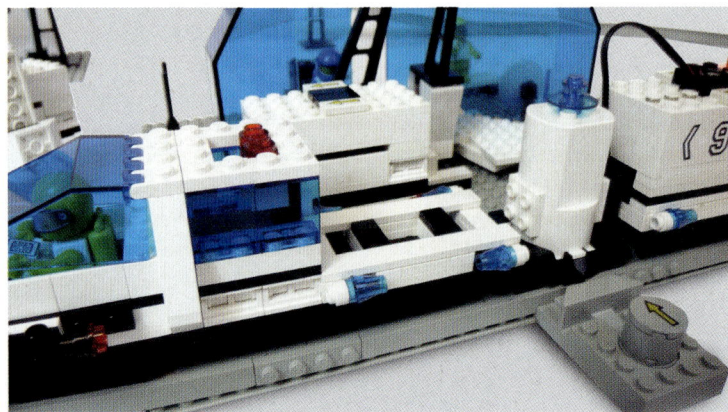

With the track dimensions finalised, Jens turned his attention to selecting the inaugural monorail's train. Multiple designers had created rows and rows of options, including some unusual variants, like one where the engine ran atop the track but the train was suspended beneath. In the end, it came down to a pair of designs. When nobody could decide between them, their respective creators were tasked with combining the best parts of each into the final design that made it into the box.

Everything came together in 1987 when Futuron was released with approximately twenty-five new elements as the first official LEGO Space faction. Shoring up its position as an evergreen theme, LEGO Space saw wave after wave of successful factions roll out of Billund throughout the rest of the 1980s and 1990s. Ultimately, only the Jedi and Sith proved strong enough to force a temporary retirement for LEGO Space in the early 2000s. When LEGO® *Star Wars*™ debuted in 1999, the LEGO Group refrained from producing other products based on a fantasy world set in space, including space backgrounds on unrelated product boxes or advertisements. Monorails would have been retired at that point, but their demise had actually come a few years earlier. Contrary to Jens Nygaard Knudsen's and Erling Dideriksen's initial vision, wide application of the monorail system within LEGO Town did not materialise. Maintaining a little-used set of moulds for just one theme was expensive and the monorail was abandoned after just three sets, the last of which came out in 1994.

However, all that was still a long way off when LEGO Space was triumphantly, if unofficially, relaunched with the monorail as its crown jewel, the culmination of Jens Nygaard Knudsen's grand vision begun so many years before.

ABOVE Set 6399 Airport Shuttle, released in 1990, connects a parking area to an airport terminal. Its monorail train has redesigned passenger windows and a new red colour scheme. Although monorails were intended to become a staple of LEGO Town as an alternative to trains, 6399 Airport Shuttle is the only LEGO Town monorail ever produced.

> "
> When we have a brainstorm, we go around the table. The first loop is always everyone's passion projects, be it helicopters or whatever. For years I would always joke about a rollercoaster, knowing that we had no way to support it, no platform for all the pieces. Everyone would laugh. Then we would say, 'OK, what are we actually going to do for next year?' But when you say it enough times, it starts to connect with people. The fairground theme was doing well, so maybe a rollercoaster could be kind of fun. But the company is, first and foremost, driven by the experience for children. So I was super-excited when it became clear that a rollercoaster seemed to be exactly what children were wanting, and, ultimately, Robert Heim designed it.
> "

Jamie Berard, Creative Lead, Senior Design Manager, the LEGO Group

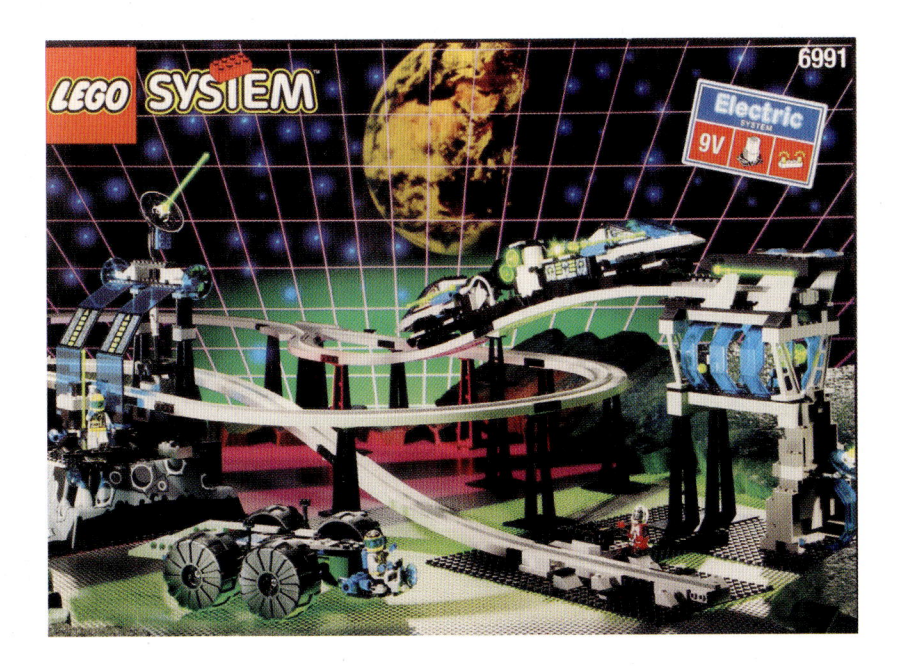

A new track

Three decades later, the small group of designers in 2016 debated whether a new monorail could bring a similar victory in response to the call for a platform which would deliver a 'new wow for children'. However, reviving LEGO Space largest set type was not the only rail system floated for consideration that day. Ultimately, three proposals were brought back to management: first, a monorail; second, a new train-track system which would facilitate different types of trains; and third, a rollercoaster track system.

Each of these concepts was then put through the ultimate gauntlet: being scrutinised and tested by the LEGO Group target audience – children. This type of test usually involves showing children concept sketches and then seeing what they 'give back', finding out which aspects of the sketches they home in on, which details connect, and which ones are missed. In this case almost all of the young subjects expressed excitement for speed, motion, upward and downward movement, and action. Only one of the proposals matched all of those descriptions: the rollercoaster.

Definitive testing alone, however, is not enough to justify the expense of a new platform. Its usefulness across the whole company must also be proven. Ambassadors from the team assigned to the project fanned out across the different design groups asking how they might use this proposed family of elements. Could such a system be versatile enough to justify the cost of development, or would it be useful only for the limited number of rollercoaster sets the market would support each year? Fortunately, designers across the company connected with the proposal and dreamed up ways the elements could be used: as structural girders, as backboards for signs, in a new *Millennium Falcon*, or even to facilitate jousting knights. In the end, management was convinced and authorised the development of a new rollercoaster platform.

Rollercoaster layouts

Despite having lost out on the new chance for production in 2016, monorails nevertheless contributed to the development of the new element family for rollercoasters. One lesson from the past in particular stood out: making sure that enough different types of track elements are

ABOVE Monorails came to an end in 1994 with the third and final iteration, set 6991 Monorail Transport Base, launched for the LEGO Space subtheme Unitron.

The Secret Life of LEGO® Bricks

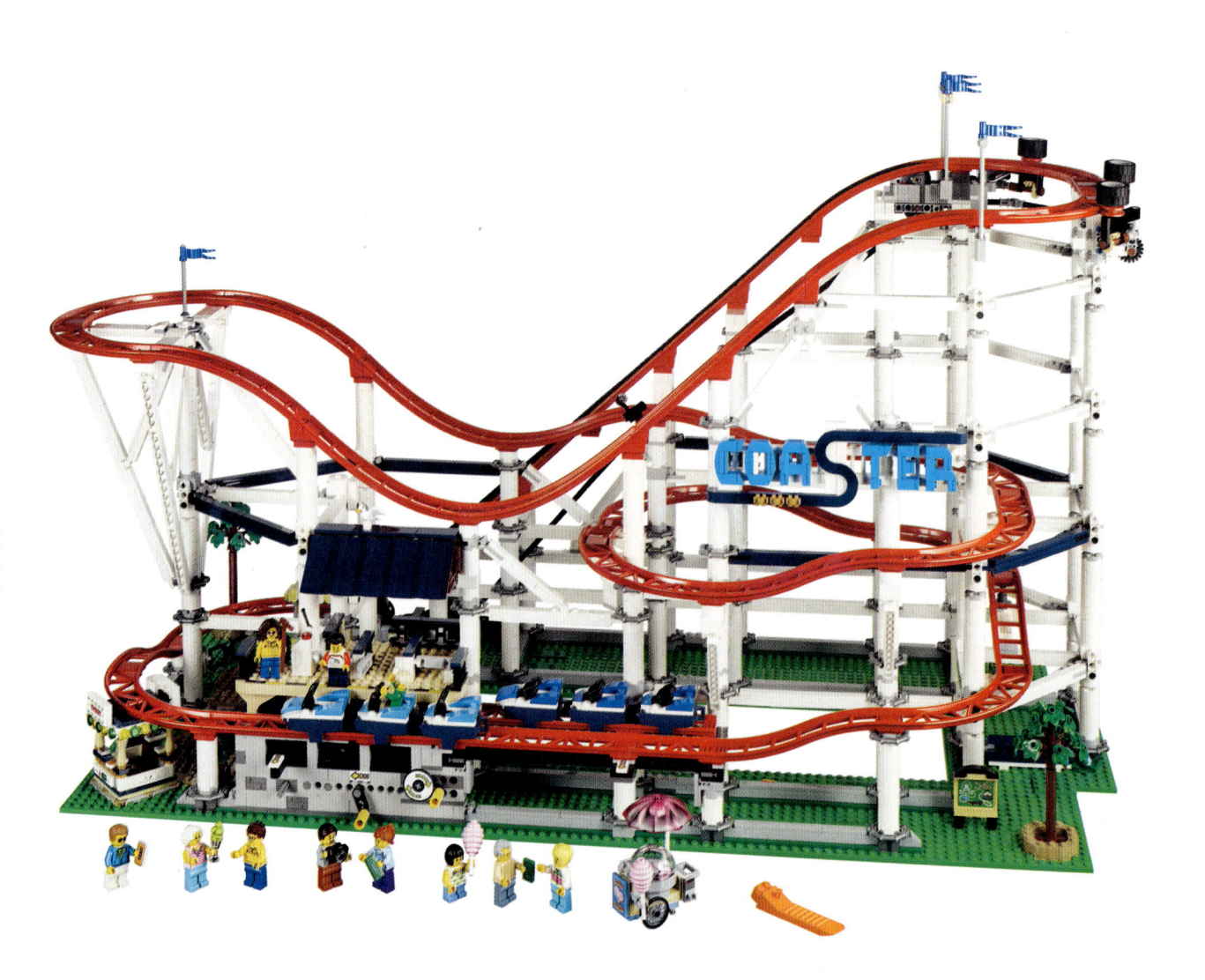

ABOVE Set 10261 Roller Coaster included every variant of the new track platform when it was released in 2018.

produced upfront to allow for versatility in layouts. That was a bit of wisdom which had been hard won back in the 1980s.

Upon completion of the initial LEGO Space monorail system, the design team quickly set out to create supplemental track sets to increase its value and design LEGO Town first monorail, which, it had been decided, would be an airport shuttle. The first monorail, set 6990 LEGO Space Monorail Transport System, had included a simple oval layout constructed from three types of track elements: curves, straights and inclines. The supplemental sets would include the same track types in greater quantities, but options for more exotic shapes was a necessity. Designers working on the project quickly ran into a problem stemming from the decision to base all the track on a thirty-stud dimension: things were not lining up. Layout after layout could not be closed with the existing selection of track elements. Eventually, in desperation, one of the team members wrote a special program on an early Sinclair computer, inadvertently becoming one of the first, if not the first, designers to develop a set digitally.

The computer program facilitated the speedy creation of many layouts and soon the problem was identified: the system was missing an eight-stud-long track element. One was quickly produced, but not before the launch of LEGO Town monorail had to be delayed in anticipation of it. The lesson to the team developing the rollercoaster platform years later was clear: make sure that all types of track elements needed are identified up front. Fortunately, computer-aided design had become the norm within the LEGO Group during the intervening years, so it was much easier to experiment with all types of layouts ahead of time.

Knowing the types of track elements was only half the battle. There was an almost infinite combination of radiuses, lengths, heights and slopes that could be utilised. On top of that, some solutions which made sense from a part-design standpoint were at odds with the physics of friction and wear inherent to a rollercoaster system. Mould engineers are always part of a platform team and in this case, they were kept very busy. The sizes and shapes found to work best for the track were much larger than elements that used an equivalent amount of plastic, which made the lattice style curve and straight components prone to warping. This would be a problem under any circumstances, but it was especially nerve-wracking within a system dependent on everything lining up smoothly.

Ultimately, overcoming all these challenges resulted in an exhaustive amount of trial and error, time, and prototyping going into developing the rollercoaster platform, but it was worth it. The track system that emerged went on to be utilised not just in an amazing flagship model, set 10261 LEGO® Creator Expert Roller Coaster, released in 2018, but a host of varied applications across the entire product portfolio. It was a perfect example of why the LEGO Group invented platforms and how they can be used to add new and exciting play possibilities or building techniques throughout the company.

BELOW LEGO® Friends contributed one of many alternative applications for the new rollercoaster track elements, using them as the finish-line arch in 41352 The Big Race Day from 2018.

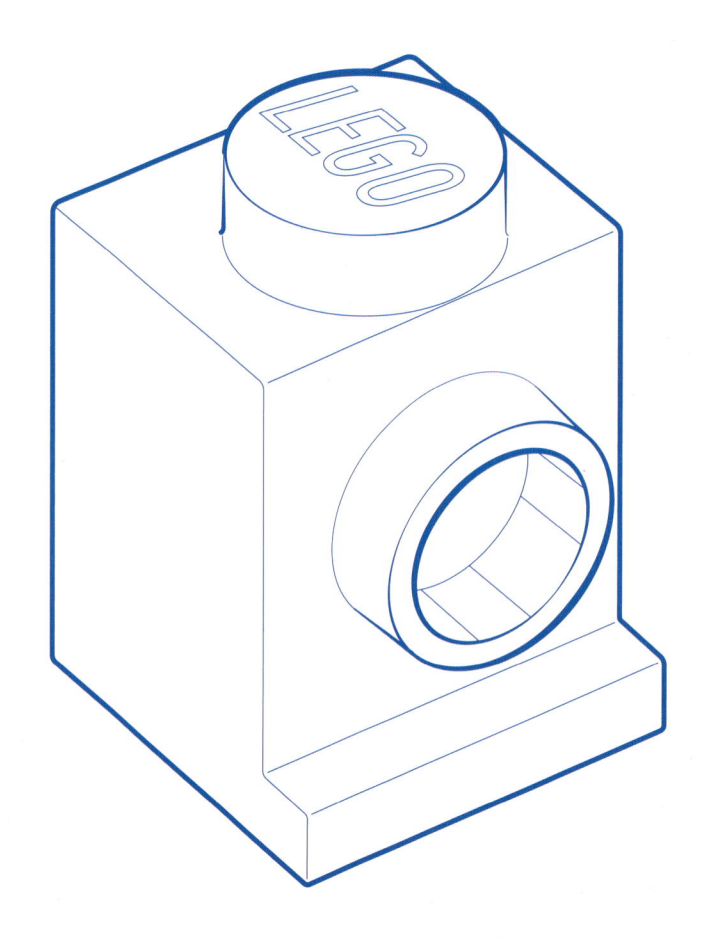

> **LEGO City is the easy step into LEGO building. The story is all around you in everyday life.**

Henk van der Does, Senior Model Coach, the LEGO Group

6
Everyday Life

How LEGO® Town – technically named LEGOLAND® Town until 1990 – and LEGO® City built on the success of Town Plan to become the longest-running theme in history

ABOVE Road baseplates were included in almost all early, large LEGO® Town sets.

BOTTOM LEFT Created for the earliest days of Town Plan, windows were repurposed as headlights in certain models before bespoke headlights existed.

BOTTOM RIGHT Called the headlight brick by fans, this element is known as the Erling brick within the LEGO Group.

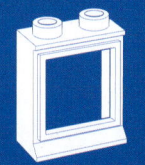

No LEGO® theme has more stories to tell than everyday life. Beginning as a line of products called Town Plan, it became an official theme in the decades immediately after the minifigure's debut in 1978. Known first as LEGOLAND® Town, the theme became LEGO® Town in 1990 and then, from the early 2000s, LEGO® World City and, finally, LEGO® City. The LEGO Group most familiar product line has served as the company's foundational subject matter for almost seventy years. It is no exaggeration to say that, without these themes, LEGO toys would not exist as we know them today. Over six decades that rock-solid foundation has been the bedrock on which innovation has been built, allowing the company to experiment in other themes. Along the way, everyday life provided a gateway for countless children to fall in love with LEGO bricks. As the longest-running and most-popular theme, it has spawned whole genres of elements.

LEGOLAND Town – which we shall refer to from here on as LEGO Town for simplicity, released in 1978 alongside set 375 Castle and the LEGO® Space theme's small inaugural wave, was the ship on which the new minifigure set sail. All the way back when Ole Kirk had first begun making wooden toys, years before the first brick was even a gleam in his eye, the LEGO Group founder believed children wanted to emulate the world they saw around them in their play. Town Plan, which was active through the 1950s and 1960s, with its realistic, if blocky, buildings and cars, was a natural realisation of that vision. When every product was rescaled to incorporate minifigures, LEGO Town took up the mantle of everyday life, though it was by that time more of a step than a leap.

Thanks to buildable figures, and especially the unarticulated 'salt pillar' figures, designers had been adjusting the size of some everyday-life sets for several years ahead of the minifigure's 1978 release. In fact, for the first two to three years of LEGO Town, its vehicles looked very similar to those that existed immediately before them.

Initially, many one-person cars and trucks couldn't contain a minifigure and those that were big enough had to be open-topped, since parts for making vehicle cabs hadn't been developed yet. Vehicle cabs would come in 1981 with a pair of elements called the 4×4 hinge roof and hinge-roof holder, which were released alongside a pair of interlocking 1×2 hinge plates. Together, these four components initiated a new family known as finger elements, derived from their

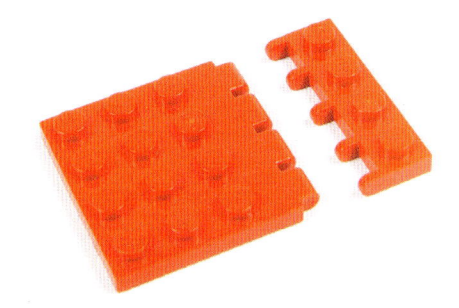

ABOVE Plates with finger hinges were ubiquitous throughout the 1980s and 1990s.

TOP Set 6678 Pneumatic Crane from 1980 could hold a minifigure, but had no roof.

ABOVE The first minifigure policeman, which came with set 600 Police Car, released in 1978, couldn't fit inside his vehicle.

ability to join via protrusions that interlaced like two hands coming together. These types of hinge would be used extensively throughout not just LEGO Town but the entire LEGO product portfolio, until being replaced by friction hinges in 1999. Considering that most vehicles in the world are not convertibles, especially industrial and construction variants, it is initially surprising that parts allowing for enclosing cars and trucks were not developed earlier. The choice gets even stranger when one learns which piece was developed ahead of them; though, as with most such stories, the explanation lies in a specific person's passion.

A brick to light the way

By the time minifigures were released, Erling Didriksen was already a seasoned employee, having designed multiple LEGO models through the years. When it was decided to create LEGO Town, Erling was asked to lead the small team of four to five designers tasked with developing sets for the new flagship product line. Several years earlier, during the mid 1970s, he had been involved with a collection known as Hobby Sets. Intended to compete with glued hobby model kits, this collection consisted of antique cars, motorcycles, a train, and, in their final outing, the USS *Constitution*, which clocked in at just under a thousand pieces, making it the largest LEGO set to date.

Headlights on these vehicles had been constructed out of components that were by this time practically antiques themselves, specifically old windows. Passable on vintage car models, Erling recognised that these would not fit in within the new world of LEGO Town. A solution was not ready for the theme's 1978 debut so, for the first two years, vehicles that were big enough included basic bricks printed with a grille and headlights in silver or black, while smaller ones went entirely without any sort of detail on their fronts. Behind the scenes, Erling worked diligently to craft a piece that was unlike anything produced before.

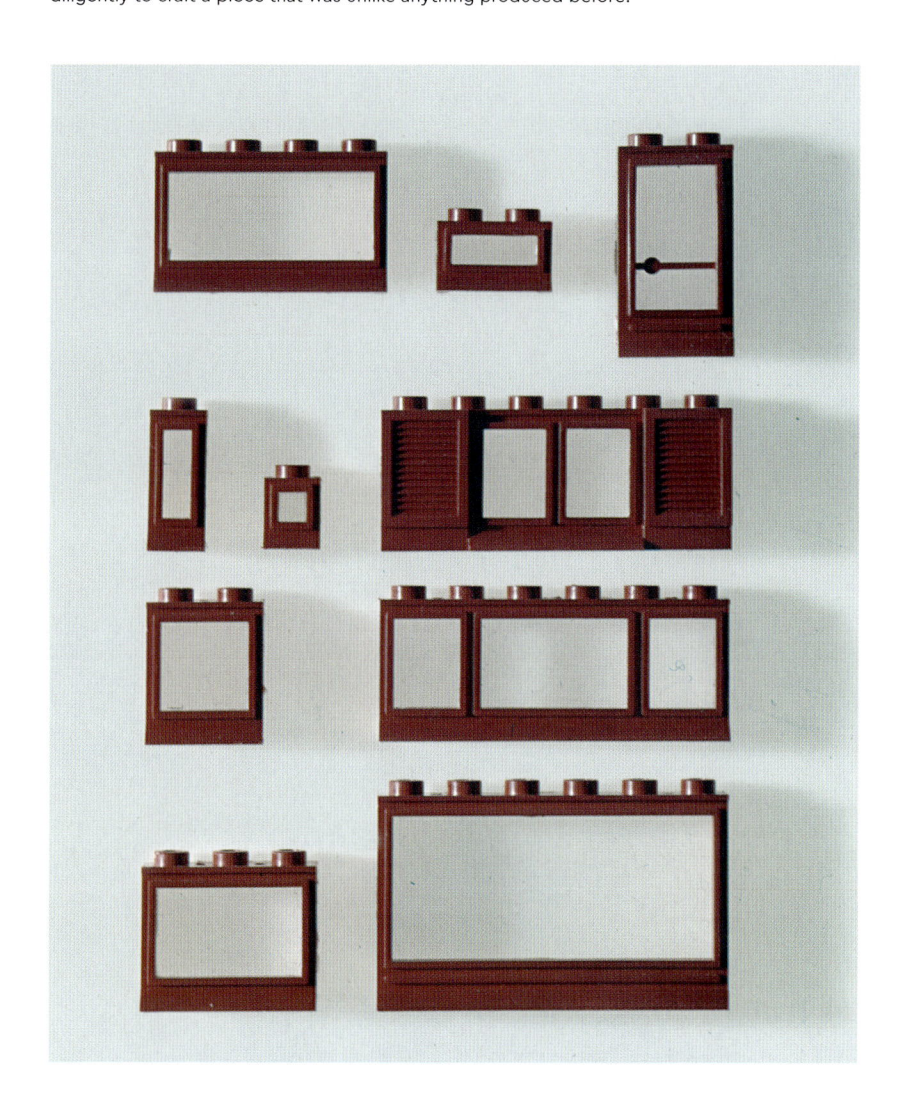

LEFT Dating back to the earliest days of the LEGO® System in Play, old windows were repurposed as headlights in Hobby Sets in the 1970s. Specifically, the 1×1×1 brick-tall and 1×2×2 bricks-tall variants seen on the left in the second and third rows.

Initially envisioning a specialised element that would depict a headlight realistically, he created prototypes by fusing a 1×1 brick with various glass-like protrusions. Placing a pair of these special parts on a vehicle's front and back simulated realistic-looking headlights. Seeking wider usability, Erling split his concept element into its two distinct components. Rather than a permanently attached glass-effect bulb, he created an independent, circular, single stud plate called a 1×1 round. The piece which emerged from this effort is known throughout the fan community as a 'headlight brick'. Within the LEGO Group it is named for its creator: the Erling brick. This piece has become one of the most universally used parts in the entire element portfolio, having been included in over 5,000 sets to date.

Having sorted that part of the task, Erling developed a modified 1×1 brick which had a hollow stud protruding from its side, onto which the new 1×1 round could be placed. Simple in concept, the small piece proved remarkably complicated, requiring a surprising number of design decisions. As this was the first time a stud had protruded in any direction besides straight up, there were no rules or precedent for the type of construction such an arrangement could facilitate. Instead, Erling and his team had to try and imagine all the various uses such a brick might be pressed into.

Their first question was where the sideways stud should be situated. Placing it directly in the middle of the 1×1 brick's face, by far the most aesthetically pleasing choice, was rife with issues. First, it meant the stud's centre would be at a height of exactly three sections. While that may not seem problematic intuitively, Erling had enough foresight to see a major issue stemming from the fact that bricks are six sections tall but only five sections wide. Any brick attached sideways at a height of three sections would not be flush with either the top or the bottom of Erling's proposed element, leaving an unsightly, and out of LEGO® System, gap of half a section. Accordingly, he elected to slide the sideways stud up, locating it at what would seem an odd three-and-a-half sections from the bottom, if you didn't know the rationale. Doing it that way meant an attached brick's edge lined up with the top of Erling's element, making it much more useful. Designers who developed what would later become known as LEGO® Technic bricks had placed the centres of their holes for snaps in the same location, so it is highly likely Erling was influenced by their earlier work. However, that brought up another challenge.

LEGO designers try to keep pieces within the LEGO System established dimensions whenever possible. The original design of what would become known as the Erling brick within the LEGO Group had the sideways stud protruding from a standard 1×1 brick. Members of Erling's team went so far as to develop finished designs for a whole family of elements with that arrangement, including 1×1, 1×2, 1×3, 1×4 and 1×6 bricks, with a proportional number of studs on their sides. Ultimately, Erling rejected all of them; he didn't like the fact that such pieces required construction that did not conform to the LEGO System. Building with LEGO components entails stacking, which Erling wanted to maintain, even if the construction orientation had been flipped

TOP For the first two years of LEGO Town, vehicles had printed grilles and headlights.

ABOVE The 1×1 round was invented in conjunction with the Erling brick to create headlights for vehicles.

RIGHT The black-and-tan striped section at middle right imitates an Erling brick if the stud had been placed in the middle. The tan brick on the right shows how an impossible-to-reconcile gap would have been created at the top and bottom. The dark blue Erling brick at middle left has a standard 1×1 blue brick joined to it. The top lines up with the pink 1×2 plate above, and leaves room for a stud beneath, which gives it many more uses.

ninety degrees. Essentially, he wanted this new brick to facilitate stacking both horizontally and vertically.

However, if the brick was the standard five sections wide, a piece that plugged into the back of it would not be able to match up with a corresponding piece building out from the stud at the face. They would be five sections apart, which is a gap that cannot be filled with pieces, since all plates are two sections thick. In the end, in order to remedy this problem, Erling created a design which not only rotated a stud ninety degrees but recessed it so that it was only four sections away from the opposite face instead of five. This created a small lip at the bottom of his new component that was both a section tall and deep.

Being able to build through in two directions was not just a conceptual exercise; Erling made it a reality by creating an opening that could receive a stud on the vertical wall opposite the one which had the outward-facing stud. Erling Didriksen did not know it at the time, but he had just laid the first foundation stone for a whole genre of building techniques, which would come to be known as sideways building within the LEGO Group and studs not on top, or SNOT, to fans.

The other designs for more standard-sized bricks with studs on their sides went into the designers' desks and files. All, that is, except for one. In 1985, a variant was approved that consisted of a 1×1 brick with studs on every face except the bottom – five in total – which led to the name 1×1 with studs on five sides. This was greenlit because the single axis one could build through the brick along, top to bottom, remained consistent with the LEGO System. Both the initial Erling element and its five-sided cousin immediately saw extensive use throughout the LEGO Group product lines.

Fortunately, designers didn't throw out the finished prototypes for other sizes, though. LEGO Town eventually provided a reason for approving them, though they would not be the first team to actually implement their idea. Designers in the mid-1990s wanted these elements because they saw exciting opportunities for realistic fuselage shapes on space shuttles and aeroplanes. Curved or angled elements could be attached to the outward-facing studs on all four sides, creating tapers, curves and other accurate shapes. That exact type of construction would go on to be a primary use for the whole family of modified bricks, which would eventually be created, including most of the originals designed during the 1980s, along with several other variants.

Designers ultimately prevailed because licensed sets required, for example, brick-built

ABOVE The five-sided modified brick was the first in what would, years later, become a family of full-sized bricks with studs on the sides.

LEFT This construct illustrates why Erling made his brick only four sections wide. The grey brick on the left is an Erling brick on its side with a red 1×1 brick connected into its back and a red 1×1 plate attached to the stud on its face. The grey brick to the right is the variant of Erling's brick released many years later. This brick is five sections wide and studs cannot be inserted into the back of it. This brick has been artificially lined up with the other Erling brick by using a red 1×1 tile on top of two red 1×1 plates so that it and the Erling brick both start at the same height. A single red 1×1 plate attached to the Erling brick on the left allows it to equal the height of a standard 1×1 brick, as shown by the dark blue element in the middle. However, the same 1×1 red plate attached to the top of the later variant on the right extends one section too far, a gap which cannot be sealed with any legal building technique.

spaceship hulls to match those seen on screen. In 2000, the next modified brick was a 1×4 with four corresponding studs on its side. This element quickly proved its worth on the first Ultimate Collector Series LEGO® *Star Wars*™ models. Regular additions to the family were developed over the next two decades, although the 1×6 variant designed all the way back at the beginning has never seen the light of day. All of that, however, was still many years away in 1980, when the Erling brick made its debut on the front and back of multiple LEGO Town vehicles.

Road plates

A priority of the LEGO Town theme was to make vehicles as accurate as possible through the use of components like the Erling brick. This was largely due to a key focus of the theme. Town Plan, the product line that launched the LEGO System in Play, had been phased out over a period of years between the 1960s and 1970s. With its retirement, the large mats that allowed a whole village to be laid out on a table or floor also ceased production. A couple of interim sets tried to mimic mats using narrow, single-lane roadways that traversed baseplates, but these were short-lived. For both these reasons, during the 1970s, fire stations or police headquarters were constructed on stand-alone baseplates independent of any intermediate roads. Towns could be created, but streets had to be imagined.

Designers engaged in several experiments aimed at creating large road components that could connect buildings and yield a comprehensive city, with some going all the way to prototype. In the end, however, none of these were released at the time. Though children would no doubt have welcomed them, the absence of road baseplates during the early to mid 1970s provided fortuitous, as their absence created a perfect opportunity to visually distinguish the new LEGO Town line from everything that had come before. Their eventual introduction in 1978

ABOVE While not released until the early 2000s, the design for the 1×4 brick with studs on its side was developed in the 1980s.

BELOW This early road-plate experiment connected a variety of models, some of which became official sets. These road plates were never produced for sale.

for the inaugural wave of LEGO Town helped communicate that, while the setting was familiar, the theme was new.

Aside from minifigures, which necessitated a huge investment in equipment, the LEGO Town theme's inaugural collection featured only a few other new elements. Even though sets scaled to salt-pillar figures had been available for years and had mostly been constructed from the same pool of elements, LEGO Town was clearly an enormous break from everything that came before, not least thanks to the long-put-off debut of road plates.

Unapologetically the spiritual successors of Town Plan's mats, road plates were a fundamental element of LEGO Town, informing nearly every set, whether directly or indirectly, and influencing designers' whole approach to the line. Initially, these large street pieces came in three variants: straight sections, curved sections and T-junctions. Crossroads would come two years later, in 1980. Each was manufactured on a baseplate that was 32×32 studs in size with the road created by omitting studs according to whichever shape was desired. Furthermore, every street, regardless of shape, was oriented so that its centre-line was perfectly centred on the baseplate's edge. This feature allowed road plates to be completely modular, with each type seamlessly joining to any other.

BELOW Road baseplates can be joined together to form different street configurations.

The initial concept for LEGO Town was literally and figuratively built on these baseplates. Conceptually, their goal was to facilitate children's ability to quickly construct a seamless, interconnected environment. Accordingly, every large LEGO Town structure included, and was erected on top of, a road baseplate in the studded areas around and beside the smooth roadways. The thinking was that families would get double value – a building and a road – which would encourage them to take advantage of the LEGO System modularity.

Many early sets included two road plates. Supplemental packs that included pairs of a given roadway shape could also be purchased. After only a few acquisitions, whole townscapes could sprawl across a bedroom floor. Interestingly, it was initially envisioned that a similar concept might be applicable to LEGO Space, which is why a pair of more futuristic road plates were developed for that theme. Children didn't take to the idea of Town Plan among the stars, resulting in both those and future LEGO Space baseplates printed with landing areas and roadways largely being novelties.

Ensuring that there was enough space for structures on either side informed the width of roads. Roads were also split into opposing lanes of traffic, which set the standard for the width of vehicles in LEGO Town at four studs rather than the six some designers wanted. Initially, nine studs stretched from a road's side to the baseplate's edge, leaving just fourteen studs' worth of space for both traffic lanes. However, even sacrificing all that real estate to provide room for buildings proved insufficient. Before long, the approach of constructing all major LEGO Town edifices on a road plate's edge led to issues. Structures both looked unrealistic and impeded play if built across all the available studs. A space needed to be left between the front walls of buildings and road edges. While sufficient for a small interior, this was not enough room for garages, parking areas or any interesting architectural features.

Minimal space to work with was not the only challenge for the designers of LEGO Town. They were also running headlong into similar issues as their counterparts on the LEGO® Castle team, specifically how to create large structures from basic elements. Like 375 Castle, structures made of standard bricks used lots of raw material, a problem often exacerbated for LEGO Town, since so many products included those two large road baseplates. Already only a single section thick, and flexible because of it, baseplates could not be made any thinner.

ABOVE Early road baseplates were manufactured using thermoforming, a process in which plastic sheets are heated so they can be formed to a specific shape in a mould.

ABOVE Set 1592 Town Square from 1980 is representative of LEGO Town early approach, which leaned heavily on road plates.

LEFT A display for LEGO Space shows how road plates were initially intended to make this theme function like LEGO Town.

TOP Set 6375 Exxon Gas Station included a vehicle lift, which required more space than was available on a single road plate. It became one of the first sets to include an 8×32-stud baseplate extension.

ABOVE An employee rounds off the edges from an 8×32 baseplate using a hand-operated machine. Such manual processes made this baseplate expensive to produce.

Both issues came to a head while designers worked on the 1980 LEGO Town releases, and two sets in particular. One set would be the largest example of dual baseplates with buildings on them, while the second was a gas station that included a mechanic's shop. For the super-sized set, a car showroom was developed, while the mechanic's shop required a lift. Both installations would need vehicles to be oriented perpendicular to the roads, and there simply wasn't enough space.

Designers rose to the challenge by creating an 8×32-stud-wide baseplate to serve as an extender for standard 32×32 baseplates. When 6390 Market Street and 6375 Exxon Gas Station hit shelves, they were the largest sets of their kind ever. Unfortunately, despite being popular, each had high production costs due to the sheer number of bricks. LEGO Town didn't have a simple answer like LEGO Castle. The LEGO Group medieval theme could make good use of a single pair of specialised wall elements, since castles were always expected to look like stone fortresses. Town buildings, however, needed to have a lot more variety.

Designers began working on the solution bit by bit. The first major salvo came in 1981. First, road baseplates were supplemented by a new design that had a single egress rather than two. That lone entrance was still the width of a normal LEGO roadway, so it maintained modularity and the ability to connect with every other road plate. This single road then widens and splits into three driveways with studs in between. Large buildings could be built over the driveways at a depth which facilitated garages. 6382 Fire Station, the first and only set to utilise that particular baseplate design, incorporated this newly possible construction style.

In addition to its baseplate, 6382 Fire Station was notable for another reason: the liberal use of windows. One of the few new pieces developed for the debut of LEGO Town was a new window frame, to which could be affixed both windowpanes and shutters. Initially, designers incorporated them only where one would expect a window to appear. However, they soon realised that the frame, especially, represented an opportunity. In 1980, a transparent sheet was created, intended to mimic a pane of glass, which could fit inside the existing frame. Together, these sheets could cover a 1×4×3 area more efficiently than filling that same space with bricks.

Several sets from the 1980 line included this element pairing, but it was 6382 Fire Station that really proved the concept. Rather than place windows only where one would expect to find them in a real-world building, they were used for around half of the exterior walls with normal bricks inserted between. Furthermore, an articulating garage door was developed, using two new elements joined in a chain with grooved bricks to serve as a track. Taken all together, these pieces and techniques allowed for sets like 6382 Fire Station to be large without blowing the budget.

ABOVE 6382 Fire Station from 1981 was notable for its unique baseplate and extensive use of windows.

> Large LEGO sets require the use of a lot of elements. Other toy companies can make an aeroplane from only a few large moulded elements. But LEGO models are built brick by brick. So we developed specialised elements that allowed models to become bigger and with more space inside for minifigures, and at the same time reducing the number of bricks.

Kim Pagel, former Design Manager, the LEGO Group

Building bigger

As the 1980s progressed, larger window-frame pieces and corresponding transparent plastic panes were developed. LEGO sets were becoming bigger, not just in LEGO Town but across all product lines. The designers of LEGO Town had originally sought to emulate in principle the earlier Town Plan sets, which had mostly been open roads with a few small buildings dotted throughout. However, it became clear that small structures on road plates would be less successful than large ones built on dedicated baseplates. By the mid 1980s, road baseplates were largely relegated to novelty parts available in stand-alone packs for those who wanted them and to airport sets, where they served as runways. In recognition of their new role, road plates were redesigned in 1986, adding four studs' worth of width to the roadways, since space for buildings at their edges were no longer needed.

BELOW After the late 1980s, road plates were usually only included in airport sets for use as runways.

Designers delivered larger and more detailed sets, including successive police stations, fire stations and airports, using a variety of new elements. Pillar components the same height as large window frames came next: these single, large elements took the place of five 1×2 bricks. Designers modelled their construction techniques after real-world buildings, which have large columns connected by thin windows.

LEGO Town was a huge success, as Town Plan had been before it. Not only were sets bigger, the number of sets in the range expanded, too. While exciting from a creative point of view, this presented a practical challenge. During LEGO Town heyday in the 1980s and early 1990s, product development cycles were three years long. Designers had no way to predict what children would be into that far in the future, which meant that they had to rely on subject matter with perennial and wide appeal. Today, these are known in the toy industry as icons, and they figure prominently in the story of big bang LEGO themes that came several decades later. Back in the 1980s, such terminology did not exist, and neither did an established way of forecasting what might be hot when a set was ready, years down the road. This led to a shift, starting in the late 1980s from playsets depicting everyday life as children might see it around them to everyday life as seen in exciting movies or in dramatic news stories. During LEGO Town early days, sets were released for public works storage yards, vehicular breakdown assistance, post offices and homes. Mailing and transporting a package was obviously a much more realistic and familiar kind of role play when set against the heightened reality of adrenaline-pumping TV shows!

Accordingly, by the 1990s, the LEGO Town team moved away from these 'ordinary-life' themes and settled on six main focuses for models. They were police, fire, medical services, racing, construction and flying. Of those, police and fire were given top billing and priority

BELOW LEGO Nautica introduced a variety of harbour-based pieces, including boat-hull elements, ship windows and supports, and booms for harbour cranes.

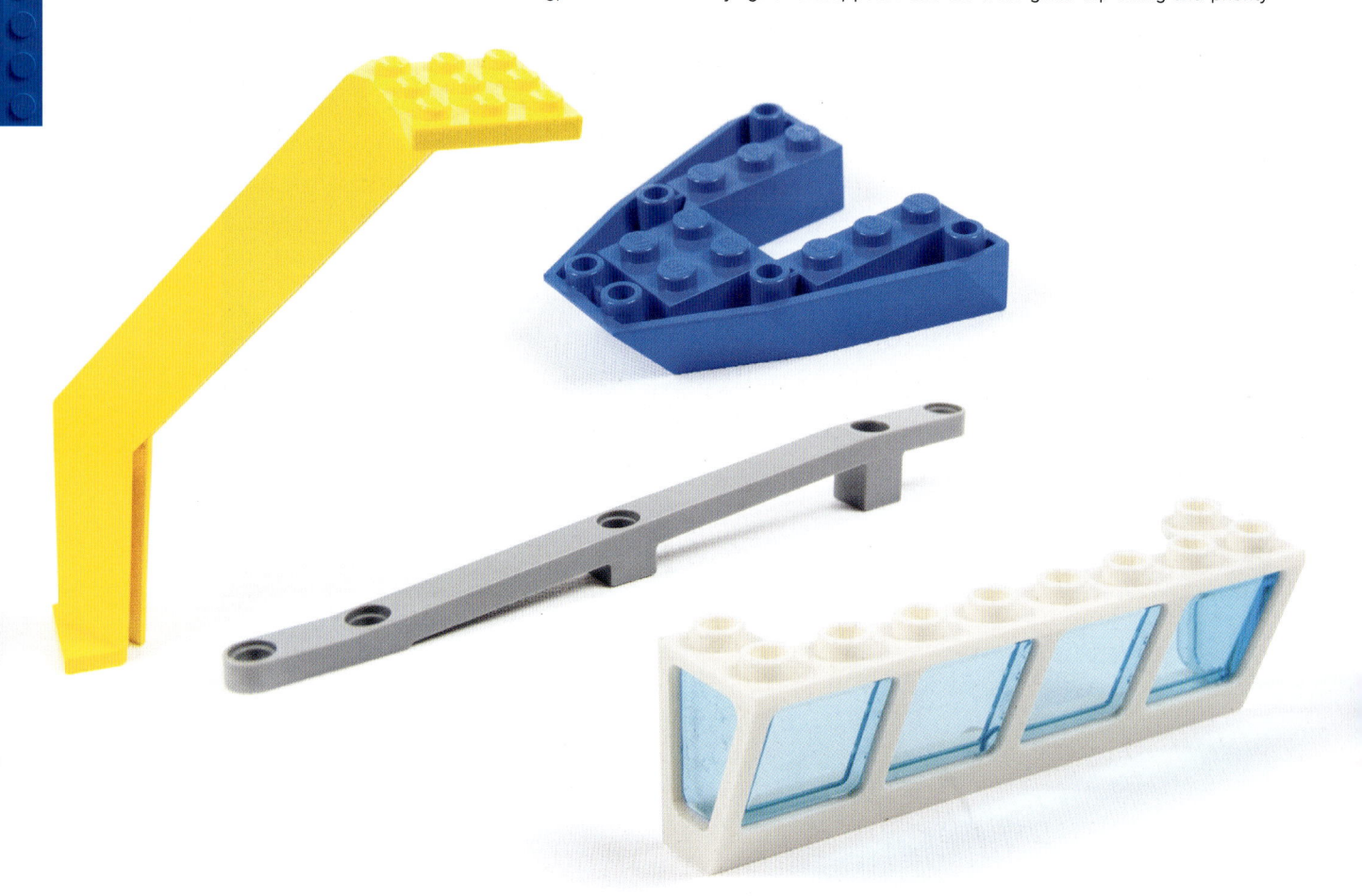

in terms of production slots. Alongside the big themes, there were plenty of one-off models that delved into other inspirations, such as trash trucks or snowploughs. Occasionally a larger experiment would be undertaken, such as 1991's LEGO® Nautica subtheme, which realised a working shipping port in brick form.

Initially, LEGO Nautica was planned as a potential ongoing subtheme. Its debut included multiple brand-new parts, including boat-hull elements, ship windows, several types of supports and booms for different harbour cranes, and two first-of-their-kind raised road plates. Taken all together, the result was a collection of the most detailed sets created to date, including the first ever product to include over a thousand pieces in 6542 Launch and Load Seaport. However, the subtheme only lasted one year, cementing the company's belief that children wanted more adrenaline. Looking for uses for all those parts, designers sought more exciting marina and ocean settings, which led to another category of regular product entries focused on sea-based models such as racing boats, coast-guard rescue stations and seaside resorts. Intercoastal trade may be unexciting but rescuing surfers from shark attacks wasn't!

Around that same time, the literal real world interjected itself into the LEGO Group product line. Despite intentionally shifting focus to more exciting subject matters, designers were still keen to, every so often, include something every town or city would need. A regular entry in this category was gas, or petrol, stations. Initially, the LEGO Group used real-world company logos – Esso, Exxon and then Shell – on fuelling stations and racetracks. However, for 1992's LEGO Town sets, the company created their own imaginary, in-world energy company called Octan. Made entirely of existing elements, the new subtheme was realised by modifying colours and creating a new logo. Octan branding was used in all future gas stations as well as racing sets and, many years later, as a central part of THE LEGO® MOVIE™.

ABOVE Two stylised oil drops are synonymous with the fictional company Octan in the LEGO world.

BEOW Branding for the fictional company Octan debuted on several sets in 1992, including 6397 Gas N' Wash Express.

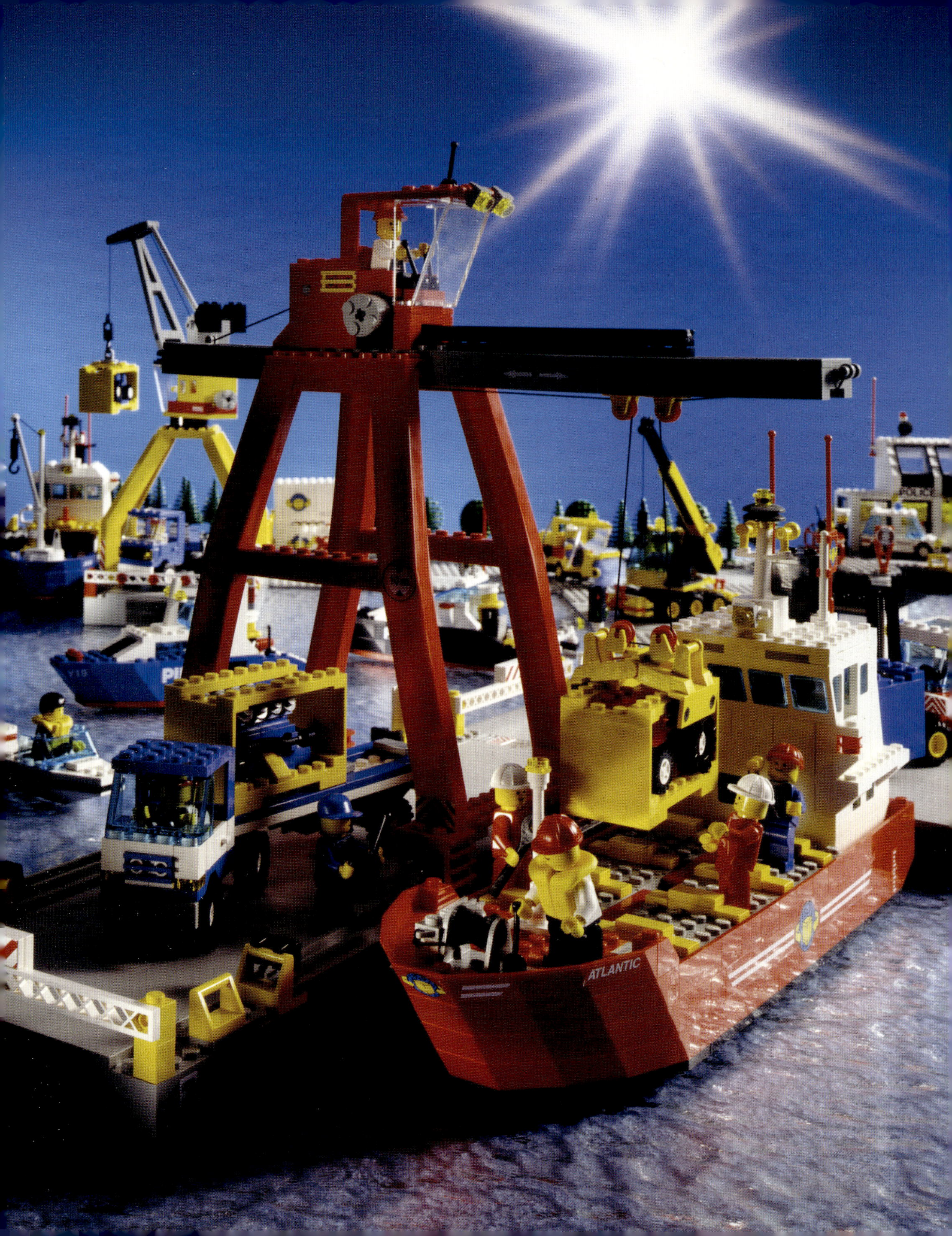
ATLANTIC
POLICE

Building with little hands

Between 1993 and 1995, LEGO Town reached an inflection point. Across almost all of its major subthemes, flagship models – police stations, airports, marinas, fire stations and more – had become as big as they could be. The flagship sets of this era towered higher and stretched wider than any of their predecessors, and were incredibly detailed, too. Quite literally, at least in terms of size, they could not be topped – a testament to designers' versatility in developing efficient new parts.

Furthermore, there was growing concern about a new competitor: video games. As game systems became more user-friendly, toy makers the world over experienced the same phenomenon: children were starting to play video games earlier and earlier, sometimes abandoning more traditional toys before they were even old enough to qualify as being developmentally ready based on standard age markers.

OPPOSITE The short-lived Nautica line included the first System set with over a thousand pieces in 6542 Launch and Load Seaport and introduced multiple new elements to the parts catalogue.

LEFT The interior of 6398 Central Precinct HQ from 1993 was an astonishing four storeys tall. To this day, it remains one of the largest LEGO police stations ever produced.

> To make the Octan logo, I designed two stylised oil drops. I was practising karate at that time and I was inspired by the yin and yang. I named the LEGO 'gasoline company' Octan because it had to be a name you can use in all countries. One country may use the term gas or petrol, but not the other. Octan sounded like octane, which is more universal. Amazingly, Octan is actually still alive. It is still in the LEGOLAND® parks and was a huge part of THE LEGO MOVIE.

Kim Pagel, former Design Manager, the LEGO Group

Challenges with age and video games came to the forefront at around the same time that all the long-established themes of LEGO Town, LEGO Space, LEGO Castle and LEGO® Pirates had reached maximum set size. A new strategy was needed, and it was LEGO Town where the first major experimentation happened. Two fundamental changes were made, both of which involved parts, and they resulted in the theme being split into two sides, with sets on each side fulfilling different purposes.

The first fundamental change was a drop in the target age range for LEGO Town most day-to-day subject matter. Sets that would previously have been intended for children who were a minimum of eight years old were recalibrated for children as young as five. Those three years are a major period for brain development and there are enormous differences between what a five-year-old can do versus an eight-year-old. The logic was that by the time children reached that higher age mark they would have no interest in acting out fireman rescues or police chases on their bedroom floor, especially not when they could be on a video-game console. Fire and police rescue were skewed towards younger ages.

Enacting this new approach meant completely revamping the complexity level of many LEGO Town stalwarts, beginning in 1997 with firefighter sets. Some techniques were deemed too advanced for the new target age group, such as the use of windows with smaller bricks filling in the spaces in between. Instead, large, specialised elements were developed, while at the same time the level of detail was simplified. The garage-door elements that had been introduced a decade earlier were not age-appropriate so, instead of being enclosed, garages became partially covered parking spaces.

ABOVE LEFT This section of the simplified fire station from 6554 Blaze Brigade avoids the use of complicated pieces and instead utilises large parts like the panel wall element originally designed for use with brick-built figures in the 1970s.

ABOVE RIGHT The fire truck from 6554 Blaze Brigade in 1997 was one of the first vehicles to be simplified in order to be appropriate for a younger age demographic.

Erling Didriksen's modified bricks with 1×1 rounds as headlights were likewise too intricate for tiny hands still working on their motor skills. Ironically, this led to a decision which came back full circle and re-implemented the very type of brick Erling had sought to replace. LEGO Town new fire trucks and police cars included basic bricks with printed headlights on them, and vehicles were open-topped to avoid the use of hinges and figures placed in enclosed cabs, which would have been too tricky for young fingers.

This wasn't the only example of revisiting the past to meet a new need. Back when the minifigure debuted in 1978, a trio of sets were released that still catered to the large, brick-built figures that had become the minifigure's progenitors. Each of these three sets – a house, hair salon and hospital – utilised the hinges that had been developed to allow 375 Castle to open up. While none of these buildings had roofs, all included four complete walls so that their interiors were enclosed. To facilitate such tall construction, a special 1×6 element was developed that rose to a height of five bricks. While eliminating four bricks' worth of studs and top faces, it was still the full width of a brick all the way up, unlike the later, thinner castle wall panels. When the minifigure took off and brick-built figures were retired, these large buildings were no longer needed and the part was shelved. Over the next two decades, it was used in just a handful of sets, before being brought back in a bigger way during the late 1990s: between 1996 and 2000 an astonishing twelve sets included the oversized 1×6×5 brick, and it appeared in many more sets through the early 2000s. This piece was perfect for allowing small hands to quickly raise large buildings.

In another nod to facilitating quick yet effective building, road baseplates were rereleased in 1997 with a fresh look and were included in some sets again. Five-year-old children can easily connect roads. Simplified models for younger hands had quickly became the norm in fire, police, cargo, race, flight and Octan-related sets, utilising these and other specialised elements, along with age-appropriate levels of complexity. Parts under a certain size or over a perceived difficulty threshold were avoided.

But LEGO Town did not completely become a younger theme. While the more everyday aspects of city life were tilted towards younger ages, designers became focused on creating adjacent settings or slightly futuristic visions of currently existing vehicles. For these models, the target age remained a minimum of eight years old, so their level of complexity and assortment of parts stayed largely unchanged. Designers relied on a mix of market research, child-testing, and their own instincts to come up with models that would excite children

For many years LEGO Town and its subthemes could almost have come from different product lines. In the same year that LEGO Town fire subtheme became greatly simplified, another subtheme known as Divers launched, which included highly detailed renditions of real-world submarines and ships. Divers reused pieces from LEGO Nautica and introduced several additional components, including a bulbous dome and a fuselage element with a porthole window, to give the underwater vessels accurate appearances. Existing sharks were recast in white to give children Great White sharks alongside a new stingray mould. Large numbers of animals were included in each set, providing lots of opportunities for divers to study marine life or be chased by teeth and stingers. Different colours of diving suit were mixed and matched as well. As with LEGO Castle, factions did not officially race each other for lost treasure, but it was assumed children would know what to do! Divers' new ships looked so different from the rest of LEGO Town line-up that they looked out of place docked at the theme's coastguard station. Very different design aesthetics in the same theme would reoccur in LEGO City, but that was still some years off.

While no other theme was aligned with the drive to capture younger children quite so intensely as LEGO Town, the new approach did spread beyond the LEGO Group everyday-life offerings. LEGO Space, too, was targeted slightly downwards in age, along with some of the

ABOVE The 1×6×5 panel allowed walls to be built more quickly and efficiently than by stacking bricks.

OPPOSITE Virtually overnight, many LEGO Town sets were adjusted to make them appropriate for younger age groups.

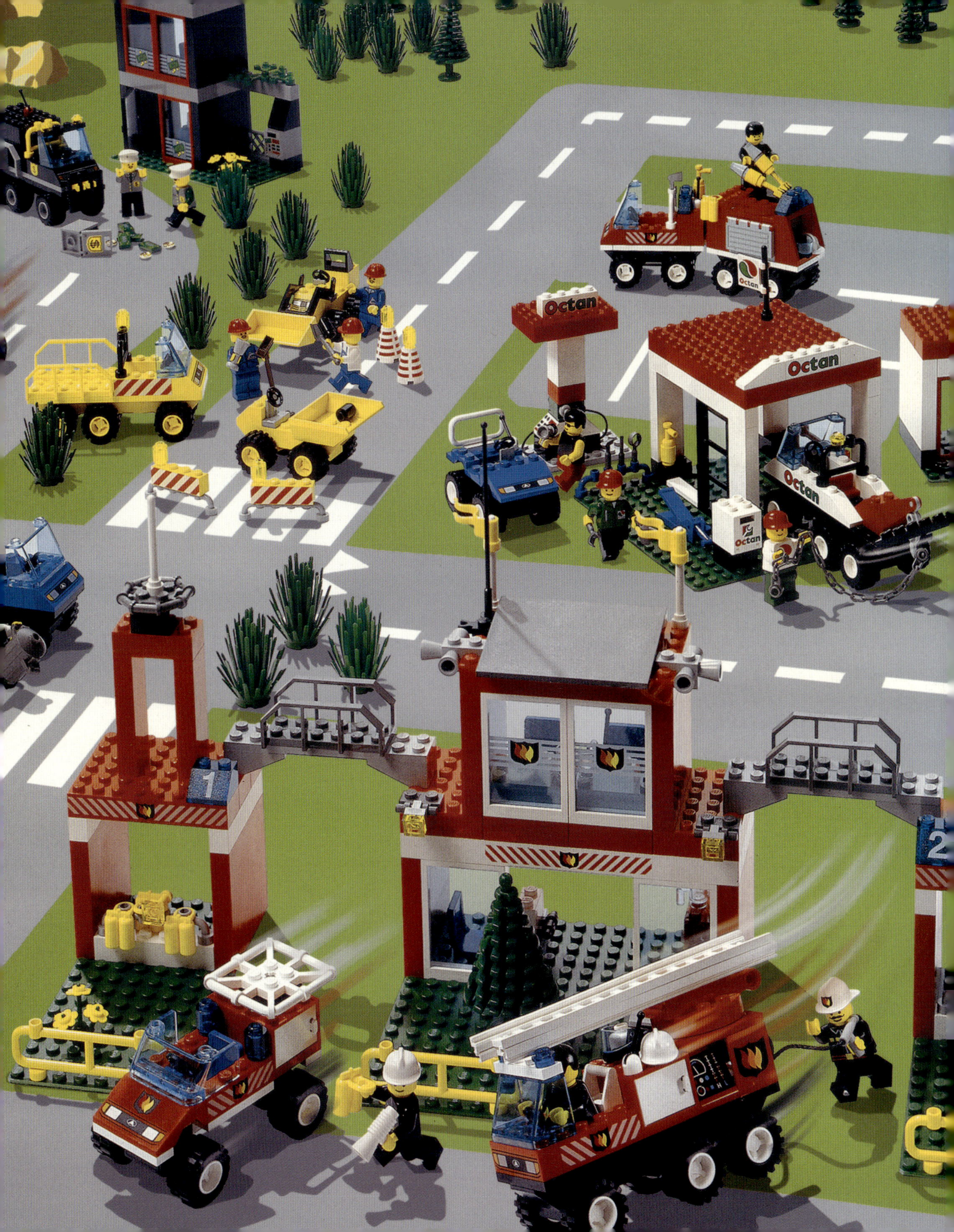
Octan
Octan
Octan
Octan
1
2

TOP Divers was one of the last highly detailed, 'realistic' LEGO Town subthemes. It included a variety of new animal elements, including stingrays and sawfish.

ABOVE Aimed at younger builders, LEGO Jack Stone used huge, moulded elements.

later waves of LEGO® Adventurers. Launched in 2001, LEGO® Jack Stone included larger, more detailed figures and super-sized specialised elements, pairing simplified building with high action. It was replaced in 2003 by LEGO® 4+, also with larger pieces and minifigures than usual, but with less focus on the character Jack Stone.

LEGO Town continued to expand as the 1990s transitioned into the new millennium. Divers began a trend as more exotic subject matter was explored, including a team of thrill-seekers in a subtheme called Extreme Team, daring search-and-rescue heroes in Res-Q, which included slightly futuristic renditions of familiar vehicles, and scientists exploring the poles in Arctic. Each of these subthemes became successively more futuristic, with existing pieces cast in offbeat neon colours alongside new, specialised elements. They also began to skew younger, blurring the line that had originally been more distinct between the sets targeting different demographics.

Through this dual-demographic strategy, designers began to recognise that children didn't just want real-life categories like police or fire; they also wanted the models within those genres to be detailed and realistic. Basic models like cars, fire trucks, police stations and helicopters must be age-appropriate and cool, but not simplistic or 'blocky'. Between 2001 and 2002, no major new LEGO Town sets were produced, aside from rereleases of past classics like the first Octan gas station and the largest LEGO Town airport. In fact, LEGO Town would never return; in its place, a new bearer of the everyday-life baton was about to debut.

Moving to the big city

Between 2003 and 2004, LEGO Town became LEGO World City and scaled back some of the simplified building techniques and oversized parts, reintroducing more detailed everyday-life models. LEGO World City also saw trains folded into the same banner as other real-world subject matter. Aiming to be edgy and cool, LEGO World City was envisioned as everyday life a decade or more beyond the present day: familiar subject matter such as coastguard helicopters, fire boats and police headquarters were given a futuristic twist. Police had an armoured tank rather than a traditional car, and brave rescuers leapt from a chopper which bore more resemblance to a spaceship than present-day helicopters.

Such unique looks were possible thanks to taking advantage of numerous elements created for other themes, most notably LEGO *Star Wars*, including hull elements and curved windshields. This growing abundance of parts enabled designers to vary vehicle sizes like never before, bringing several of them up to six studs in width, as some of their predecessors had wanted to do back in the 1980s before the first road plates precluded such an option. This trend would continue until widths of six studs became the new standard.

While LEGO World City offered detailed sets, they were still slightly futuristic and it became clear to designers, through customer feedback, that children wanted pure, unadulterated renditions of the world around them. A fire truck or boat should look like the real vehicles that children could see in their own town and should include relevant details that even a young child familiar with the subject matter would expect to see. Fire stations needed huge garages. Harbours must have cranes. Trains should feature lights, and so on. Everyday life needed to be just that: everyday life. Designers began working on what some of them dubbed the 'back-to-basics' strategy. Just because a model needed to be simple enough for a certain developmental age did not mean that it could forgo detail or realism. The standard bearer for this new direction was 7239 Fire Truck, released in 2005.

LEGO World City had launched with the focus primarily on police sets, with fire sets planned for the following year. When the decision was made to rebrand everyday life simply as LEGO City, designers had been working on LEGO World City fire assortment, so this became the first major genre produced under the new LEGO City banner. Every designer on the team had, at the outset, been given the same task: to build a fire truck. The intent was to look at multiple interpretations of a model that was appropriate for younger age groups while maintaining realism. The winning model would be used as the design style for everyday life in the new theme. The model that was selected became 7239 Fire Truck and the key to its design rested on two new elements, a roof plate and wheel arch.

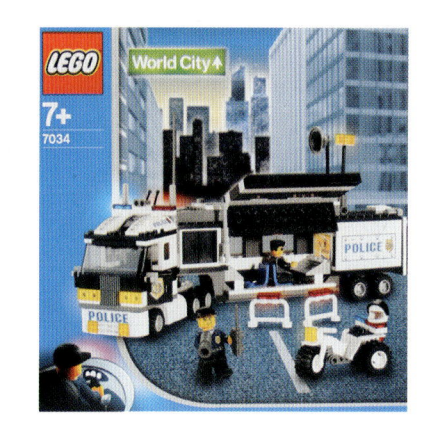

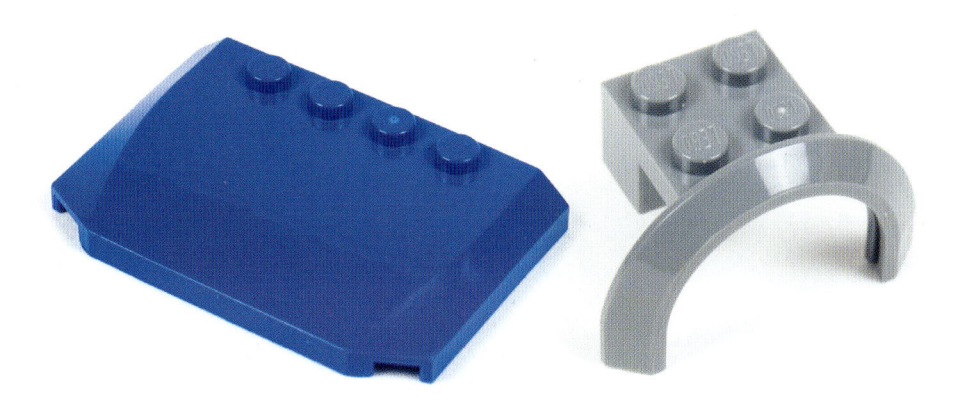

ABOVE LEGO World City bridged the gap between LEGO Town and LEGO City. It pioneered many of the techniques that would be used in the later theme, including six-stud-wide vehicles and greater levels of detail.

FAR LEFT Roof plates largely replaced hinged elements for covering the cabs of vehicles.

LEFT Wheel arches were created to add more realism to cars.

> The idea with LEGO World City was everyday models but with what we called a twist. Models were designed to look subtly futuristic. When LEGO World City was about to become LEGO City, every designer was asked to build a fire engine. The one I built is very close to the first one we launched in LEGO City. It got picked to be the representative design style for the new theme, with the wheel arches and roof.

Henrik Andersen, Design Master, the LEGO Group

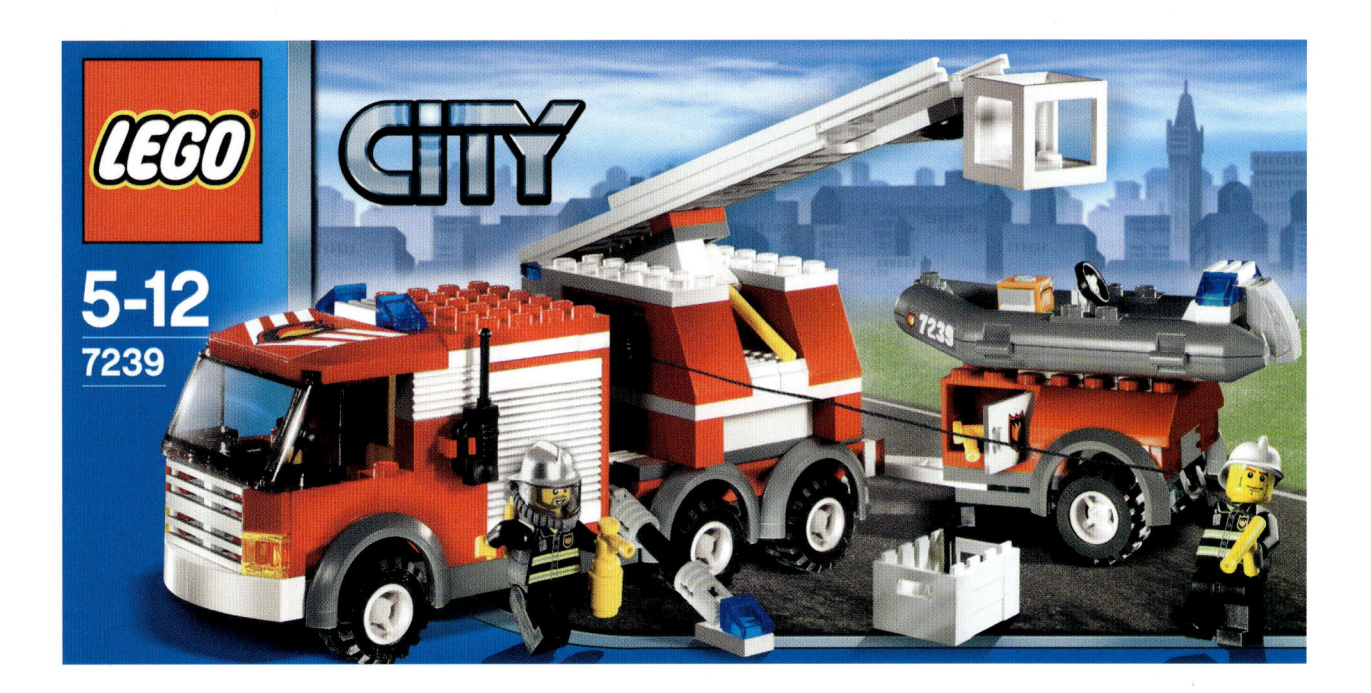

LEGO World City had used the old finger hinges, which could prove tricky for little fingers to assemble. The new roof plate didn't pivot to open; it simply attached somewhat loosely to a vehicle's top so it could be easily removed. Designers intentionally omitted window pieces on either side of the cab so that children could reach their fingers in and easily pop off the roof plate.

Wheel arches replaced a variety of different parts that had served the same purpose through the years. Doing so had the triple benefits of reducing the overall number of active elements, creating a distinctive component that defined the aesthetic of LEGO City new vehicles and making building more straightforward, since the same arches were used on all vehicles throughout the theme, which had not been the case before.

Once this aesthetic and approach to LEGO City was defined, it became formalised over the years. Alongside going back to basics, the LEGO Group expanded testing with children in the early 2000s. Feedback from those interactions helped the company define ever more thoroughly what a five-year-old child was, and was not, capable of. Today, models for younger children aged five and below, despite never being that large, are some of the hardest sets to design because they have the most constraints and rules governing what is allowed in their creation and they go through one of the most intense vetting processes of any LEGO product. All of this is to ensure that young children don't get frustrated. Bricks of similar lengths in the same colour are avoided. Designers aim for symmetry down at least one axis. Bricks of dramatically different colours are used to form the insides of models so that children can easily see where things go and which direction a model should be oriented in relation to the instructions. Certain types of connections are avoided since they require too much strength to attach or remove.

The focus on user-friendly building goes even further. At model committee reviews, attendees intentionally build prospective sets incorrectly and make recommendations for changes to both design and instructions so that, if a child veers off track, they will still have a good chance of creating a fun model to play with. While it may not be the exact aeroplane or car shown on the box, it should still be reasonably close.

ABOVE 7239 Fire Truck from 2005 defined the design style for LEGO City vehicles and introduced new roofs and wheel arches.

Thanks to getting back to basics and striving to make LEGO City as user-friendly as possible, the theme became what is known within the LEGO Group as a recruiter. Capturing the interest of young children is a challenge: they need stories to be simple and engaging. Typical scenarios from LEGO City are perfect, such as a robber escaping jail and getting chased or a cat being rescued from a burning building. To that end, LEGO City designers have, through the years, striven to create a cohesive style and approach to their subject matter that is consistently inviting and teaches children how to build. If a child can experience success in this theme, chances are they will want to try something more challenging when they reach the appropriate age.

As the years went on, other themes joined LEGO City in enticing new fans into the fold. Among the most counterintuitive of these were brands for licensed Super Heroes. Logic would dictate that these themes would appeal only to older children who could proficiently read comic books, but this turns out not to be the case. These Super Heroes and Villains have become so ubiquitous that they are as familiar to many young children as firefighters or police. Put a Super Hero into a four-year-old's hand and they will immediately be able to start playing.

Each year the company creates a balanced portfolio with a certain percentage of sets spread across all themes that are appropriate for younger ages. Sometimes this has been done in tandem with special branding, such as LEGO® Juniors or LEGO 4+. Other times, smaller sets from various themes are aged down, with no special branding. If a new theme is aimed almost entirely at younger children, space can be freed up elsewhere for an additional set targeted at slightly older children. Every year is a balancing act.

As LEGO City took off in the early 2000s, it followed a remarkably similar trajectory to LEGO Town, albeit a little more accelerated. Correctly recognising that larger sets from the theme would

RIGHT Once LEGO City designers had established their style, seen here in 7641 City Corner from 2009, it stayed remarkably consistent. Buildings and vehicles from many years later do not look out of place next to their older counterparts.

be bought primarily by or for children on the upper end of the age range, more complicated elements were used, though building techniques were kept as straightforward as possible. Garage doors came back in a big way, alongside a new technique to stretch building sizes even larger. Now, instead of the sides of structures being mostly windows, entire sides were largely omitted. In their place, columns were used for support, with the spaces between them left empty.

In 2005, a key element was introduced that quickly rose to prominence: an updated version of the large 1×6×5 panel brick that had been resurrected from the 1970s for the final years of LEGO Town. In its revised form, the piece was moulded more like the old castle wall panels, with a single wall and ridges supporting it on the edges incorporating full plates and studs on top and bottom respectively. Like its predecessor, this allowed for a huge amount of surface area but also efficient use of raw materials. Thanks to parts like this, used in tandem with strategic open spaces, LEGO City buildings became bigger and bigger.

New generations of children would want their own fire stations, police stations and construction vehicles: there was no doubt such offerings needed to remain evergreens. Accordingly, during the first few years of rebuilding after LEGO Town demise, the main focus was on reviving these classic subthemes and incorporating the new style and design approaches. Airports, planes, construction vehicles, gas stations: all returned in glorious new six-stud-wide scale thanks to the roof plates, wheel arches, garage doors, updated wall panel and another new element, the 2×2×10 girder. Girders were another example of achieving size through the strategic use of support elements to cover large areas with minimal material while not compromising strength.

To this day, the scale of some of the resurgent models that first incorporated these new elements has not been topped. To add further novelty, designers introduced more varied locales that existed adjacent to or just outside LEGO City limits, such as an offshore coastguard base.

The first major deviation from traditional subject matter came in 2009. LEGO Castle was in the final year of its Fantasy Era line and a unique opportunity emerged for synergy between the two themes – centred around cows! LEGO Castle was developing the first non-military-based set in a generation: a village square with market that would become set 10193 Medieval Market Village, released in 2009. LEGO City designers had developed a potential farming subtheme that included a prototype pig element, as well as cows, the latter of which both teams jointly launched. Farming had never been rendered in LEGO System bricks before and served as the first experiment with subject matter that existed adjacent to LEGO City. Farming was just the beginning.

Around this time, LEGO City designers created at least ten fully developed subthemes set in exotic locales, including space, jungle, volcanos, underwater, and a realistic return to the Arctic. They did not just create a single, representative set, but fashioned complete lines with models in a range of sizes. At this point, they were not that different from their predecessors who had

TOP Set 7993 Service Station was inspired by the first Octan service station in 1992 but has been given a modern twist through the use of new elements.

ABOVE The revised 1×6×5 panel is an even more efficient way to build walls than its predecessor.

OPPOSITE Set 7905 Building Crane used multiple girders to create the largest crane set ever produced.

Everyday Life 163

ABOVE Set 7994 City Harbour from 2009 included the largest single element ever produced for an everyday-life theme in its enormous boat hull. This hull element would never be used again, as soon after this, LEGO City sets were reduced in size.

conceived the subthemes Extreme Team or Res-Q in the late 1990s. However, in the late 2000s, a pair of key tools were available that had not been present before: testing with children and accelerated development schedules. While in years past designers had largely been left to guess what children would be interested in three years later, now products could be brought to market in less than half the time and with a lot more certainty.

A new pattern began. LEGO City designers would bring ten to fifteen fully developed subthemes to a series of tests. The results would be tallied to see which ones children responded best to. Potential subject matter included classic icons such as space and underwater exploration, but also some more unusual ones, including volcanic and jungle exploration, as well as a few conventional themes like mining. Year after year all the options were presented to a new batch of children, with the winners being turned into official products, provided enough time had passed since a given subject matter was last selected.

Designers soon learned that it was impossible to predict which subtheme children would pick in a given year. Sometimes they wanted an old stalwart, while in other years a previously unexciting theme was red hot. Children are impressionable. Sometimes larger cultural trends or even recent discoveries figuring prominently in the news come into play, while in other instances better colour selection might be the key. The process consistently yielded popular LEGO City-adjacent offerings to keep the line fresh. As with LEGO® NINJAGO® and LEGO *Star Wars*, novelty-driven sets relied largely on a few exciting new parts centred around their given setting. Since cows started the trend, animals have remained a consistent favourite, especially in the wilder settings such as jungle and underwater, and include leopards, sharks, crocodiles, stingrays and more.

Within the LEGO System range of themes, everyday life, and specifically LEGO City, continues to be one of, if not the, primary recruiter for the LEGO Group. It is a role the subject matter has played for over six decades and, thanks to the sustainable approach the company has developed for researching and designing new sets which are age appropriate, satisfying to build, and yet retain novelty year after year, it feels safe to say that everyday life will continue as the product line's foundation for many years to come.

ABOVE Two prototypes stand alongside the final version of the cow created for the joint venture between the LEGO City and LEGO Castle themes.

LEFT 7637 Farm, released in 2009, is the largest set from the LEGO City subtheme, Farm.

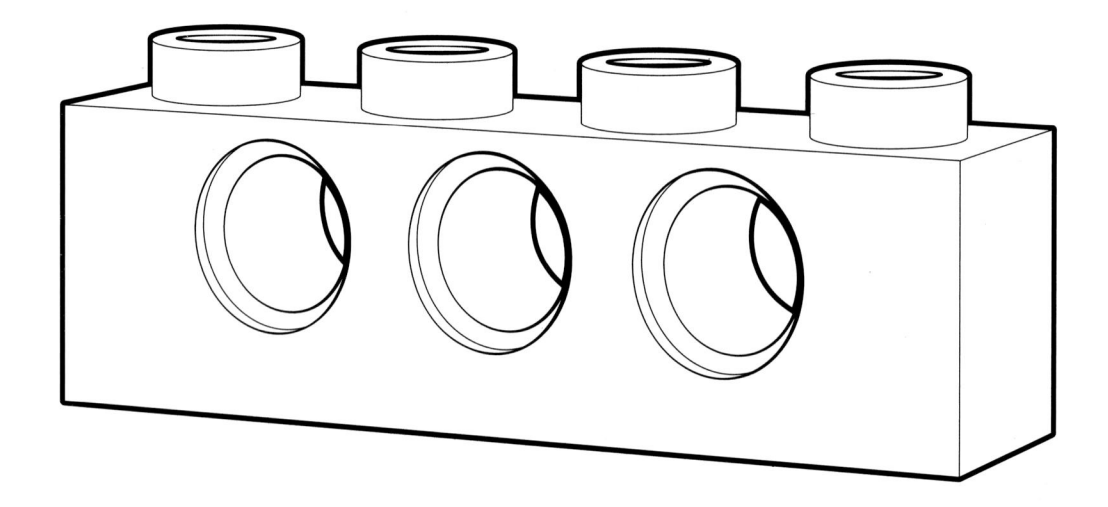

> **"**
> We wanted to make a big car with a strong chassis, so we used pins to lock the bricks with holes together. That was actually the start of LEGO Technic.
> **"**
>
> Jan Ryaa, former Design Master, the LEGO Group

7
Building at the Highest Level

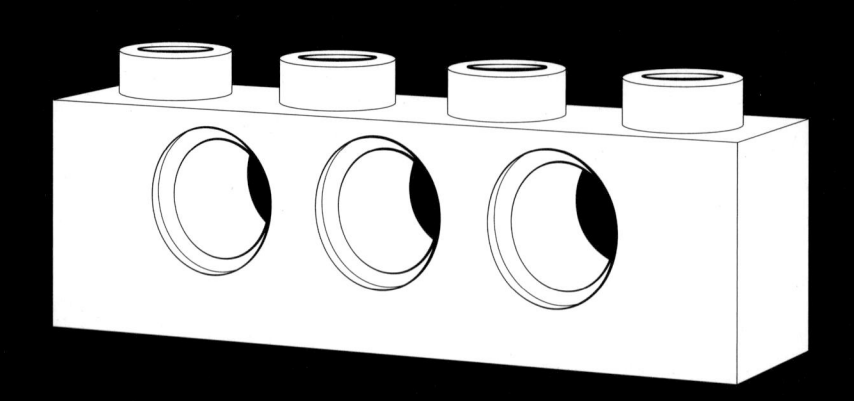

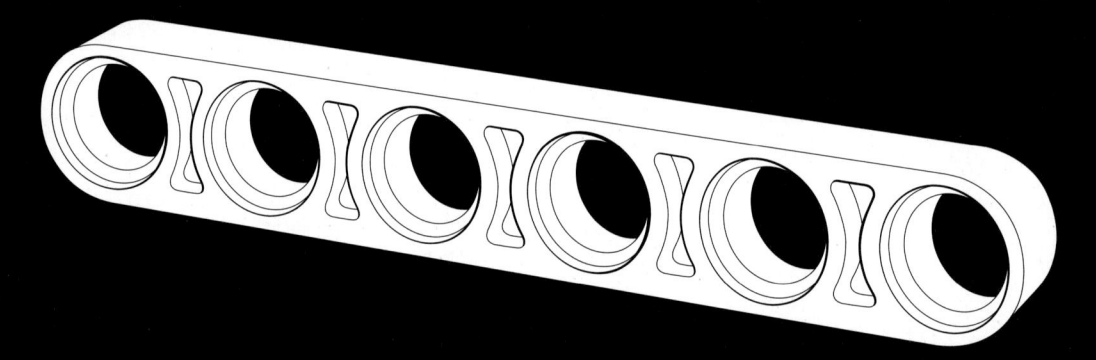

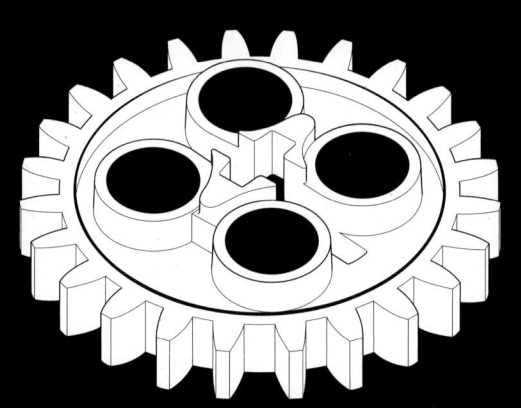

TOP LEGO® Technic bricks are the oldest structural LEGO Technic elements.

CENTRE LEGO Technic beams have no studs and are a single module tall.

BOTTOM Gear sizes are based on a ratio developed in the 1970s.

LEGO® Technic has one of the most fascinating stories of all LEGO® lines. Every new LEGO theme had to beat the internal competition on potential new ideas, then offer continual novelty to endure on store shelves. But LEGO Technic stands apart as a theme that evolved its own unique building system out of an existing one, eventually becoming something so different it must be classified as its own species. Both in the beginning, and at various stages throughout its history, LEGO Technic did not set out to become its own system; however, through key choices and element designs, that is exactly what happened. More than anywhere else in the parts catalogue, individual, unassuming elements have followed the hero's journey, getting plucked from obscurity to play a role of outsized importance.

LEFT The LEGO train motor and battery box helped launch the precursor to LEGO Technic.

BELOW Aside from changes in colour, LEGO Technic axles have remained the same since their inception. An early, milky-white axle shown on the right, with a modern axle on the left.

BOTTOM Set 802 from 1970 showcased several new parts on its box, including gears, cross axles and a modified 2×4 brick with holes through it for axles.

By the late 1960s, a family of electrical components for motorised trains had been established. At its heart were two vital members on which the whole contingent literally ran: a 4.5V motor and a battery box. The mould for the battery box would one day go on to play an unexpected role in the LEGO® *Star Wars*™ line, but not for several decades. Producing such specialised and expensive electrical pieces led designers to look for applications beyond the world of trains. Eventually, they settled on introducing a new type of movement to LEGO products: mechanical functions.

There had been some experimentation with gears across a few unrelated products during the 1960s, but this was the first formal effort to make something uniform out of the concept. Designers eventually developed three new classes of parts which, all together, contained nine elements. Up until this time, LEGO wheels were all still variants of Knud Møller's original design that affixed non-removable metal axles to plastic wheels. This arrangement was perfect for models of cars, but gears required more versatility. They needed to be able to be positioned at different locations along the axle, and a fixed metal axle rod made such variation impossible.

Out of that need was born the first independent LEGO axle, which, aside from being cast in a milky-white colour, looked exactly like the modern LEGO Technic cross axle, so named for the shape of its cross section. These elements have remained virtually unchanged, aside from the establishment of rules governing their colours. Both cross axles and snaps – snaps are what designers call the pins that hold LEGO Technic elements together – are now colour-coded based on length or type. Sorting them this way helps builders avoid making errors while following instructions. During the 1980s and 1990s, all cross axles were black, which made it easy for builders to mistakenly place similar lengths in the wrong places. Eventually, cross axles came in four different colours: red, yellow, grey and black. Each increase in length is assigned the next colour of the sequence so that no axle of the same colour is anywhere close to the same size as another that shares its hue.

In the early days, cross axles were produced at lengths equivalent to the space between four, six, eight and twelve studs. A short adapter was also made that could plug into the train motor, which was sized for existing wheels, not cross axles. In order to have enough strength, the new cross axles had to be larger in diameter than their metal predecessors, so a new brick for anchoring them was also required. Despite technically being new, the design of this anchoring brick closely mirrored the modified 2×4 Knud had come up with for the original LEGO wheel.

Once again, holes were passed through each of a 2×4 brick's walls. However, this time, instead of one hole per side, a bisecting tunnel was cast in between each pair of studs on all four walls; three on the long sides and one on the short faces. Finally, three sizes of gears were created, with cross-shaped holes in their centres that could attach to all the axles. Designers had started this effort trying to find some additional applications for the train motor and battery box. Little did they know they had just unwittingly laid the first stone in what would become the foundation of LEGO Technic.

BELOW The new gear and axle elements released in 1970 made it possible to build working vehicles like this tractor.

ABOVE Several sets from the mid 1970s used tyres of the wheel-over-gear construction, including 392 Formula 1 from 1975, seen in the middle here. Other more specialised wheel variants were also produced.

The new parts first appeared in 1970 in three unnamed sets: 800, 801 and 802. The sets allowed a variety of mechanical contraptions to be built, which, when paired with regular bricks attached to studs on the gear's faces, created a whole new level of functionality, including lifting arms, turning bases and much more. Two years later, the concept was expanded further through an additional pair of new parts. The first of these opened up numerous possibilities thanks to mitigating a previously limiting factor. The initial trio of mechanical sets had lots of parts that could turn, but none of them were actual wheels, meaning models were still largely stationary or moved in a clunky manner. So designers created a flexible rubber tyre that could fit over the smallest gear's circumference, thereby repurposing it into a rim. Further flexibility was provided through a joint element that allowed two axles to connect at an angle while still being able to rotate, which created the possibility for installing drive trains.

The complete collection of parts allowed the construction of motorised vehicles. Between 1972 and 1974, the parts were offered in a number of collections of bricks, with ideas for multiple models, rather than formal sets. The parts – especially the independent axles, small gears and rubber tyres that fit over them – also saw use in Hobby Set models during the mid 1970s. The next step towards LEGO Technic was about to be taken.

Jan Ryaa, before he worked on LEGO® Trains, along with another designer named Eric Bach, wanted to push the LEGO® System and create larger models than ever before. Specifically, these two designers dreamed of making a giant car set. However, the normal method of stacking System bricks would make a sturdy build, but would require too many elements. So, rather than abandon their idea, the pair began experimenting with ways to make existing bricks capable of stronger connections. Computer-aided design was decades away, so the two designers employed far more analogue methods by modifying existing elements with drills and saws. Their idea was to introduce holes through the sides of bricks into which pins, later dubbed snaps, could be inserted. Then a second brick with holes could be mounted across the pins, securely joining the whole assembly. Their goal was not to create a whole new building system, but simply to modify existing bricks slightly in order to open up new possibilities.

Jan Ryaa and Eric Bach placed holes in between the studs of the bricks, making a similar decision to their predecessors, who created the modified 2×4 for those first independent axles. They didn't know it at the time, but this was a foundational decision. System bricks are based on even numbers of studs, which means that placing a hole between each pair results in an odd number of penetrations. A sixteen-stud-long brick will have fifteen holes, a fourteen-stud one will have thirteen holes and so on. Later, this would prove a fortuitous, if inadvertent, feature. In many mechanical constructs like drive trains, the ability to place the axle from the motor directly through the centre of an element is highly advantageous, since it allows all the moving parts to be mirrored on either side of the vehicle. Jan Ryaa and Eric Bach worked for several years on their project, with timing that could not have been better.

Concurrent with the development of minifigures during the late 1970s, Kjeld Kirk Kristiansen also wanted to clearly define and segment the ages at which different LEGO products were targeted. The car that Jan and Eric were developing could be perfect as the first model in a new range aimed at older children looking for more challenging building experiences. The car project had begun largely as an experiment, but it quickly garnered official backing and support. Later, the idea of a challenging building experience would become one of the three principles to which every LEGO Technic model must adhere: Authenticity, Functionality and Challenging building, known internally as the 'AFC promise'. Every LEGO Technic set must meet this promise, which is partly the reason that there are no historical or highly futuristic LEGO Technic sets, since it is difficult to make something feel authentic when people don't see it around them in their daily lives. Despite not having that formula at the time, Jan and Eric unknowingly foreshadowed it with the other feature they decided to include in their car.

Jan Ryaa and Eric Bach wanted the car they were designing to be big, but also to have some authentic functionality. They considered working steering or pistons that fired when wheels rolled along, which would allow the model to behave like a real vehicle. Knowledge and experience gained from examining the earlier gears and their models allowed Jan and Eric to home in on what worked well and uncover improvements they could make. They determined that the existing gears were too large and had teeth that were too big. Because the holes drilled in each brick fell exactly between studs, the distance from the centre of each hole to an adjacent one was the same as that between the centres of studs: a distance equal to one module. As a result, the same foundational dimension laid down all those years ago by Godtfred Kirk Christiansen and Axel Thomsen became the basis for the LEGO Technic System as well, though the implications of this would only come to full fruition several decades later, when LEGO Technic Beams were invented. For their gears, it meant Jan and Eric also started with the basic module dimension.

Work began with the smallest possible gear, which was defined as being sized so that a pair of them could sit side by side in sequential LEGO Technic holes. This meant that each one's teeth needed to intertwine across the one-module distance between holes (see FIGURE 1). Accordingly, Jan and Eric determined that their gear's nominal diameter should be a single module. (In practice, LEGO Technic gears are not exact modules in diameter, especially when the teeth are included, but they are close enough that designers can use these designations

ABOVE The modern twenty-four-tooth gear maintains Jan and Eric's initial relationship, as it is nominally three modules in diameter.

> We wanted to make a big car with a strong chassis, so we used pins to lock the bricks with holes together. That was actually the start of LEGO Technic. But we also wanted to give this car a working function, with an engine that has pistons that go up and down, with the pistons driven by the wheels. Thankfully, we didn't have to invent all the elements, because at that time there was an existing LEGO product with small holes in a 2×4 brick. We also already had cross axles and gear wheels, so it was just a matter of making those gear wheels smaller. We evaluated what we had, incorporating elements where we could and improving pieces that were hard to incorporate.

Jan Ryaa, former Design Master, the LEGO Group

for simplicity). Through trial and error, they further concluded that eight teeth evenly spaced around the resulting circumference worked well and left enough space for a strong centre through which cross axles could be passed. Thus, the foundational gear relationship of eight teeth for every module of diameter was born.

Ultimately, three gears in total were developed for the car project: the small one at one module in diameter and then two more at each odd numbered interval in sequence after that: three and five modules respectively. Multiplying the number of modules by the relationship of eight teeth per unit gave the other two gears counts of twenty-four and forty teeth respectively.

After three years of work, Jan Ryaa and Eric Bach's project was ready for its debut. In 1977, an assortment of six sets was released: four models, including the car that had started it all, and two supplementary packs containing more of the new parts. The initial assortment included several new classes of elements, such as LEGO Technic plates, snaps and connectors, along with bricks and gears. Snaps were the pegs which fitted into holes, and connectors allowed axles and snaps to be joined together, while LEGO Technic plates were normal System plates with holes through the centre of every group of four studs. These sets were released under the name Technical Sets; the LEGO Technic title would be established later.

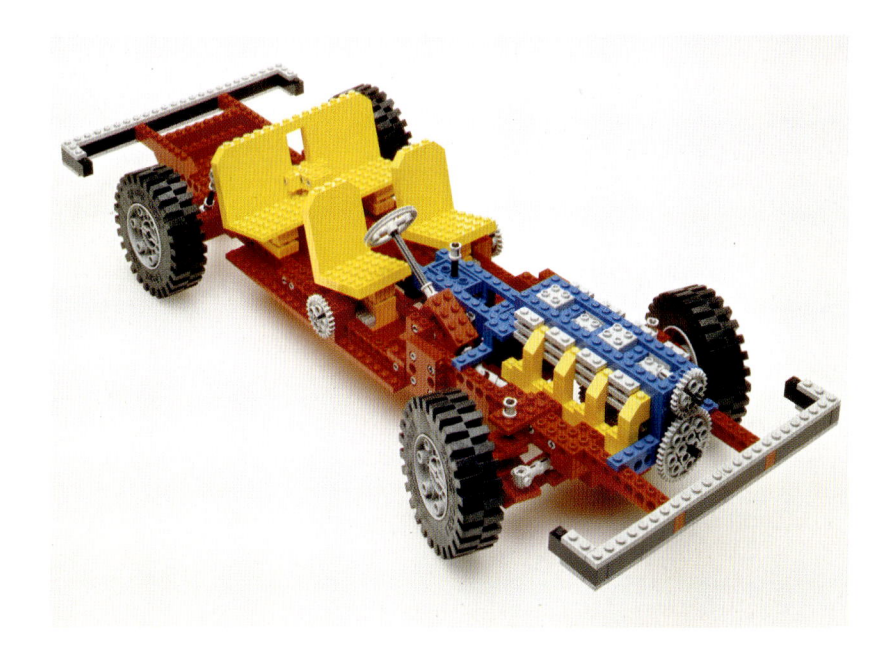

ABOVE Gears are based on odd numbers of modules so that they can be centred more easily in LEGO Technic bricks and beams.

LEFT Designers Jan Ryaa and Eric Bach's dream of a LEGO car unlike any before it came to fruition in set 853 Car Chassis, released in 1977.

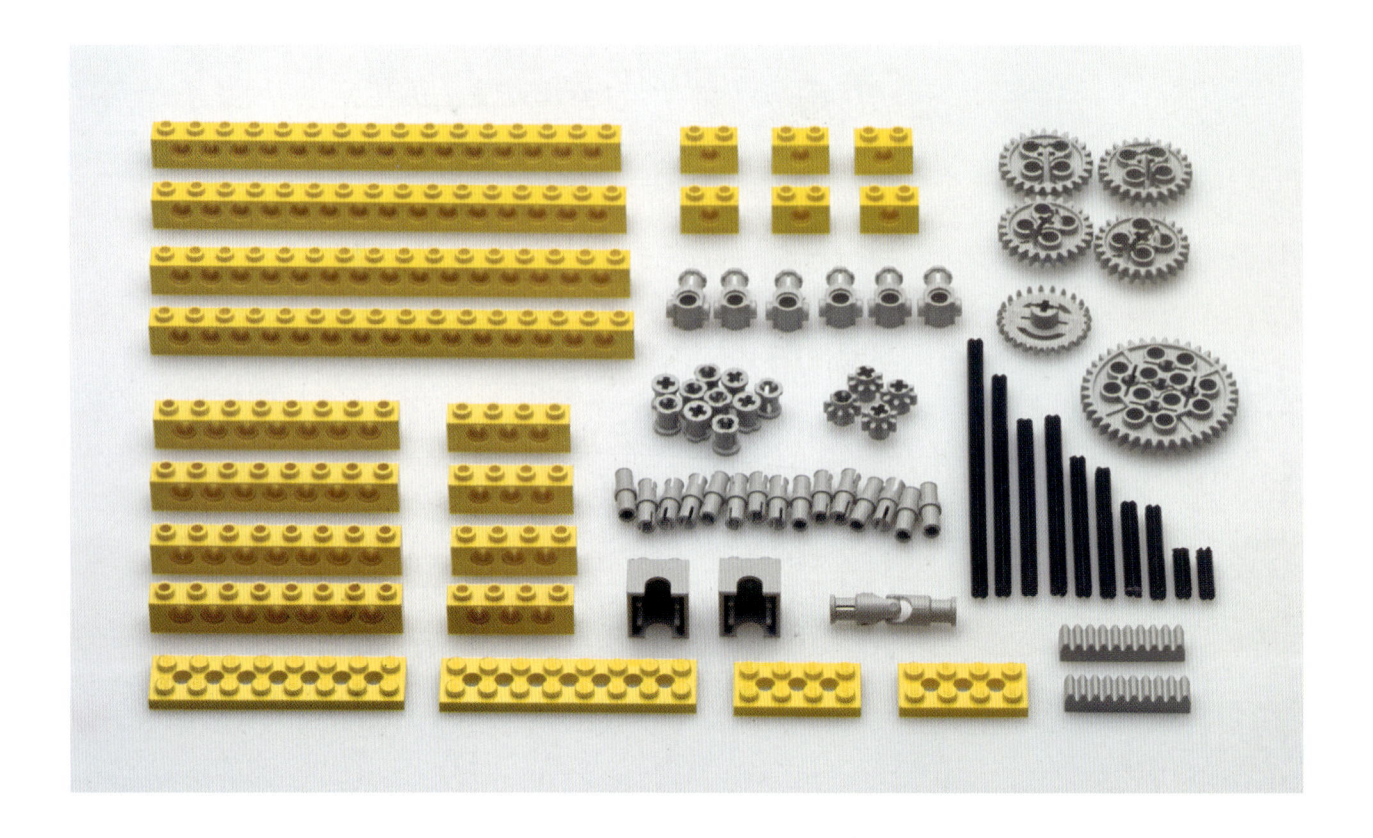

TOP In 1977, the theme that would later become known as LEGO Technic launched with a range of new elements.

ABOVE Friction snaps (*left*) are distinguished from smooth snaps (*right*) by the ridges along their length. These ridges resist turning when the snap is fitted into a hole.

Thanks to being fully compatible with normal System bricks, Technical Sets, which included vehicles and accessory packs, were able to expand for the first several years with only a few dedicated new parts being created for it; instead, it incorporated components developed by other LEGO themes. The subject matter was new and different, though, which provided novelty, and the range of bricks and plates used in LEGO Technic were cast in a range of colours beyond their original yellow.

By 1982 the line had become well established and was rebranded LEGO Technic. At the same time, a new part was added that greatly aided construction. Previously, the single snap invented by Jan Ryaa and Eric Bach had been used as the primary method of connecting various LEGO Technic bricks together. With an eye towards rotating functions, the two designers had designed the snap to fit securely but loosely in the hole. It was free to rotate without a lot of friction. While great for certain movements, it was less sturdy in some of the structural applications in which it was now often used. Accordingly, a new, tighter-fitting snap, known as a friction snap, was introduced, allowing for more secure model construction.

Showcasing functionality

The evolution of LEGO Technic had begun. Initially, models in the new theme were similar to the Hobby Sets from the 1970s, built with standard elements underneath which were hidden functions. However, as more parts became available and the theme's designers gained experience, products began to evolve into a new style. By the mid-1980s, the models being created were markedly different from those that had come before. Designers began to embrace the mechanical nature of their models by removing plating and walls that had previously hidden functions; showcasing the functions became a prominent part of set design. That approach was cemented as the theme's future after a brief experiment during the mid 1980s.

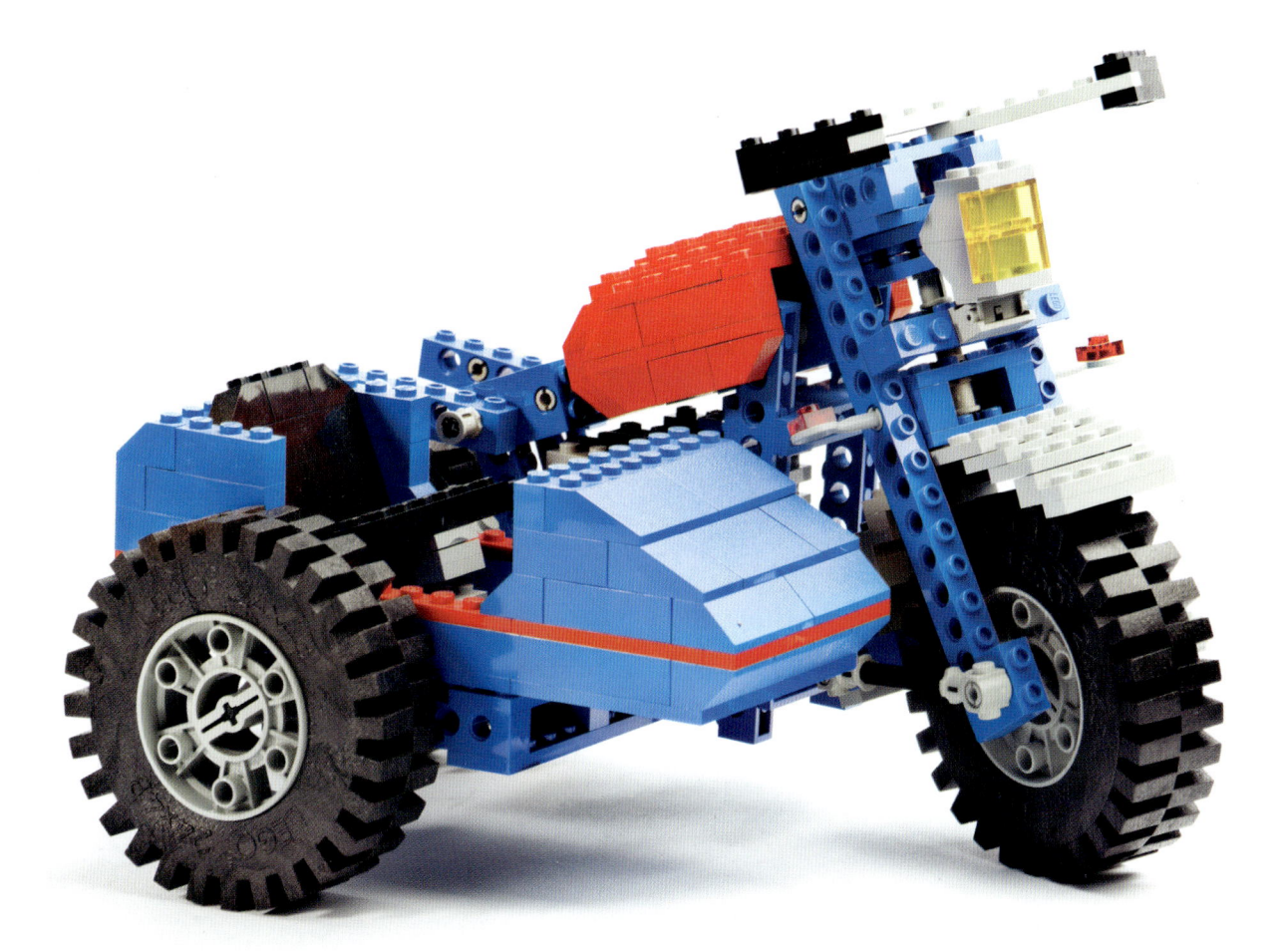

Like their counterparts in LEGO® Town, LEGO® Space and LEGO® Castle, LEGO Technic designers were aware of the growing popularity of action-oriented playsets in the 1980s, often based on TV shows or feature films. Thanks to the concurrent effort to develop new figures for sets targeted at girls, LEGO Technic ended up with a unique opportunity in the form of its own figure – and designers took a diversion into role play. LEGO Technic figures were taller than minifigures, with additional points of articulation, and hands that could grip snaps. The new figures debuted in 1986, in a four-set LEGO Technic subtheme called Arctic Action. The theme included vehicles for traversing frozen terrain, as well as explorers' accessories that fused role play with the functionality of LEGO Technic. Arctic Action only lasted one year, but the LEGO Technic figure would go on to be included in various sets for many years and the large skis created for the figures were used extensively in the LEGO Space Ice Planet subtheme several years later.

After the foray into role play, LEGO Technic returned to its core strength as a technical theme with models that were packed with functions. Nevertheless, the impulse behind the frozen subtheme inadvertently prefigured a new approach that would emerge within the LEGO Technic theme, and the first step was taken the very next year.

During 1987 the LEGO Technic team was developing products intended for launch in 1989. Occasionally during the development process, a product will be dreamed up that would require more new parts than there are frames available in any given year. Teams will develop precursor models that utilise a couple of the parts needed for the ultimate goal and therefore justify creating them. Within a few years, all the necessary elements will have been gathered.

ABOVE Early LEGO Technic sets like 857 Motorbike with Sidecar, released in 1979, hid their functionality behind standard System elements. Later models would be much more open.

ABOVE Set 8660 Arctic Rescue Unit, released in 1986, fused LEGO Technic building techniques with role play revolving around the new LEGO Technic figures.

    The LEGO Technic team had conceived of such a project, which would be the most technical and complicated product the theme had ever seen. The first step in the process had been an excavator vehicle, released in 1984, for which a small bucket element had been created. This was followed in 1987 by a loader, which included an even larger bucket on its front. The team's ultimate aim was to create a model that incorporated both of those elements into a pneumatically operated backhoe with the excavator bucket articulating on its back and the bigger loader bucket attached to its front.

    As designers got to work, however, they discovered an issue. These types of vehicles had a key feature, without which the model wouldn't be authentic: outriggers. Used for stabilisation, outriggers are protruding legs that come out from the side of many construction vehicles to keep them from tipping over or shifting when moving heavy loads. Such a function had never been incorporated into a LEGO Technic set before and designers quickly discovered why: scaling them realistically required tolerances between bricks that were impossible. Designs were either too bulky or caught on neighbouring parts of the vehicle. Solving the problem involved a new element dubbed a lift arm, which was distinctive in several important ways from other LEGO Technic components.

Building at the Hightest Level 179

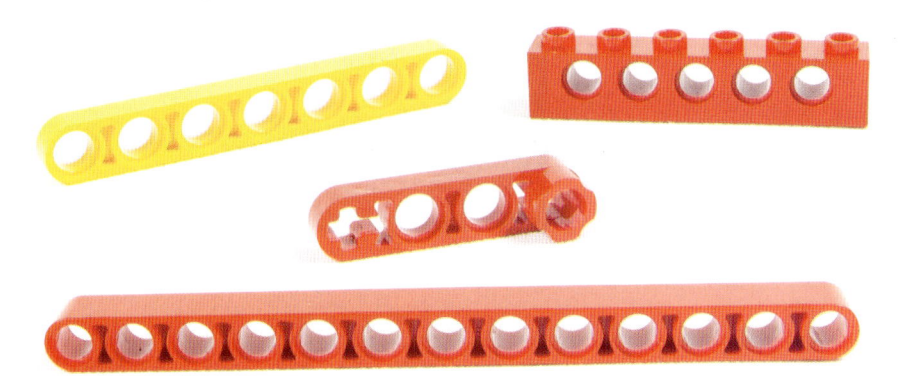

First, along most of its length, the lift arm was half the width of a normal brick, or two-and-a-half sections. At one end, a full module of width was cast for extra stability due to its second feature: the inclusion of cross holes. Cross holes, so named for their shape, are designed to hold axles securely and keep them from rotating. Their inclusion at either end of the four-module-long initial lift arm meant that lift arms could be joined to, and rotate with, a gear. Arranged in that configuration, they became arms which could lift, hence the name.

Casting them at half a regular brick's width helped with the space issue on the backhoe, but it wasn't quite enough, which led to the final two, and arguably most important, decisions. Designers both rounded the lift arm's edges and made it only one module tall, slightly less than the height of a regular brick. These features meant that rather than the blocky, ninety-degree nature of normal bricks, lift arms were comprised of thinner profiles and graceful arcs that allowed them to fit in far tighter spaces.

They were perfect, solving all of the outrigger's problems, and ended up being included in that role on two models in 1989: set 8862 Backhoe Grader and set 8854 Power Crane. The significance of lift arms was easily missed among all the other LEGO Technic bricks, but they began a new stage of evolution that would culminate in an entirely independent LEGO Technic System based on beams.

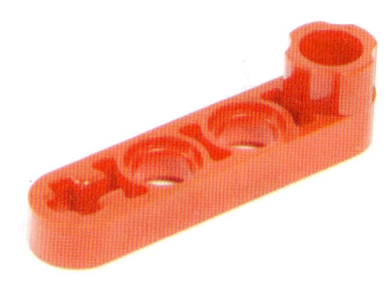

TOP A quick primer on the four main classes of LEGO Technic structural elements. The LEGO Technic brick (top right) was first released in 1977. The lift arm (middle) was released with LEGO Technic sets in 1989, and then evolved into the half beam (top left) in 1995 and the full beam (bottom) in 1996.

ABOVE The first lift arm included a full module of width at one end, which was omitted by the later variant.

LEFT Set 8862 Blackhoe Grader from 1989 utilised the new lift arms in its deployable outriggers. These elements would eventually evolve into LEGO Technic beams.

Securing a niche

By the early 1990s, LEGO Technic had found its niche. Due it the level of challenge, it was a theme that existed largely for children who stayed with the brand's toys longer than some of their peers; children who graduated from the eight-to-twelve-year-old range and wanted to keep building. Successful and unique on its own terms, LEGO Technic was never expected to compete on the level of LEGO Town or LEGO Space. It was allocated a proportionate number of frames each year for new elements and colour changes, and allowed to develop organically.

If the wider significance of lift arms was not initially easy to see, the next key element in LEGO Technic progression was virtually invisible. In the lead-up to the assortment for 1993, designers wanted to add more detail to models. Lots of vehicles, especially industrial ones, have lights that can shine on whatever they are working on. Erling Dideriksen and the LEGO Town team had introduced transparent 1×1 round nubs years before, initially for use as headlights, and the LEGO Technic team wanted to find a way to incorporate them into its sets. After much brainstorming and sketching, they focused in on a simple element that would have a cross hole and a standard LEGO Technic hole sitting side by side but perpendicular to each other. The cross hole could be anchored to an axle protruding from a model, while the LEGO Technic hole would have a 1×1 round nub's stud inserted into it. This piece would be the latest in the class of elements known as connectors, and the smallest to date; indeed, at only two modules wide, it was impossible to become any smaller and still join pairs of components.

Once designers got their hands on a prototype of the new piece, they realised they had just created a treasure, especially when paired with lift arms. Thanks to both pieces being nominally five sections tall, instead of a standard brick's six sections, this new piece, eventually named a cross block, could join two lift arms directly adjacent to one another. Because LEGO Technic bricks were the standard six sections tall, it was impossible to join them right up against one another, but such tight tolerances were possible when using cross blocks and lift arms due to their unique geometries. Designers loved it, and they wanted more. A few years later an opportunity presented itself.

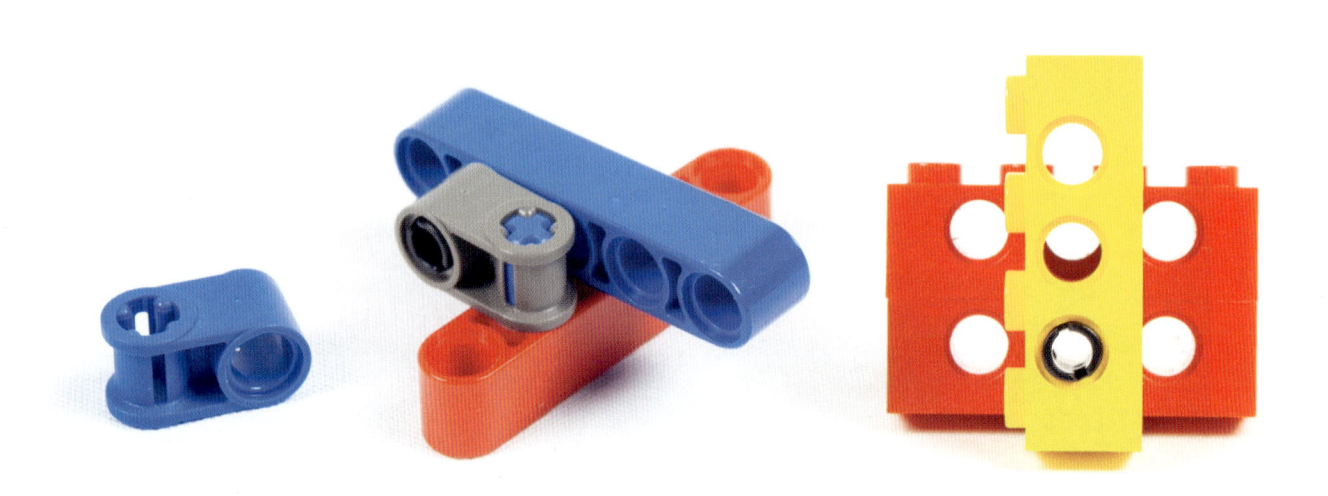

BELOW The unassuming cross block (left) was a crucial element in the evolution of the LEGO Technic system because it allowed elements to be joined more closely. The advantage of Technic beams is that they can be joined adjacent to each other. Compare this to two LEGO Technic bricks stacked on top of each other, which, due to the position of their holes, cannot be joined by a third brick pinned to their faces (right). To make such a connection would require a gap between the bricks.

During the mid 1990s, LEGO Technic reached a sort of crescendo. Having steadily added new elements year after year, designers had built up a catalogue of parts that allowed for ever-larger models that included more functions of greater complexity. Released in 1994, set 8880 Super Car was the largest LEGO Technic model to date and an item which is still highly sought after by fans to this day. In 1995, set 8485 Control Centre II came with over a thousand pieces to construct a remote-controlled helicopter, hovercraft or dinosaur – a sort of preview to what would become the programmable robotics theme, LEGO® MINDSTORMS®, a few years later.

In 1996 and 1997, designers continued the pattern of alternating a highly technical model with a wide array of functions and a model with some sort of unique electrically powered element. For the technical model, they opted to recreate the iconic Space Shuttle. However, there was an immediate challenge with that choice. Until now, LEGO Technic vehicles had been depictions of vehicle types or classes, not recreations of exact vehicle models that existed in the real world. 8880 Super Car was clearly a car with many accurate details. However, it was not a make or model that actually existed, so there was nothing to judge its appearance directly against. Likewise, all construction vehicles, aeroplanes and boats that had occupied shelves

TOP Set 8880 Super Car from 1994 is a phenomenal feat in terms of both size and complexity, considering the parts available at the time it was developed.

BOTTOM Set 8829 Dune Blaster from 1994 was one of the first LEGO Technic models to depict curves using semi-rigid, flexible hoses.

ABOVE Set 8480 Space Shuttle, released in 1996, was the first model to use LEGO Technic beams in its construction.

since the 1970s were generic versions of their inspirations. In contrast, Space Shuttles were specific vehicles with distinctive shapes, proportions and features.

LEGO Technic models had always used pegs, holes and right angles to approximate the curves and bends of real-world vehicles, rather than depicting them in an exact way. In 1994, however, flexible, semi-rigid hoses were introduced. Thanks to being bendable, hoses could be positioned to approximate the outlines of windshields or fuselages without impeding the view of a model's internal mechanisms. Their use would increase steadily throughout the 1990s, allowing designers to instil greater realism into the bodies of vehicles.

However, flexible hoses weren't right for the Space Shuttle's cargo bay. NASA's famous vehicle devoted about half of its length to open space for transporting payloads to and from orbit. This section of the fuselage had a distinctive arc shape and the split curves that formed its doors when opened were a well-known visual the world over. Authenticity required that the LEGO Technic model replicate both the cargo-bay doors' shape and their opening function. After several experiments using existing parts, it was agreed that a new component was needed. Through that element design process, a fateful decision was made.

At this point, all the team wanted was a part for their Space Shuttle model, but they inadvertently ended up facilitating the next big leap in LEGO Technic evolution. They developed a special element with both a straight and angled portion. Such unique shaping meant that there was no logical place to incorporate studs, since mounting them on any surface would mean they inevitably bent away from each other. In what was at the time a radical departure, designers eventually elected to model their new part's geometry more on a lift arm than a LEGO Technic brick. Accordingly, they cast it with the same nominal height of one module but, instead of making the width half a module, the width of this element was a full module in order to give it more strength. The first LEGO Technic beam had been born. Taking further inspiration from lift arms, the final connectors along each of the beam's sides was done as a cross hole so that it could be anchored and turned, vital for making the Space Shuttle's cargo bay doors open and close.

BELOW Three angled LEGO Technic beams create the profile of the Space Shuttle's cargo-bay door, the first use of these elements on a LEGO model.

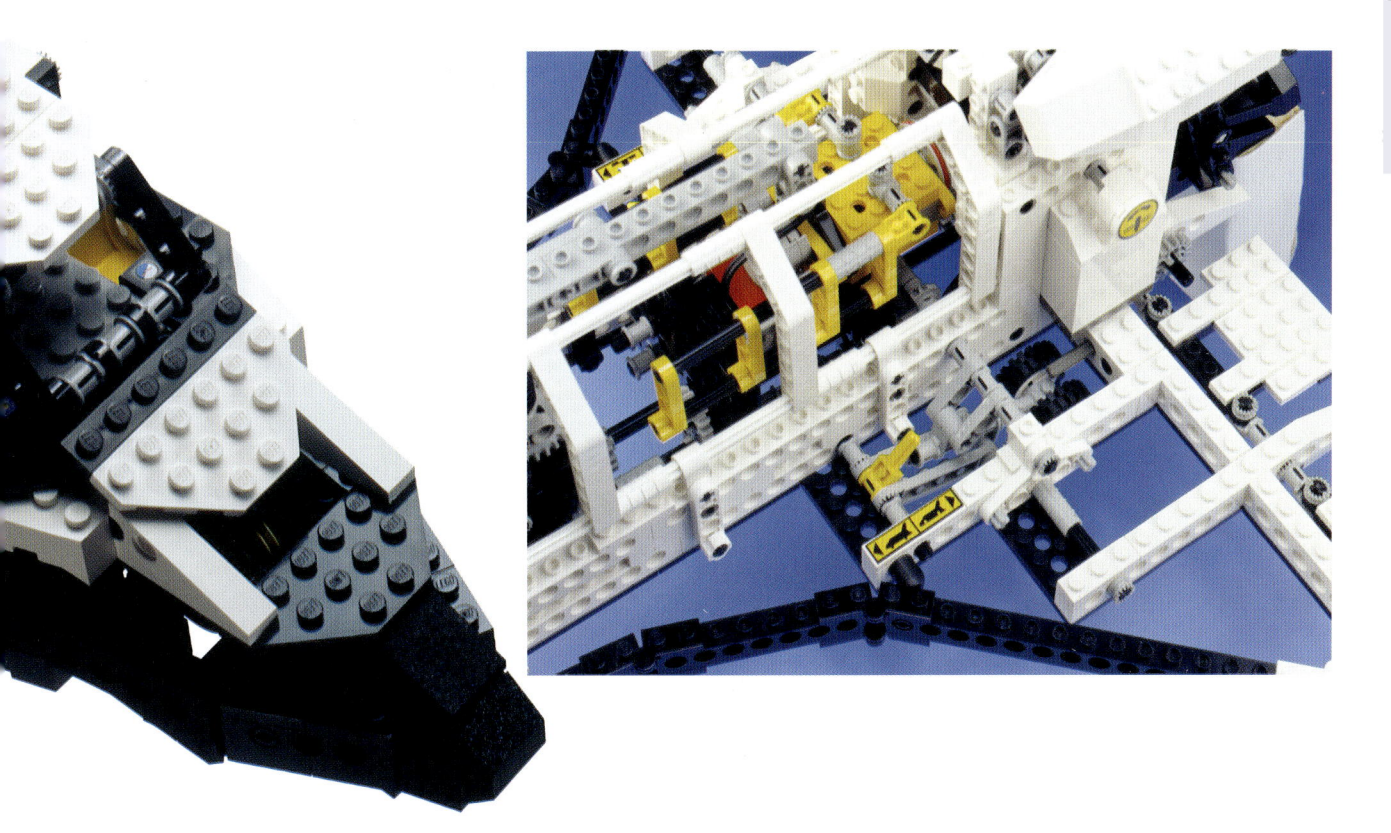

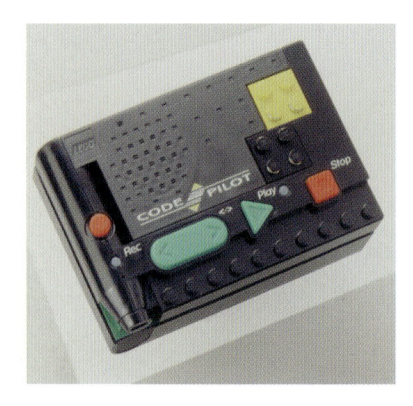

ABOVE The barcode reader developed for 8479 Barcode Multi-set allowed the set's dump-truck vehicle to be programmed using a sheet of printed barcodes.

BELOW The dump truck from 1997's flagship set, 8479 Barcode Multi-set, included the newly created second LEGO Technic beam in the construction of its bed.

Everyone was delighted with the new element's visual and functional appeal in 8480 Space Shuttle, released in 1996. The following year's flagship model was slated to be a set powered by an electrical motor, 8479 Barcode Multi-set. A unique barcode reader, which allowed the dump-truck vehicle to be programmed to perform a range of functions, was developed for this one set. Designers also created a second angled beam to give the dump truck a more realistic rear bed. Already, designers were beginning to see the benefits of this class of elements.

Both angled beam variants imbued vehicles with dynamic new shapes, and were used as grabbing claws in different models released in 1997, such as set 8250 Search Sub. Paired with the growing number of flexible tubes, a whole new aesthetic became possible for LEGO Technic sets. During the late 1990s, the LEGO Technic team mixed these two new families of parts and added new variant parts year by year as frames allowed. Designers could construct more realistic shapes than ever before, while still maintaining the open-for-viewing construction that had long been the theme's trademark.

In 1999, even more possibilities became available when several plating components were created that could also anchor the semi-rigid hoses and, later, tubes. Each was sleek and cool-looking. While plating components were used in a variety of models, designers were careful never to conceal too much of a vehicles' interior; the plates were mostly used to add flair or as the aforementioned anchoring point for tubes.

During those first years, the combinations of beams and other elements were mostly decorative. Frameworks of LEGO Technic bricks would form a model's interior, with beams contributing to certain functions and exterior details, along with tubes and plates. However, as the family of beams grew, its uses began to change. Initially, the shift was most prominent in a class of models that almost hadn't existed before: small LEGO Technic vehicles. Due to the spacing required to pin LEGO Technic bricks together, small products had never been possible before. As the number of beams and half beams increased, their tight tolerances allowed for stable, small depictions of all kinds of vehicles, from motorcycles to aeroplanes, and more. Now, with smaller sets, children could experiment and see if they liked the LEGO Technic theme before moving onto higher-priced sets. In around the year 2000, discussions took place over several years concerning future plans for LEGO Technic, and one of the points discussed was the increasing prominence of beams in models.

Other points of discussion included LEGO MINDSTORMS, BIONICLE®, and studs. MINDSTORMS was a new product line released in 1998 after a decade of development. It combined LEGO Technic elements with a new programmable, computerised smart brick. Known as the Robotic Control System, RCX, it was the end result of a partnership initiated by Kjeld Kirk Kristiansen himself with Seymour Papert, a renowned professor of mathematics and computer science at

ABOVE Set 8448 Super Street Sensation from 1999 was the first flagship LEGO Technic model to include beams, flexible hoses and the new decorative plates all in the same set. The result was one of the theme's most realistically shaped vehicles ever created to that date.

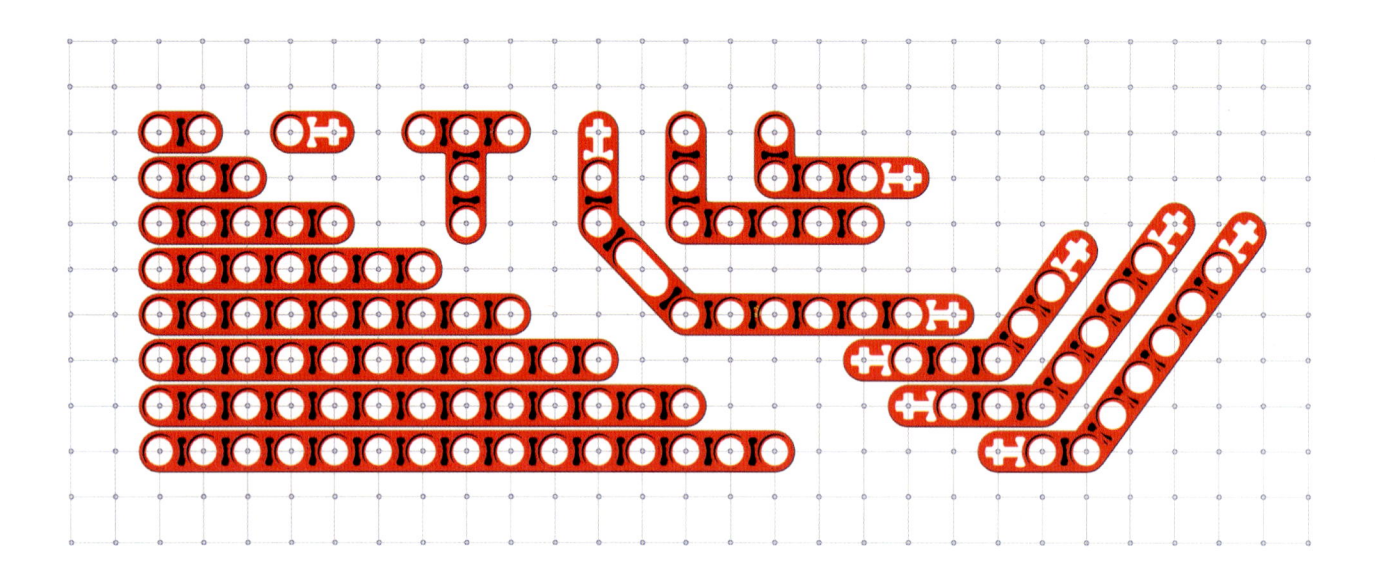

ABOVE The family of beams has continued to grow since the first introduction of this type of element in 1996.

BELOW LEFT The inaugural LEGO MINDSTORMS Robotic Invention System, set 9747, from 1998, was mostly composed of LEGO Technic bricks and beams.

BELOW RIGHT The initial RCX component that was at the heart of LEGO MINDSTORMS.

the US-based Massachusetts Institute of Technology (MIT). LEGO Technic team members were involved in creating the designs for robots that were constructed mostly from LEGO Technic elements. Over its first several years, between the late 1990s and early 2000s, MINDSTORMS released a variety of accessory sets and upgrades, along with a few experimental offshoots. Almost every set included instructions for more than one model, all of which were designed within the relatively small LEGO Technic team.

Furthermore, another new theme, BIONICLE, utilised a building system known as Constraction rather than standard System elements, but used LEGO Technic connectors and axles. All of which provided several possible directions for LEGO Technic to take: should it continue to evolve the types of models for which it had become known over the last two decades, or should it move into robots, or perhaps to BIONICLE style action figures made from almost entirely new pieces?

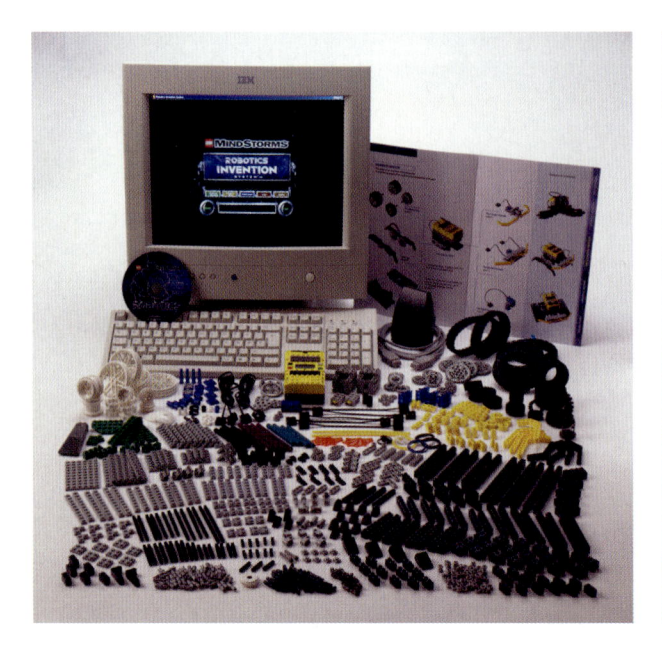

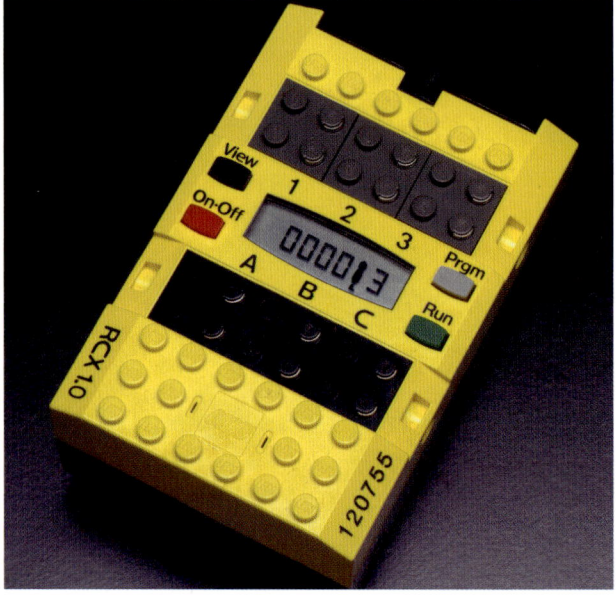

The other matter under discussion was the question of studs, which stemmed from an experiment that took place during the development of the range of models released in 2001. The flagship set 8466 4×4 Off-Roader was prototyped using two different construction methods. One version relied on a mix of LEGO Technic bricks for the internal structure, with beams, hoses and plates adorning the exterior, along with a variety of functions like a working suspension. The other version used only LEGO Technic beams, both for the details and the interior structure. It was not sturdy enough for release quite yet – there were still not quite enough connectors to lock all the beams together with the same strength as LEGO Technic bricks. Even so, everyone could see that they were only a couple of components away from an entirely independent LEGO Technic System with not a stud or tube in sight. That possibility raised the question: was a model without the iconic studs a LEGO model?

In the end, in the 2000s, the LEGO Group continued to release MINDSTORMS sets alongside LEGO Technic sets and BIONICLE. With their programmable RCX and robotics elements, MINDSTORMS had a high bar to entry, while LEGO Technic provided more modestly sized options for children who loved technical building.

Many models released from 2003 onwards were constructed exclusively of LEGO Technic beams, although some of the bigger ones still mixed old LEGO Technic bricks with new. Partially, this was to allow some studs be kept visible in LEGO Technic products. Other times it was required for achieving certain details that only the greater number of standard System parts could achieve. It was the latter which kick-started the final, major evolution in the LEGO Technic family of elements.

ABOVE Set 8466 4×4 Off-Roader, released in 2001, was prototyped using both a mix of LEGO Technic beams and bricks as well as just beams.

"

Studs have always been our brand. When you build a model with LEGO bricks and plates, you have the most stable construction you could imagine. However, there was an in-between time where we had two systems in play. We had the LEGO System to make a stable skeleton and we used the new LEGO Technic beams and other elements to make the shapes around it. But eventually we had to decide. We had made a big truck with large wheels. Then I tried to make this big truck, the same model, using just the new beams. It was completely soft because we only had a single cross block and there wasn't anything we could use to strengthen it. This showed us that we would need to develop new beams if we wanted to move away from the old LEGO Technic bricks. But there was concern over whether customers would recognise a set as a LEGO model if they didn't see bricks with studs. So we often deliberately used some of the old bricks on the model just to allow studs to be visible, because they are such a huge part of our brand.

"

Realism *and* functionality

Smaller, more accessible LEGO Technic models meant that greater numbers of children were getting into the theme at a younger age. Thus, the company began receiving more requests and feedback than ever before on LEGO Technic products. A consistent message was that children wanted vehicles. They loved the functions, but also wanted their models to look like a real plane or car. Designers had talked about doing this for years but resisted it every time out of a desire to keep the cool mechanisms highly visible.

During the mid-2000s, the LEGO Technic team, now operating independently of MINDSTORMS and BIONICLE, began to experiment with the range of new elements. Set 8421 Mobile Crane, released in 2005, became the largest LEGO Technic set by piece count to date. Although it featured a few bricks with studs, these were largely for show: the model's size and strength were derived from the new beam elements. Next, a second experiment was developed.

In the lead-up to 2007, a pair of streams converged. The first came from BIONICLE, which was looking for ways to add new novelty to its characters. Early on, BIONICLE had followed a lot of the same rules as LEGO Technic, and its characters had classic open skeletons. Over the years, though, functions, mechanisms and internals had been progressively covered with more exotic armour and plating. Children loved it and, combined with the feedback they were sending in about wanting their LEGO Technic sets to similarly cover up, designers decided to test a theory.

BELOW Set 8421 Mobile Crane was the largest LEGO Technic set by piece count ever produced when it was released in 2005.

They had recently rediscovered a large System plate element originally invented as the base for couches and other larger items in LEGO® Belville back in 1994. This plate was extremely useful for covering huge spaces in the larger models that were being created. Designers used these plates, along with more recently developed LEGO Technic plates, to create a LEGO Technic model unlike anything before it. A flagship model in 2006, set 8285 Tow Truck, was highly realistic, both in its visual appearance and its functions. Its mechanical interior was so well-covered that the set almost bore more resemblance to a Model Team design than a LEGO Technic one, prompting some concern in the company that the distinctive LEGO Technic attributes loved by consumers would not be visible.

Achieving the amazing looks of 8285 Tow Truck was a design challenge. Designers had to painstakingly make the transition from odd-number-based beams without studs back to System elements with even numbers of studs. To allow future LEGO Technic models to have enclosed interiors would require more specialised elements and, for some within the company, hesitancy over breaking fully from studs remained. In light of this, the final stage of LEGO Technic evolution came not from within, but from without in two different ways.

By the late 2000s, the Construction family of elements within BIONICLE had grown into an expansive system. Designers combined it with LEGO Technic beams to construct ever larger products. Throughout most of its history, BIONICLE had been almost exclusively figure-based, with the occasional vehicle or accessory. However, the 2008 line was slated to include several large battle vehicles akin to flying scooters or planes. They were not intended to be LEGO Technic style models inclusive of numerous, intricate functions. Rather, they were envisioned as tools for role play in the same vein as a pirate ship or police car; children could hold the models in their hands and swoosh them around a room. In light of this, while being made of predominantly LEGO Technic elements, there was no expectation that these battle vehicles' interiors should be exposed for viewing. In fact, it would have been odd for them to be anything other than enclosed. Furthermore, BIONICLE had never included elements with studs in its building system and it would have been unusual to introduce such construction nearly a decade after the theme's debut.

RIGHT Set 8285 Tow Truck, from 2006, was the first LEGO Technic model to feature a full, realistic exterior using a combination of early LEGO Technic plates and standard System variants.

All of these factors led to the development of new elements, the first of what became known internally as LEGO Technic shells. Included on two BIONICLE models released in 2008, 8941 Rockoh T3 and the larger 8943 Axalara T9, this new part was different from the LEGO Technic plates that had come before. It was designed to integrate seamlessly with beams connecting into them across multiple orientations in order to cover large areas. Only one type was created for this pair of BIONICLE sets: a curved shell that was based on an odd-numbered geometry of eleven and three studs, but designers immediately saw its potential and set about literally sketching out LEGO Technic future.

The lead LEGO Technic element designer who developed the part for these BIONICLE models sat down after completing it and proceeded to design over forty more shells of various shapes, sizes, geometries and orientations: large, small, angled, curved, straight and everything in between. The LEGO Technic theme had never pre-planned on such a massive scale before and the team pored over these designs, suggesting tweaks and developing a rough priority list. Over the next ten years they would slowly acquire many of them, using a couple of frames year by year.

Copious numbers of designs based on that first shell for BIONICLE proved that there was a whole class of elements waiting to be created that would open up lots of new opportunities for different types of LEGO Technic vehicles. That was, however, only the first of two outside factors that moved the theme into its final evolutionary stage towards breaking completely away from its System roots.

After the highly realistic and largely enclosed 8285 Tow Truck, the next LEGO Technic sets returned to the aesthetic established throughout the early 2000s of vehicles with open frameworks that allowed easy viewing of internal functions. Once the 2008 BIONICLE line inaugurated LEGO Technic shells, however, LEGO Technic team members immediately began to incorporate them, both the first variant and successive ones, as more of the initial forty designs became available. First in 2009 and then again in 2010, LEGO Technic products were made virtually entirely of their own beams, shells and connectors. Only an occasional transparent plate or cheese slope depicting a headlight, or some other small detail, sported studs. It was at this time that the second outside factor came into play: licensing.

LEFT In its final years, BIONICLE expanded to include a variety of large vehicles for its heroes to ride. The first LEGO Technic shells gave vehicles such as 8943 Axalara T9, released in 2008, a unique look.

ABOVE LEGO Technic shells were specially created for BIONICLE.

Licensed models

LEGO Technic had produced licensed sets before, but they were few and far between. Initially, the Mercedes-Benz proposition didn't seem like it would be anything different. The LEGO Group partnered with the world-renowned vehicle manufacturer to release a commemorative model of the Mercedes-Benz Unimog U 400 for the sixtieth anniversary of these multi-purpose all-wheel-drive trucks. Thanks to the newly available range of shell elements, designers were able to execute specific vehicle models to a never-before-possible level of realism, both in functions and appearance. The media took notice, including the automotive press, which broadcast the set's existence to an audience that normally didn't buy LEGO sets. The next several years saw an expansion in both licensing and the use of shell elements in LEGO Technic models.

It became clear that consumers were keen to see larger and more complex models, so in response, the LEGO Technic team began evolving the building system to allow for these models to be created. The team also introduced storytelling into the development of its models, to enable role play and a stronger link to reality. Designers added relevant functions to, for example, an excavator, so the experience would be closer to controlling the real thing. New details were included with the models, such as loose elements for a dump truck to carry. These details gave context to the model and helped fans understand its scale and functions.

Finally, the team began exploring partnerships that allowed for the creation of more realistic models with unique functions specific to their real-world brands.

Licensed models like the Unimog had made it clear that there was a whole genre of fandom, both young and old, that loved branded vehicles – not just cars as a general category, but specific makes and models; not just the category of tractors or bulldozers, but makes and models created by beloved companies. Many of these fans longed to live out their fantasy by owning, or at least driving, the objects of their obsession, but most never could.

RIGHT Set 8110 Mercedes-Benz Unimog U 400 from 2011 began a new era of licensed models for LEGO Technic.

Andy Woodman, a self-confessed Porsche enthusiast, who joined the LEGO Technic team in 2015 after leading the LEGO® Legends of Chima™ design team, had a background in automotive design. His vision was that LEGO Technic models could become part of the stories aficionados told about themselves and the vehicles they loved by giving people a way to, at least partially, get wish fulfillment. LEGO Technic fans would still get the intricate building experiences they loved and fans of an automotive brand would also find something to love even if they had never built a LEGO product before. This new approach would transform LEGO Technic from niche product line within the portfolio into a growth driver and key theme within the LEGO brand.

Practically, this new approach played out in two ways. First, where possible, models should depict versions of vehicles that actually existed. A tractor was slated for development so the LEGO Group reached out to CLAAS, one of the world's foremost agricultural manufacturers, and received permission to design a LEGO Technic version of their XERION 5000 TRAC VC. Volvo happily partnered on a EW160E Excavator and both models were released in 2016, sporting shells and beams cast in new, accurate colours. The second part of executing this new approach to LEGO Technic was even more bold. It was called the Ultimate Concept.

The Ultimate Concept was envisioned as a new line of LEGO Technic products that would be larger and more realistic than ever before. Its centrepiece would be supercars. The LEGO Group reached out to several high-end vehicle manufacturers to ask about partnering on this exciting idea. Porsche stood out for their can-do attitude to the concept and the launch timing of the latest GT3 RS model. Creating a LEGO Technic version to correspond with the official unveiling was an opportunity too good to pass up. However, it meant a very tight development schedule, especially considering this was envisioned as the first in a line of supercar models which would

BELOW LEGO Technic designer Uwe Wabra works on the Porsche model, surrounded by prototype models and pieces.

ABOVE Designers compare the Porsche's real wheel to the LEGO version.

all need to follow the same scale. Not only would the Porsche be the first Ultimate Concept car, but it would also set the size, detail level and precedent for everything that followed.

The Porsche model required the combined efforts of practically the entire LEGO Technic team. One designer was tasked with constructing the sequential paddle shift gearbox. Another worked on suspension options. Previously, suspension had been a major visual function, with the goal being to make the vehicle as bouncy as possible. But such exaggerated movements would look out of place on a supercar. It took highly skilled design work to allow the model to move up and down a little but not enough to appear ridiculous.

Early on in the process, everyone agreed that the wheels need to be unique and define the entire scale of the Porsche and, by extension, all future cars. However, LEGO wheels and tyre size were governed by definitive rules. Any new scale of tyres would need to conform with these internal standards. Designers selected a diameter that was closest to the scale of car they thought would allow them to include all the relevant functions.

Having selected their tyre diameter, designers began creating a unique rim element to match the real-world car, which they had seen at a top-secret Porsche test facility. Initially, these rims were to be cast in silver but, after 3D-printing some prototypes, a challenge revealed itself. The rims were just a little too small proportionally compared to the tyre. While subtle, it just didn't quite look like it should next to an image of the actual car. Due to the compressed development schedule, there was no time to work on a different solution. Initially, these rims were to be cast in silver, but, after 3D-printing, the rims were instead moulded in black to match the tyre so it was almost impossible to see where the transition from one to the other occurred. While an effective

> We launched the Ultimate Concept with a Porsche. We had plans for more models but, of course, you don't know at the start whether a line will continue. Because it was the first, we had to do a lot of pre-work to understand what scale would be sustainable. We didn't want to do something that was so small that we wouldn't be able to give people that ultimate building experience. It had to have enough volume to put functions into it like a gearbox, suspension and steering. And then we had to review the LEGO Technic building system. It is incredibly versatile because we have a lot of elements, including box sections and structural parts. But we had to see if there were any elements that we needed to create to allow us to make these large structures.

Andrew Woodman, Design Manager, the LEGO Group

> The Porsche project was intended it to be the ultimate building experience. We chose not to make the model remote-controlled or motorised, so we could focus on the accuracy of the interior, gearbox and other functions. Must-have functions included steering and suspension. Then Porsche told us about the sequential paddle-shift gearbox, which we had never done before! One function from the real car that we deliberately left out of our model was the rear steering because, with LEGO Technic, wheels must move quite a lot to see that the steering is working. In the real car, you don't really even see the wheels move. Also, the rear wheels turn in the same direction or the opposite direction to the front wheels, depending on speed. We loved that as a function, but it was impossible to replicate in a working LEGO Technic model!

Andrew Woodman, Design Manager, the LEGO Group

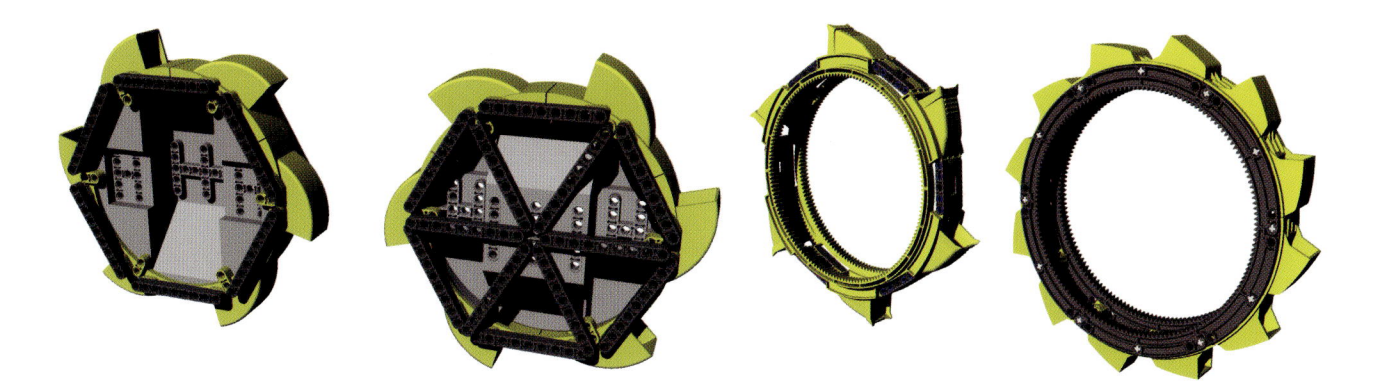

solution, it didn't stop designers from noting the issue and vowing to correct it on the next car, should the opportunity present itself.

Supercars were only one half of the Ultimate Concept; the other was construction vehicles. Long a LEGO Technic staple, the plan was to take them to a whole different level in terms of both size and functionality. Intending to impress with its first large-scale model, the team chose a bucket wheel excavator, as these massive mining machines had never been attempted in a LEGO Technic model before. Determined to create a new category of products larger than ever before, the team lead repeatedly sent team members back to their work tables with the instruction to 'make it even bigger'!

Two new components were developed specifically for the massive mining set, both relating to its bucket wheel, the construction of which proved challenging. After multiple prototypes, each of which ended up having a fatal flaw, the set's designer created a curved gear rack which, with four copies, could be assembled into a full, smooth circle. This part went on to be a foundational element in the Ultimate Concept line: the giant turntable could be placed horizontally so that huge models could sit on it. A second new element frame had to be used for a revised bucket, as the existing version couldn't fit within the space available.

LEGO Technic new strategy was released upon the world in 2016. The CLAAS Tractor and Volvo Excavator sat alongside both inaugural entries in the Ultimate Concept's supercar and construction categories, 42056 Porsche 911 GT3 RS and 42055 Bucket Wheel Excavator respectively. Nothing like this assortment had ever been produced and LEGO fans loved them. Each part of the strategy was continued, with licensed models being inserted wherever possible and entries in the Ultimate Concept line coming every other year. For the second supercar, 42083 Bugatti Chiron in 2018, designers didn't forget about their challenges with the Porsche's wheels. This time around, the rims were expanded with a lip that overlapped in front of the tyre by just a few millimetres. This provided just enough cover to get the proportions right so the Bugatti's rims could be cast in a distinctive blue and silver mix.

While the appearance and level of detail within LEGO Technic models has evolved to a truly astonishing degree over the last almost fifty years, the goal that Jan Ryaa and Eric Bach set out to achieve has remained remarkably consistent: to make the largest models possible. Today, the holes and pegs they developed have achieved that goal many times over. Furthermore, their LEGO Technic brick lives on. While almost never included in standard LEGO Technic sets any more, nearly the whole assortment has found a new home in System sets across almost every theme, where they form incredibly strong skeletons for many models, from the largest spaceships to police stations and much more. LEGO Technic evolved from a family of elements, and has come to define its genre of technical LEGO models of vehicles – a feat that no other theme has achieved so completely.

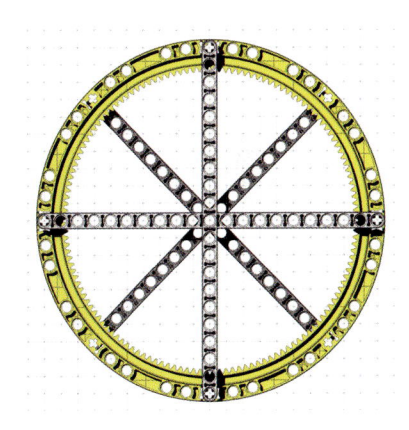

TOP Early concepts for the bucket wheel excavator's rotating wheel.

ABOVE The Curved Gear Rack was developed for set 42055 Bucket Wheel Excavator. Clever part design enables the construction of a perfect circle using an arrangement of four identical elements.

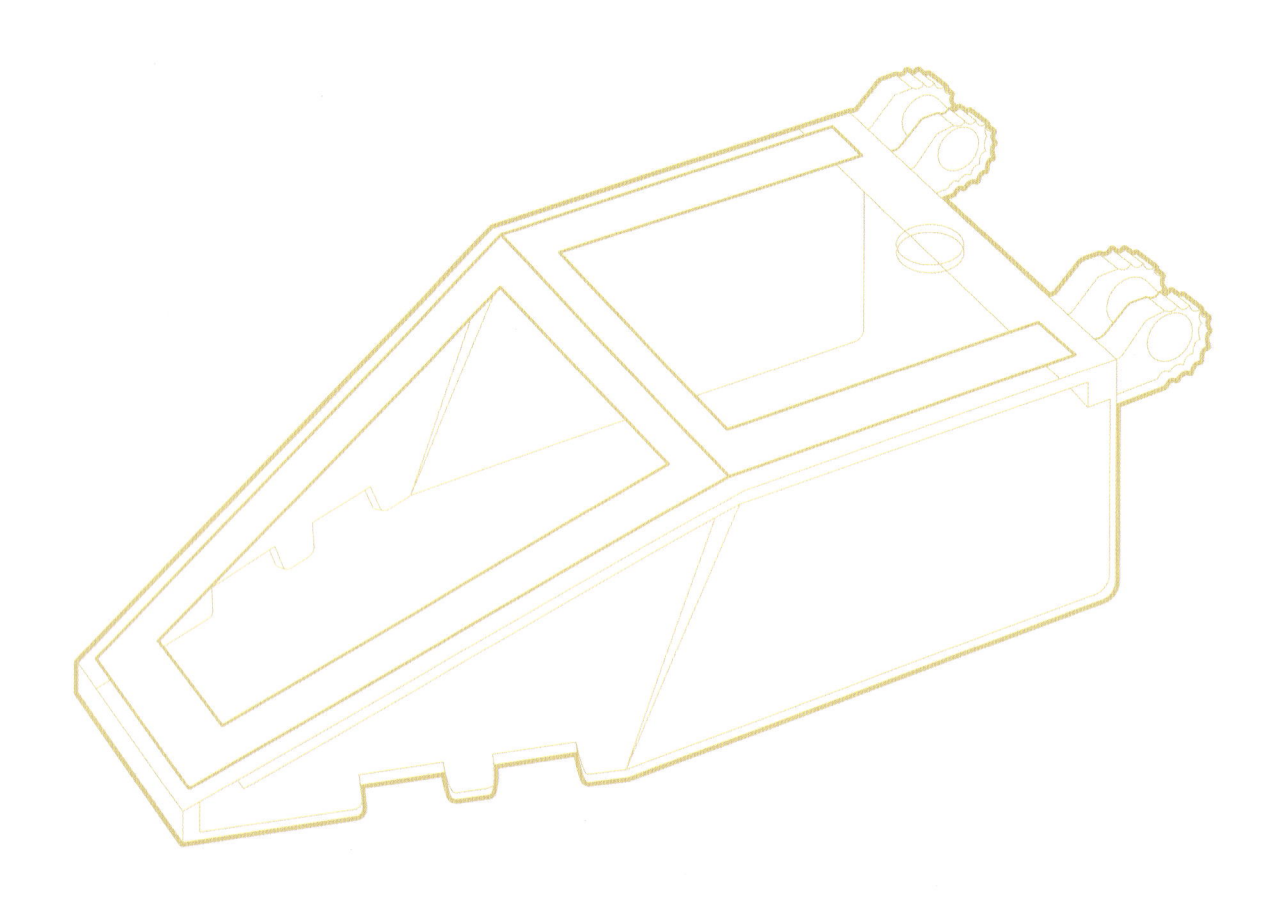

> "The cockpit element is actually made in an old mould casing, just with new inserts."

Henrik Andersen, Design Master, the LEGO Group

8
New Worlds

LEGO® BIONICLE® and LEGO® *Star Wars*™ transform the LEGO Group and set the stage for future successes.

TOP The new cockpit windscreen element was key in capturing the iconic look of *Star Wars* in LEGO® bricks.

CENTRE Friction hinges provide greater strength than earlier hinges, allowing new kinds of building techniques.

BOTTOM Masks of power were key to the concept for LEGO® BIONICLE®.

Designers had no doubt in their minds which set should be the flagship for the launch of LEGO® Star Wars™ in 1999: Han Solo's iconic ship, the *Millennium Falcon*. It was designed and ready to go, along with several other models depicting classic vehicles from George Lucas's original trilogy.

Elsewhere on the Billund campus, another team was busy honing a brand-new platform, with a family of parts that was unlike any other in the company's history. Ball joints and corresponding torsos emerged from sculptors' tables. Far larger than even the 1970s LEGO® building figures, the pieces in this 'buildable figure platform' were so radical they were hardly recognisable as LEGO elements.

LEGO® BIONICLE® and LEGO *Star Wars* represented seismic, foundation-shattering shifts. Out of the rubble would emerge two of the LEGO Group most legendary themes and an iconic collection of parts that would define childhood for a whole generation of children. For the company, their arrival would prove hugely inspirational.

Throughout the late 1990s and early 2000s BIONICLE and LEGO *Star Wars* circled each other, interacting and feeding off one another in interesting ways. They offered two approaches to the challenge represented by the changing play habits of children, and in particular the growth of video games. The LEGO Group looked at the challenge in two ways: one view stated that the future remained in classic LEGO building; another perspective was that bricks had to evolve and be more specialised to keep up with the computer revolution.

In this bid to meet the demands of the present, greater innovation was encouraged and designers were empowered to come up with new approaches, seeking the 'cool factor'. Consequently, many new moulds were produced, including large, specialised pieces that enabled children to start playing with LEGO products quickly without having to build models completely from scratch. This was an exciting new burst of creative freedom born of necessity, where radical ideas were considered. Into the breach stepped a small clutch of designers and a creative partner named Christian Faber.

New elements, new stories

Since the 1980s, Christian Faber had worked in a team that assisted the LEGO Group with product development and launches. For a while, this group had been excited about the possibility of telling more developed stories through LEGO sets. At one point they had even used George Lucas's galaxy far, far away as an example of the world-building they thought could inspire new themes. At the time, however, the goal for LEGO toys remained the sparking of open-ended imagination in children, rather than the serving up of pre-made narratives.

In 1995, Christian and his team developed and pitched a new idea for a narrative-led theme. In this concept, humans had created artificially intelligent robots, called Cybots, and sent them deep below the Earth's surface to collect energy crystals. Once there, a contingent rebelled and his storyline then centred around a conflict between the rebels and those still loyal to humanity.

Underground exploration was something of a trend for LEGO designers in the mid 1990s. Several themes were fully developed, including one which nearly edged out Exploriens, a LEGO® Space subtheme that had launched in 1996. Ultimately, this underground space theme was deemed too similar to LEGO® Aqua Raiders, a subtheme of the underwater line LEGO® Aquazone. Prototypes for drill bits and other mining-type elements abounded at LEGO Futura during those years. Eventually, all these streams would converge, becoming LEGO® Rock Raiders in 1999. Cybots did not make it to market, but several of its story beats were incorporated a decade later into both LEGO® Exo-Force and LEGO® Power Miners. These later product lines, however, were not Cybots' most enduring or important legacy.

The Cybots team wanted its proposed concept to stand out, so the designers set about creating a new type of LEGO element. Their objective was realistic, almost organic movement. Taking human limbs as inspiration, they used modelling clay to craft a ball at the end of an arm, which slotted into a receiving socket. Brick-built accessories supplemented this invention and the end result was something wholly different. It was clearly still a LEGO toy, but also very unusual.

The pitch went nowhere, but designers stored away the 'ball joint', as it was dubbed, into one of LEGO Futura many drawers. Nothing at the LEGO Group ever truly dies. Talk to any LEGO designer and you will hear stories of them developing a model believing it was a wholly original concept, only to be told upon showing it to a colleague that their idea had been fully developed years before, quite possibly multiple times. Fortunately, the ball joint's story followed that script. In 1999 Christian was brought in to assist with the launch of a new line called Slizer (or Throwbots

BELOW Set 8506 Rock Slizer (in US, Granite Throwbot), released in 1999, features the new ball joints and flexible throwing arm.

in the US market). Designers had taken the earlier prototype components and developed them into a small collection of new LEGO® Technic elements which facilitated the construction of something completely original: buildable LEGO Technic figures. Each part was cast in exciting colours and, thanks to a special flexible arm, the Slizer robots could fling small disks. This ball-joint concept also allowed the robots to pose and be moved in ways in which no previous LEGO product had been capable.

Slizer/Throwbot robots were intended to be short-lived novelties. LEGO designers sometimes refer to these as 'in and out themes', which are intended to last a year or two to spark an exciting fad and 'fill in' around higher-profile 'big bang' themes. Christian and a team of designers, however, wondered if the elements could be used for an even more ambitious concept. They dreamed of a product line that used ball-and-socket joints to construct action figures that could live for five or more years in a fully realised universe.

In 1999, amid worldwide anticipation for the first of the upcoming *Star Wars* prequel, *The Phantom Menace*, Christian's team hit upon a perspective that framed their effort. They decided to act as if the LEGO Group owned a big property that could support a blockbuster movie. What would its story be, where would it be set and what types of products would children

BELOW Prototype Genesis elements and constructed figures.

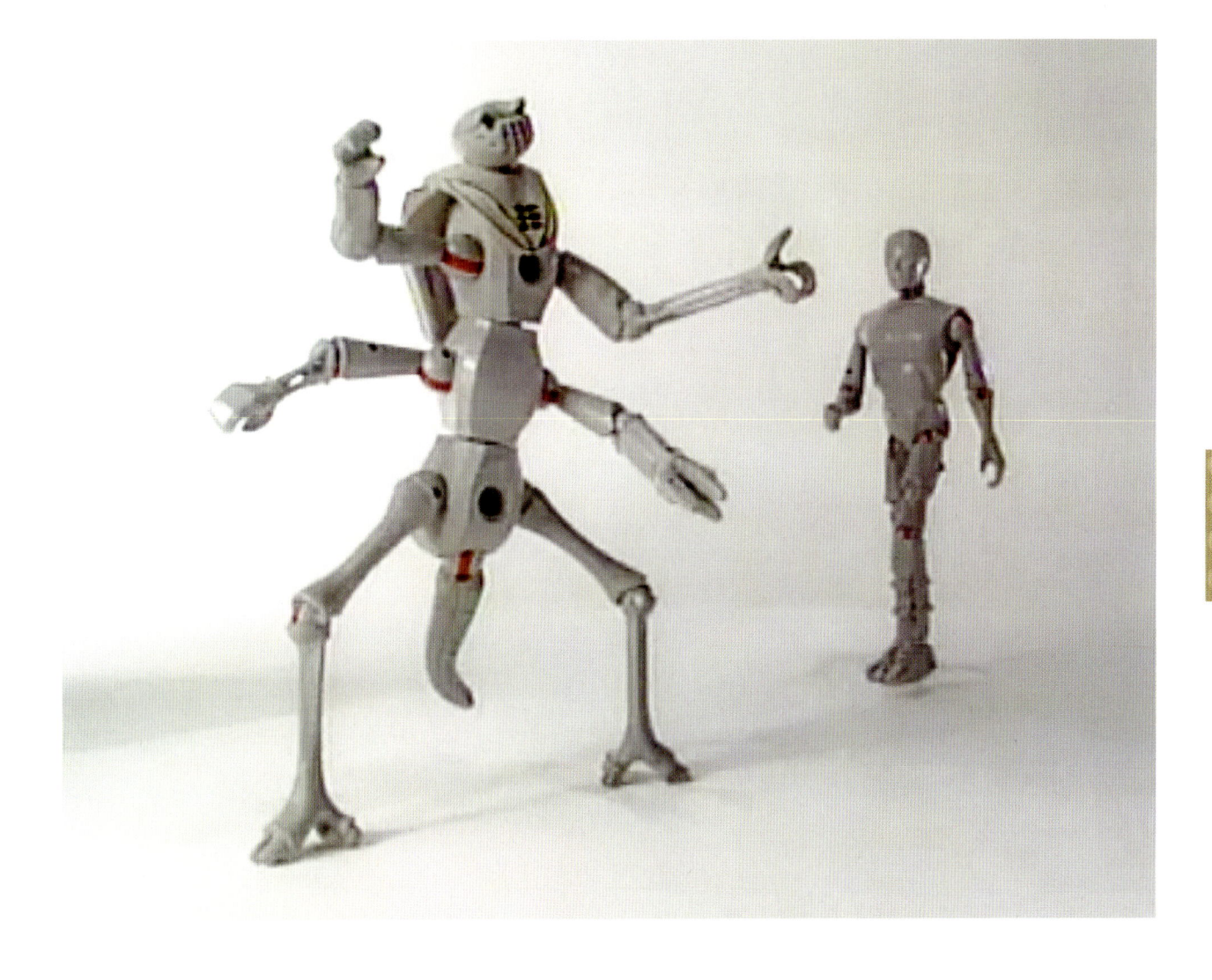

want in order to interact with it? Here *Star Wars* again exerted an influence. While the galaxy far, far away had spawned all manner of tie-in merchandise, action figures had by far been the most successful. Could the few elements used for Slizer be expanded into a system that could support buildable figures? The idea was radical, but it turned out that the way had already been paved, thanks to something called Project Genesis, which was being explored concurrently elsewhere in the company.

Genesis – so named because children were going to be able to play the part of creator in a new universe – was intended to be an entirely separate line of toys consisting of no elements compatible with the LEGO® System. Instead, children constructed creatures with large, moulded, interchangeable heads, arms, wings, torsos and tails. These appendages, which were sculpted to look like they came from animals, humans, robots and fantasy creatures, were joined to one of several central torso variants. Torsos had multiple ports for jointing them together or for connecting the various appendages. Creatures could be large or small, bizarre or recognisable. Construction was facilitated by a brand-new prototype friction hinge, which could lock into a socket then both rotate and articulate. Far from BIONICLE, which would go on to be compatible with LEGO Technic parts and marketed under that brand name, Genesis was separate and made

BELOW In the TV show *Galidor – Defenders of the Outer Dimension*, the central character Nick Bluetooth has the power to alter his limbs to gain additional powers. His LEGO figure also featured swappable body parts. Set 8313 Nick Deluxe, shown here, includes cyber-wings, which can be swapped out for the figure's arms.

up of detailed organic components meant to look like real, if slightly fantastical, body parts. There were no studs, pins or anything else in the whole system that were recognisable as LEGO DNA. These other-worldly elements were, however, just the beginning of Genesis' unique new collection of parts.

On top of that foundation of articulating pieces was envisioned another layer infused with technology. First was a voice unit embedded in a neck-wrap component that was held in place between a creature's head and torso, allowing it to speak. Even more daring was the sonic receiver integrated within another element, for which there were huge plans. The piece was endowed with technology that could hear sounds tuned out by human brains, the intent being to embed signals in all manner of media that would trigger responses in the constructed creatures. The LEGO Group planned to build a huge multimedia empire around Genesis, with video games, TV shows, commercials, live events and more. Each of these would be laced with audio signals discernible by Genesis' sonic capabilities, allowing children, and their creations, to interact directly with what they were watching. Sets would have instructions for creatures that would appear in this media and, if built, would respond to what happened to their character on-screen. It was the toys-to-life idea more than a decade before *Skylanders* and far more ambitious.

The first, and only, application of Genesis' platform was called Galidor, an in-house theme that was intended to become a hit TV show and game, in keeping with the grand vision for this new direction. Galidor debuted in 2002, a year after BIONICLE was released, when it seemed that systems like this were the future. Designers developed action figures and vehicles that matched the onscreen actors and sets but kept construction to a minimum. The challenge was that Galidor didn't easily fit into a single toy aisle, which confused toy retailers: was it a building toy, an action figure, an electronic product or a TV tie-in? Consumers didn't immediately recognise Galidor as a LEGO offering, nor was there any precedent for a live-action TV show based on LEGO products of any kind. Designers had to unlearn many hard and fast rules to come up with the products. Finally, since none of the toys used existing elements, every single component required a new mould, making the theme incredibly expensive to produce.

Galidor, however, was still a few years away. Back in the late 1990s, the concept for ball-and-socket elements was still being worked out. Realising that these parts suggested robots, the team naturally proposed an outer-space setting for the new line, dubbed for the time as simply 'Constraction', an amalgam of construction and action that referenced that these would be buildable action figures. Then came an amazing announcement, and simultaneously a significant challenge. The LEGO Group revealed that it would be embarking on its first-ever major licensing deal, producing toys for none other than Lucasfilm and *Star Wars*.

The advent of LEGO *Star Wars* made another theme based on intergalactic conflict with robots not only redundant, but off the table. While a new team began working on LEGO *Star Wars*, the Constraction team went back to the drawing board.

LEGO *Star Wars* faced a very interesting challenge. Up to this point, LEGO designers had always come up with their own models – now they had to depict not only a fantasy world developed by others, but some of the most iconic movie props and vehicles in the world. There was no doubt in anyone's mind that the required accuracy called for new elements, but management counselled caution. In the unlikely event that consumers didn't embrace the new LEGO *Star Wars* theme, the LEGO Group would be left with some very specialised bricks and moulds which could be hard to use elsewhere. Designers were therefore charged with what seemed initially like two mutually exclusive mandates: to design new LEGO elements that would enable the creation of recognisable models from the *Star Wars* universe but which were also generic enough to be used in other product lines. Realistic weapons were also avoided, in line with The LEGO Group long-standing policy against the use of military armaments. One weapon was a necessity, though, and this one was futuristic enough to pass muster: the lightsaber.

206   The Secret Life of LEGO® Bricks

Lightsabers and spaceships

Initially, the lightsaber hilt element followed standard LEGO design logic: a stud at one end and an open tube at the other end, which would receive the transparent bar that represented a glowing blade. In Lucasfilm's initial review, LEGO designers were told, 'You should probably make it so that a blade can be inserted on both ends.' Confused, since the request was unprecedented based on films released to date, the LEGO folks asked why. 'No reason in particular, but you should definitely do it,' came the response.

Everything made sense after the first previews of *Star Wars: The Phantom Menace* showed Darth Maul igniting his double-bladed lightsaber. The change also ended up being fortuitous as, when lightsaber handles were made available for use outside the LEGO *Star Wars* line, their ability to connect bars end to end made them inestimably more useful: as downspouts for Modular Buildings, masts for miniature-scale boats, engines, antenna, a host of minifigure accessories and more.

While lightsabers were a given, other elements depended on what the final line-up of sets would be. Designers, many of whom were *Star Wars* fans, were excited to get the chance to depict their favourite ships, but from the outset it was clear to all what the flagship set should be. The *Millennium Falcon* was the most famous spaceship ever seen on screen. There was, of course, no way that it could be scaled to roughly match minifigures. LEGO models couldn't be built that big, reasoned the designers. As a solution, they scaled down the ship, shrinking all its proportions equally. They borrowed rounded panel elements from UFO, a recently developed subtheme of LEGO Space. In conjunction with a new wing plate, these panels were used for the ship's front fins, among other uses.

Delighted with the result, the LEGO *Star Wars* team pitched the *Falcon* to Lucasfilm, but the model was not taken forward. For the initial wave, Lucasfilm were keen that sets were accurately scaled to minifigures. Starfighters and new vehicles called podracers would therefore be the upper limit in terms of size. Undaunted, designers persevered.

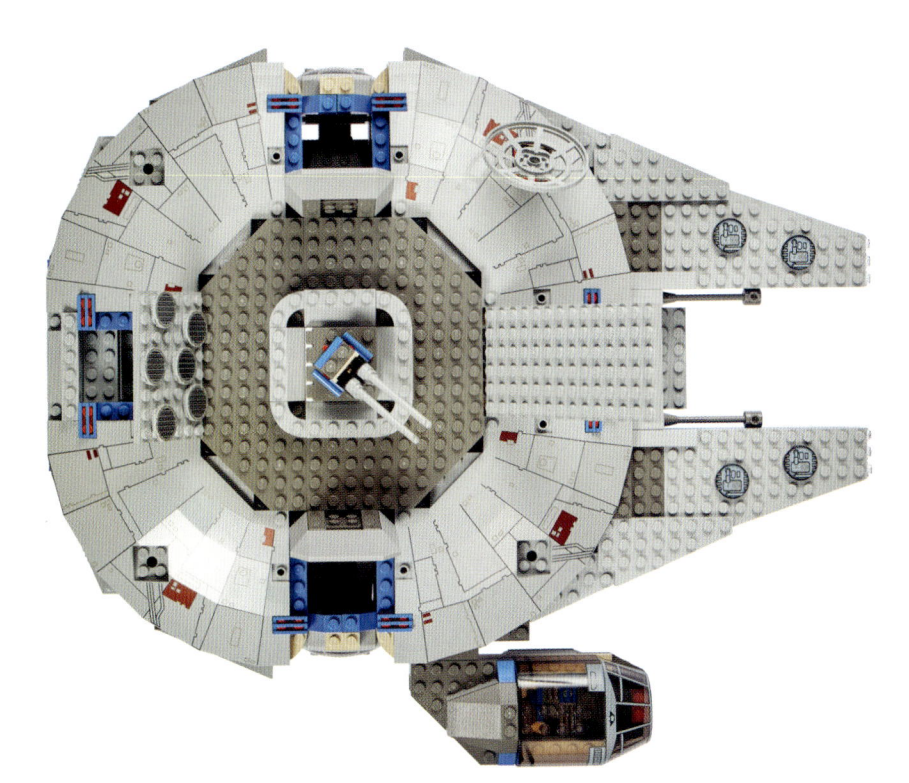

OPPOSITE An early sketch of a LEGO *Star Wars* logo.

ABOVE Lightsaber elements were essential to creating an authentic LEGO world that looked and felt like the *Star Wars* galaxy.

LEFT The proposed scaled-down version of the *Millennium Falcon* was held back from the first wave of LEGO *Star Wars* toys in 1999 and moved to the second year.

Ball joints and ejector elements

Construction was also recovering well from its initial setback. During subsequent discussions, the team decided its central characters still needed to be robots. A whole platform of elements based on the ball-joint system had been authorised, so it would be all but impossible to create figures that didn't look like robots. The team's conundrum became how to distinguish them from LEGO *Star Wars* so as not to confuse consumers.

Then the team had an epiphany: it would go in the opposite direction with its setting. Instead of placing Construction's robots in a high-tech futuristic world, they would put them somewhere more archaic and primeval. Boneheads of Voodoo Island was born.

Wanting a feature to give the figures more play value, designers drew inspiration from another recent LEGO Technic experiment: Cyber Strikers. In what would prove to be one of the long-lived LEGO Technic figure's final outings, Cyber Strikers pitted two figures against each another in vehicles equipped with mechanical functions that either extended arms or launched projectiles aimed at a target on an opponent's model. If struck, ejector functions flung the figures sky high, James Bond-style.

Similar action-oriented mechanics were incorporated into Boneheads. Each sported a chest element that, if pressed, popped off its figure's head. The intent, similar to the long-popular Rock 'Em Sock 'Em Robots, was to enable boxing-style matches where children could engage in parts-oriented pugilism, not just role play.

Excitement was high as the team took the new elements and figures into an inaugural test with children. Between ball joints and ejectors, they thought Boneheads would be an instant hit. However, hopes were quickly dashed when the feedback was received: children didn't want heads popping off their toys. Work on Boneheads of Voodoo Island was halted and a question mark was placed over Construction and ball joints altogether.

ABOVE The first wave of LEGO *Star Wars* sets in 1999 consisted only of vehicles that could match the scale of minifigures.

A galaxy of new pieces

Meanwhile, LEGO *Star Wars*, launched in 1999, was a smash success. Designers had succeeded in making the toys accurate to *Star Wars* while using almost uniformly generic parts. Aside from a variety of new torsos and face prints depicting Jedi and other characters, the only elements that were exclusive to LEGO *Star Wars* were related to heads, aliens and astromech droids. The balance of new pieces had little struggle making themselves useful in many other LEGO play themes. However, among Darth Vader's iconic mask, scout trooper helmets and battle-droid components, one new piece was especially significant.

A minifigure's distinctive head, torso and leg configuration had remained almost unchanged since 1978, aside from a few variations such as pirates' peg legs in 1989 and a skirt piece in 1990. Heads had appeared in different colours and with a wide variety of prints, but the basic shape had remained untouched. During the 1980s, designers had considered making special heads for aliens in a prototype LEGO Space theme called Seatron. In the end, however, the decision was made to vary helmets, hair and armour but keep the basic minifigure shape unmodified. The first prototype of a LEGO skeleton figure had been developed in the early 1980s during the first revamp of LEGO® Castle, but it was only released in 1995 after a relaxation of the rules on minifigures. Even the LEGO Space subtheme UFO, released in 1996 and premised entirely on aliens, saw minifigures with standard heads made transparent but not otherwise modified. But the Gungan alien from *The Phantom Menace*, Jar Jar Binks, cracked that wall, starting a small trickle, which, before long, became a torrent.

While Jar Jar's head element would be unique, every other element created for LEGO *Star Wars* could be used throughout the LEGO System – from Qui-Gon Jinn's hair to starfighter canopies and spaceship engines, and especially a new type of hinge, which introduced friction so that even heavy appendages would stay in. As the offering for the second year of LEGO *Star Wars* began taking shape, circumstances converged to create something truly special.

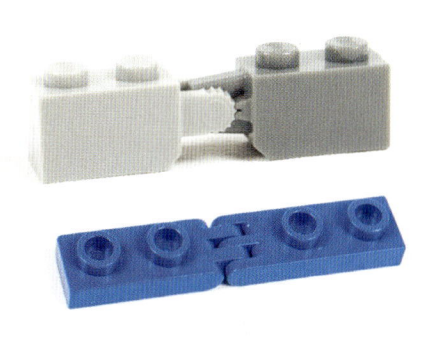

ABOVE Friction hinges (*top*) were stronger but also bulkier than their predecessors (*bottom*).

BELOW Several prototypes of the Jar Jar Binks head element.

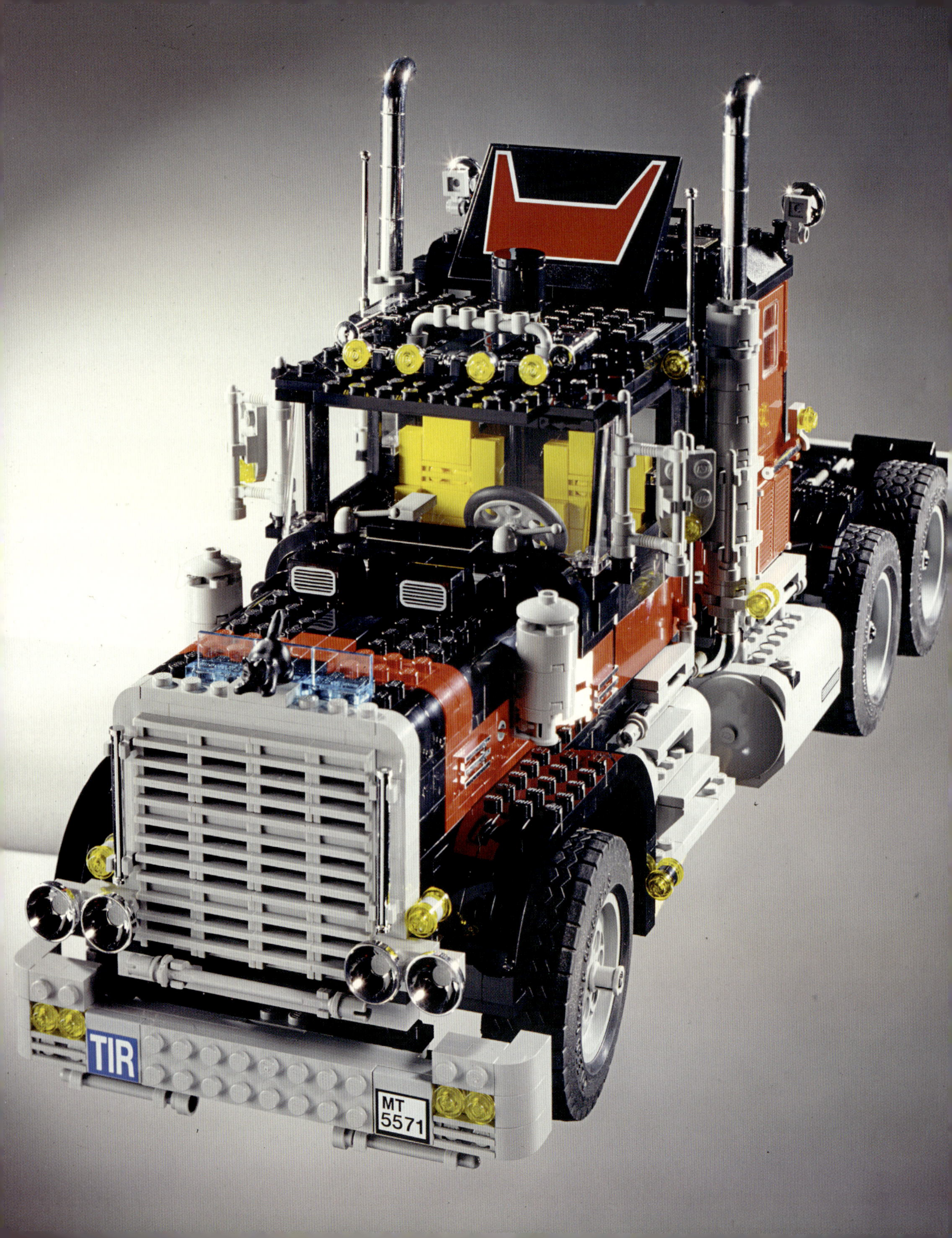
TIR
MT
5571

The search for the perfect cockpit

Ironically, just as emerging adult fan communities began to appear on the LEGO Group radar thanks to LEGO® Train, another theme that was popular with adult fans was wound down: LEGO® Model Team. Launched in 1986, LEGO Model Team had been a niche product line, ultimately tallying just sixteen sets over a thirteen-year run. Exclusively made up of vehicles, every LEGO Model Team masterpiece was a highly detailed rendition of its subject matter – boats, cars and planes, each far larger than minifigure scale. Over those years, LEGO Technic went for internal accuracy, whereas LEGO Model Team, as the name suggests, targeted external detail in the vein of hobby models.

When the line was discontinued, its skilled designers moved onto other teams, including LEGO *Star Wars*. Just before this, though, team members had begun experimenting with applying the detailed approach of LEGO Model Team to several of Lucasfilm's spaceships. For the second year of LEGO *Star Wars* sets, the team pitched a new concept that could be summed up as 'LEGO Model Team in space'.

While their effort was greenlit, no new element frames were available. This was a challenge. Designers had already built several stellar prototypes, an X-wing and a TIE Interceptor chief among them. Both had been designed to incorporate LEGO Technic figures with Imperial

OPPOSITE Set 5571 Giant Truck, released in 1996, was one of largest models produced for LEGO Model Team.

ABOVE The LEGO *Star Wars* team created a new X-wing cockpit canopy element by using the mould for a 4.5-volt battery box, seen here in a promotional picture from its release in 1976.

> We had permission to make a new cockpit element for the prototype X-wing, but we were short on budget. However, somebody in the team knew somebody in the factory. They found out that there was a mould casing standing around for the old 4.5-volt battery box. It's a large piece with a switch on one side. The cockpit is actually made in that mould casing, just with new inserts. The mould itself had a big cavity, so the technicians were able to insert small pieces into it to form our cockpit at a fraction of the cost for a whole new mould. The mould casing didn't have room in it to make a hinge on the element, which is why it only has a one-by-four plate on the back. We had to build a hinge in the model separately. When we redid the X-wing many years later, we made a new version of the element with two click hinges. This later element was also used in Benny's spaceship [in THE LEGO® MOVIE™].

Henrik Andersen, Design Master, the LEGO Group

or Rebel printing. One designer had even sculpted a classic Rogue Squadron helmet for the X-wing pilot, assuming these larger-scale figures would be included. At this time, though, the LEGO Technic figure was cancelled, rendering the idea moot. Multiple iterations of both ships had been developed, including one where a pneumatic system operated the X-wing's opening wings. Transparent domes had originally been created for the underwater theme LEGO Aquazone released in 1995. One of these large domes now worked splendidly when flipped on its side for the TIE Interceptor's windscreen. But no existing window component looked right on the iconic X-wing.

In the end, the team decided to create two final versions of the X-wing for presentation. One featured an existing four-stud-wide cockpit that had been used for a decade in LEGO Space. The other model incorporated a new movie-accurate prototype element that had been vacuum-formed out of foam. Side by side, there was no question which direction was more impressive.

The designers got the go-ahead to move ahead with their preferred version, but they would have to arrange for a new element frame themselves. Fortunately, the LEGO Group had kept some of its old moulds and a large, retired part from LEGO Train's 4.5-volt days came to the rescue. Manufacturing engineers were able to repurpose its mould at minimal cost for making the new X-wing canopy.

Named Ultimate Collectors Series (or UCS) models, 7191 X-Wing Fighter and 7181 TIE Interceptor were released in 2000 in the second year of LEGO *Star Wars*. These amazing models, which were all the more impressive considering how few specialised elements were available at the time, became the first of what would grow into a storied line of products. UCS sets in one form or another have continued to this day. 'LEGO Model Team in space' was a concept that worked.

ABOVE The original UCS X-Wing set 7191 with the special canopy element for its cockpit window.

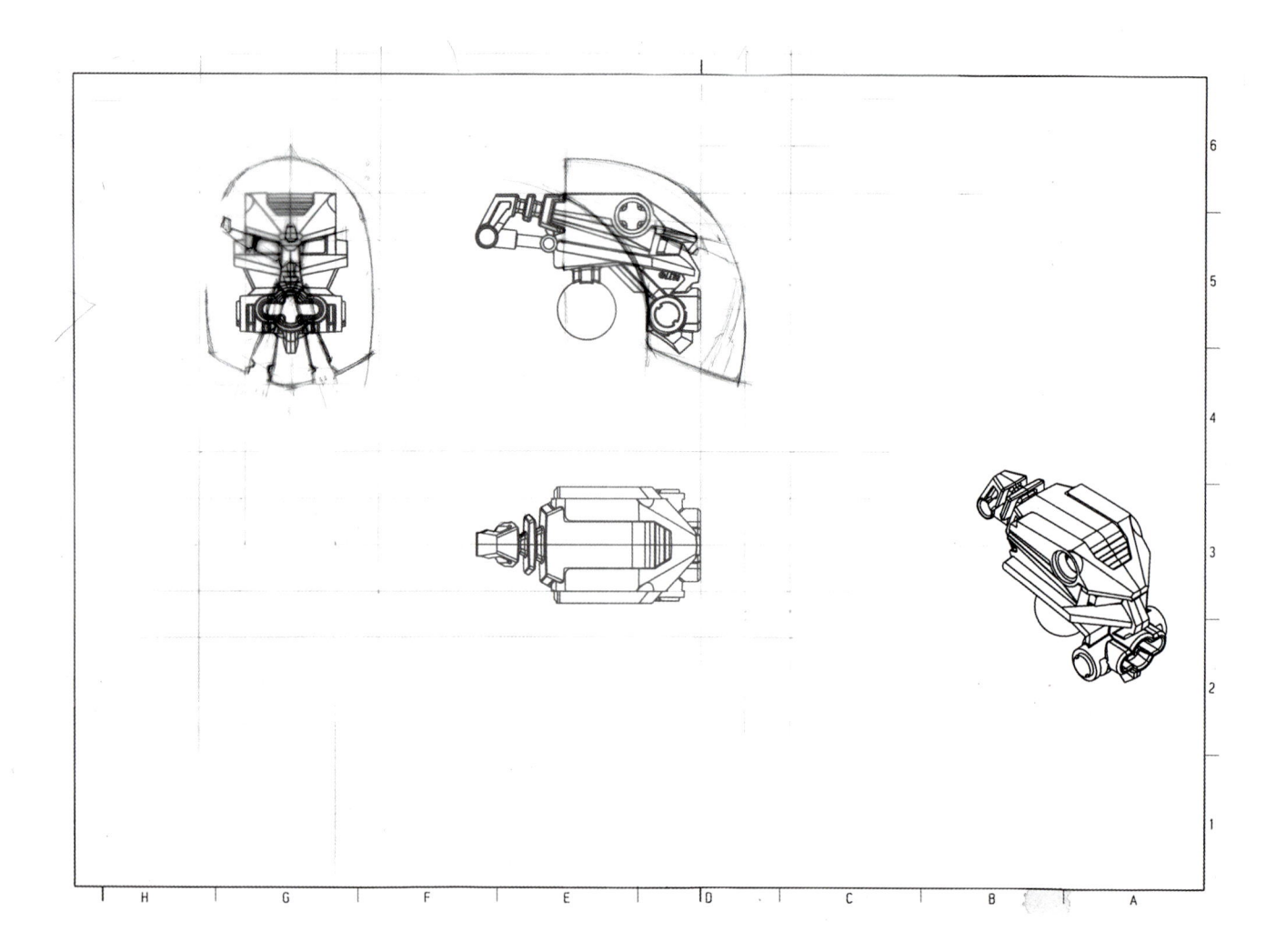

Masks of power

As LEGO *Star Wars* ramped up, the Constraction team went back to square one following their disappointing Boneheads of Voodoo Island test. Fortuitously, Christian Faber's nephew needed a babysitter and his uncle answered the call. Over several visits, he watched as his young charge played superheroes, dressing up as his favourite ones. Before long, Christian noticed a pattern formulated around one particular article of clothing: masks. Upon donning a character's face or cowl, his nephew immediately took on a different persona and traits. Instantly he was fast, strong or invisible. Masks bestowed power. The epiphany proved to be a breakthrough, requiring only minor tweaking to Boneheads' basic concept.

Instead of losing heads, Constraction figures could acquire and wear masks, each imbuing the character with various attributes. Gaining the right mask granted power, while losing it made the character vulnerable. In a moment of further inspiration, the team realised that they could make all the masks collectible, which played into the cool school-playground vibe they had originally wanted; children could gain cred by having more or rarer ones than their peers.

Designers pored over mask designs, creating selections for their six main heroes, later dubbed Toa. They also developed special face elements in the same ball-joint style, to which masks could attach. Now their world just needed a name. Christian eventually suggested BIONICLE, an amalgam of biological and chronicle, the latter a testament to this universe's size and sweep.

ABOVE A technical drawing shows concepts for a BIONICLE mask and the head element to which it would be attached.

Some voiced concerns as to whether 'LEGO DNA', as it is called, could be seen in the bizarre, gangly BIONICLE figures. But in the end the company felt confident that children would be able to see that the LEGO System was clearly present, just manifested in a different way. BIONICLE was released in 2000.

Along with six Toa heroes, the designers produced a collection of enemies built from both standard LEGO Technic and new Construction elements, along with civilian characters. Their story was told in another first for the LEGO Group: regular comics. Each was professionally drawn and were included for years with the free LEGO Club magazine sent to households all over the world. Across hundreds of pages, children were introduced to these new characters and the island of Mata Nui they inhabited.

BIONICLE connected with a whole new contingent of consumers, many of whom had never collected LEGO toys before. BIONICLE story, as told over numerous issues of comics, pulled people into the world and the ball-joint-based system kept them there. Clicking together figures was simple, intuitive and fast. Children could get quickly from building to playing. Each also included some sort of mechanical function, facilitated by LEGO gears and other LEGO Technic elements, which could join with the frames of the BIONICLE figures. Initially, all the characters were skeletal-looking, but this changed as the years went on. Designers established a selection of basic figure parts that could be used over and over as base layers, with new elements added on top. Teams of Toa remained at the centre of every successive BIONICLE wave. However, to distinguish them, different armours were grafted onto the interior skeletons, endowing each year's figures with different shapes, sizes and abilities. Some armours were removable and had special powers, like the masks. Masks, however, remained the focal point throughout the entire BIONICLE run and eventual, short-lived reboot in 2015. Hundreds of different variants were developed and whole storylines revolved around key masks, such as the Masks of Creation, Light and Life, which figured heavily in climactic comic runs and several direct-to-video movies.

After the setback of Galidor and the cancellation of Genesis, BIONICLE was unique in the assortment – and so successful that at one point the team suggested taking it, and Construction as a whole, in an almost unimaginable direction. With several years of new element frames having been allotted to BIONICLE, the assortment of Construction pieces compatible with the ball-joint had grown. The BIONICLE team observed that the LEGO Group now sold two completely unique building systems, one based on studs and the other on ball joints. These systems were so different that they could be their own brands. They proposed pulling the Construction system entirely out of the LEGO Group and turning it into an independent brand. This would allow them to target an older age demographic and tell stories with edgier tones. They envisioned worlds that were darker and grittier, inspired by steampunk, fantasy and the tabletop game *Warhammer*. Construction would be expanded so that it, like standard LEGO System bricks, would have multiple themes under its banner, set in different universes from BIONICLE, all built with the ball-joint elements. Decorative elements compatible with Construction would be developed to depict demons, monsters, griffins, mecha and more. In the end, however, the company decided to keep everything under a single banner.

New shapes

LEGO *Star Wars* also evolved through the years alongside BIONICLE. Depicting the galaxy far, far away went through several distinct phases, all of them fuelled by LEGO elements. First came the honeymoon stage, where every set was a ship or location that had never been seen before, fresh and new. X-wings and Y-wings in year one were followed in quick succession by A-wings, TIE fighters, the *Millennium Falcon*, Jedi starfighters, and even Jabba the Hutt's sail barge. Nearly all of these were built with that initial collection of pieces developed for the inaugural wave. Then came a new challenge: how to turn an already highly detailed model for a specific *Star Wars* vehicle set into an evergreen set.

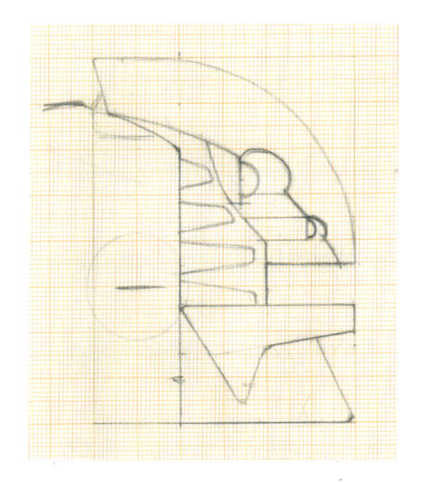

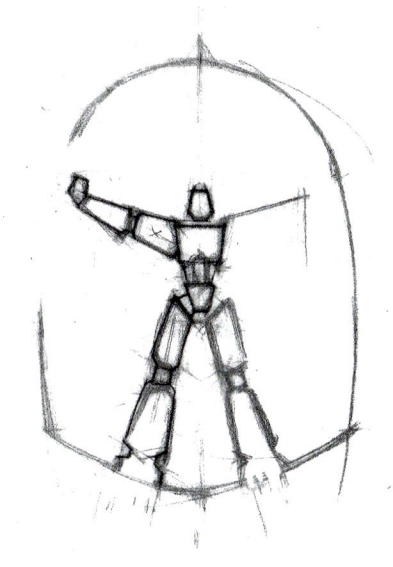

TOP Often, designers sketched out new ideas for BIONICLE masks by hand.

ABOVE One of the first concept sketches for the Mask of Life, which would feature prominently in a later BIONICLE storyline.

Evergreen sets had long existed within evergreen themes. Police stations, for example, had been part of the LEGO portfolio of products even before minifigures ushered in the modern LEGO® Town theme. However, successive police stations could vary widely in architecture, shape and size. LEGO *Star Wars* was different. An X-wing has specific proportions, lines and an overall look that could not be significantly changed. Several vehicles, including TIE fighters, the *Millennium Falcon* and Jedi starfighters, were identified early on as ships that needed to always have some variant available on shelves. Accordingly, designers began allocating a certain number of new element frames each year to refreshing portions of those ships. New cockpit elements, wings, engines or bubble canopies provided stark visual distinctions from what came before, improving the overall accuracy of each new version. Play features were another tool used for distinguishing successive iterations. The wings on the original X-wing were pried open by hand, which locked the then-new friction hinges into place. Later versions did away with hinges altogether, opting for wings that popped open mechanically when a knob was turned – and which snapped shut through the use of rubber bands. Incremental change through better elements and play features became the hallmark of the second phase of LEGO *Star Wars*.

A platform was tasked specifically with developing a key class of elements. Its name was shape elements. With graceful curves and facets, these pieces were used to create ever more movie-accurate spaceship hulls. Even as they focused on LEGO *Star Wars* sets, designers never strayed from their initial push to make components as widely usable as possible. Shape elements were embraced throughout the company, showing up in contemporary themes like LEGO Exo-Force, LEGO® Dino 2010 and beyond, all the way to the present.

Building for size

With a passionate fan base, both young and old, hungry for LEGO *Star Wars*, boundaries of size kept getting pushed further and further. Early on, designers would create one or two higher-price sets a year to see if the market would support them. Every time the answer was yes, and the bar continued to rise. These larger models provided a home for a group of elements that might otherwise have been retired.

ABOVE Shape elements gave vehicles more realistic curves and angles.

Concurrent with the rise of LEGO *Star Wars* was the transition in LEGO Technic from bricks to beams. Prior to the early 2000s, designers of LEGO System sets had used LEGO Technic elements sparingly, preferring to make their structures and frames exclusively of studs and tubes. As LEGO *Star Wars* models grew bigger, however, they demanded greater strength, which only LEGO Technic bricks could provide, with their ability to incorporate pinned as well as stud construction.

Slowly, the interior structures of LEGO *Star Wars* sets became increasingly reliant on LEGO Technic bricks until the methodology became almost universal. LEGO *Star Wars* rescued many such elements from retirement, including one whose future hung in the balance after the cancellation of the set it was originally designed for.

The L-shaped 5×5 LEGO Technic brick was developed in the late 1990s for what would have been the largest LEGO model ever released and whose identity was so secret that designers are still not permitted to reveal it. Slated for release in 2001, this cancelled set was so massive that it justified the development of the L-shaped brick all on its own. Set 8466 LEGO Technic 4×4 Off-Roader was the only model to include the element for the first four years of its mould's existence, showing that the LEGO Group had big plans for it. Just before the 5×5 was deleted from the element library, designers in the LEGO *Star Wars* team needed it. 10143 Ultimate Collectors Series Death Star, released in 2005, used several in its superstructure, but the major coup came two years later. Returning full circle, the L-shaped 5×5 served as an integral part of 10179 Ultimate Collectors Series *Millennium Falcon*, released in 2007 – the largest LEGO set at the time.

ABOVE The L-shaped 5×5 LEGO Technic brick has found use in a variety of products, notably for LEGO *Star Wars*.

BELOW The incredible progression of detail in LEGO *Star Wars* minifigures can be seen clearly in the evolution of Yoda's head and body printing.

Eventually, LEGO *Star Wars* models became so large and minutely detailed that designers found it challenging to up their game between variants. Instead, minifigures became the go-to for novelty. Thanks to LEGO *Star Wars*, as well as other themes such as LEGO® Legends of Chima™, printing technology at the LEGO Group expanded, enabling levels of detail on minifigures never before imagined. Designers created sculpts for ever-more-obscure and diverse aliens and re-visited previously produced characters to give them makeovers. Eventually, sustained enthusiasm for miniature Jedi and much sought-after Rodians led to a much-needed re-examination of a key *Star Wars* prop.

Blasting off

Initially, special elements depicting guns were avoided in LEGO *Star Wars*. So, to create that most iconic of *Star Wars* weapons, the blaster, designers flipped an old megaphone piece around and placed a transparent nub on the end. By 2007, it was ready for an update, especially as shape elements were allowing for more-movie-accurate ships. Accordingly, two moulded blasters were created: a rifle and standard-size gun. These new parts in turn necessitated another. Battle droid minifigures had originally been released with slightly bent arm components sporting identical claw grips at either end. Oriented vertically so that the upper claw could connect with the droid's shoulder, this meant that its megaphone blaster's handle protruded sideways. Despite it being unnatural in appearance from the beginning, designers had reasoned that the piece would be more useful as a generic piece with that orientation. But with formal blasters available, a more realistic grip was required. Accordingly, a new arm was produced, straight this time instead of curved, with claws alternating in direction on either end so that blasters could be held more naturally.

ABOVE In 2007, the original megaphone-style blasters (top) were replaced by blasters that more accurately represented the weapons seen in the *Star Wars* galaxy.

RIGHT 7141 Naboo Fighter, from 1999, features the original battle droid arm holding the megaphone blaster sideways.

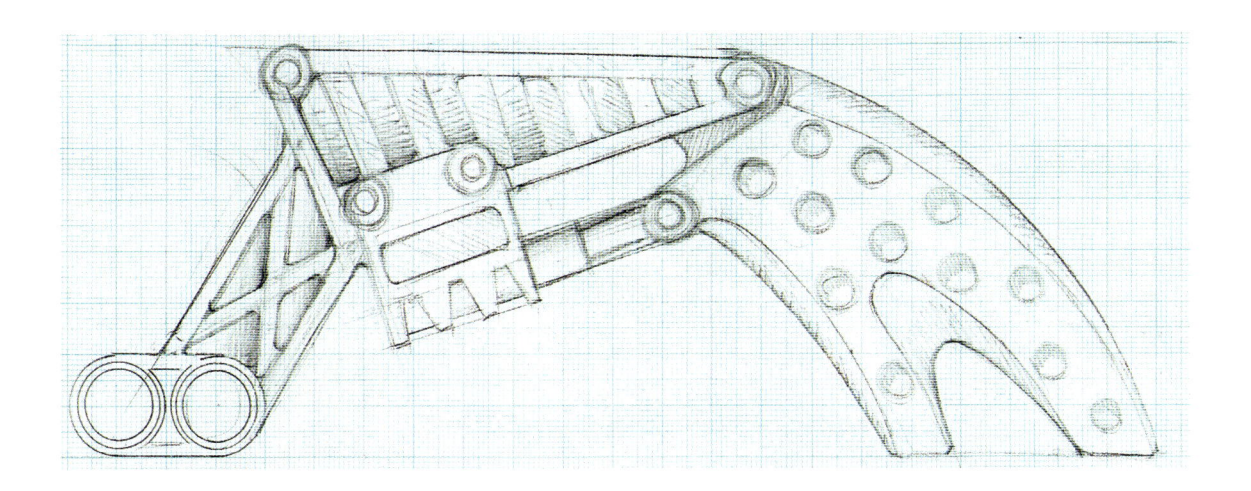

Evolving world

BIONICLE took a slightly different path. Without external influences, designers and storytellers could evolve the Toas' world ever larger, but freedom brought with it a very different type of challenge. Designers were able to change the look of the characters year by year by creating new parts. Hundreds of masks with various powers came and went as the universe grew. Children loved and stuck with BIONICLE because of its amazing world-building; many of them came of age reading the comic books and consuming other media that featured the Toa and their world. However, after several years, BIONICLE had become an evergreen LEGO theme where its own history mattered. LEGO® City could be completely reborn every five years or so to greet a new generation with no ties to previous storylines, but similarly rebooting BIONICLE would disrupt the universe and alienate children who loved the story. Keeping it going, though, meant that new fans had the challenge of having to catch up on years' worth of lore and world-building without the benefit of the easily accessible movies and TV shows provided by other major franchises such as *Star Wars*.

The initial inspiration behind Construction had been to treat it as if it had a movie, and in this designers succeeded beyond their wildest dreams. Eventually the BIONICLE universe became ever-more massive and complex. The theme began to slow around the mid-2000s as the children who fell in love with it during those first five years began to grow out of playing with toys. Due to the high bar of entry, their younger siblings' generation did not embrace BIONICLE nearly as enthusiastically, leading to the storied theme's cancellation in 2010, only halfway through a planned twenty-year run.

It is not an exaggeration to say that BIONICLE and LEGO *Star Wars* changed the LEGO Group forever. Construction lived on, initially in its successor theme, LEGO® Hero Factory. Buildable figures using its elements also appeared in LEGO *Star Wars*, LEGO® DC Universe Super Heroes, LEGO Legends of Chima and more. LEGO *Star Wars* continues to be an evergreen theme to this day and has spawned countless new elements, with both specific and general uses.

But the legacy of BIONICLE and LEGO *Star Wars* goes beyond the incredible diversity of LEGO elements used to realise these worlds. These themes showed that world-building, strong characters and rich storylines, whether born within Billund or from without, could enhance children's play rather than detract from it. Blockbuster success for both lines pointed towards the type of toys that would be needed in an ever-more technologically saturated world – and proved that it was viable to both partner with big brands *and* develop in-house universes. Throughout the 2000s these lessons would be further developed and honed, with incredible successes to come.

ABOVE Hundreds of different BIONICLE elements were designed through the years. This sketch shows a fang piece that would be used on insect-like creatures called Visorak.

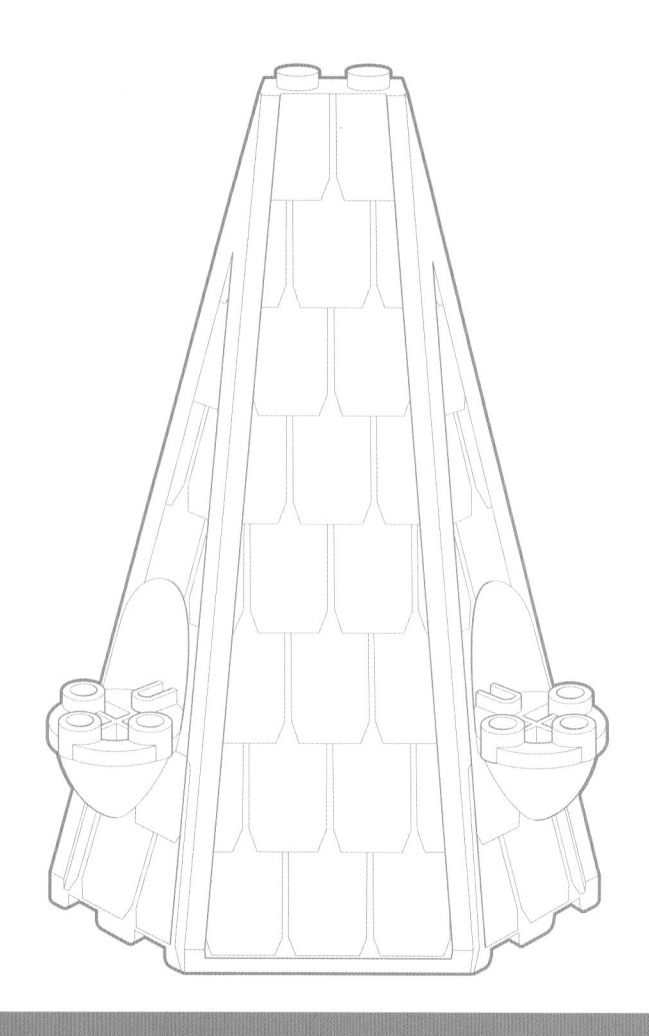

> **Depending on the concept, sometimes we will choose some or all the characters first and then design sets around them.**

Adam Corbally, Design Master, the LEGO Group

9
Playing with Story

How licensing and a focus on storytelling led to an explosion of LEGO® themes and laid the groundwork for even bigger things to come.

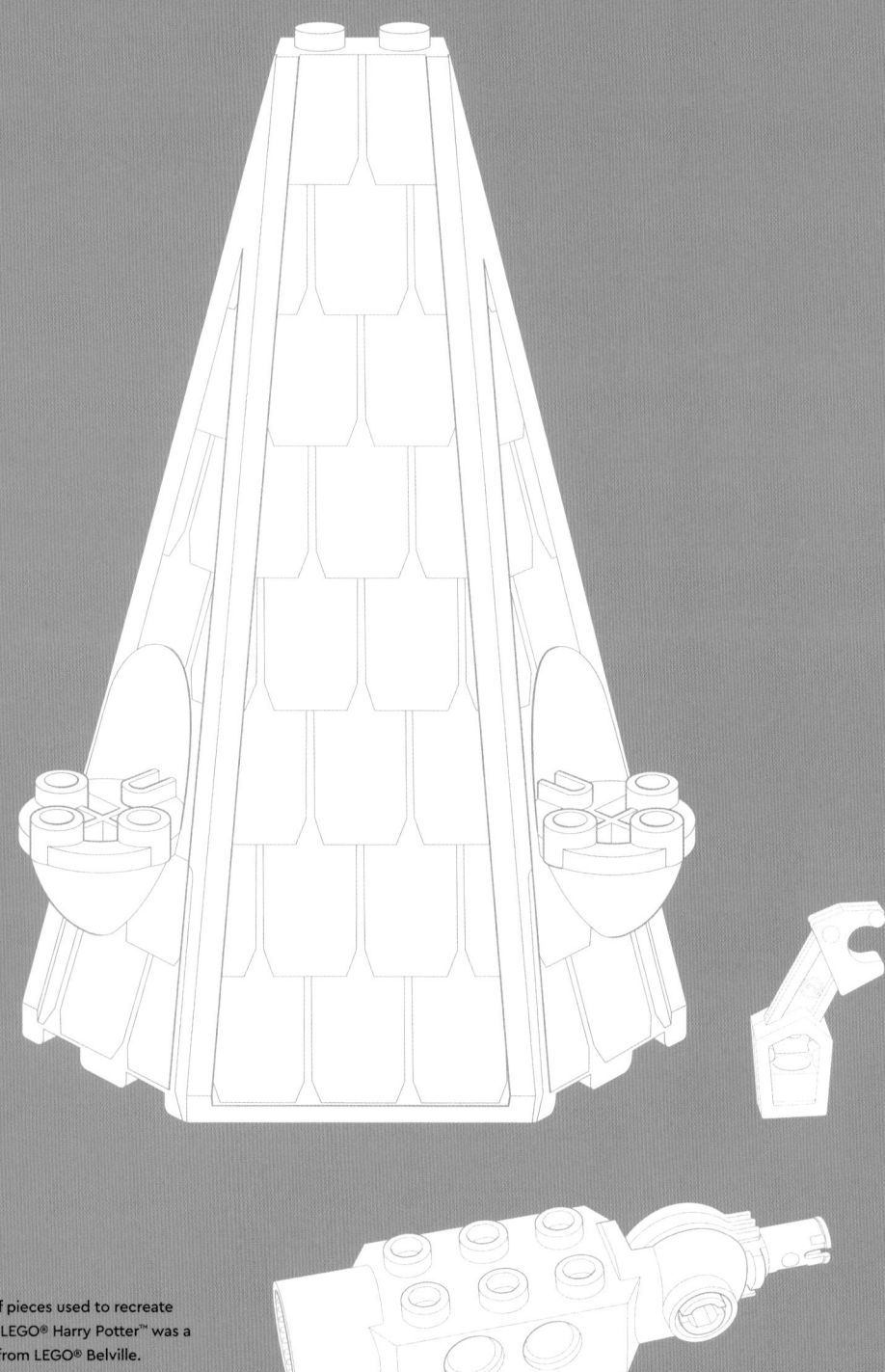

TOP The original roof pieces used to recreate Hogwarts™ Castle in LEGO® Harry Potter™ was a recoloured element from LEGO® Belville.

ABOVE RIGHT Robot arms used in LEGO® Exo-Force are one of the theme's biggest legacies, since they are used extensively throughout the product portfolio.

RIGHT The friction hinge used in LEGO® Knights' Kingdom™ could articulate in multiple directions.

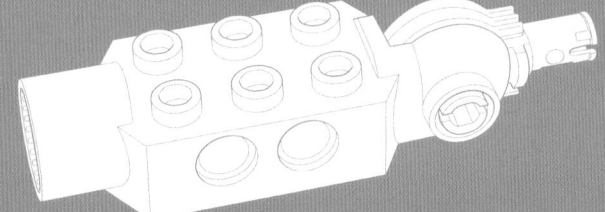

After achieving blockbuster-level status, it is difficult to overstate the influence of LEGO® BIONICLE® across all corners of the LEGO Group. For top-level executives to packaging, advertising and every department in between, the success of such a ground-breaking experiment had proved revelatory. Designers had multiple takeaways, one of which was to wonder whether buildable action figures could work in other themes. While throngs of children adored BIONICLE, there was a belief among multiple product leads that significant numbers of fans would never buy it, not because they didn't like the concept or play options, but due to the fact that its parts were not uniformly compatible with System pieces. The triumph of BIONICLE was that it had been designed to bring children into the tent who had never touched LEGO® bricks before. But what about children who loved building and had bins full of LEGO® System parts that didn't always join intuitively with Construction elements? This key question, and others, would revolutionise the LEGO Group product lines and design processes.

Throughout the 1980s and 1990s, four core themes had comprised four fifths of System product lines: LEGO® Town, LEGO® Space, LEGO® Castle and LEGO® Pirates. Over the course of several years before and after BIONICLE release, the core themes had begun to play a lesser role in the overall portfolio. In the lead-up to 2004, when the LEGO Group experienced financial difficulties, frames for new elements became understandably scarce, so it was decided to reboot LEGO Castle, for which so many existing moulds were available. However, the theme needed reimagining and novelty. Breathing new life into the old stalwart led designers to embark on their first experiment at recreating some of the magic of BIONICLE elsewhere. Breaking with the past went all the way to branding: instead of LEGO Castle, the rebrand would be called LEGO® Knights' Kingdom.

Designers of the new theme intended to mimic BIONICLE template, which was distilled down to two key traits: story and action figures. Large, buildable knights were created, but the designers were mindful of not alienating children who loved building structures and playing with LEGO minifigures. So a dual strategy was developed. LEGO Knights' Kingdom would have as its core several fully fleshed-out minifigure characters: a king named Mathias, several loyal knights, each with a name and basic backstory, and an arch-enemy called Lord Vladek. This was largely unprecedented. Past LEGO Castle subthemes had included a few named minifigures, but most were generic cannon fodder. There was no comparison between previous LEGO Castle plots and the narrative built around the five heroes and villain of LEGO Knights' Kingdom. Designers were clearly channeling the Toa from BIONICLE, with each knight given a distinctive colour palette and individualised helmet visor, making them easily distinguishable. This was a huge break from previous knights and a nod to BIONICLE masks.

Other than new helmet moulds, the minifigure-scale LEGO Knights' Kingdom sets brilliantly repurposed existing elements, using several strategic colour changes, including brand new shades called violet blue and dark purple. However, since the minifigures were so vibrant and different thanks to their never-before-seen hues and distinctive helmets, visually the whole theme looked fresh and new.

The few new element frames that LEGO Knights' Kingdom did have were largely devoted to its riskier venture: brick-built action figures. Construction elements did not mesh seamlessly with LEGO System parts, both technically and aesthetically. These figures were going to be knights, not robots, so a variety of new parts were sculpted. Visually, the most noticeable were large chest pieces, shields and helmets, which matched the distinctive colours of their namesakes' minifigure-sized versions. These parts were relatively straightforward, since each was static. The challenge was to work out how to impart dynamic movement.

Friction hinges were the new standard for System-compatible parts since being introduced

RIGHT Knight Danju in his dark purple armour faces off against minifigure Lord Vladek in 8777 Vladek Encounter, released in 2004.

in LEGO® Star Wars™. Designers wanted to create joints with the strength of friction hinges so that they would be useful in all sorts of applications, but with the same mobility and poseability of Constraction ball joints. Ultimately, they devised a new composite part which utilised LEGO® Technic pin connectors and could rotate and articulate simultaneously. They also developed several types of receiving elements for the pins. These sported traditional studs and tubes so they could be built into models and used as anchor points for hip, knee, elbow, hand and foot joints on the figures. Other designers received enthusiastically the new system of hinges, which were used across multiple product lines upon release in 2004.

ABOVE The new friction hinge developed for the action figures of LEGO Knights' Kingdom could rotate and articulate simultaneously.

LEFT The supersized action figure version of Lord Vladek, the villain of LEGO Knights' Kingdom, with the new hinge elements.

A new scale of castle

The LEGO Group didn't know it yet, but an organic sea change was underway. Lessons learned in ventures like LEGO Knights' Kingdom were meshing with others acquired from adjacent themes. Over the next decade these would form a foundation that would be built upon, leading to a complete transformation of the philosophy of how and why bricks are developed. Developing the successor theme to LEGO Castle reinforced what would prove to be one of the most vital lessons learned from a new theme launched in 2001, LEGO® Harry Potter™.

LEGO *Star Wars* had required many new elements. In addition to minifigure parts like helmets, spaceships required new generic pieces. Lucasfilm's galaxy was such an established franchise that it justified the expansion of the parts catalogue, but when the LEGO Group first looked at Harry Potter, it was still a purely literary property. Before even the public announcement of a film based on the first book, a member of an early incarnation of what would become the LEGO Group inbound licensing team (now known as Entertainment Partners and Content) brought back a few books from the UK that were 'apparently quite popular'. A LEGO product had never previously been developed based on a book's descriptions, which can be imagined very differently from reader to reader. Furthermore, the LEGO Group experience with licensing to date had focused on vehicles, thanks to their natural facilitation of action play. Children could easily swoosh a spaceship around their rooms, but, by contrast, the Harry Potter settings relied on physical spaces with much of its action taking place in rooms. Historically, location-based LEGO products had almost exclusively been 'base of operation'-style sets. Action was launched from a castle, police headquarters or pirate island, but was acted out on the floor or in the air around it. The Harry Potter series, by contrast, took place almost entirely within its primary locale, Hogwarts Castle, a place so beloved by fans that it was almost a character itself.

Tackling this challenge led the early inbound licensing team members to establish what has become a staple of evaluating possible new licensees before striking deals: the development of prototype models. Naturally, Hogwarts Castle was chosen, but the sheer size and scale of the building presented a complication.

Facilitating meaningful play within a building meant that the model that would become LEGO® Harry Potter™ Hogwarts™ Castle needed to be much bigger and more open than any previous LEGO structure. There had been police stations four storeys tall, but every room was cramped. Larger interior spaces would necessitate more bricks, driving up costs. The challenges were compounded by the need to mimic spires atop ramparts, which had historically been created in LEGO models via brick-built construction. Both features were needed for a realistic Hogwarts™ Castle. Solutions came from an unexpected source.

Designers realised that the LEGO Group had actually developed product lines with these characteristics. Two 'dollhouse' themes had done it: LEGO® Belville, beginning in 1994, and LEGO® Scala, starting in 1997. Designers built proof-of-concept models using parts from these two themes, which helped sell the viability of Harry Potter as a LEGO theme. The influence of these two earlier themes did not stop there. Both LEGO Scala and LEGO Belville sets were open and spacious, giving the illusion of greater size by using large, porous pieces. Rooms would have supports only at the corners and many walls were constructed of enormous lattice elements, which imparted a convincing illusion of enclosure while actually being anything but. These techniques facilitated the creation of large interior spaces, necessary for hands to reach in and play with oversized figures. LEGO Harry Potter designers found they could achieve similar results through the use of columns and arches. In another nod to its brick-spiration, the Hogwarts model was topped by an enormous roof element from the LEGO Belville fantasy line. Designed for dolls several times bigger than minifigures, its imposing size matched the castle's enormous scale, which dwarfed any previous medieval LEGO structure.

Designers were delighted with their recreation of Hogwarts Castle in LEGO bricks. They felt their creation was distinguished from what had come before. It communicated a sort of magical air due to incorporated hinges, which allowed for the rearranging of castle sections, and an ingenious new rotating staircase element which, when stacked, could be 'magically' set into any number of orientations. Their final coup was designing every set that depicted Hogwarts in a modular system so that anyone lucky enough to own all of them could combine everything into a single, enormous playset.

Strategic repurposing and re-colouring of Belville elements, along with rotating wall and trap-door parts from the LEGO® Adventurers line, meant that all of Hogwarts could be produced using existing moulds. Set 4707 LEGO Harry Potter Hagrid's Hut was prototyped as a simple, easy-to-build, square structure with mostly traditional LEGO Castle pieces. This design had to change when the film series was announced and reference material showed Hollywood had imagined the gamekeeper's home as a more challenging round stone building. Set 4708 Hogwarts Express rounded out LEGO Harry Potter first wave in 2001, though not before an issue in getting source material.

ABOVE *The repurposed LEGO Belville tower roof element featured prominently in the original LEGO Harry Potter Hogwarts Castle set from 2001.*

> The LEGO Harry Potter theme was quite challenging at first because, even though the movie was being filmed in London, reference material had to come from Warner Bros., in Burbank, California. We could visit the film sets in London – which was only an hour's flight from Billund – but we couldn't take any photographs. With the first Hogwarts Express train set, we had to rely on images that were available on the Internet. So we used these as reference and were able to bring the model to the next meeting with Warner Bros.

Henrik Rubin Saaby, Senior Designer, the LEGO Group

It's all about the unique elements

Throughout the process, designers were delighted to discover that through stringent review of past product lines, they could usually find what they needed to capture the essence of the Harry Potter universe. With few new parts frames being consumed by the structures, the new frames available were free to be used on unique character elements, accessories and animals, including Norbert the dragon, Fluffy the three-headed dog, owls, elaborate keys, brooms – and the first ever double-sided minifigure head, produced for Quirinus Quirrell/Lord Voldemort. Most of these constituted small components whose moulds were far less complex and expensive, allowing the frames that were available to stretch even further. In aggregate, it was a revelation. Requiring little more than colour changes, the LEGO Group had managed to produce, with almost entirely existing parts, a unique and instantly identifiable take on the Harry Potter universe. Executives wondered whether they had discovered a formula which could be applied to other valuable partnerships. In short order, that theory would be tested more thoroughly than management ever could have imagined.

Hollywood is a very connected town, and once word got out that the LEGO Group had successfully turned two of the world's biggest franchises into successful construction-toy lines, other potential partners came knocking. First it was companies with existing ties: Lucasfilm, for its upcoming Indiana Jones movie, and Warner Bros., for its Batman™ The Dark Knight Trilogy. Then came introductions to Nickelodeon, riding high on its twin hits SpongeBob SquarePants and *Avatar: The Last Airbender*. Success brought more offers through the years. New Line was doing a Hobbit trilogy, Warner came back with *Speed Racer*, and Fox eventually brought them *The Simpsons*.

In every case, new frames were used primarily on developing the essential components for minifigures, accessories, animals, and any other iconic props that were part of the public consciousness around specific properties. These were taken in and given LEGO makeovers so that they were instantly recognisable as both LEGO elements and their subject matter. Batman's cowl,

TOP Set 4730 LEGO Harry Potter Chamber of Secrets, released in 2002, incorporates the design aesthetics established in the wider LEGO Harry Potter theme: open-building techniques, modular construction and green roof pieces.

ABOVE Professor Quirrell sported the first ever dual-sided head. This novelty would go on to become a common feature of minifigures.

Indiana Jones' whip, the One Ring, Marge Simpson's tall blue hair, Aang's beloved flying lemur Momo, SpongeBob's rectangular head, and, of course, numerous Jedi and Harry Potter characters – all leapt from concept drawings to sculpts, and finally onto production lines.

Secrets of construction

While mesmerising to fans, the stories of these seemingly unique elements are all remarkably similar. Model makers are provided with reference material, after which they work with mould engineers and part designers to create specific key components. Finally, those are incorporated into finished products. Understandably, fans go wild over new novelty characters from beloved film properties, while LEGO designers are generally able to make most of the rest of the set from recoloured existing pieces. Special elements are locked to preserve novelty until such time as contracts expire, at which point all but the most iconic are released for wider use.

The LEGO Group successful approach to licensing allowed it to easily and swiftly incorporate other opportunities, including many individual movies. In between blockbuster movie releases, comic books and much-loved evergreen characters offered inspiration for further licensed LEGO models.

This sort of ubiquity was reserved only for the largest entertainment giants; other lines lasted only the length of a movie or show's popularity. As licensing brought with it both experience and success, the LEGO Group began wondering if similar formulas, and subsequent positive results, could be applied to their own in-house lines. Unfortunately, those worlds were different in some important ways, and some lessons were yet to be learned.

TOP LEFT Several iconic accessories from the LEGO® Batman™ theme. Moulds for such elements are easy to produce yet help make the theme feel authentic and recognisable to fans.

TOP RIGHT LEGO® SpongeBob SquarePants™ recreated Bikini Bottom in 2006 using newly designed minifigure elements and a range of existing parts and wings developed for LEGO *Star Wars*, cast in new colours.

ABOVE Momo, Aang's beloved flying lemur from *Avatar: The Last Airbender*, was one of the few new moulds created for that theme; LEGO designers created all the other models from recoloured existing elements.

> A lot of us in the Super Heroes teams are big fans of comic books, movies and TV shows. We like to include lesser-known or fan-favourite characters in the sets, where possible. Depending on the concept, sometimes we will choose some or all the characters first, and then design sets around them. Part of the process includes shuffling figures between sets, depending on what makes sense with our partners, what would be appealing to consumers, and what is possible for us to produce. With movie tie-ins, we are dependent on reference very early on in the development of the films, so we often have to approach things with an open mind. Occasionally, the challenge is ourselves: it can be easy to fall into a rabbit hole of weird versions or obscure characters when creating concepts, but ultimately it needs to make sense to the children. Although, if it is a larger set with many minifigures, we can sometimes squeeze in a fan favourite or two...

Adam Corbally, Design Master, the LEGO Group

Making mecha

LEGO Knights' Kingdom was discontinued after three years, but a small cadre of designers had watched its development with keen interest. United by a mutual love of Japanese manga, they saw an opportunity in the buildable figure hinges. When, separately, LEGO *Star Wars* spearheaded development of shape elements, the designers knew that LEGO models of mecha (large armoured robots with human pilots) were now possible, something which the parts catalogue had previously precluded.

Mecha had appeared in the LEGO Space sub theme Life on Mars from 2001, but, since only LEGO *Star Wars* friction hinges were available then, they had been limited in both size and mobility. This team's pitch was simple: to create a poseable robot line based on LEGO System bricks set in its own imaginative world and populated by characters with a manga aesthetic. Additionally, they proposed building on the lessons of LEGO Knights' Kingdom and taking the experiment further by creating an expansive storyline – inspired by the success of BIONICLE – for their theme to inhabit.

LEGO Exo-Force, as the theme was named, got a green light. Taking cues from both LEGO *Star Wars* and LEGO Harry Potter, designers' early focus was on characters, and specifically how to use them for creating that all-important novelty. There wasn't a simple answer. SpongeBob and Batman were intrinsically exciting by virtue of being beloved characters rendered in minifigure form. Once established, interest could be maintained through a new suit or face print from different storylines. The LEGO Exo-Force team believed its best chance was going all-in with the manga inspiration.

RIGHT The intimidating-looking battle machines called mecha in LEGO Exo-Force incorporated hinges from Knights' Kingdom and shape elements from LEGO *Star Wars*.

Hairpieces, arms and eyes

Designers working at a scale factor of three lovingly crafted enormous, spiky, brightly coloured hairpieces that seemed like something from another world, which, of course, was exactly the point. Speaking of points, those turned out to be a challenge. Initially the hairpieces were cast in ABS (acrylonitrile butadiene styrene), used for all previous minifigure hairpieces, but when samples came back from product safety tests, they had failed: the sharp points on the hairpieces could present a hazard. LEGO Exo-Force designers went back and forth, ultimately arriving at a solution utilising a softer plastic, which was, at the time, quite new for the LEGO Group. Unfortunately, this new material did not perform as expected: while the rubbery plastic looked great, it lacked proper clutch power. The never-before-seen connector pair of minifigure head stud and soft plastic tube turned out to be insufficient for achieving the proper function. All of which meant that the characters in LEGO Exo-Force were prone to losing their hair.

LEGO Exo-Force minifigures did, however, look awesome. As the LEGO Group expanded into more licences, a softer plastic would go on to be the answer for many product-safety concerns and the challenges faced by LEGO Exo-Force became a key lesson that gave value many times over in future elements. To this day, if a set contains rubbery plastic, safety concerns will have driven the decision. Furthermore, if the element is a headpiece, it has been adjusted to fit much tighter than the original manga wigs.

Pitted against the colourful LEGO Exo-Force heroes, the team created an army of robots that, in a storyline that could have come straight out of the Terminator franchise, had rebelled against humanity and now sought to drive humans from the fictional Sentai Mountain that served as the theme's setting. Drawing again from manga, designers set out to make robots roughly to scale with a minifigure, and also poseable. The legs on their nearest brethren, LEGO *Star Wars* battle droids, did not move independently of each other, so the figures could do little more than bend over. The designers' goal here was to make it so that minifigures and their robot nemeses alike could be staged in cool action positions. Battle Droids were not menacing, which was something else that needed to be different for Exo-Force.

ABOVE When LEGO Exo-Force launched in 2006, unique hair and face prints made what were otherwise standard minifigures look completely new and different.

BELOW The final design of LEGO Exo-Force poseable robot enemies features an arm element that would go on to see extensive use throughout nearly every product line in future years.

Bulk and independent leg elements proved the right mix, leading to a trio of special robot components that incorporated two very clever features. Battle droids may have had limited mobility, but designers across the LEGO Group had found one aspect of them incredibly useful: their arms. These had been incorporated into sets across nearly every theme, a practice which continues to this day. Instead of reusing these arms, the LEGO Exo-Force team opted to create their own, but with different capabilities so designers would have more options in future products. They intentionally maintained the unique elbow bend of battle-droid arms. But rather than a clip-on both ends, the new arm piece had a clip at one end only. Instead, the other end had receiving holes for bars placed in two orientations (on the end and in the side).

Additionally, designers envisioned the robot's eyes to be different colours. Dual-colour moulding was still not possible and tacking on 1×1 transparent round bricks looked ridiculous rather than menacing. Both conundrums were solved by casting a cross hole into the robot's head, which allowed for a small, red LEGO Technic axle to be inserted, effectively suggesting menacing, glowing eyes.

Epic world-building

With distinctive characters developed and imposing mecha coming together, building on the LEGO Knights' Kingdom click-hinge system, all that remained was to define the LEGO Exo-Force storyline. Ultimately, the theme's setting would be robotic battles and a mountain split apart by humanity. Numerous bridges connected each side of this mountain, pinch points where battles would take place. Figuring out a story and setting was not an isolated challenge during the early 2000s. Thanks to the inspiration provided by BIONICLE, many LEGO themes were seeing the need for vivid world-building and interesting narratives.

Media saturation was increasing, and it took more to hold children's attention than ever before. LEGO Exo-Force came into being concurrently with two other product lines, which both ended up beating it to market by a year: LEGO® Vikings and LEGO® Dino 2010 (called Dino Attack in North America). Together, this trio of themes represented a collective shift in the types of worlds the LEGO Group was willing to explore. Each had its own story and focused most of its new part frames on making it distinctive. LEGO Dino 2010 used as its backdrop mutant dinosaurs which had appeared for... unknown reasons! The LEGO Dino team's strategy was to give each of its creatures its own special abilities. Not surprisingly, they focused nearly all their new element frames on giant, surprisingly realistic reimaginings of various dinosaurs.

The LEGO Dino 2010 theme's novelty rested in its prehistoric beasts, and no expense was spared. Brand new variants of legs, arms, heads and torsos were developed, all utilising a version of the LEGO Knights' Kingdom friction hinge system. The new connectors imparted superior strength and mobility, allowing body parts to be combined into four huge, specialised creatures that reused only very few elements across the range and were exceedingly expensive to produce. Lesson learned: they would never appear again, and their lack of versatility was a major motivator in the eventual creation of an *Animal Building System Platform,* which undergirds modern Jurassic Park dinosaurs and other large creatures. To this day, however, no moulded LEGO animal has ever topped LEGO Dino 2010's mutant T-Rex for sheer size.

LEGO Vikings inadvertently ended up on a similar path. A theme based on what are arguably Nordic countries' most famous denizens seems such a natural fit for the Danish LEGO Group. One could be forgiven for wondering why it hadn't been done before. In fact, designers had tried many times over, going all the way back to 1978, when the theme was pitched against the famous LEGO Castle, set 375. LEGO Castle won then, and continued to do so when later generations made similar proposals throughout the 1980s and 1990s. However, with LEGO Knights' Kingdom exploring action-figure sets and LEGO Harry Potter covering fantasy, designers tried again. This time they pitched a concept that would cater to those who loved traditional LEGO Castle: pitting two factions against one another in good old-fashioned melees. That idea, however,

ABOVE Arm elements had clips on one end for attaching to the robot's shoulders and holes on the other end, into which modified bars with clips could be inserted. A LEGO Technic axle inserted from the back of the head gives the robot its sinister red eyes.

quickly ran into challenges, most notably answering the now all-important question of where novelty would come from. For that and other reasons, team members instead proposed an idea involving Viking warriors battling giant creatures – both from Norse mythology as well as generic dragons. There was just one problem: parts.

LEGO Dino 2010 had been able to invest virtually all of its limited capital in specialised, moulded dinosaurs because, similar to licensed themes, everything else it needed could be had for a few colour-change frames. The LEGO Vikings theme was not so lucky. Capturing novelty would mean new weapons and minifigure accessories, most notably distinctive horned helmets, but also larger, structural elements for longboats, as well as new components for building unique animals. It was too much, so designers got creative. First, they tried brick-built creatures. Alas, while this is possible today in themes like LEGO® NINJAGO®, the parts catalogue in the early 2000s did not have enough of the types of pieces that make such construction possible; they simply hadn't been invented yet. Every attempt was either too fragile for play, or unsightly and unrealistic. Furthermore, the new friction hinges their peers were using so extensively did not help. Such obvious joints were fine for mecha, and borderline acceptable on action figures, but they stood out like sore thumbs when integrated into animals. Designers needed that level of functionality, though, and eventually hit upon it not through inspiration from BIONICLE, but by essentially becoming BIONICLE. In the only major example of Construction and LEGO System elements ever being sold in large quantities together, LEGO Vikings included large-scale creatures.

This solution required few new pieces: special heads and wings. All other parts needed for their animals already existed. The designers rationalised such a unique choice by observing that the aesthetics of mixing would be novel all on its own, and large numbers of children were already fans of BIONICLE. Regardless, there really wasn't another economical choice. Having solved that problem, next up was Vikings' figures and weapons.

ABOVE The moulded creatures in LEGO Dino 2010 are the largest the LEGO Group have ever made.

> We wanted to do something that was a little bit different from LEGO Harry Potter and LEGO Castle, so it seemed obvious to try a theme involving Viking warriors. At first we had opposing minifigure armies. But we realised it was difficult to tell the good guys from the bad guys. So we decided to put creatures into the mix. Concurrently, our research and testing discovered that children like to have goodies and baddies in the same box. In the old LEGO Castle theme, sets alternated with goodies or baddies in them. But this meant that on Christmas morning, if you only got one set, even a really large one, you might not have anyone to fight against. With LEGO Vikings, we solved that problem by having a bad-guy creature in every box. It was a success, and it became common practice.

Bjarke Lykke Madsen, Design Master, the LEGO Group

Viking helmets and axes

Two precious new element frames were allocated towards a pair of components deemed essential for LEGO Vikings: a double-bladed axe and iconic, if not historically accurate, helmet. They were initially envisioned as monolithic parts, but when initial prototypes came back to designers, nobody liked them. Both looked wrong cast in a single colour. Horns on Viking helmets may very well be a fiction, but thanks to years of Hollywood films they were absolutely the public's perception of medieval Norse warriors. Grey horns sticking out from the side of a grey helmet just wasn't right, and the LEGO Group did not yet have the expertise in casting dual-colour elements that would come in later years.

One designer proposed a solution: develop the metallic grey helmet with two holes on either side into which a separate white horn, which he had specifically created for that purpose, could be placed. Mixing the colours solved the aesthetic problem and inspired a tweak to the LEGO Vikings axe as well. Rather than make a whole new weapon, only an axe blade was made. Thanks to clever design, which offset the attaching clip from the centre, two of the blades could be affixed to an already existing bar element, creating an imposing double axe, or used alone for a single-blade variant. This kind of versatility is the stuff ideal LEGO part designs are made of,

ABOVE LEGO Vikings mixed articulating elements from BIONICLE with new wing and head components to create impressive dragons, such as the one seen in 7019 Viking Fortress, against the Fafnir Dragon released in 2005.

but there was a final catch: they needed three pieces and had only two remaining new element frames. Appeals are always allowed, and in this instance the LEGO Vikings design team had a solid argument. They petitioned management for an additional frame, pointing out that their new horn could prove extremely versatile. History would go on to prove them correct. The horn has been used for teeth, animal horns, claws and much more across hundreds of sets. Higher-ups caught that vision and approved the extra frame.

The need for novelty

LEGO Knights' Kingdom, LEGO Exo-Force, LEGO Vikings and LEGO Dino 2010 were all released between 2004 and 2006. These themes, along with early licences such as LEGO Harry Potter and LEGO Batman, served as a phase one of sorts as the LEGO Group rebuilt the strength of its product portfolio. Designers took away key lessons from each successive release, which they would eventually use to create even more ambitious sets and themes. LEGO Dino 2010 established cool, enormous creatures and, in that vein, many later products would continue to focus on creatures. The knights in colourful armour from LEGO Knights' Kingdom gave children easily differentiated minifigure characters with personalities they could connect with. LEGO Exo-Force had been boldest with its story, told via web comics, and laid a foundation for even grander multimedia storytelling to come. In Exo-Force, in which both humans and robots piloted mechs, designers could see that even greater differentiation of good characters from bad would be even stronger. Ever since, designers have been very intentional about instilling different aesthetics across opposing factions wherever possible.

Short-term, novelty-driven themes could create a lot of excitement, fuelling engagement with the toys. Now, instead of relying primarily on four long-running evergreen themes, a wider array of offerings would supplement the always-available stalwarts. Licensed sets were tied to current movies or TV shows, while homegrown offerings were envisioned to run for a year or two, as by that time it was assumed children, and Hollywood, would have moved on.

While the company laid the groundwork necessary to further develop their own big worlds, designers reimagined stalwarts like LEGO Castle, LEGO Space, LEGO® Aquazone, and LEGO Pirates, building literally and figuratively on lessons learned and parts invented. Within familiar themes there was latitude to experiment with instilling novelty while relying on familiar worlds to tell simple narratives. Since core themes had been off shelves for a few

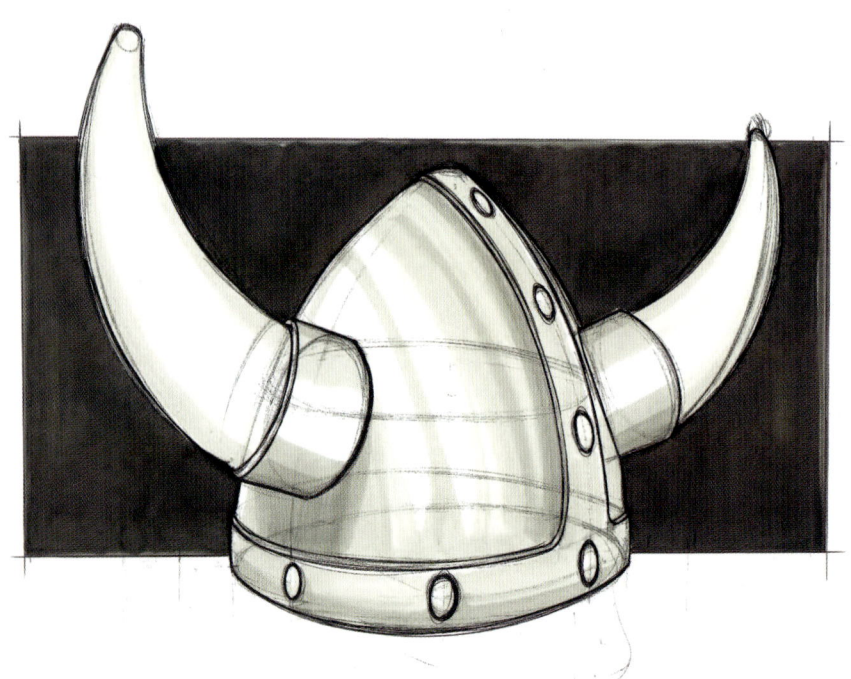

TOP Viking axe heads were designed so that they could facilitate both single- and double-blade orientations.

ABOVE Originally the Viking helmet was to be a single element with integrated horns. However, designers realised that a separate horn would be extremely useful and were able to secure an additional frame to create it.

BELOW Sketches of the original single-mould Viking helmet and the final version that included detachable horns.

years, short-lived offerings based on them felt fresh. Taking a page from licensing, designers focused new parts primarily on figures, accessories and animals. LEGO Castle returned in 2007 with a fantasy-heavy portfolio that took the creature wings from LEGO Vikings and placed them on beautiful, fully moulded dragons. No mixing of BIONICLE here; this was pure LEGO System. Giant Trolls became one of the first of what would be called 'big figs' – large, moulded creatures standing about twice the height of standard minifigures. Prior to them, only LEGO® Rock Raiders and LEGO Harry Potter had experimented with the concept. Specialised big figs would go on to represent many licensed characters in the LEGO® Super Heroes themes.

During the first year of 'fantasy-era' LEGO Castle, undead warriors rode atop skeletal horses. In the second year, minifigure-scale trolls with special helmets battled with knights. LEGO® Mars Mission, first launched in 2007, utilised many previously developed components from the theme's long history mixed in with new alien figures and shape elements originally developed for LEGO *Star Wars*.

Underwater, LEGO® Aqua Raiders took over where LEGO Aquazone left off. Running with Vikings' insight that goodies and baddies in every set did well, the new theme pitted not two factions of competing humans, but man versus giant underwater sea creatures. Thanks to new parts developed in the years immediately preceding Aqua Raiders, these could be satisfactorily rendered with normal pieces, becoming some of the first large-scale, brick-built animals ever created. This was a testament to the good work done by element designers and the new platform system for developing parts. The limited number of new, non-minifigure-based parts

ABOVE This dragon's mould was developed for the new fantasy-led LEGO Castle theme in 2007.

BELOW Giant Trolls from LEGO Castle in 2007 were the first detailed 'big figs'.

TOP Shape elements help create the distinctive styling of 7691 LEGO Mars Mission EXT Alien Mothership Assault from 2007.

ABOVE LEGO Mars Mission introduced new alien figures.

being invented was more versatile than ever. These homegrown themes, along with licensed lines like LEGO® Indiana Jones, LEGO SpongeBob SquarePants and LEGO® Avatar™: The Last Airbender, became phase two in the LEGO Group rebuilding effort and proved that short-lived, novelty themes worked. They also bought the necessary time: a system was emerging, or, more accurately phrased, a funnel.

A new system for innovation

During the 2000s, the LEGO Group experienced many seismic changes but none may have been more profound than those that rocked how product lines and elements were developed. Since the minifigure's debut in 1978 and even further back than that, LEGO toys had been inspired by children but developed almost solely by their designers. Themes and sets were, in every sense of the word, passion projects. Initially those individual passions inspired whole themes, leading to the core of LEGO Town, LEGO Space and LEGO Castle. Once the themes were established, creatives plied their art through the models within them. The whole process was almost completely devoid of any outside input or interference. Designers worked under the watchful eye of a creative lead on one of five primary teams: Present Day, Future, Historical, Basic and LEGO Technic. Within those loose confines they were free to dream up almost anything they wanted. Twice a year, management and regional market heads would come to Billund, where new, fully developed lines were presented, and they would choose which ones would go into production. For every Blacktron, Lion Knights, Aquanauts or Fort Legoredo, there were at least two or three other options, with a full range of products from small to large, that were rejected: Jules Verne, Romans, constructable musical instruments called Band Booster, Seatron, Space Miners, multiple early rounds of Wild West, Aquazone, and Vikings, to name just a few.

Playing with Story   241

ABOVE A concept sketch of a Troll warrior from LEGO Castle ('In and out' Castle) in 2007.

LEFT A dimensional sketch of the skeleton horse from the first year of LEGO Castle in 2007.

BELOW This Wild West diorama is an example of the practice of presenting new sets to management mixed in with earlier concepts or other models designed to showcase the theme's larger environment.

242   The Secret Life of LEGO® Bricks

THIS PAGE AND OPPOSITE The largest LEGO Aqua Raiders set, 7775 Aquabase Invasion, included a large brick-built octopus for attacking the underwater station.

Playing with Story 243

Within each theme, designers also developed parts. Some worked in clay and tin; others made sketches; nearly all sawed, cut and glued existing components into crude prototypes. The overriding trait of the whole process was that it emanated from and centred around individual designers. Even though testing of various kinds had been done directly with children since the 1950s, mainly to ensure they could easily follow the building instructions, it was only later that it became more fully developed and thorough, as part of the product-development cycle. This methodology worked well until it collided with the modern digital world emerging in the late 1990s and early 2000s. The LEGO Group needed to open up and allow outside influences, so it created a new process, which operated like a funnel for creative ideas. Everything within product design is now driven by and interacts with this process. During the 2000s, potential themes were run through early versions of the funnel, and by the decade's end it had more or less become what it is today. Phase three of the design department's transition was comprised of the early themes to go through the new process. These included LEGO® Power Miners in 2009 and the LEGO Space subthemes Space Police III, also in 2009, and Alien Conquest in 2011.

The funnel begins at its widest with ideas sourced from just about anywhere. Through the years the LEGO Group has cast ever-wider nets and opened up more sources for inspiration. Potential licensees come with them. Designers can, of course, still propose their own passion projects. LEGO Ideas is a way to get input from fans directly: fans propose product ideas for potential realisation as sets on the LEGO Ideas website. Most important, however, is an internal

BELOW An early brainstorm at Front End for LEGO Power Miners.

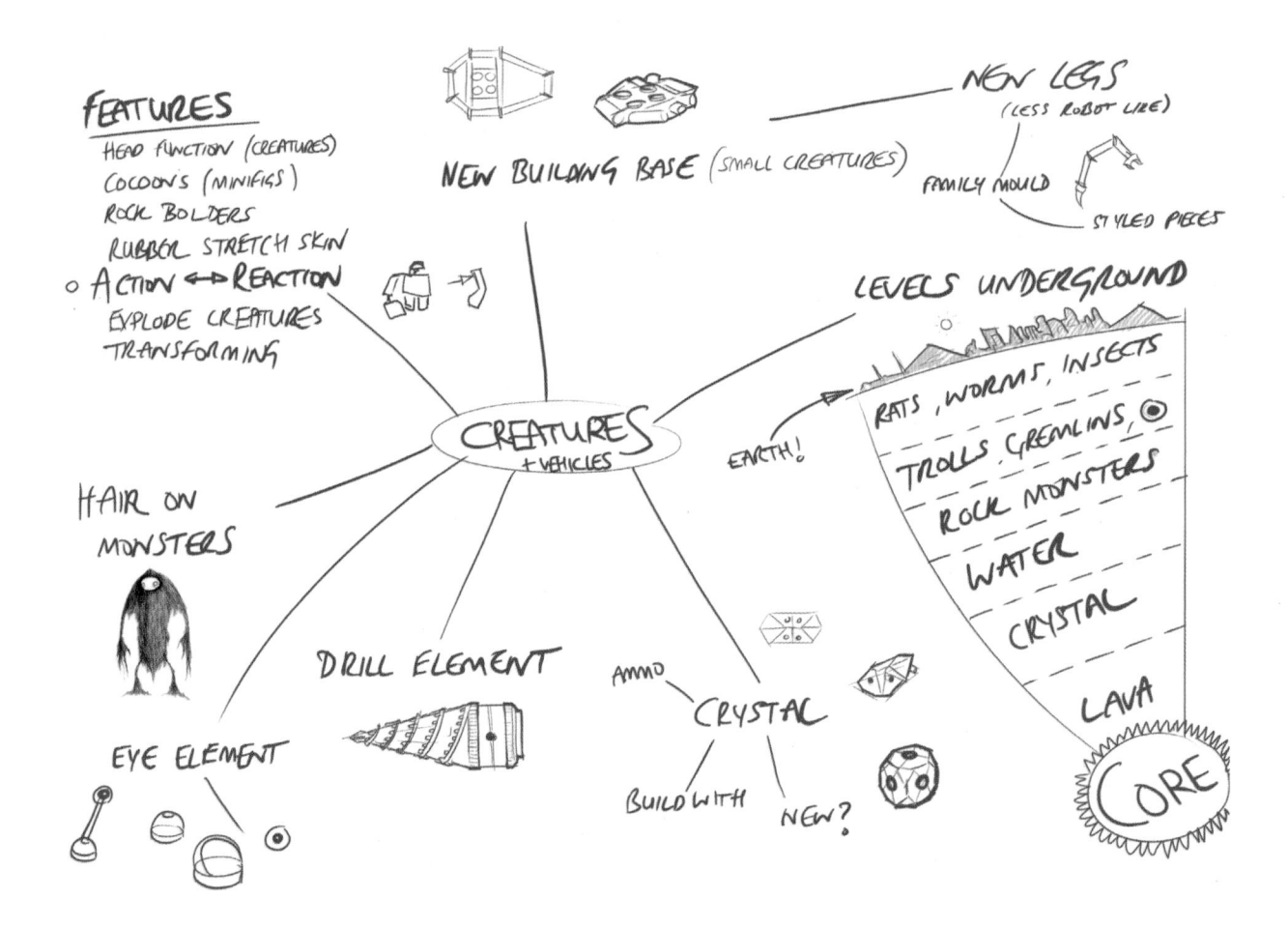

team within the company itself for whom this is their sole purpose. Currently that group is called Creative Play Lab or CPL; previous incarnations were named Front End and Concept Lab. There is also Advanced Concept Group or ACG, but their job is to look more at long-range trends than to develop specific product ideas.

Inputs from all these sources, often numbering in the hundreds, are eventually collected for a given brainstorming window. This was how what would become LEGO Power Miners, LEGO® Alien Conquest and LEGO® Space Police III began their journeys. Ideas can be very undefined and vague at this point. The whole idea might be 'underground explorers fighting rock monsters with big machines' or 'interstellar cops rounding up an eclectic collection of

ABOVE A designer in Concept Lab draws an idea for a future model.

ABOVE This early concept board shows the original idea of aliens versus farmers for the LEGO Space subtheme, Alien Conquest.

RIGHT In one concept tested with children, the LEGO Power Miners fight undead dinosaurs rather than Rock Monsters. This sketch also shows the beginnings of some of the theme's key vehicles.

space gangsters'. Then teams of designers, managers, marketers and others consider each idea. During this selection process, the funnel narrows from hundreds of ideas to several dozen. These are then developed further. What would this world look like? Who would the characters be? What types of models could be cool?

While designers may create early builds known as sketch models for some of these, the vast majority are drawn on storyboards. The designers use these boards to experiment and play with answers to all the questions about a new concept, mixing and matching different ideas. LEGO Alien Conquest would ultimately pit a high-tech defence force against the interstellar invaders, but an early concept, inspired by the cow abduction trope, pitted farmers in specially built farm equipment against the aliens.

BELOW The final aesthetic of LEGO Alien Conquest was very different from the original concept art, illustrating how themes change as they go through the development process.

BOTTOM This line-up of potential LEGO Space Police figures was shown to children to gauge their reactions. Most of these did not make the cut.

ABOVE A prototype model of a lava monster from LEGO Power Miners.

Concepts that test well move through the process. At this point there will be far fewer ideas so each one can receive more resources. Sketch models of potential key sets are built in droves. Characters are developed more deeply. These will all then be tested with children, along with more concept boards of possible minifigures and other aspects of potential themes to work out which aspects work best. Whole product lines may not make the cut if they cannot find a cohesive vision that consistently tests well.

Successful ideas for themes or models are consolidated into a brief for the designers, which explains the theme, lays out its test results, and makes a case for the number of frames which should be allotted to it. A new team is assembled for every short-lived theme, and designers who worked on concepts may well stay with it into the next part of the process. The brief will contain everything the newly minted design team needs: how many new models are required, how many of each type of frame they have, as well as sketch models and prototypes.

Even when themes have been determined, options within them are still open. Key models and elements may have prototypes and there will be a lot of sketches, but plenty of work remains to be done. Multiple options for each model are developed and tested with children. For every new set that finally makes it to shelves, between five and ten other possibilities may

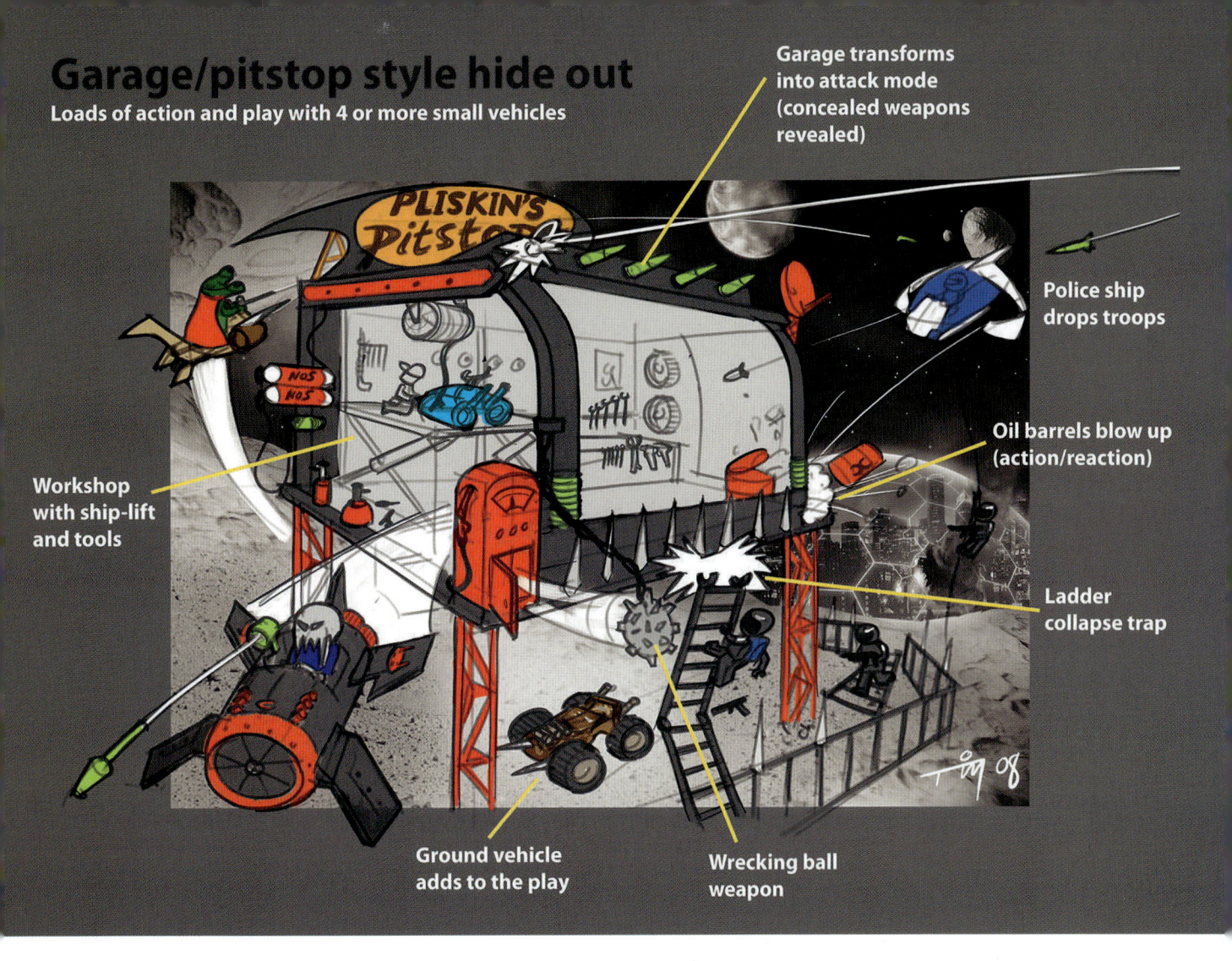

Garage/pitstop style hide out
Loads of action and play with 4 or more small vehicles

Garage transforms into attack mode (concealed weapons revealed)

Police ship drops troops

Oil barrels blow up (action/reaction)

Workshop with ship-lift and tools

Ladder collapse trap

Ground vehicle adds to the play

Wrecking ball weapon

have been considered and rejected. Team members work together to develop new elements that will be useful across their assigned theme, eventually utilising all their various new element frames, graphic-design frames and colour-change frames to instil that all-important novelty.

The options for each model are then peer reviewed by the Model Committee, Element Coach and Building Instruction teams. At this point the model is locked in the system, meaning its inventory can no longer be changed. The final step is generation of the all-important bill of materials, or BOM list, which goes to the factory.

When LEGO Power Miners and LEGO Space Police III hit shelves, phase three of product development's transformation was complete. The LEGO Group now had a functioning system for developing new ideas. Furthermore, provisions were in place to manage its all-important element count, ensuring that variants of pieces like wheels or cockpits are kept under control. Finally, there was a proven methodology for vetting new ideas to determine which had the best chance at succeeding. The importance of novelty had been recognised, in addition to the power of partnering with narrative powerhouses through licensing. The final mountain to conquer was the development of in-house stories as gripping as those of blockbuster movie franchises. To date, BIONICLE was the LEGO Group most successful venture on that front, but team members were learning, and believed some of their next ideas would produce bigger bangs than ever before.

ABOVE Notated sketches, such as this one from LEGO Space Police, are passed from conceptual teams to the model designers.

> "We realised this play theme, with its characters, world and mission, could be more than the sum of its parts!"

Philip McCormick, Discovery Facilitation Lead, the LEGO Group

10 Big Bangs

How the LEGO Group captured lightning in a bottle and developed its own universes.

TOP Designers created numerous prototypes before they perfected the innovative LEGO® NINJAGO® spinner.

ABOVE LEFT Ball joints opened up new building opportunities for figures, unique angles for vehicle panels and much more.

ABOVE RIGHT Collectible treasure keys in LEGO® Atlantis open the portal to the lost city of Atlantis.

In 2009, LEGO® designers began to think up ideas for a new, collectible play theme experience that was aimed primarily at boys ages seven to nine, which would also invite new children into the world of LEGO toys. For nearly a decade since its launch in 2000, BIONICLE® had been the standard bearer for this concept. With its collectible masks, expansive in-house universe and appeal to children who had never before touched normal LEGO bricks, BIONICLE was unique in the LEGO Group portfolio. Now, with the theme about to be retired, a new theme needed to take up the torch, and Front End, the LEGO Group internal think tank, had been tasked to work out what it was.

The LEGO Group recent play themes each had its own signature elements centred on creating unique figures. LEGO® Castle, launched in 2007, boasted a slew of new parts for different fantasy creatures, while in 2009 LEGO® Power Miners featured several Rock Monster variants, and LEGO® Space Police had a cadre of moulded alien minifigures. Each theme had successfully created novelty through the use of cool figures and accessories and the development of great sets around these figures and accessories, utilising mostly colour changes of existing parts.

Throughout the company, however, a desire to try something new was growing. Not since 2006, with the Japanese manga-styled LEGO® Exo-Force, had a theme with a big storyline been developed. Themes created alongside and after LEGO Exo-Force employed popular genres such as space gangsters or miners. Characters from these themes had names and unique elements, and their worlds had simple storylines that facilitated open-ended play. But now designers began thinking up ways to create bigger stories.

A team was assigned to develop the next theme and in the back of many minds was a growing desire to do something more ambitious – if only the opportunity would present itself. What happened next was so organic and multi-faceted that even those who lived it have a hard time remembering where all the ideas came from. However, all agree that a key piece was icons.

Looking for an icon

An icon, in this context, is something widely recognised and appealing to children across different cultures and countries; categories of characters or settings that immediately evoke certain universal images. Pirates, knights, extra-terrestrial invaders, cowboys, ancient tombs, distant moons, underwater exploration, dinosaurs, post-apocalyptic dystopias and ninja are all icons. These motifs represent go-to subject matter for toy makers, entertainment companies and authors due to their near-universal recognition and appeal. Each are reimagined every few years for a new generation. Competition within pop culture for icons is fierce and there is rarely room for more than one franchise to concurrently focus on any given subject.

The LEGO Group had always been careful to avoid icons that were actively being used in current movies or television shows. This was not a recent phenomenon, with examples of unreleased themes going back all the way to when minifigures were new. For example, in the 1980s, a LEGO theme based on ancient Rome was developed and nearly released. Centurion helmets, legionnaire shields, Corinthian column elements and more were all crafted by chopping up existing bricks or casting in tin. However, this theme never saw the light of day for fear that it too closely resembled *The Adventures of Asterix*, a popular European TV show at the time, which pitted the titular Gaul against the Ancient Romans. Children might have bought a LEGO set thinking it was licensed Asterix material and then been disappointed when none of the minifigures matched the on-screen characters.

Hosts of icons are fed into the LEGO Group product funnel at the start of every new development cycle and most are quickly discarded due to overlap with existing external properties. This was especially true in years past when, if any other entity, including both entertainment companies and fellow toymakers, were exploring a given icon, the LEGO Group would choose to pass and wait for it to become available another time. Such was the case this time around, with three icons that entered the pipeline as no major entertainment properties were currently exploring them: deep sea, robot dinosaurs and insect invasion. Alongside them was another one, a 'wild-card concept', which denotes the idea as being a little 'out there' but thrown in out of curiosity to gauge reactions: future ninja. (At the time, the most well-known ninja property, Teenage Mutant Ninja Turtles, was in between major TV shows and would not appear in Michael Bay's movie reboot until 2014.)

Initial concept boards were sketched for all four proposals and shown to children. Somewhat surprisingly, future ninja tested better than robot dinosaurs, so it joined deep sea and insect invasion on P-gate's other side, where general ideas for elements and characters began to be developed.

Heads, keys and tentacles

Not surprisingly, alien figures were a focus for insect invasion. Designers sketched possible methods for adding elongation to minifigure heads through a hair-like attachment, as well as creating options for new hands, arms, legs and feet. Each could be configured with freshly imagined faceprints to create different named invaders with disparate personalities. These would eventually be abandoned in favour of entirely special head elements of more generic aliens, the insect concept having been shelved for later.

Under the sea had been explored just a few years previously with LEGO® Aqua Raiders, a one-year-only theme from 2007. Customer feedback had indicated that children loved the oversized, brick-built sea creatures included in every set, but the challenge had been to create sustained play scenarios with fighting animals. In order to provide an engaging objective, each set had included a treasure for the divers to find, but these recoloured goblets and jewels dated back to Johnny Thunder and his LEGO® Adventurers almost a decade earlier. 'Fantasy-era' LEGO Castle in 2007 and LEGO® Power Miners in 2009 had sought to provide a great deal more character-based conflict, as well as compelling missions. Now, for the new underwater theme, designers were itching to add even more drama. Before long, the mythical lost city of Atlantis was floated as a possible execution for underwater exploration, and with it the idea of keys.

Atlantis would be accessed through a portal which could only be opened via special keys. Searching for them would be the mission's backbone and the focus of most sets. Once collected, each key would be put into a corresponding slot on the lost city's doorway to open its portal. Such an approach hit all the brief's high notes. Since multiple keys would be needed, each could be unique and collectible. In an attempt to further distinguish itself from the brick-

ABOVE A sketch shows possible approaches for creating new alien figures for the theme that would become LEGO® Alien Conquest.

built animals from the LEGO Aqua Raiders theme, designers developed multiple concepts for large moulded elements. These elements would snap together into sea creatures, including enormous serpents and turtles, in the style of LEGO® Dino 2010 from 2005. Several of these pieces were designed and prototyped to various extents before ultimately being abandoned: the number of frames available meant it would not have been possible to give each set a unique creature. Instead, special minifigure-compatible elements were sculpted, which enabled the creation of hybrid human/sea creatures. Octopus legs and shark heads were particular favourites – and, as a bonus, such pieces ticked the box for novel figures, which was a universal goal during these years.

But it was one of the other new proposals, future ninja, that proved the most challenging. While it had passed initial testing, support for it was not entirely universal. In the popular imagination, ninja were sneaky assassins who worked alone and had almost no variation in their looks or mission; how could interesting, long-lasting play experiences be made out of them? However, exploring ideas which may initially seem doomed is the whole point of wild-card concepts, so work continued. Even at this early date, the ninja team believed it might be on to something special and had already started to think of how to make ninja work, using Batman as a precedent.

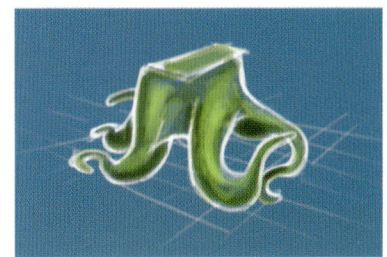

ABOVE A concept sketch and subsequent detail drawing for a human/octopus hybrid, which would become the Squid Warrior minifigure in LEGO Atlantis. The brand-new tentacles element would fit beneath a standard minifigure torso and opened up whole new worlds of LEGO minifigure modification and character building. Similar techniques would be used for snakes in LEGO® NINJAGO®.

The Secret Life of LEGO® Bricks

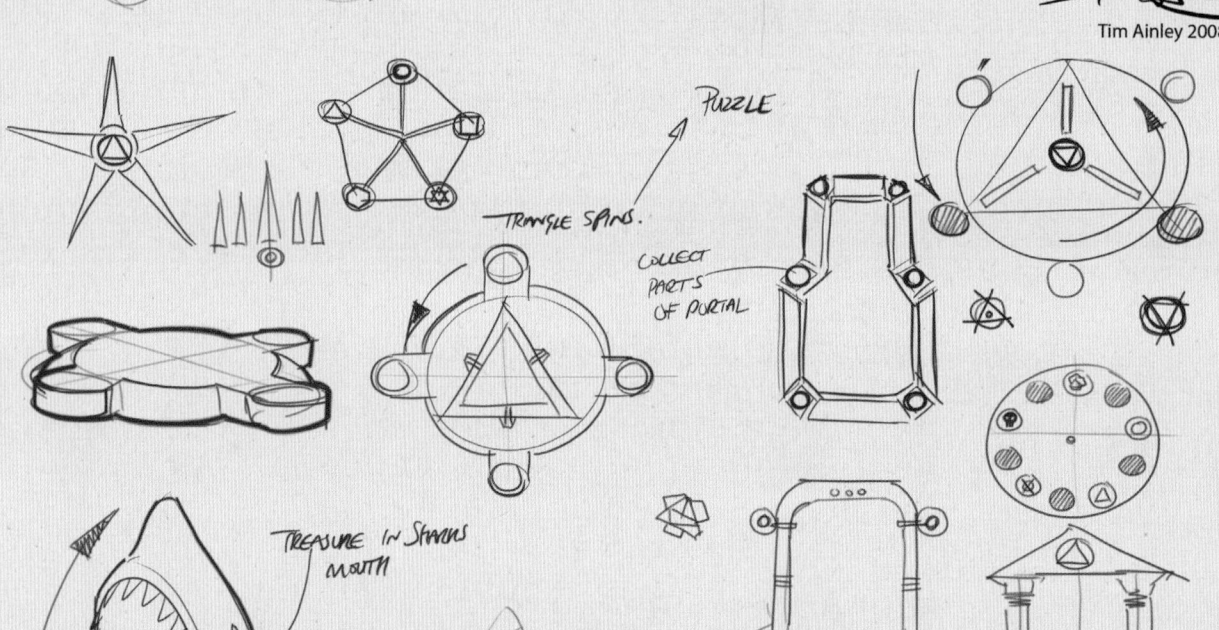

CAN BE MOULDED

TECHNIC TRI-PIECE

3.18 ELEMENT

3.18 SYSTEM

Tim Ainley 2008

PUZZLE

TRIANGLE SPINS.

COLLECT PARTS OF PORTAL

TREASURE IN SHARKS MOUTH

PORTAL IN SHARKS MOUTH

ROTATES

Tim 08

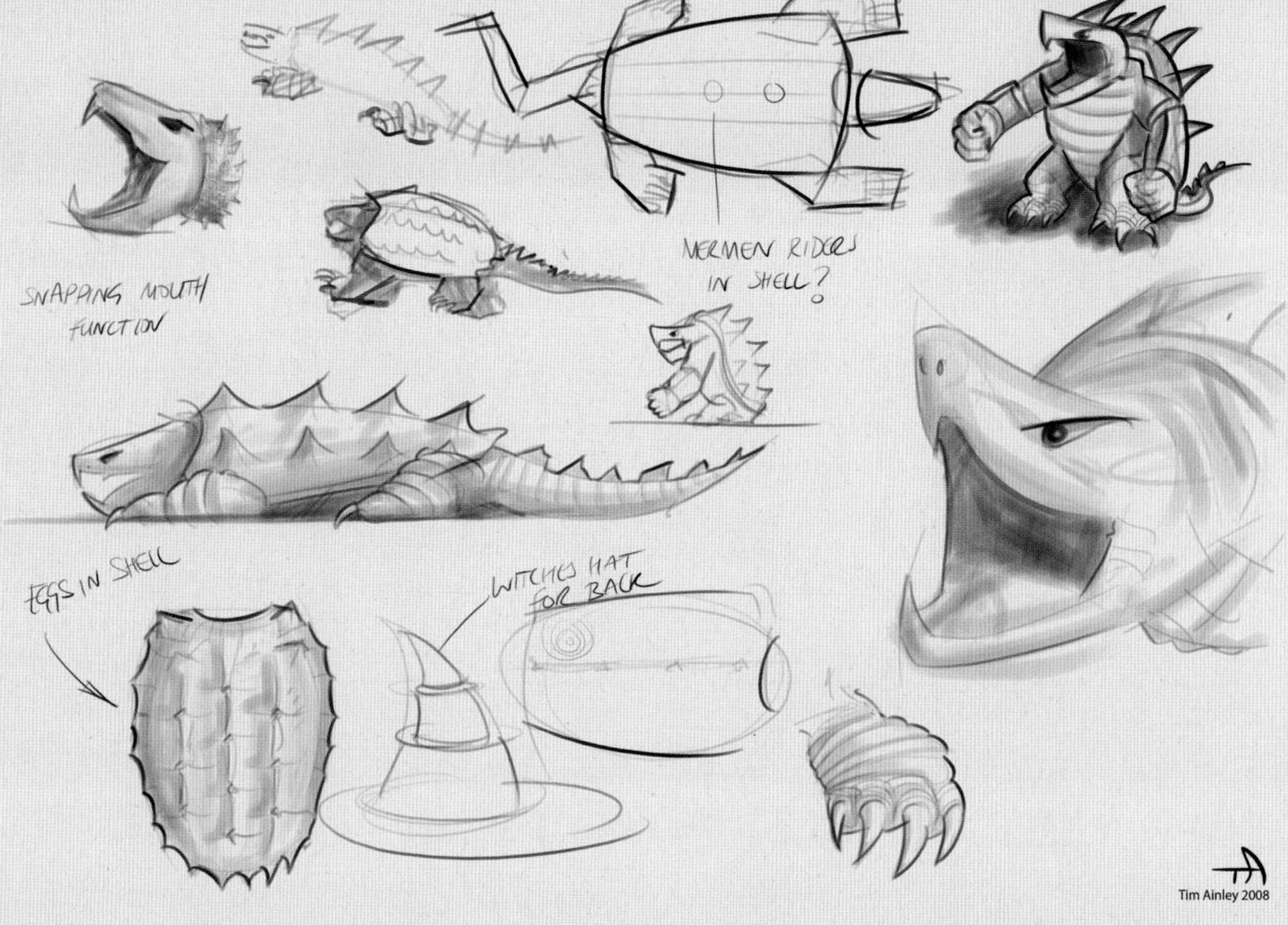

Big Bangs 257

ABOVE Conceptual artworks created for LEGO Atlantis, showing a giant turtle, which became set 8079 Shadow Snapper, and a head element for a sea serpent.

ABOVE LEFT These early sketches show ideas for possible 'treasure keys' for the theme that would become LEGO Atlantis.

BELOW LEFT Initial ideas for a portal into which the various key elements would be placed in LEGO Atlantis.

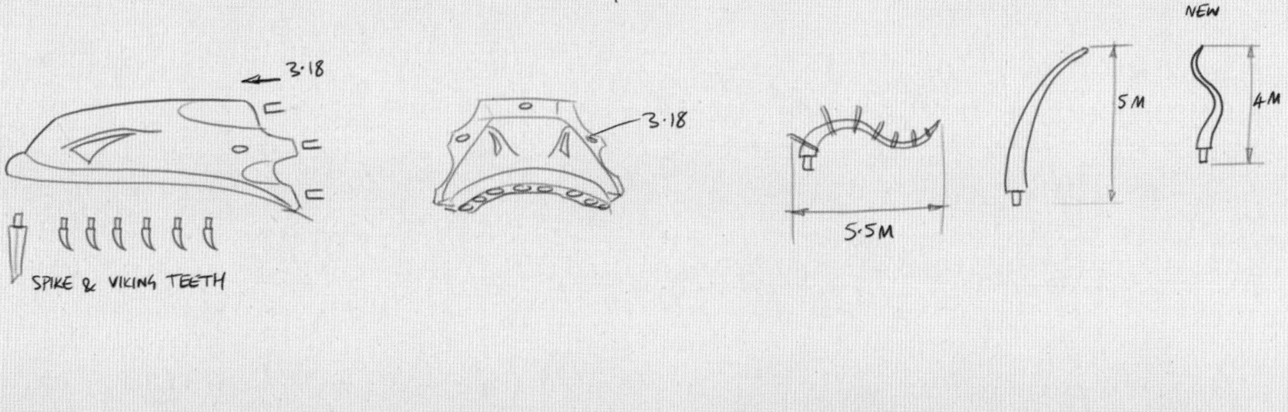

Dark inspiration

The Dark Knight provided inspiration for the team developing the ninja concept. While Batman did dress in black then stealthily sneak around to get the drop on enemies, he also utilised an array of cool gadgets and, most importantly, vehicles. The Dark Knight had been popular with every generation of children since his introduction at the end of the 1930s. Initially, the LEGO designers' idea was to make their ninja team more like a group of secret agents. An early development note at Front End goes so far as to draw inspiration, and possible direction, from a previous LEGO theme. The note read, 'Alpha Team done in Japanese style'. Front End was referencing a theme that dropped three waves between 2001 and 2005. LEGO® Alpha Team included a group of agents, each with a name and a special skill, facing off against supervillain Ogel. There was little character development beyond generic traits like 'pilot' or 'demolitions expert' and that was how future ninja was originally imagined; except, instead of general skills, the figures would be masters of various weapons. Conceptual elements for realising this vision soon followed.

Initially, the future ninja concept included four ninja students, each with a weapons specialisation, setting off on a mission to rescue their kidnapped 'old master' from the ominously named 'Dark One' and his troop of ninja clones. Matching each team member's mastery would be new parts, specifically shurikens, spears, swords and nunchakus. Additionally, in a throwback to the masks created for BIONICLE, unique hair and visor elements complemented each armament. All these various parts were brought together into a new concept board that was once again presented to children.

Showing the concept board highlighted some challenges with the new theme. One early idea was to give each ninja their own visor or helmet that would correspond to specific skills and powers. While masks worked well on large BIONICLE figures, similar concepts didn't scale well at minifigure size. It was also not intuitive for children to distinguish between the good guys and bad guys when face wear was this small. Front End took several important messages from this test. First, they needed to regroup and develop characters more. Each side needed to be distinctive; everything was on the table at this point, including non-human options for both good guys and bad. Second, children were responding well to images of special armaments and

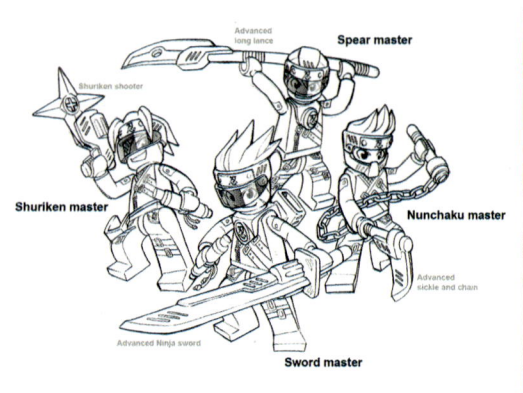

ABOVE One of the earliest element concept sketches from Front End's ninja theme gave an indication of the range of new LEGO pieces that designers had in mind, including ninja weapons, cool visors and unique hairpieces.

RIGHT This concept board shows the first ninja concept, with evil ninja clones and the heroes wearing similar, white outfits.

> "There was a big moment in the development of LEGO NINJAGO in around 2009 where we realised that it didn't have to be just generic ninja; it could be an IP. Previously, we'd had generic miners, ghost hunters, police, space police and so on. But this was the first time where we felt we could create a cast of characters that could have more than just names but also back stories and developed character traits. We felt that the theme could resonate and potentially compete with all the other stories that are occupying the head space of children. We realised this play theme, with its characters, world and mission, could be more than the sum of its parts!"

Philip McCormick, Discovery Facilitation Lead, the LEGO Group

armour, which suggested that missions that revolved around trying to acquire sacred weapons might work well. Despite solid progress, it was clear to everyone that 'future ninja' still needed work. For this reason, it was eventually decided to proceed with LEGO Atlantis first, which would buy more time for developing ninja. That decision would prove more important than anyone could have possibly realised.

Alien Clingers and ninja hoods

Setting was the next major consideration for all three themes. Atlantis tested and scored well; children knew that legend. The lost city was almost an icon in its own right and hadn't been utilised extensively since Disney's 2001 film, far enough back in time that a new LEGO play theme would feel fresh and new. Insects were officially shelved for the alien-invasion theme, though they would serve as villains just a few years later in LEGO® Galaxy Squad, launched in 2013. This LEGO Space subtheme transitioned the action from Earth to conflict between intergalactic bugs and spacefaring humans, more akin to the long-popular *StarCraft* franchise. For this round, now officially called LEGO Alien Conquest, a more straightforward storyline and setting was selected. Saucer-shaped UFOs would invade LEGO® City, allowing for easy crossover play with that theme's products, meaning Alien Conquest could skew slightly lower in its target-age demographic.

ABOVE One of the ideas for non-human ninja heroes: dragon ninja!

An element emerged as a key aspect in the invasion story: the 'alien pet' (later called an Alien Clinger). Moulded as a cute, if vaguely creepy, extra-terrestrial, it could also fit over minifigure heads like a hat – to suck out its victim's brainpower! Defending humanity would be the Alien Defence Unit, a futuristic agency whose vehicles were not so advanced that they looked out of place in LEGO City. Thanks to an extensive catalogue of spaceship elements from LEGO® *Star Wars*™, designers could easily generate models for Earth's defenders. Once again, future ninja emerged as the challenge.

Front End wasn't sure where in time to place its new theme. While future ninja had been the original idea, initial responses to super-futuristic versions had been muted. Children expected to see ninja, not secret agents with ninja-style weapons. The LEGO Group think tank realised that a key part of the ninja icon was distinctive hooded robes. Whatever headpieces were ultimately developed would need to be traditional and immediately recognisable. This realisation would, conveniently, free up a new element frame. The LEGO Group had previously delved into ninja during a short-lived theme from the late 1990s. All the minifigure outfits had been strictly traditional ninja and shogun garb, exactly what children were now indicating they wanted. Amazingly, these moulds were still in existence. Deference for classical outfits raised another important question: if children wanted traditional heroes, did that also mean they would prefer a historical setting with almost generic heroes? In other words, did they want the exact opposite of 'LEGO Alpha Team in Japan'? Resolving that query became vital, as it would heavily inform everything else.

Defining the ninja world

Front End representatives returned to testing rooms armed with three new boards, each showing a drastically different time period for their theme: past, present and future. Past borrowed heavily from the recent success of 'Fantasy-era' LEGO Castle and even a bit of LEGO® Vikings. Undead warriors rode ships and skeletal horses under the watchful eye of a reanimated dragon built, at least partially, of Constraction elements. Ninja dressed in matching traditional outfits rode forth to meet this nightmare army from a Japanese-style castle equipped with catapults. The ninja were mounted either on horses or a flying bird, whose headpiece would eventually be used in sets such as 75952 LEGO® Fantastic Beasts™ Newt's Case of Magical Creatures, released in 2018.

An option for setting the theme in the present utilised the backdrop of a modern-day Asian-style city in which vehicles, just slightly futuristic in appearance, were placed. Essentially, this was 'LEGO Alien Conquest in Japan', but with cyborg shoguns as the invaders. Ninja rode cool motorcycles and cars built from shape elements. They battled against mechanised animals that looked like hybrids of scorpions and snakes, each constructed of the ball joints that had been utilised in LEGO Exo-Force short-lived final wave.

Finally, the concept board for a futuristic setting depicted an advanced cityscape with layers of roads and buildings. This option was the purest incarnation of 'LEGO Alpha Team in a Japanese setting'. Teams of ninja faced off high above the metropolis amid buildings crackling with electricity; the ninja wielded energy-based weapons in addition to more typical ninja armaments. Shown these three concepts, children were definitive: the present-day setting was the clear winner.

With the timeframe now defined, designers turned to creating characters and an overall mission for their theme, using what was now a familiar pattern: new concept boards and tests. Again, they presented three possible approaches. In each, the ninja characters were completely generic, all wearing exactly the same outfits, which concealed their different faces beneath. No trace was present of what would eventually become Kai, Jay, Zane, Cole, Nya and Lloyd. These traditional ninja faced off in three different missions against a trio of possible options for bad guys.

ABOVE The Face Clinger – LEGO Alien Conquest version of the Facehugger from the *Alien* films!

TOP The cityscape from the future-based option for LEGO NINJAGO would be used later as inspiration for NINJAGO City in the theatrical movie.

ABOVE An early sketch model depicting the action shown in the metropolis concept board. This approach would eventually become Nindroids in the rebooted LEGO NINJAGO toy range in 2014 and the dragon temple would be refined into set 2507 Fire Temple, released in 2011.

One option depicted cyborg shoguns in a Japanese metropolis fighting over sacred weapons ensconced in a dragon temple. In another option, the dragon temple was placed adjacent to an evil-looking cityscape belching out pollution and populated by rough-looking biker gangs with a penchant for purple. Finally, the dragon temple, with its weapons to be defended, was placed among mountains across a lake from an evil fort, which looked to have drawn inspiration from He-Man's Castle Grayskull! In this scenario, bird men with unique heads flew dragons against the ninja heroes.

What is fascinating about these boards is that aspects of each would eventually get produced in some form. The cyborg shoguns and aesthetic style of their mechanical creatures map almost perfectly onto the Nindroids from what would become the rebooted line for LEGO NINJAGO in 2014. Biker gangs who loved purple would eventually serve as the primary antagonists in 2018's Sons of Garmadon wave. Most notably, the mountain scene's bird creatures looked like they were straight from LEGO® Legends of Chima™, the next big theme that would follow LEGO NINJAGO. LEGO Chima would, in fact, grow out of discarded ideas for animal-based bad guys from LEGO NINJAGO. Finally, the dragon temple housing sacred weapons had already emerged as a must-do and that conclusion was only reinforced by further testing. After multiple prototypes, it would eventually be refined into 2507 Fire Temple, the flagship set from the first wave of LEGO NINJAGO.

Even after so many tests and concept boards, Front End wasn't even halfway finished by this point in the story. Eventually some members of the team would be present for tests with over 800 children. In order to facilitate such high volumes, a selection of concept-board backgrounds would be reused with different combinations of options for good guys, bad guys, vehicles and accessories inserted on top of them. Sometimes twenty different options would be tested in one go to see which aspects children responded to. If a motorcycle, sword or villain was consistently noticed across multiple boards, it was a sign the team was on to something. Popular inclusions would then be taken back and developed into prototype parts, sketch models and further concept boards.

ABOVE Prototypes of ninja weapons were brought to tests with children as the theme became further developed.

Through this testing process, the team learned dozens of important lessons. First, villains shouldn't be other ninja: ultimately undead skeletons would be selected as the villains, winning out over both traditional samurai variants and a version reminiscent of the Terminator! Second, good guys should ride dragons – but bad guys should not. Third, vehicles should be big, cool and used primarily by villains, though some use by ninja was ok too. Finally, children didn't want generic ninja – they wanted personalities underneath those traditional robes. Children wanted to connect with their characters, to see a bit of themselves reflected in the robed heroes. The developers at Front End eventually settled on the idea of unique ninja distinguished by colour, preferred weapon, skill set (musician, adventurer, tech-savvy, and so on) and, most importantly, their own small dragon. That last aspect was key, since it was going to be how the ninja theme met the brief's demand for collectability. Entry into this product line would be through inexpensive dragon sets, each with a ninja minifigure included. Best of all, the team had an idea for new elements to create these creatures.

BELOW LEFT In tests, children looked at various options for skeleton-based bad guys for LEGO NINJAGO – including a Terminator-style, cyborg version!

BELOW RIGHT An early idea for how the ninja might look underneath their robes, with interests suggesting personalities.

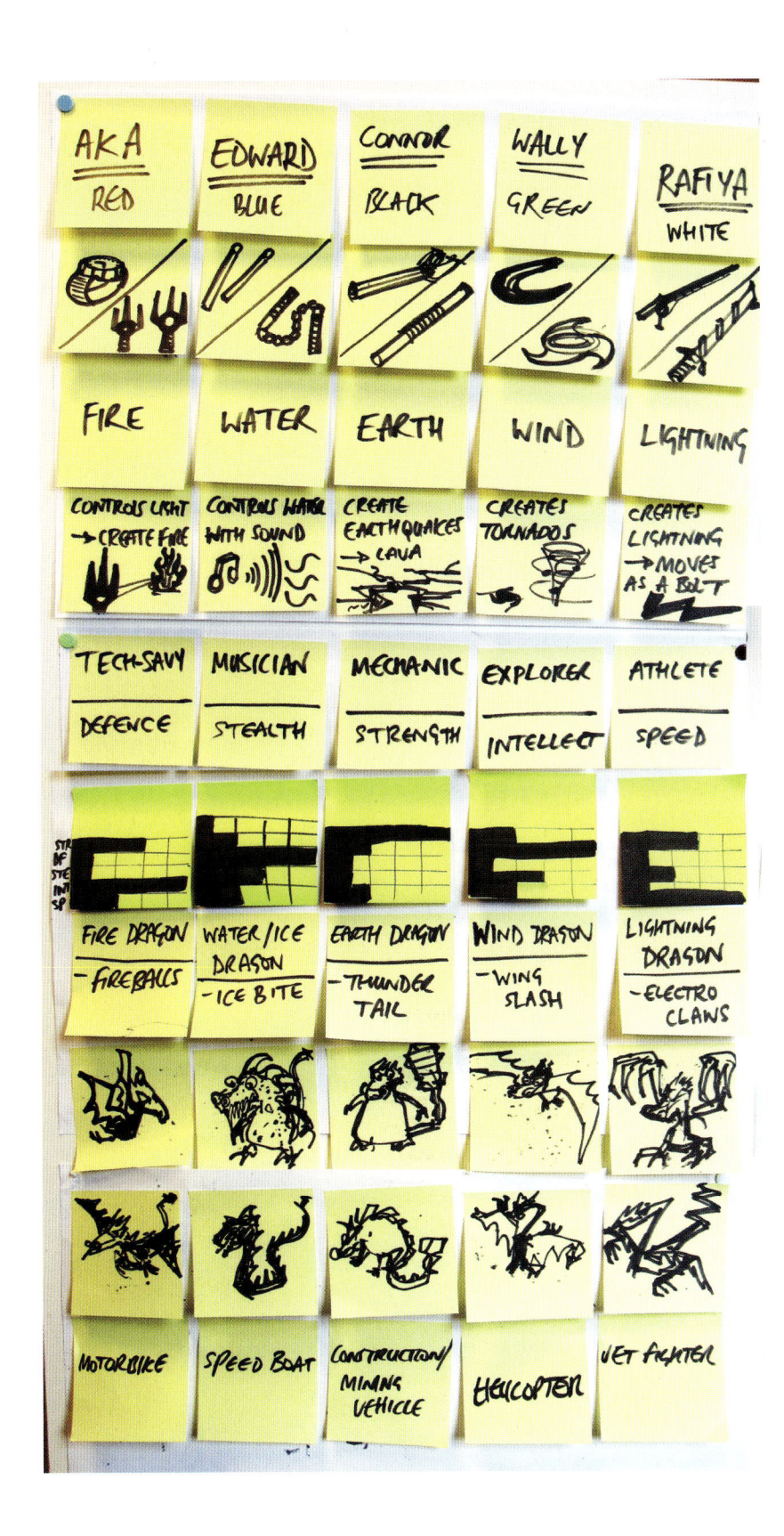

LEFT Developers made grids of sticky notes to map out the unique features of the ninja. Each character's unique dragon has been sketched towards the bottom.

Collectible dragons and ninja spinners

Setting out to create collectible ninja dragons, the development team wanted to avoid using construction-style ball-and-socket joints, which didn't look organic enough. Instead, the developers envisioned a new class of components: mini-ball joints. Each would work in the same way as their larger cousins, but, at a fraction of the size, they would not stand out so much in a model and be easier to conceal, while still imbuing excellent functionality.

Prototypes of mini-ball joints were made for inclusion in the collectible dragons envisioned for the first wave of LEGO NINJAGO. However, they turned out to be far trickier to get right than expected. Obtaining enough friction so that limbs wouldn't droop, but not so much that they were hard to move, proved challenging on the drastically reduced surface area available. It quickly became clear that there was no way they could be perfected in time. Mini-ball joints were not abandoned, however, and all the kinks were eventually ironed out. Several designers who worked on LEGO NINJAGO went on to join the team for LEGO Legends of Chima and they resurrected them for a similar use. Mini-ball joints debuted in LEGO Chima in rideable creatures called Legend Beasts, with essentially the exact purpose for which they were originally envisioned. Those elements have gone on to be used extensively in numerous themes.

Eliminating small-scale dragons meant that something different would be needed for meeting the brief's mandate for collectability. Fortunately, side efforts had been churning along in parallel. A creative lead had come to one of the element designers with an idea: spinning. He asked: 'Could the ninja be turning when they fought, spinning super-fast like a tornado?' He then asked if an element could be developed that would facilitate this type of play to such an extent that there could be a clear win-lose outcome. In other words, could minifigures spar?

Initially, brick-built attempts at the idea were constructed but none proved acceptable. Next, moulded versions were sculpted, inspired by traditional spinning tops. Designers resisted using weights for a long time in an effort to keep costs down, but eventually acquiesced to integrating brass because it dramatically improved performance. Ultimately, over a hundred different prototypes were developed for what would become the famous spinners used in LEGO NINJAGO, as the designers homed in on what they believed was a dynamite play experience. They tested multiple types of methods for competition before settling on a final approach. Children would mount their minifigure characters on spinners

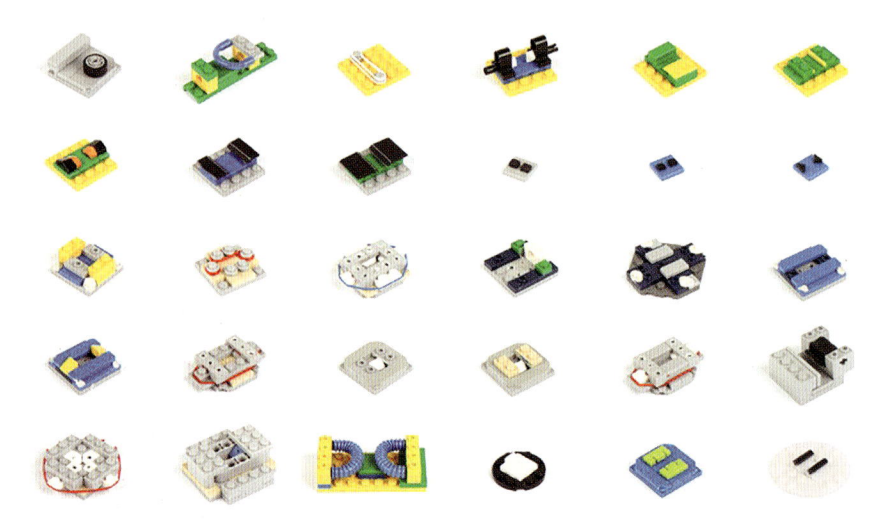

RIGHT Early brick-built prototypes of what would become LEGO NINJAGO spinners.

> Product safety said the spinners won't work because of the risk of a minifigure with a weapon in its hand flying into someone's eye. So then we were back to zero and I was almost crying. I had to get out of the office, so I went sailing. I was sitting there in my dinghy, and looking at the waves gave me an idea. I made 3D-printed prototypes of a part that holds the minifigure's feet, but which can go up and down as the spinner rotates, allowing the minifigure to 'fall' out instead of springing out. My name is on the patent for this eject function!

**Klaus Elias Nielsen, Manager Specialist,
Student Front End, the LEGO Group**

and launch them towards one another in jousting matches, with the loser getting flung sky-high. After countless hours and more prototypes than they could keep track of, a successful version was finally developed that utilised a spring-loaded ejector function. Then came a major setback.

Product testing determined that the spinner design would never pass toy safety standards. The risk of a ninja minifigure holding weapons getting accidentally shot into the eyes of children would not fly – or, rather, might fly too well. Thankfully, the lead prototype designer got some inspiration from a nearby waterway and solved the problem.

Spinners nearly blew the roof off the testing facility when children got their hands on them. The coordinator confided to the team that she had never seen such strong positive reactions. In her words, 'You have a megahit on your hands.' Her words would prove prophetic. LEGO NINJAGO, as the theme which began as 'future ninja' was ultimately named, began to form into something truly special. Up until this point there had been many disparate 'streams', as they are called within the LEGO Group – meaning teams who look after story, elements, characters, collectability and so on. With LEGO NINJAGO, all the streams were coalescing into something unlike anything the LEGO Group had ever created. Something much greater than the sum of its parts was emerging. Then came the final piece.

As LEGO Atlantis was in its final stages of development, someone suggested a new idea. By that time multiple licensed themes had proved successful. The LEGO Group had seen first-hand the power of a movie, both with *Star Wars* and several direct-to-video BIONICLE films. What if LEGO Atlantis had a short movie? Its distinctive elements, especially the minifigure/sea creature hybrid pieces, were perfect for creating compelling visuals. However, creating animation for the small screen was no simple task. The LEGO Group would have to finance the entire venture itself and then find a network willing to broadcast it. Eventually they took the gamble and it paid off. LEGO Atlantis received a twenty-two-minute TV special, which helped increase awareness of the theme and drive upfront sales. LEGO NINJAGO team pushed for a similar approach and then suggested an even more daring idea. What about an entire TV show?

Big bangs

The term 'big bang' had floated around the LEGO Group before LEGO NINJAGO as the description of a new theme's dream outcome: that it would produce a big impact on customers. LEGO NINJAGO, however, changed the term from an aspiration to the proper name for a new class of LEGO theme. This was accomplished by inadvertently creating the formula that every subsequent big-bang theme has followed. This formula consists of four parts: a well-developed universe to explore, strong characters for children to explore it through, a TV show or similar

ABOVE Prototypes were created to test different methods for holding a minifigure in a LEGO NINJAGO spinner.

media for telling the world's story, and the vague X-factor. X-factors are the great challenge of big bangs, and are what ultimately allowed LEGO NINJAGO to succeed so much more than LEGO Atlantis, which had the other three traits. X-factors are something cool and different that attract children who were not previously interested in LEGO toys. Difficult to pin down, and highly variable in their success, X-factors have become the de facto trait that distinguish big bangs from regular themes. LEGO NINJAGO spinners reign supreme as the single greatest X-factor ever developed, but every big bang which followed would have their own as well. Now, creating X-factors is a separate stream in the development process, with teams devoted exclusively to developing them, working alongside more traditional set and element designers.

LEGO NINJAGO launched in 2011 with the novelty spinners and its own TV special. Reception for the special was high enough to justify an entire TV show. Thankfully, several key people within the LEGO Group had foreseen this and pushed for investment in writing a full season of episodes before the special even aired. When it succeeded, they were able to transition completed scripts into production and get the show on air quickly enough that LEGO NINJAGO was still on the public's radar. Children tuned in and the show would go on to notch season after season.

Spinners were modified into actual tornados for the TV show, coining a new phrase, 'spinjitzu', which became common parlance for the toys as well. While the LEGO Group realised they had a megahit on their hands – LEGO NINJAGO spinners were the top-selling toy in Germany for 2011 and schools in Sweden had to ban them from the playground – the company still planned for

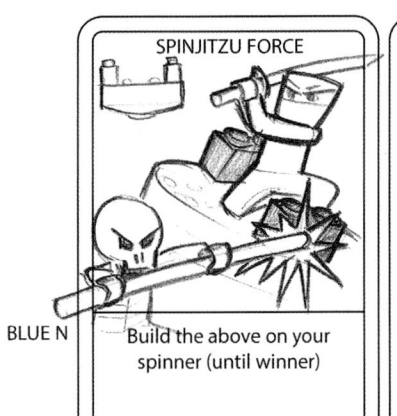

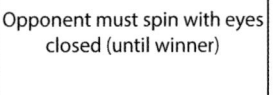

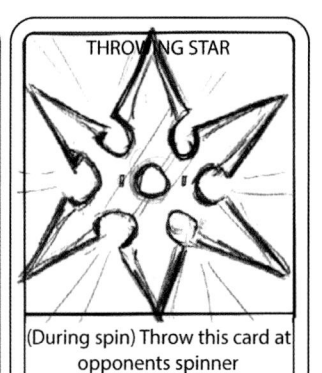

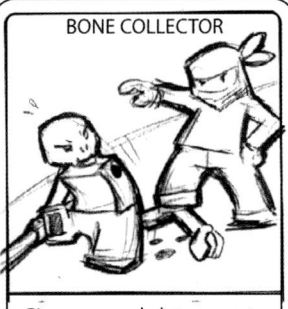

BELOW Playing cards served as an important link between the LEGO NINJAGO TV show and its toys. They were included in spinner starter sets and described different powers and rules for sparring.

ABOVE The LEGO Group uses this tool to evaluate possible themes. A healthy product portfolio should have entries in all four quadrants and never have two concurrent themes that occupy the same spot on the graph.

ABOVE The designers in the LEGO Legends of Chima theme considered making a tribe called Prehistorics, which would have included minifigures sporting dinosaur heads.

BELOW Legends of Chima included new animal-head-shaped 'helmets' that fitted over regular minifigure heads, as well as the brand-new olive-green colour for the crocodile tribe.

LEGO NINJAGO to be replaced by a new theme in three years' time. So it greenlit the next idea that had been testing well in the funnel, a world based on anthropomorphic animals inspired by discarded concepts for animal-based ninja villains. When LEGO NINJAGO flamed out in a couple years, they would be ready. To protect this future theme, no LEGO NINJAGO bad guys would be animals, other than snakes for year two.

The complexity of colour

In many ways, LEGO Legends of Chima was even more ambitious than LEGO NINJAGO. The LEGO Group had developed a simple tool for evaluating possible play themes that graded concepts on two scales: fantasy versus reality and high- versus low-conflict play. (For the LEGO Group, healthy conflict is a natural part of children's play but never means products that promote or encourage violence.) This pair of continuums were represented on a simple graph, with level of conflict on the x-axis and realism on the y-axis, thereby defining four quadrants that specified the major types of themes that could be developed. The pairing of high reality/low conflict found its truest form with LEGO® Friends. High reality/high conflict can be seen most clearly in offerings like the police subtheme within LEGO City, where cops chase robbers, only for them to escape from jail and start the cycle over again. High fantasy/low conflict is well illustrated by LEGO® Disney Princess. LEGO NINJAGO occupied a spot that was deemed low reality/medium conflict. Its world and elements should be somewhat familiar, and the ninja hung out and had other interests beyond just fighting. LEGO Legends of Chima would be different, occupying the furthest extreme of the final quadrant: high fantasy/high conflict.

The types of elements needed by themes are also influenced by where the theme lies on the grid. Offerings which are utterly realistic will need eye-catching elements to infuse novelty within otherwise everyday scenes. LEGO City has introduced pieces that mimic squirting water from fire engines, launch nets from police helicopters or allow for creating modular roadways. All involve new components or, in the case of roadways, new families of elements. The goal is simple: to bring novelty to a familiar context. Conversely, high fantasy entails making products that look completely different from everyday life. This can be accomplished in two ways using parts: either by generating a range of new components or by effecting extensive colour changes on large swathes of existing elements. LEGO Legends of Chima chose the most extreme version of option two: creating a whole new colour.

New element colours are, in some ways, more complicated than original elements. The LEGO colour palette has a set total number of entries that does not change, so the addition of a new colour requires the deletion of an existing one. This can be a monumental logistical effort, as the entire company must be canvassed to make sure no team needs the colour up for deletion. The world of Chima evolved through the design process to consist of multiple animal tribes all vying for the mystical CHI, an energy source represented by a new element that looked like

> LEGO NINJAGO was successful as the first mover – a theme designed internally as if it were a big franchise. It had an action toy: the spinners. But timing was also important. It came out at the right time and there was a void to be filled: there was a space for it.

Tommy Andreasen, Senior Manager, Entertainment Development, the LEGO Group

a transparent crystal. Numerous species of animals were considered for tribes, and the theme would eventually count gorillas, elephants, wolves and even skunks within its ranks. At one point, designers contemplated creating extinct animals, including a tribe of dinosaur minifigures with special moulded heads. Eventually, however, it was decided that the setting was fanciful enough and only living animals should be included. To that end, lions and crocodiles were selected as the initial warring tribes. Special 'helmets' in the form of these animals' heads were moulded, but designers wanted more distinction. They wanted a new colour for the crocodiles.

Ultimately, LEGO Legends of Chima secured permission to introduce olive green, and used it extensively alongside traditional and dark green to create a distinctive aesthetic for the crocodile tribe. Their muted, marshy tones stood in stark contrast to the bright yellows and dark reds of the opposing lion tribe. Together, these colours helped give the whole theme the fantastical quality that designers wanted.

Securing permission to introduce a new colour was not the only parts-related logistical challenge LEGO Legends of Chima faced. Another challenge was much more technical: printing. Having spent almost all of its frame allotment on casting a number of existing elements in olive green, the team's remaining budget honed in on the unique animal helmets for its characters.

Graphic designers had dreamed up a range of ultra-detailed figures with exquisite face printing and colouring. Originally, they created moulded heads, but eventually those were

ABOVE Lion leader Laval and his team went through a lot of iterations. An early version saw the tribes more as groups of allies than uniform species. Every iteration, however, included detailed face prints.

> Sometimes new elements have surfaces that require the manufacture of a new machine part just to hold the element firmly enough to allow the print to be done. That was the case for LEGO Chima. There are also challenges with getting the machine to print everything in the right place on certain designs. Minifigure heads, if they are printed, need to be printed back and front at the same time. It's why the LEGO torso has a little colour strip on the stub that sticks out for the head to attach to. That little colour field is for the machine to know which side is front and back when the arms are coming on.

**Tore Magelund Harmark-Alexandersen,
Senior Designer, the LEGO Group**

replaced in favour of the helmet approach so that they could be swapped around to different figures more easily. Such an ability was deemed important so that children could easily play storylines where someone from one tribe disguised themselves as another while still retaining their identity. The level of detail on those helmets, however, needed to remain the same as fully moulded variants and this was where challenges emerged. Chima heads had more irregular surfaces that needed printing than any previous elements. A single component might feature furled brows, double curved surfaces, bulges, protruding teeth and concave curves – all at once. The LEGO Group utilises a printing technology where flexible pads pick up paint and then press onto elements to apply graphics. Each piece must be held firmly in place in order to resist the force as designs are stamped onto it. Pads can flex, but that also means they will deform slightly, which is a challenge for graphic designers, who have to take into account how much the pad will have deformed at each point along a graphic's length and width. LEGO Legends of Chima had all these challenges at once and required the implementation of new equipment and techniques in the printing department. These technologies and the new capabilities they enabled were utilised throughout the company, which is why minifigure decoration became even more detailed after Legends of Chima. There was only one thing missing: an X-factor.

The search for a new X-factor element

Spinners for LEGO NINJAGO had been the result of an internal idea, but the X-factor for LEGO Legends of Chima came about somewhat by chance through an almost throwaway graphic. Like its predecessor, an enormous number of concept boards were created and tested with children throughout the development process. One batch of them included what was called a 'small lion motorcycle'. This particular board was intended more to test environment and creatures; the few vehicles included were primarily filler, sitting in the mid background and having little action centred around them. However, each tester noted that children were drawn to the little motorcycle, which was so small they could have been forgiven for not noticing it all. Design notes in the test report contained the following quote: 'Not many vehicles in this board! But boys liked the ones shown – especially the small lion motorcycle, which attracted a lot of comments and attention.' Developers homed in on that interest and began to wonder whether this little vehicle could be turned into something competitive like the spinners in LEGO NINJAGO.

Eventually, that tiny 'lion motorcycle' became a key element of LEGO Chima: Speedorz, small vehicles which could be propelled using a pull line. Every aspect of them was new,

RIGHT The concept board with the little 'lion motorcycle', which first sparked interest in what became the Speedorz in LEGO Legends of Chima.

from their coverings to the gear mechanism that allowed them to speed across floors, to the large wheel at the front. Designers imagined that all sorts of competitive play could be facilitated by Speedorz. They made prototype sets and elements for jousting, stunt ramps, obstacle courses and more. Eventually, a small selection of these were released in wave one, with more held in reserve, assuming Speedorz took off like LEGO NINJAGO spinners had. In the event, children found them less intuitive to use than their spinning ninja predecessors and harder to master. That ended up being just the start of the challenges faced by LEGO Chima at the hands of LEGO NINJAGO.

ABOVE Early design sketches for Speedorz for LEGO Legends of Chima.

LEFT Early ideas for Speedorz sets included various 'challenges', which would feature a buildable set as well as a vehicle.

LEGO Legends of Chima was all set to replace LEGO NINJAGO, but the ninja were still riding high. However, the design pipeline had already stopped creating more LEGO NINJAGO products. Announcements of both the show and theme's cancellation were met with howls of protest from fans. Parents were writing and calling customer service, sometimes with the sounds of crying children in the background, pleading with the LEGO Group not to discontinue their child's favourite toys in the whole world. Before long, management made the executive decision that LEGO NINJAGO would continue alongside LEGO Legends of Chima.

Can a minifigure fly?

With LEGO NINJAGO being relaunched, designers got to work. The theme would need a new X-factor. The creative lead who had initiated the spinning idea, Erik Legernes, had another dream: making the minifigure fly. By his own admission, it became an obsession. Multiple attempts had been made to get minifigures airborne as far back as the 1980s. The designers for LEGO® Town

BELOW Successful follow-up themes, such as ninja pitted against snake tribes, contributed to the ongoing popularity of LEGO NINJAGO. This image shows different design complexities based on how many new element frames would be allotted.

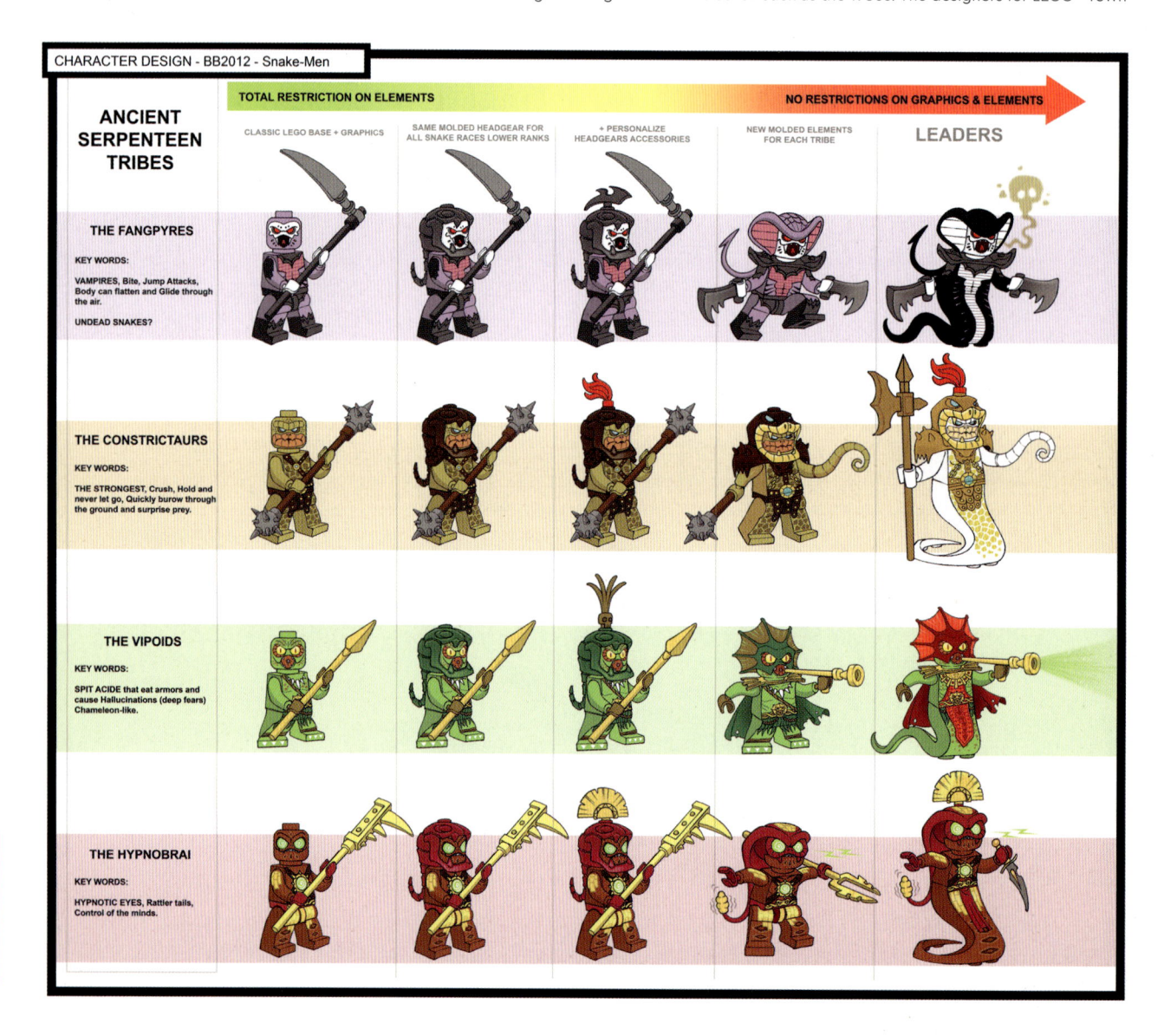

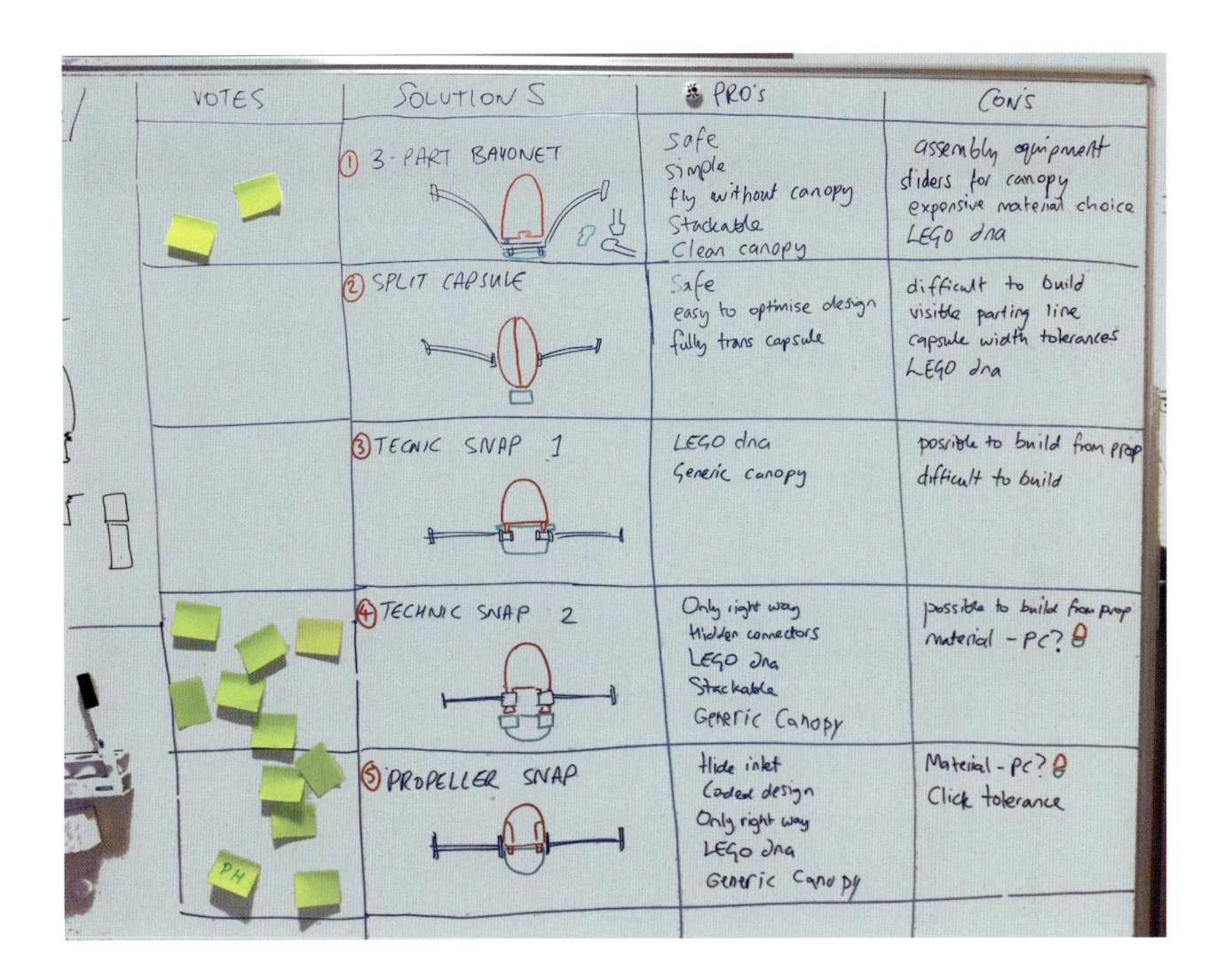

VOTES	SOLUTIONS	PRO's	CONS
	① 3-PART BAYONET	Safe Simple Fly without canopy Stackable Clean canopy	assembly equipment sliders for canopy expensive material choice LEGO dna
	② SPLIT CAPSULE	Safe easy to optimise design fully trans capsule	difficult to build visible parting line capsule width tolerances LEGO dna
	③ TECNIC SNAP 1	LEGO dna Generic canopy	possible to build from prop difficult to build
	④ TECHNIC SNAP 2	Only right way Hidden connectors LEGO dna Stackable Generic Canopy	possible to build from prop material - PC?
	⑤ PROPELLER SNAP	Hide inlet Coded design Only right way LEGO dna Generic Canopy	Material - PC? Click tolerance

had attempted it with helicopters and, most recently, LEGO Exo-Force had experimented with flyers as well. None had succeeded, with many prototypes meeting untimely ends as piles of pieces on the ground after test flights had been initiated from the roofs of buildings in Billund. Making the models stable enough to fly properly had proved challenging, to say the least.

The designers in the LEGO NINJAGO team, however, were determined to succeed. As with the spinners, they developed countless prototypes. Before long, sculptors determined that the solution was to place the minifigure at the centre of the flyer, and that stability was best achieved via three rotors held together by a perimeter ring. Combined with a slightly modified version of the Speedorz rip cords from LEGO Legends of Chima, designers finally succeeded. LEGO NINJAGO flyers, both as stand-alone sets and incorporated into several larger models, were front and centre in the theme's relaunch in 2014.

LEGO Legends of Chima followed the path LEGO NINJAGO had been expected to take, retiring after a healthy run, which would have been deemed a smash success had LEGO NINJAGO not shattered the expectations for what a big-bang theme could do. The funnel had never stopped churning, however, and in the years prior to LEGO Chima riding off into the sunset, Front End had been hard at work. Developers returned to those rich waters of time-tested subject matters to

ABOVE The LEGO NINJAGO design team kept track of the different designs for flyers on large whiteboards.

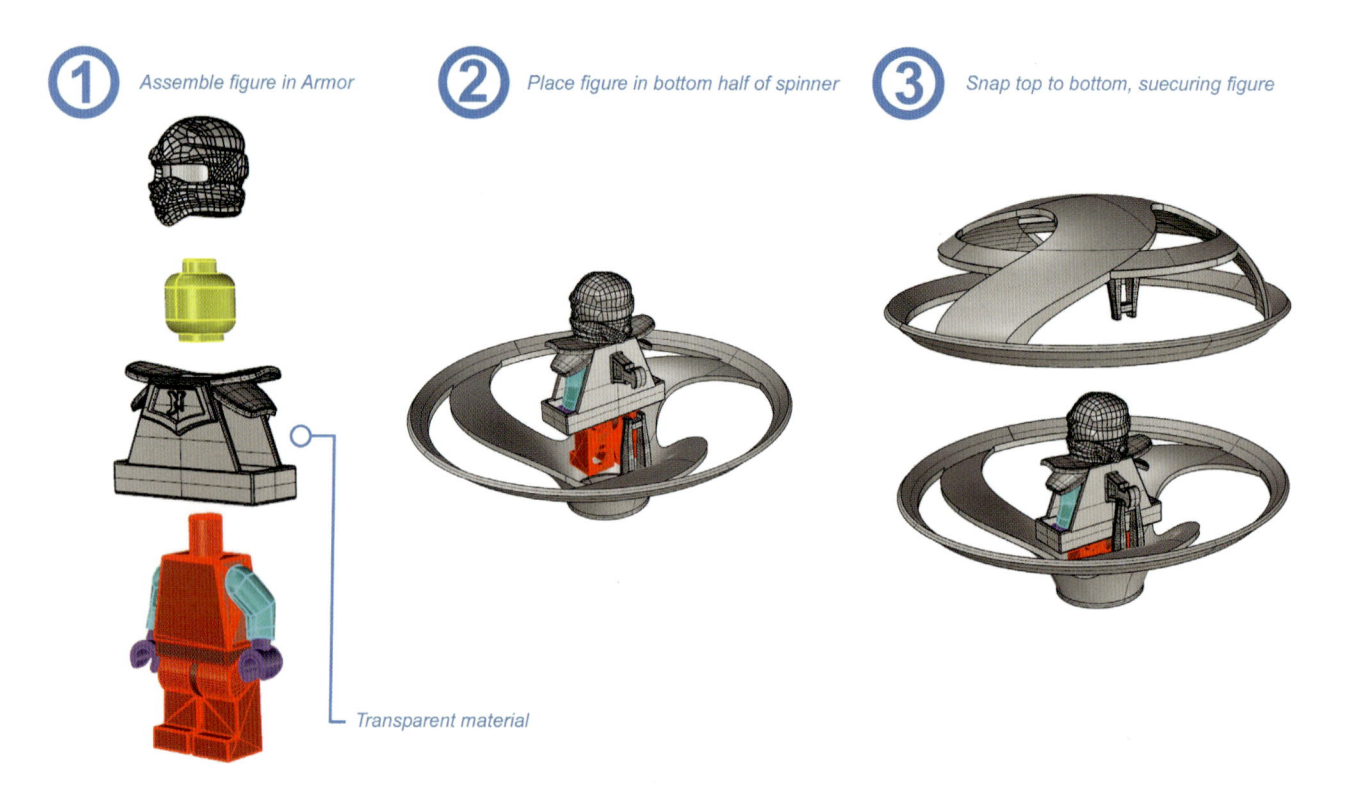

① *Assemble figure in Armor* **②** *Place figure in bottom half of spinner* **③** *Snap top to bottom, suecuring figure*

Transparent material

ABOVE This discarded flyer prototype used a central element to lock the figure in place.

see if they could give one of them a twist that would connect with consumers. There was now even a specific name for product lines based on icons: power themes.

Immediately, developers realised they had a new challenge: LEGO NINJAGO was still going to be around. They needed to create a theme that was different enough not to steal any glory from the mighty ninja. The X-factor also needed to be worlds apart from what had come before. LEGO Chima Speedorz had been too similar to LEGO NINJAGO spinners: the types of children who liked competing with spinners were likely to be the same ones who would love jousting with Speedorz. Whichever icon they used this time would need a strong X-factor, alongside a different category of play from that of LEGO NINJAGO.

Lessons learned from LEGO Legends of Chima had also led to another conclusion: it wasn't enough just to do colour changes and novelty figure parts. Coexisting with LEGO NINJAGO meant the new theme had to be dramatically different visually. LEGO Chima vehicles, if you stripped away the fresh colours and animal details, could almost have fitted in to the LEGO NINJAGO world. Greater differentiation was needed, and the answer was a new category of parts: structural elements.

To date, families of elements had been the purview of special platforms, which existed outside of any given theme, similar to those used for bow slopes or rollercoaster tracks. Once completed, platforms would immediately be available for any team that wanted to use them. Shape elements may have been designed primarily with LEGO *Star Wars* in mind, but they were not limited to a galaxy far, far away even in their first year. That made them less expensive to produce, since other toy themes could quickly use them, but this also diluted their novelty. Structural elements would be different.

Essentially, these elements were envisioned as theme-specific platforms that would be developed, at least initially, solely in service to their product line of origin. Structural elements could then endow a unique aesthetic or style impossible to achieve via the current parts catalogue. Every set in LEGO Legends of Chima, barring figures, could have been built, or nearly built, using parts available the year before that theme's launch, albeit in different colours. The goal of structural elements was to make that impossible. Once completed, they would be locked in the system, as with licensed themes, for a period of time in order to preserve their novelty, before eventually being released for wider use. That new approach was reflected in the eventual number of new element frames granted to the successor to LEGO Legends of Chima: an astonishing forty-two!

Pirates, cowboys and more had all gone into the funnel, but there was too much overlap on those with other properties. Eventually, a clear winner emerged: knights. Medieval warriors were largely absent from pop culture at the time and children seemed hungry for them. The question was, in what form? Front End set out to explore various executions of the knights' concept. They developed concepts for police knights, fire knights, classic knights, *Warhammer 40,000*-style knights, and, in a throwback to the first iteration of LEGO NINJAGO, tech knights.

BELOW In testing, children were shown various approaches to knights, ranging from historical to futuristic.

Designers on the team favoured an industrial *Warhammer 40,000*-style approach. Ninja were light-footed and relied on stealth, while *Warhammer* was the complete opposite: it relied on big, heavy machines that didn't need to hide because they could take the hits. Such a distinction would help differentiate the new theme from LEGO NINJAGO.

The designers developed concept models based on that aesthetic. Unfortunately, these concepts kept testing poorly with children, who liked the bulkiness but consistently preferred tech knights. Children were also responding well to an element that kept showing up in concept boards: a book of monsters. Eventually prototypes were created for a simple pair of new elements that mimicked the front and back covers of a bound volume on which faces could be printed. This particular piece of literature was alive: open the book to the correct page and images of monsters would become real, emerging for battle. Building on that solid concept, more good ideas began to come. What if the knights countered this magic not through alternate spells but downloading powers from the cloud? That would bring in the tech aspect. Children loved it: this was the right X-factor.

The shield piece

Over time, all the various ideas merged. Physical models would consist of minifigures armed with massive new sword and shield elements. Each knight would have a different personality, mimicking the approach that LEGO NINJAGO took to its characters. Shields were vital, since they would double as mechanisms for downloading powers from a digital wizard's server. Figuring out how to depict that exchange physically became an interesting challenge.

Initially, designers prototyped shields with mesh covers. Inserts depicting powers could be slid behind the mesh. That approach proved tricky to manufacture and lacked connectors. However, making separate parts for the shields and the powers seemed a sound idea. More brainstorming and ideas for synergies led, eventually, to the breakthrough moment. Shields and their powers could be a link between digital and physical play.

A smartphone game could be developed that would allow scanning technology to recognise the images printed on LEGO shields. Scanning would endow digital players with a shield's powers, encouraging collection in both the physical and virtual spaces. It was a perfect solution, but also put an incredible burden on shield designers. This single element had to facilitate scanning, be fun to play with, compatible with other LEGO bricks and have a distinctive look that would define the theme's aesthetic, since they would be its centrepiece. The designers' first priority was to establish the shields' shape: round, square or something else?

TOP Early prototypes for a more *Warhammer*-style approach to what would become NEXO KNIGHTS.

ABOVE The Book of Monsters became the central villain in NEXO KNIGHTS and crystallised the central play pattern for the theme.

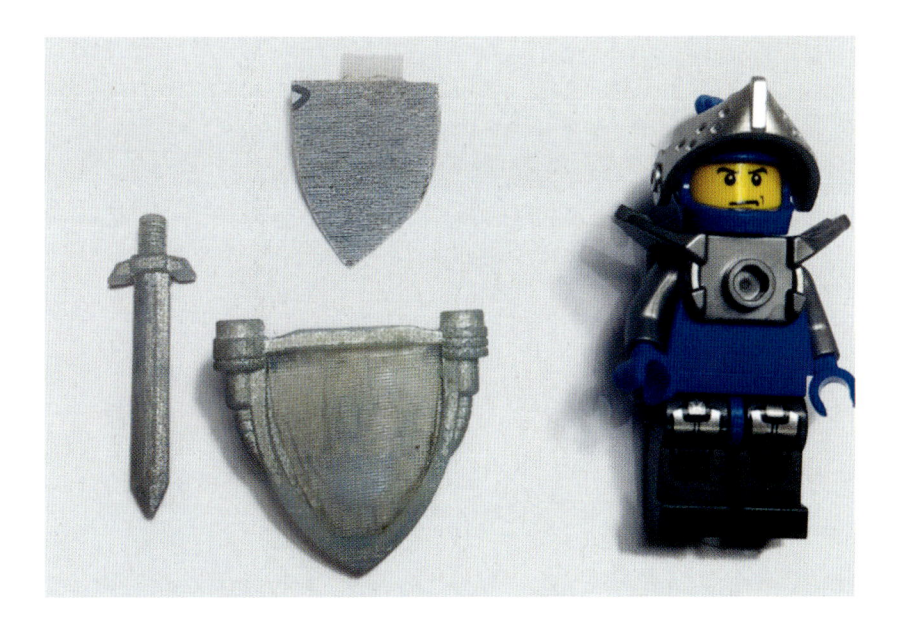

In the midst of this, one of the team members picked up a prototype 3×2 studless plate which was being circulated for review as the latest expansion of the tile family of elements. In a moment of inspiration, he clipped off the last third from both long sides at an angle, to create a pointed end. This became the element on which powers would be printed, now known among LEGO designers simply as 'the NEXO shield piece'. That description, while a good shorthand, is technically inaccurate, as the element became the power piece that was attached to a shield. Nomenclature aside, its distinctive look set the tone for the theme's eventual aesthetic: sharp had joined heavy. It was just in time.

Structural elements needed to be created so that final set designs could be developed. That distinctive point on the power tile led to facets with dual slopes being incorporated into nearly all the theme's family of pieces. LEGO® NEXO KNIGHTS™, as the theme was now called, was the first extensive foray into structural elements, which have since become the norm. Themes are assigned most new element frames in their first year, but reduced numbers of structural elements are also allocated to subsequent waves of evergreens, helping to inject a measure of novelty there as well. Sometimes the process can prove maddening to other teams hungry for a chance to incorporate the requisite 'new shiny thing' into their own models. That was the case with the 'NEXO shield piece', which ended up being unlocked earlier than originally intended due to high demand within the company. Other teams were allowed to use it, on the condition that they wouldn't print anything on it for the first year. The LEGO® Creator Expert team was especially happy, as they were able to use it for an ornate floor on a massive LEGO Disney Castle set.

TOP One of the early shield concepts for LEGO NEXO KNIGHTS featured a see-through mesh cover on the shield, behind which power elements could be slid.

ABOVE Printed power tiles were unique to LEGO NEXO KNIGHTS for a period of time before this element became used more widely.

LEFT LEGO NEXO KNIGHTS featured new LEGO minifigure accessories as well as a family of faceted elements.

It's movie time!

LEGO NEXO KNIGHTS ran for two years, while LEGO NINJAGO still remained a hugely popular theme. One big-bang theme, however, exceeded even the impact that LEGO NINJAGO had and catapulted the LEGO brick from beloved toy to cultural icon.

When the LEGO Group was originally approached about doing a theatrical movie, the idea percolated for several years before the initiative began to build momentum. It still remained relatively under the radar in Billund right up through release. Despite being an in-house movie, the product-development process closely mirrored that of other licensed themes, with the one major difference being that model designers worked closely with animators to develop designs that would work both on-screen and off. Almost all the new elements created specifically for the film were characters' accessories, such as Wyldestyle's hood, Unikitty's tail, Lord Business's overbearing hat, Metalbeard's namesake metallic facial component and Vitruvius's hair. All the villains' minions were either existing figures with new prints or entirely brick-built. There was only one major exception, the Piece of Resistance, which figured prominently in the movie's plot.

BELOW Early drawings for THE LEGO MOVIE show some of new elements created for minifigures.

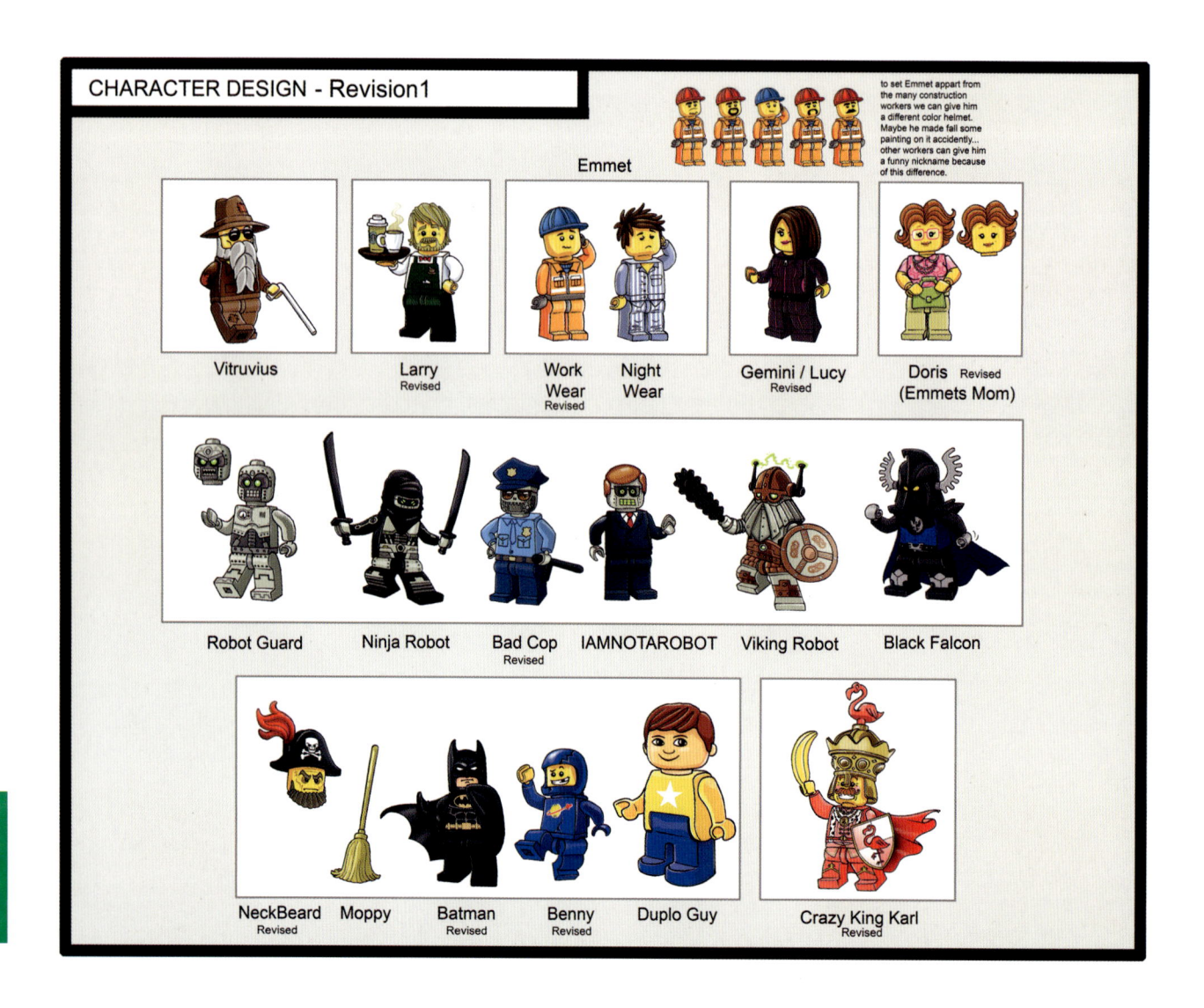

Upon release, THE LEGO® MOVIE™ became a massive blockbuster, spawning a cinematic universe that would eventually include films for both LEGO® Batman and LEGO NINJAGO. It also catapulted LEGO bricks to the apex of the cultural zeitgeist, bringing legions of new fans into the fold. A surprise blockbuster became the ultimate X-factor.

Big bangs continued after LEGO NEXO KNIGHTS. First came LEGO® Hidden Side™ in 2019, which pitted a pair of ghost hunters against a horde of ghouls haunting their town. This was followed in 2020 by LEGO® Monkie Kid™, an expansive theme inspired by Chinese legends. Both followed the approaches laid down by their predecessors, incorporating X-factors, structural elements, multimedia exposure, expansive worlds and strong characters. LEGO Hidden Side brought augmented reality to LEGO play through a smartphone app that facilitated digital ghost hunting in the space around physical sets. LEGO Monkie Kid relied primarily on new elements and colours to instil a fresh and distinctly Chinese aesthetic, a novel X-factor in its own right.

Big-bang themes after LEGO NINJAGO have followed the path originally anticipated for that initial theme: they generate a huge buzz for two to three years, then are replaced by the next novel offering. That was always the vision, and it has become a reality. The LEGO Group took the unexpected mega-success of LEGO NINJAGO and was able to turn its lessons into a creative process for evaluating and producing a string of successful themes, and now, years later, a cornucopia of elements which have helped make all sorts of new building opportunities possible.

LEFT Lord Business's hat and armour were new elements created for the character.

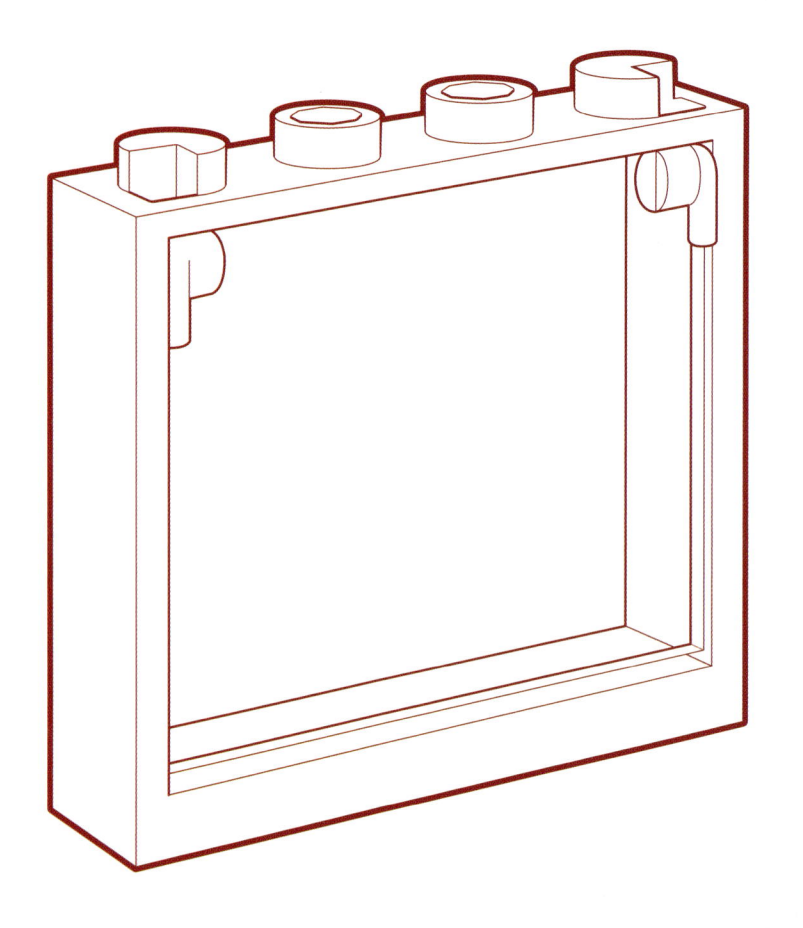

> **"In the LEGO® Creator 3-in-1 team, we didn't do decorations on elements because we wanted the bricks to be as versatile as possible."**
>
> Jamie Berard, Creative Lead, Senior Designer, the LEGO Group

11 Everything is Awesome

Thanks to wide exposure from the LEGO® Cinematic Universe and Big Bang themes, the LEGO® brick became a cultural phenomenon. Fortunately, designers were ready, having spent the previous decade experimenting with ever larger and more daring products.

TOP LEFT LEGO® Creator designers love to 'celebrate what is available' and find unique uses for elements that were designed for vastly different purposes, such as Unikitty's tail.

ABOVE LEFT The 1×1 slope, or cheese slope, is a favourite element among both fans and professional LEGO designers.

ABOVE RIGHT The 1×4×3 window frame was one of the first requested by the LEGO Creator team after successfully launching the Modular Building line.

'**W**hy is this set selling so well?' asked an executive. His curiosity was justified. Set 4886 LEGO® Creator Building Bonanza was nobody's idea of a blockbuster, yet the numbers didn't lie. Sales were exceeding all expectations by a wide margin, requiring more production runs than anticipated. While a good problem to have, Building Bonanza was such an outlier that it prompted something almost unprecedented: a special investigation.

The results turned out to be more important than anyone at the time could have imagined – and it set in motion a chain of events whose effects still reverberate. Years later, when the LEGO® brick skyrocketed to the centre of global consciousness on the heels of THE LEGO® MOVIE™, unintentional preparations had been made, in part, thanks to innocuous 4886 Building Bonanza.

That strangely named set hailed from what was, at the time, a very traditional corner of the LEGO Group toy portfolio. LEGO Creator, launched in 2001, was the most recent incarnation of what the company called its free-building line. For as long as there have been LEGO bricks, these types of products had been sold. Containing mostly basic elements, they are intended to provide lots of raw materials for imaginative building with little to no formal instructions. That idea had been memorialised in the very names of these themes, which had been both LEGO® Basic and LEGO® FreeStyle. Creator had been handed that baton at a time when the LEGO Group was becoming aware of just how little free building children were doing. Instead, many children were acquiring sets, assembling them and then leaving them together. Creator sought to promote a different approach.

LEFT LEGO Basic was the LEGO Group free-building product line from 1985 until LEGO FreeStyle replaced it in 1996. LEGO Basic was brought back in 1998, but was eventually superseded in 2001 by LEGO Creator and LEGO Designer.

Building can be daunting, especially for children just starting out with LEGO toys. What was needed, designers realised, was a way to encourage rebuilding so that children would get more value from their sets and would develop confidence as they succeeded multiple times. Initially, there was a bit of overcompensating when directions for different models from the same box reached double digits. That quickly became unsustainable. Over time, it was found that a far more reasonable three options per set achieved the best results with customers. LEGO Creator 3-in-1 was born.

From its inception, LEGO Creator utilised only existing elements. Frames, if any were even granted, would be for a graphic or two and the occasional colour change. Over time this limitation evolved into a cornerstone of the theme's identity. Designers describe it as a fierce pride over 'celebrating what is available'. Novelty is instilled not by new parts, but by using existing elements in fresh and exciting ways, or through incorporating subject matter not being explored elsewhere in the product portfolio.

Novel subject matter became a hallmark early on. For example, LEGO Creator did mechs before LEGO® Exo-Force, brick-built dragons years ahead of LEGO® NINJAGO® and giant sharks before LEGO® Aqua Raiders. Many years later, LEGO Creator would become the home for pirates, castles and other beloved themes when the wider portfolio could no longer accommodate them, but that was still a long way off. After initial success with smaller sets, vehicles began entering the mix. Then, in 2004, came 3-in-1 Building Bonanza. In this case the

ABOVE LEGO FreeStyle sets sought to inspire creativity by showing unique uses for parts.

> At the start of LEGO Creator, there were a lot of ideas for what it could be. We know that we wanted to get creativity back into building because many people were just getting the model, playing with it and leaving it on the shelf. We wanted to encourage people to rebuild. That was the reason we started up what became LEGO Creator 3-in-1. Some of the first models we made were actually eighteen or twenty in one! We made eighteen building instructions for some of the early cars and dinosaurs. But people were just choosing one of them and leaving it built instead of rebuilding them all, so it ended up becoming the Creator 3-in-1 concept.

Steen Sig Andersen, Designer, the LEGO Group

name referenced not the act of construction but the set's subject matter, which consisted of options for three structures, each requiring a different level of skill to assemble. The most advanced was a two-storey house with dormer windows, a small lawn and a fence. It was an empty shell, with nothing inside, ergo management's confusion when it flew off shelves. What was going on?

Sleuthing with customer service eventually yielded an answer, but it only deepened the mystery. Children were not buying 4886: adults were, and not just one copy but multiple ones. By this time, the LEGO Group had its ambassador programme in place, giving the company direct lines to the fan community. Utilising that communication pipeline, they asked a simple question: why are you buying so many of this one set? The answer proved revelatory. Fans explained that in their quest for novel and exciting themes, the LEGO Group had neglected sets based on everyday life. Houses had been staples of the product line during the 1980s when many of those now-adults were children and they loved including such vintage models in their displays. During the 1990s, houses fell out of favour. Building Bonanza was the first to come along in years, and fans were snapping it up in the belief that this might be their only chance for a long while. Management was surprised by every aspect of the answer and it got them thinking. Trains had proved successful with this emerging adult market; could it perhaps support other types of products as well?

Inspired by adult fans

Eventually a small experiment was greenlit, resulting in a brief that gave wide latitude for exploration: 'Take existing elements and see if they can be used to develop a house that LEGO fans would want.' Two employees were tasked with the assignment – Jamie Berard and Steen Sig Andersen, who were respectively one of the newest and one of the most veteran model designers. With the help of LEGO ambassadors, they further probed the adult market in order to discover what these fans were up to and what they wanted.

At that time, a major focus of the adult community was something called the Moon Base Project. It was an open-source venture which defined a universal set of measurements and rigid coupling specifications for modules of a Moon base. Anyone could participate as long as they complied with the established rules that ensured that any two builds, no matter who their creator was, could join together. Fans would then gather at conventions and assemble massive bases. This focus on modularity caught Jamie and Steen's eye.

Almost immediately the designers realised that incorporating modularity precluded a neighbourhood full of different houses: it would not make sense for such structures to join together. However, an urban setting with closely packed buildings would facilitate such construction while also technically meeting the desire for houses. Like the Moon Base Project, they further concluded that for such a layout to work they would also need rigid rules for how models coupled together, which could never be altered. Accordingly, they began their design process by laying down constraints and measurements as well as brainstorming how they could make their models novel without any new parts.

One of their primary concerns was ensuring that their eventual buildings did not resemble doll's houses, which they assumed would put off many adults. This meant that creating facades that opened to allow access to interiors was not an option. Likewise, LEGO® City style buildings with open backs, known internally as Hollywood sets, were also non-starters: their buildings needed to be fully enclosed. While a necessity, there was also an inherent advantage in that approach. Such structures would require a lot of bricks. Only a few basic pieces came in most sets and while LEGO Creator had more than most, they were all cast in basic colours. The buildings being envisioned would be huge, demanding large numbers of the most rudimentary elements. If they could include those basic bricks in unique or rarer colours, that would add novelty all by itself.

ABOVE Set 4886 Building Bonanza had three different options of models to build.

Eventually Jamie and Steen established an approach with set widths for sidewalks and the spacing of connectors so that buildings could scale up to 16×32, 32×32 and even 48×48 baseplates. Horizontal rules complete, they transitioned to vertical, deciding that, if at all possible, each building should have a repeatable middle section so that fans who were inclined to buy multiple copies could, theoretically, stack floors up to infinity. Specifications were soon finalised, establishing their modular system's foundation. Now they just needed products.

The challenge of windows and doors

The designers pitched three initial models to management based on a simple argument: testing modularity would require multiple sets. Their presentation included approaches for all three which would not only test their new specifications, but probe how adults would react to different architectural styles: a San Francisco-style grocer, a New York fire station and a French café, each of which would be a LEGO Creator 3-in-1 set with two alternative models. Approval was granted and the French café was chosen to inaugurate this new line.

LEFT Set 10182 Café Corner, released in 2007, became the first modular building in the LEGO Creator 3-in-1 theme.

Work began on what would become set 10182 Café Corner and very quickly the lessons started piling up, nearly all of which related to pieces. Simply put, the parts catalogue was not ready to support this style of building. Nowhere was this more obvious than windows and doors. The buildings for LEGO® Town and, later, LEGO City required little variation in these elements, so the parts catalogue had a limited selection. Urban buildings, however, rely heavily on different window and door styles to instil unique architecture and aesthetics. To complicate matters further, the great parts purge was in full swing, and many of the few pieces that had been available were now retired and those that remained were mismatched. A four-stud-wide by six-brick-tall window frame existed, but there was no corresponding door element to fit inside it. For doors, only a free-standing variant that was five bricks tall was available, meaning that café doors and windows would be mismatched. There was another challenge with the transparent windowpane component which fitted in the frame – something which wouldn't bother children but may very well annoy adults. It was called the bullet hole.

LEGO elements are made by plastic injection. Moulds with cavities in the shapes of whichever brick is being produced have molten plastic injected into them at high pressure. While small, that point of injection inevitably leaves a small mark behind, usually in the form of a little nub or circle. Part of the process of designing new moulds is to think through where these nubs will appear and hiding them as much as possible. In the case of the large windowpanes, their injection points had been placed right in the centre, about two-thirds of the way up, leaving behind a large, circular blemish, later christened the bullet hole by model makers. There was nothing to be done in the moment, but Jamie made a mental note of the problem and, as luck would have it, several years later was in a position to do something about it.

BELOW A mould from the 1950s clearly shows the channels that feed plastic into the cavities. Today, the process is done very differently via an automatic process in the machine.

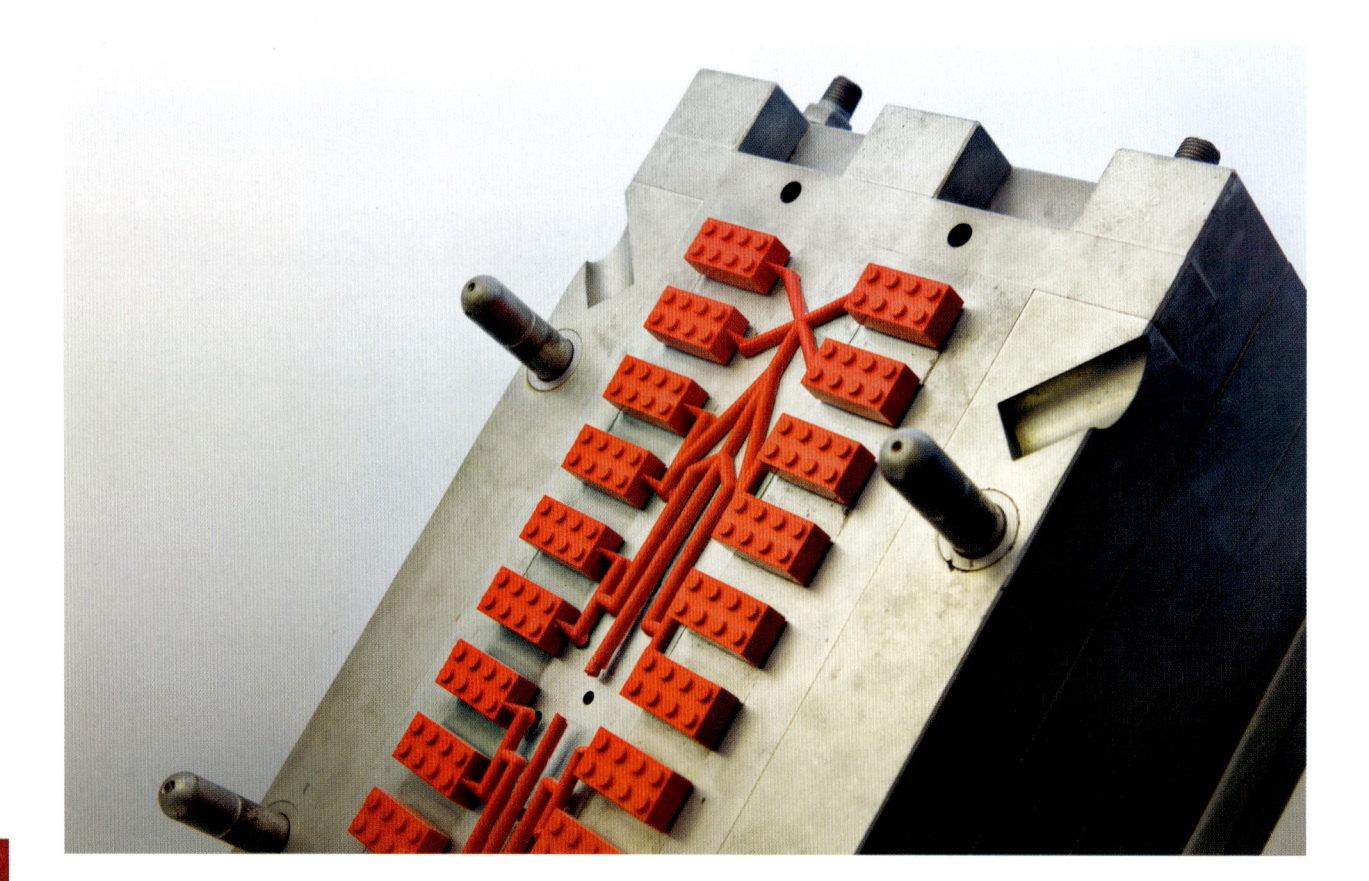

The LEGO Group injection moulds are made of top-quality steel, but they do not last forever. As an element's moulds near the end of their useful lives, an internal operation called the reordering process kicks into gear. First, an evaluation is done as to whether this particular piece still needs to be produced. If not, it gets retired and no new moulds are ordered. However, if a component is to stay in production, it goes through an evaluation to see if changes should be made to improve the part that would require modifying its mould. Input comes from across the company and changes may be suggested for a host of reasons, ranging from part usability to more efficient manufacturing. While often subtle, these minor alterations are sometimes significant enough to be noticeable, as was the case with jumper plates.

LEFT A special division in the LEGO Group factory in Billund, Denmark, regularly maintains moulds.

Jumper plates had been around since the 1970s and were designed from inception to fulfill a very specific purpose. They were a 1×2 plate with a single stud in the centre that allowed for moving construction over half a module instead of a full module. Underneath, they were just like any other 1×2 plate with a centre rod for creating clutch power – and that was the problem. For years, model designers were frustrated by that rod, as it precluded having another brick's stud attach directly to a jumper plate's centre from beneath. If that type of connection were possible, it would open up many new building opportunities. While making such a change may seem straightforward, it wasn't – and evaluating all the pros and cons in a situation like this is part of the rationale for having a thorough re-ordering process.

In the case of jumper plates, nothing was cut and dried. LEGO elements are primarily intended for children and a key part of their design is not only ensuring that children can use them correctly but also to make sure, as much as possible, that they can't use them incorrectly either. More often than not, if there are two ways a brick could be designed, simplicity wins out, even if that means less versatility. It is better for an element to work only one way so that children can't go wrong, fail in building and get frustrated. This argument prevailed with the jumper plate over multiple reorderings, as different designers argued for eliminating the rod – each time their request was denied. Ultimately, it was the LEGO Creator team that finally prevailed, convincing everyone that, with the advanced building techniques they were employing on ever-more complicated models, greater functionality was needed. Jamie Berard became an element ambassador and led that charge. He also reduced the bullet hole in the large windowpane and moved it to a corner so it would be less obvious.

A new family of parts

Unfortunately, none of those changes had happened yet during Café Corner's development, so designers had to get creative. Bullet holes were hidden as much as possible under protruding eaves. Doors were mismatched in size to windows, but those same eaves helped mask that discrepancy. Nevertheless, these tricks only worked on the bottom floor; moving

BELOW LEFT This older-style door was the only kind available for Café Corner. Every future Modular Building would use newer variants developed in the years after Cafe Corner.

BELOW CENTRE Café Corner made use of a window that was originally from LEGO Castle and LEGO Pirates.

BELOW RIGHT A whole family of windows were envisioned during Café Corner's development, including this 1×2×3-bricks-tall variant.

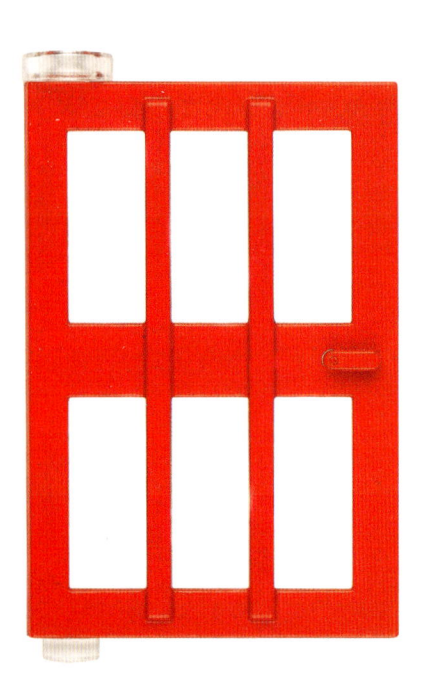

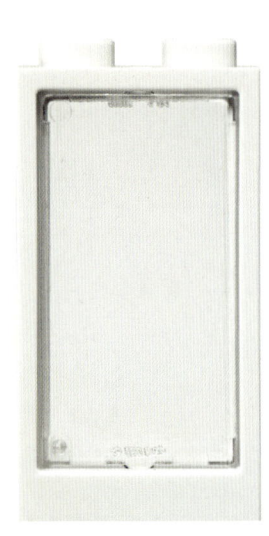

upwards, finding the right windows became more challenging. Only two frame sizes were available: a curved 1×2 variant that was three bricks tall, which hailed from LEGO® Pirates and LEGO® Castle, and a 2×4 version, also three bricks tall, which had mostly been included in offerings from LEGO Basic and LEGO FreeStyle. Lattices were available for each option, but no windowpane components. When a rectangular 1×2 window three bricks tall became necessary, pairs of panel pieces had to stand in, with nothing between them but empty space. With so many gaping openings, Café Corner's upper floors would be very expensive to keep heated during the winter months!

Even as that first set was being developed, LEGO Creator team members began working on a solution to the challenges being encountered. Right then and there they sketched out a whole family of windows and doors, with windowpanes to match: 1×2, 1×3, 1×4, with variants two studs high, three studs high, six studs high and so on. Being in the LEGO Creator theme, they knew that a windfall of new element frames allowing for a large number of parts was not on the cards. Instead, they campaigned for a doors-and-windows platform and obtained approval. A schedule for release, with new entries from their wish list ranked by priority, was developed as part of that process, with a 1×4 door six bricks tall at the top. Over the next decade most of their platform would become reality.

Despite having so many parts limitations, Café Corner had one distinct advantage: the element of surprise. Simply put, nothing even remotely like it had ever been produced throughout the LEGO Group entire history and the LEGO Creator team was outdoing itself in terms of celebrating what was available. Clever usage of existing pieces abounded. Skis, originally produced a decade earlier for a subtheme of LEGO® Space called Ice Planet, were strung together across a flexible tube to create an ornate decoration above the café's door. Wheel mudguards for cars became arches over upper windows. Fortuitous timing also played a role. LEGO® Belville was being retired, which meant its catalogue of unique parts, which had previously been locked for use anywhere else, became available. Looking to add novelty, designers selected an ornate lamppost for inclusion in Café Corner. Although it had been intended as a one-off, managers in the warehouse said they would hold off on destroying the mould until after Café Corner was retired. When that piece proved popular with fans, it was included in subsequent Modular Buildings, becoming a staple of the line. Eventually, the lamppost mould ended up having to be renewed, which left the warehouse managers good-naturedly shaking their heads in bemusement. They wouldn't be getting that space freed up on the shelves after all.

Having succeeded in overcoming parts limitations and creating a drop-dead-gorgeous set, designers turned to the final aspect of Café Corner's development: its alternate models. In keeping with the agreed approach, two additional options were made, which could be constructed from the included parts. This was, after all, a Creator 3-in-1. However, that process exposed several flaws in applying such an approach to products of this scale. Inordinate amounts of time were required both to figure out the builds and develop useable instructions. This represented a huge resource drain for what everyone realised was minimal gain: few, if any, consumers were going to take apart and rebuild a set made of more than 2,000 pieces. In this one instance, though, the additional effort did not go to waste. As the inaugural entry in what was supposed to be a modular building system, there was no easy way to illustrate for consumers what that vision could look like. Ultimately, the back of Café Corner's box presented an alternate model, along with multiple copies of the base set stacked and joined together in different configurations, in order to showcase what was possible. Any doubts that the Creator team was on to something were put to rest when reports began coming in from the company's shop-at-home arm: high volumes of customers were ordering six copies of the set, exactly the number needed to recreate the biggest combination shown on the back of the Café Corner box.

ABOVE LEGO Creator Modular Buildings saved an ornate lamppost, originally used in the LEGO Belville theme, from deletion.

ABOVE The back of the box for Café Corner showed an alternative model as well as builds requiring multiple copies of the main model. It also highlighted some of the unique building techniques.

The LEGO Creator team did not rest on its laurels. Its designers had been authorised to create three buildings and there was no time to waste. Many of the large products which hit shelves during the early 2000s began as passion projects, initiated by designers in their own time. As the LEGO Group around it transitioned to the formal funnel system, the LEGO Creator team remained beholden to the old ways where products began life not as briefs, but as an idea a designer loved and wanted to share with others. Café Corner was the first of these passion projects to be officially commissioned ahead of time rather than being greenlit for production only after a designer had built it and brought their finished product for consideration.

Thus began a several-years-long stretch of time that everyone involved looks back on fondly. LEGO Creator and its line of adult-focused products, eventually dubbed Creator Expert, flew mostly under the radar. The company as a whole still saw them largely as a cauldron for experimentation. Accordingly, designers were given wide latitude to try unusual things to see if they worked and were allowed to work on off-hours passion projects which could, of course, be whatever a designer wanted. Even so, risk was managed by keeping a tight lid on the number of sets targeted specifically at adults that could be produced each year. Initially that number was four across the whole company, inclusive of LEGO® *Star Wars*™, which almost always took a pair of them, leaving the remaining two for Creator Expert. For 2008, one of those would be the next Modular Building, as they had now been named: the San Francisco grocer.

Set 10185 Green Grocer got to benefit from the new doors-and-windows platform prompted by Café Corner. There were still challenges, but nobody in the LEGO Creator team could deny that their cries had been heard. Two new doors were now available, each sized to fit in the large window frame. Joining them were the first two alternative window sizes they had requested: 1×2 at two bricks tall, and 1×4 at three bricks tall with transparent panes to fill them. In short, there were a total of six new parts from the platform, an unprecedented, immediate windfall; filling out the rest of the platform would take years. Investment in these parts had been warranted because multiple other project teams had expressed enthusiastic interest, and all six components quickly saw wide use. Not only did designers use them on the Green Grocer's exterior, they also incorporated them inside. Café Corner had not included an interior, in keeping with the LEGO Creator houses that had inspired it, which had all been empty. Having since determined that Modular Buildings would not be under 3-in-1's banner, model makers had decided to create full interiors going forward.

Being a grocer, cold storage was needed, which provided more opportunities for utilising the new, clear doors for refrigerators. Despite their windfall, not every window needed was available. Flanking the Green Grocer's right side was a gorgeous two-floor bow window projection, which featured multiple copies of the new 1×4 windows at three bricks tall stacked up the protrusion's centre. Flanking them were spaces not quite large enough to accommodate 1×4 windows; however, 1×2 windows three bricks in height had not made the initial cut and wouldn't be available until the following year. Designers found a clever workaround: train windows, which were the right size, were flipped around backwards and used instead. Missing windows aside, there was no doubt that LEGO Creator Expert adult-orientated offerings were gaining clout, as evidenced by the theme having also received a couple of frames for colour changes – and the team knew exactly how to use them.

Grey cheese

'Cheese slopes', as 1×1 slopes are affectionately known both inside the LEGO Group and among fans, are universally regarded as one of the most useful parts ever created. By the time Green Grocer was under development, they were already circulating widely, but astonishingly not in light grey, one of the most basic colours. Fans were clamouring for them in that hue, and the Creator Expert team, who worked diligently to keep tabs on the community's pulse, were aware of that desire. Alongside forty cheese slopes in light grey, further novelty was added to the set by using the ultra-rare sand green colour as the namesake green in Green Grocer. To date it had only been available through a couple of offerings, most notably an Ultimate Collector Set of Yoda for LEGO *Star Wars* and a scale model of the Statue of Liberty. Bricks from those production runs were still available, meaning only a couple of fringe parts, like the special grooved elements for wall decorations, needed colour-change frames. Between rare colours and much-loved bricks in a useful new hue, Green Grocer would make adult fans happy based on components alone: but the model was also gorgeous and it proved a massive hit with its audience. Modular Buildings, along with another surprise product, began to put Creator Expert on the map.

10179 Ultimate Collector Series (UCS) *Millennium Falcon* was designed as a passion project free from any price-point requirements or parts limitations. Its designer had achieved the previously unthinkable: a proper minifigure-scale version of Han Solo's iconic ship. Incredibly, this feat had been achieved using entirely existing parts; no new element frames would be needed to make it an official set. However, that didn't mean there were not major hurdles. Producing the model would require nailing down the logistics of sorting and packing an unprecedented number of

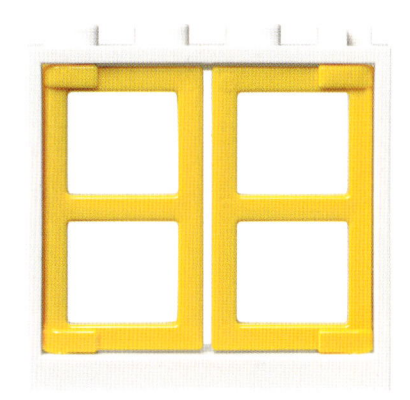

ABOVE The 1×4×3-bricks-tall window frame was one of the first new elements developed from the doors-and-windows platform. It could be fitted with either a single transparent pane or two opening windowpane elements.

bricks, and call for a fairly large leap of faith: would people actually buy a toy that was this big and expensive? In the end, 10179 practically flew off shelves and the LEGO Creator Expert team realised that they were in a whole new world.

The LEGO Creator Expert team was able to increase the number of adult-orientated sets they made. Other teams began coming to its designers asking for help with upper-end offerings across the product portfolio. This was extremely exciting for the team, not least because it meant more chances to raid their drawers for previously shelved ideas.

During the 2000s, some designers had a ritual of making pilgrimages to the new-element wall. This is the place where prototype or freshly minted parts are displayed to let designers know they are available or to comment if development remains ongoing. Every piece has an intended use, of course, but one of the keys for the designers of LEGO Creator Expert and others

ABOVE LEGO *Star Wars* Ultimate Collector Series Millennium Falcon, set 10179, from 2007.

Everything is Awesome   299

who were experimenting with big builds was to not see purpose but instead see shapes. Pieces which caught an eye would be gathered, usually multiple copies of them, and brought back to desks. Designers might stack, place or position two at an angle to each other, looking for unique interactions, relationships and shapes. This was how Unikitty tails ended up being used as an architectural element in the roof of Modular Building 10246 Detective's Office. Lined up together they yielded a very distinctive and pleasing look. Often these unique uses of parts are figured out ahead of time in isolation and then incorporated into models when opportunities present themselves. To this day, the team responsible for Modular Buildings had remained small and close-knit. They alone come up with subject matter for each year's structures, and sometimes ideas sparked by pilgrimages to the new-element wall will lead to whole buildings, or at least parts of their architecture.

ABOVE Unikitty tails are used as buttresses in the roof of 10246 LEGO Creator Expert Detective's Office, released in 2015.

> The first UCS *Millennium Falcon* was a real conversation piece within the LEGO Group. We asked whether people would really want a model that big, complicated and expensive. It took a leap of faith on the part of [LEGO *Star Wars* design manager] Jens Kronvold Frederiksen and his team. But it really opened doors. When the model just flew off the shelves, we said, OK there is a market for this. It was almost our first insight into the passion side of LEGO toys. If people care about it enough, they can justify it in their life. A casual person might say, 'I would never spend hundreds of pounds on a toy.' For other people, it's not hundreds of pounds for a toy, it's money well spent on reliving a memory or nostalgia moment. That set really opened our eyes.

Jamie Berard, Creative Lead, Senior Designer, the LEGO Group

A bigger wheel

After UCS *Millennium Falcon* exceeded all expectations, the LEGO Creator Expert team began getting more opportunities; in particular, one that had been bubbling just beneath the surface for a while. The LEGO Creator 3-in-1 team had made Ferris Wheel, set 4957, released in 2007. It was not intended for minifigures and was relatively basic in many respects, built from a combination of System bricks and LEGO® Technic elements. Put simply, this was a Ferris wheel for children. However, some people within the LEGO Group had become aware that such fairground-related subject matter was popular at fan conventions and they wondered if there would be a market for official offerings. When the UCS *Falcon* blew the roof off, plans to explore fairground sets were accelerated. The LEGO Group was also introducing the new catalogue of Power Functions parts as the 9V system was phased out, so the timing was perfect; it was another opportunity to showcase this new system with an older audience.

LEFT The LEGO Creator theme's first Ferris Wheel set, released in 2007, led managers to wonder if adults would buy a more detailed model.

ABOVE The overall weight of 10196 Grand Carousel was reduced by the use of lightweight fabric roof elements – they also added to the set's aesthetic appeal.

The LEGO Creator Expert team was given permission to aim high with their inaugural fairground model. Should it prove a success, there was a possibility that fairground-themed models could become a new line, similar to Modular Buildings. Carousels were chosen as the subject matter, both due to their iconic nature and their unique movements, which would highlight the capabilities of the new Power Functions. Pretty soon, however, a challenge was encountered: weight.

In order to make a circular shape for the carousel's base with the parts available at that time, its diameter had grown beyond the bounds of a 32×32 plate. This had already necessitated a first, the inclusion of a 48×48 baseplate in a set. The LEGO Group extra-large baseplate had debuted in 1980 but had only ever been sold as a stand-alone item. It provided a large surface on which children could free-build, with the only expectation being a brief stint as the backing for a short-lived early 2000s mosaic theme. What became 10196 Grand Carousel would notch two milestones for this enormous element. Grand Carousel was its first use as the base for a structure in an official set and the sole time it was ever cast in green, having only ever been manufactured in grey before. That jaw-dropping size was great from a visual perspective, but it made the whole apparatus very heavy. Even with the new Power Functions, a brick-built roof would increase the weight beyond the capabilities of the motors. That problem was solved through specially designed fabric elements, called foils internally, which not only provided an elegant, lightweight, circular shape for the roof, but also more closely matched real-world carousels.

Upon its release in 2009, 10196 Grand Carousel was a masterpiece in every respect: size, functionality, beauty – this set had it all. Unfortunately, it also had an Achilles heel: that big 48×48 green baseplate. Having been sold exclusively in isolation for its entire existence, model makers were unfamiliar with some of the challenges such a large, sprawling sheet of plastic brought with it when released out into the world with a giant set built on top. The LEGO Group line of baseplates, which have come in numerous sizes through the years, are only a single section thick, half of a standard plate. This was done for purely economic reasons: areas that are 32×32 and 48×48 studs-square require a lot of plastic, so casting baseplates at minimal thickness kept them affordable. It also meant they were flexible, which became a noticeable issue for consumers when they tried to move the enormous carousel. Although the set was prematurely cancelled as a result, sales were strong enough before that to convince management that fairground sets had potential. This eventually led to more amazing products, including a second carousel built on more rigid plates two sections thick, a Fairground Mixer ride, and more.

BELOW Set 10244 Fairground Mixer, released in 2014, followed the Grand Carousel in the fairground theme.

"
Steen Sig Andersen was just brilliant in coming up with this gorgeous Grand Carousel for the first fairground set. But unfortunately, it had a very limited run because the only baseplate big enough at the time was 48×48 and it ended up being so flexible that there were challenges with people moving it. When they would go to pick it up, it would separate too easily. We actually had to prematurely stop the Grand Carousel just because some people were disappointed with how hard it was to move. It did really well, people were excited by it, but we had to exit it early. At least it showed the potential here. I then made a concept for the Fairground Mixer, which actually didn't go forward because of uncertainty about what it was. It's a truck, but it's also a ride. How does this work? Is it for adults or children? There's a lot of play there, but it's also complicated to build. It ended up getting parked. But when I came to lead the team, we made the Fairground Mixer, which did well enough that we could then do the Ferris Wheel, then the second Carousel and eventually my holy grail, the Roller Coaster.
"

Jamie Berard, Creative Lead, Senior Designer, the LEGO Group

Seasonal success

The fairground theme's inaugural Grand Carousel was not the only experimental model being developed in the late 2000s. Concurrently, management came to Creator Expert with another brief that they assured team members would not count towards one of their precious adult-oriented slots. It would, in their words, be a 'freebie'. As with many such briefs, it was more of an idea than a directive: 'Can you make a holiday [seasonal] item that creates a tradition that people will come back to?'

The LEGO Group had been making winter-themed sets for years. Printed 1×2 bricks with angels' faces, mouths open in song, had been part of brick-built sets depicting carolling cherubim, on and off since the 1980s, alongside similarly blocky renditions of Santa and snowmen. All were stocking-filling size and never played a significant role in the overall assortment. Now, however, management was wondering if there was an opportunity to do more with the subject matter and wanted LEGO Creator Expert to take the lead. Team members got to work. The original idea for what became Modular Buildings had not been forgotten. Soon, a concept began to form. The desire for brick-built houses and depictions of everyday life would be merged with the cute and cosy aesthetic of whimsical porcelain winter villages that many families collected. If they proved popular, a new product could be released each year, creating a holiday tradition – and fulfilling the product brief.

Whether because it was a LEGO Creator set, an experiment, or both, no new parts frames were allocated to the project. The novelty of a seasonal offering would have to be enough. Designers intentionally distinguished this new line from Modular Buildings by foregoing a rigid system of connectors. These sets should be more free-form so they could be easily arranged in different configurations around a Christmas tree or fireplace, where families often displayed their porcelain villages. Inaugural subject matter was obvious: a toy shop. It was festive but could also easily fit into a LEGO City layout if this new line was not successful.

Ironically, the LEGO Creator Expert team's recent victory with new doors and windows presented a challenge for which the older pieces would have been perfect. Versions of those elements used throughout the 1980s and 1990s were five bricks tall. In an effort to help build up the facades of Modular Buildings, as well as other LEGO structures, all the new versions were six bricks high. Extra size was great for a storefront at the base of a three-storey building, but on a little winter village structure they were too dominant. Large sheets of glass didn't enhance the cute and cosy aesthetic. Designers got clever both with their initial set, 10199 Winter Village Toy Shop, and many other subsequent entries. Overhanging eaves, sometimes laden with snow, as well as exterior log pillars and other architectural features, were utilised to cover up around a third of the new window elements. The Creator Expert team also raided one of its favourite sources, LEGO Belville.

ABOVE Brick-built Christmas sets like these jolly Santas had been mainstays of the product line for years.

The Toy Shop's small upper floor contained a workshop with two of the new window variants stacked on top of each other. With the large plate windows on the lower level mostly covered, these upper ones now stood out as too big. An element which was originally used as a large fireplace front on LEGO Belville sets was repurposed as a decorative arch, which partially covered the windows. In the bowels of the parts catalogue for LEGO Belville, designers also stumbled upon a part that had been created for that theme's early 2000s fantasy subtheme. Originally used as crystals to top the spires of a palace, they were the spitting image of snowflakes. One of these was recoloured in transparent yellow and placed atop a large Christmas tree in the square beside the Toy Shop. It proved to be fortuitous that this part's mould was saved from destruction as many of the sets based on the film *Frozen* have made use of it.

Winter Village Toy Shop was a hit and launched a seasonal festive theme with a new entry for the village every year. Before long, all of this success with adult-orientated products forced a logistical reckoning within the company.

Logistical challenges

With all of these experiments, the LEGO Group had been probing to find the upper limit of the adult fan market. How big was too big for a set and how many products were too many? During the early years, the LEGO Creator team had needed to be very selective, since production slots for large, adult-oriented sets were limited. Now the team began finding itself in the great but nevertheless challenging position that every time they experimented, people clamoured for more of what was meant to be a one-off. Trains, landmark buildings, vehicles, fairground rides: there simply wasn't capacity in the factories to churn out regular entries in each of these categories, especially considering how many parts each set contained. Economics of production are extremely challenging for LEGO products. Most toy-industry wares go through a two-part process within factories: manufacture and assembly. In the first, their various components are created before being put together during the second. As construction toys, LEGO bricks are, of course, manufactured, but then those parts must be sorted, counted and bagged for consumers to build. That whole process – ensuring no parts are missed throughout – is a logistical challenge of such magnitude that it is hard to comprehend, and it only gets more complex when a product's piece count grows larger.

TOP LEFT The front view of 10199 Winter Village Toy Shop clearly shows all the various ways that designers partially covered the set's windows to make them look less prominent.

TOP RIGHT The large LEGO Belville star is placed on top of the brick-built Christmas tree in the Winter Village Toy Shop set.

ABOVE From inside, it is possible to see how much of the large new window elements was covered over in 10199 Winter Village Toy Shop.

> In the LEGO Creator 3-in-1 team, we didn't do decorations on elements because we wanted the bricks to be as versatile as possible. You should be able to rebuild the pieces into anything. And that's stuck with me for quite a few years. When we were doing the first Winter Village set, we didn't even decorate the male caroler's torso – we used a pilot's torso. We only decorated the faces because we needed to show singing – which was a big discussion! So the hanging shop sign has nothing on it, you have a pilot as a caroller – we were just really clever using what we had. When we relaunched the Toy Shop several years later, we added the decorations. But the first time, the ongoing joke was that a snowstorm had blown snow all over everything, so you couldn't see the decorations!

Jamie Berard, Creative Lead, Senior Designer, the LEGO Group

ABOVE Set 10256 Taj Mahal, released in 2017, was a designer's passion project that started a LEGO Creator Expert subtheme of landmark buildings.

OPPOSITE TOP Shown here in the late 2000s, the final step of a packing line involves filled bags of elements being dropped into boxes.

OPPOSITE BOTTOM The LEGO Group factories house many production and packing lines like this one, photographed in the late 2000s.

Each bag of elements within a LEGO set must run down what is called a packing line. Along the way, sorting machines drop bricks into bags as they pass underneath. Larger sets require more machines and the logistics of sorting and bagging represent one of the most complicated aspects of bringing products to market. Each LEGO product is quantified for various factors, including moulding capacity, sorting and bagging, expected demand and more. Another factor is market tolerances: even if dragons are top-sellers, there is still a limit on the number consumers can reasonably be expected to want in a region? Furthermore, overall sales are helped when product portfolios include lots of different toys on shelves, so there are places for niche products if they are tied with certain licences or can be expected to generate outsized positive buzz. This latter trait would become especially important as social media took off – and would become the hallmark of another experiment, which got its start just as adult-oriented sets from LEGO Creator Expert were picking up steam.

Everything is Awesome 309

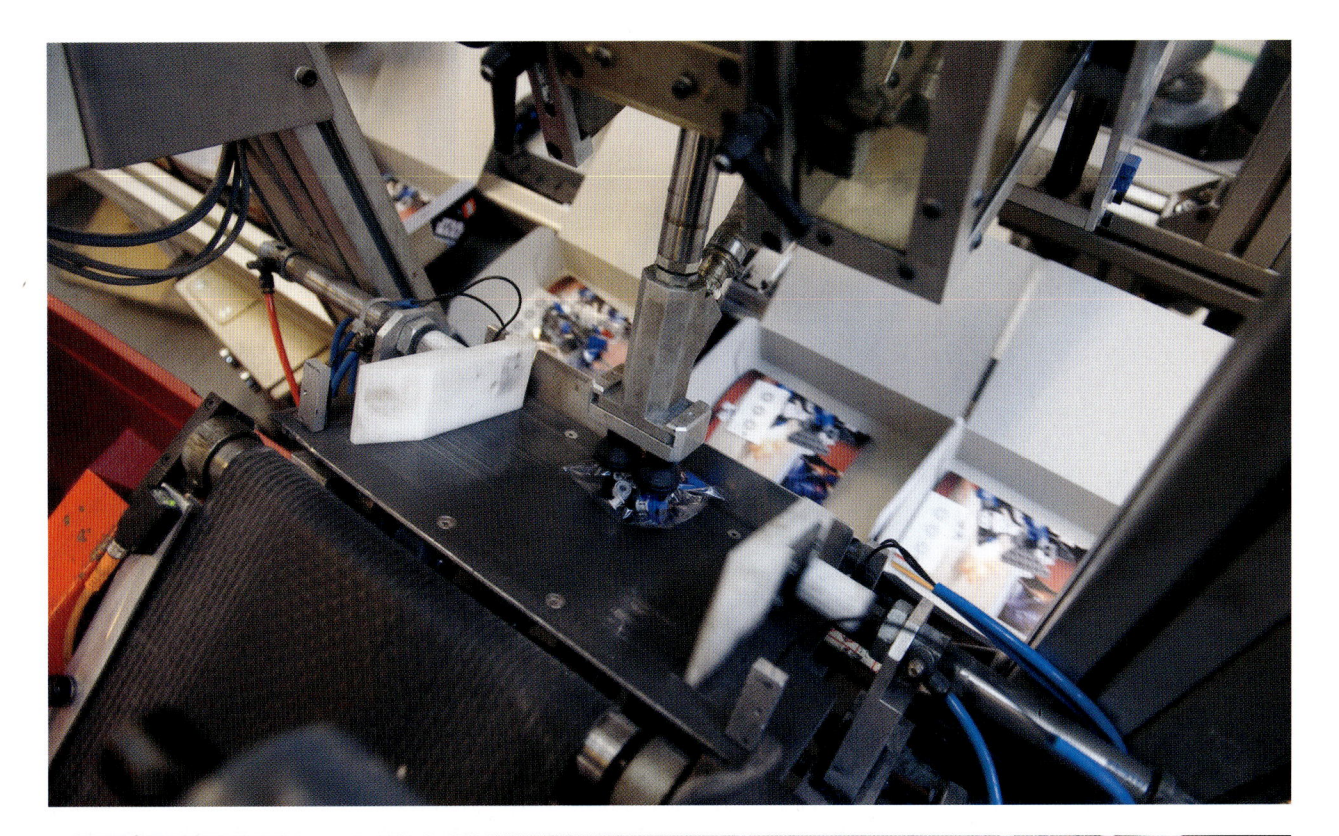

RIGHT Modular Buildings like 10224 Great Hall might require hundreds of packing machines.

New dreams

New Business Group was an internal team whose task was pretty well described by its name. Its task was to look for new opportunities and potential revenue streams for the company. During a brainstorming session, one of the team's members brought up a website he had recently become aware of, called CUUSOO. Based in Japan, its name was derived from a word in that country's language, *kuusou*, which translates as 'to imagine and wonder about something unlikely to happen or exist'. What this website did was allow people to, in a nutshell, make wishes. Ideas for anything could be uploaded and then users reacted by 'wishing' a company to turn those concepts into reality. What was intriguing to New Business Group was that several LEGO models had already been uploaded. One of those was a small submersible built by Japanese fans. Secretly, an internal initiative was launched.

New Business Group prepared a proposal for CUUSOO about a potential partnership. The group's concept was a system where, if enough users voted for an idea, the LEGO Group would turn it into reality. However, before any overtures were made, the company needed certainty that this submersible model could successfully be delivered if enough people backed it. A senior model designer was tasked with studying pictures posted on CUUSOO and seeing if he could recreate the sub, following all internal rules and guidelines. Just because this would be a special product did not exempt it from the LEGO Group high-quality standards. His prototype passed muster and contact was made.

LEFT The first LEGO® CUUSOO set was 21100 Shinkai 6500 Submarine, released in 2010.

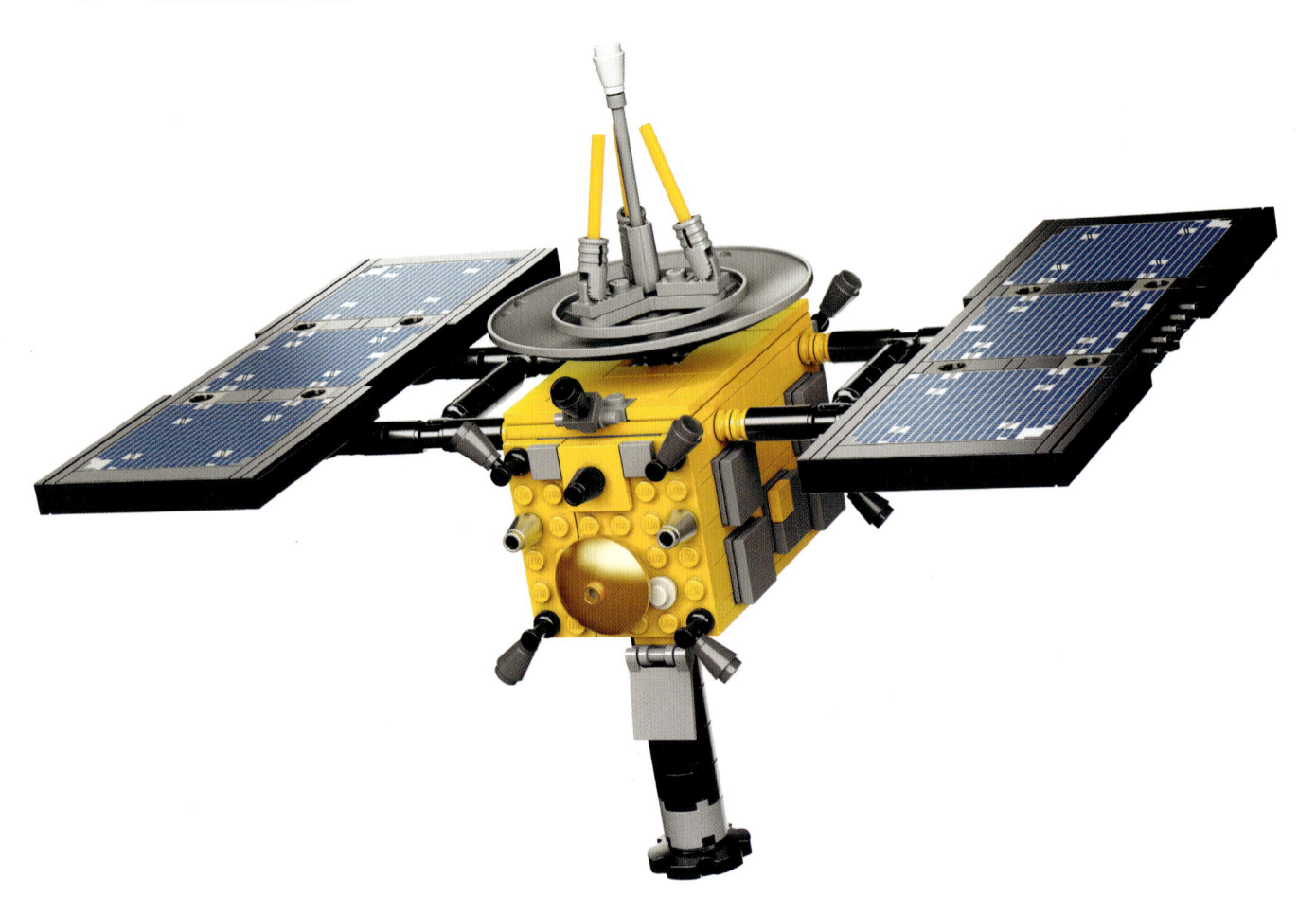

CUUSOO leapt at the opportunity to partner with the LEGO Group, and Japanese fans enthusiastically backed the submersible model when that opportunity presented itself. 21100 Shinkai 6500 Submarine was released in Japan only during 2010. It contained no special parts but was enough of a hit in that regional market to justify a second effort, which resulted in 21101 Hayabusa, which depicted a Japanese robotic spacecraft that collected samples from an asteroid. This set included a minifigure of Hayabusa's real-life project manager Junichiro Kawaguchi. While the character was exclusive to the set, all of his components were from other models, including a bespectacled face graphic from Alien Conquest which, humorously, had a second print of the character screaming in terror on its back, hidden behind a grey hair element.

After Hayabusa also succeeded, the programme was expanded beyond Japan. Eventually, in 2014, the LEGO Group ceased partnering with CUUSOO and launched its own platform called LEGO® IDEAS. On the site fans could submit their own model ideas and, if 10,000 other users voted for it, their creation would be evaluated for possible production. Evaluation looks similar in many ways to the initial effort with the submersible. Proposals which reach 10,000 votes are first evaluated internally by legal and design leads to see if they conflict with any external IPs or projects already under development. If that test is passed, a prototype model or two is built for verification that an idea can successfully be turned into a viable product. After those two tests are passed, a formal evaluation of a potential product's viability begins.

Initially, LEGO IDEAS products were made with existing elements only, but this changed as the programme grew and began to include one-off licensed products. First, it was special minifigure prints for characters from *Back to the Future* and *Ghostbusters*. Additionally, special

ABOVE The second LEGO CUUSOO set was 21101 Hayabusa, released in 2012.

elements were made for iconic props such as Doctor Who's famous Sonic Screwdriver. Despite those exceptions, unique prints on figures and elements are usually all it takes to bring an IDEAS set to life.

LEGO IDEAS sets often generate an outsized buzz. Many successful submissions tap into other interest groups for whom that first set may serve as a gateway into becoming proper LEGO fans as well. All four members of the Beatles have become minifigures, along with famous female NASA scientists, the *Flintstones*, the cast of *The Big Bang Theory*, characters from *Sesame Street* and all six main characters from *Friends*, among others. Expansive reach outside of traditional LEGO markets has been one of the greatest strengths of LEGO IDEAS, along with supplying fans with sets, characters and parts that would have remained dreams otherwise.

Between LEGO IDEAS, Winter Village, Creator Expert's expanding portfolio, and products targeted at older fans appearing in multiple other themes, the LEGO Group had built an incredible repertoire of desirable sets and successful lines by the mid 2010s when THE LEGO MOVIE hit. This proved extremely fortuitous. As untold numbers of parents were reminded of just how awesome LEGO toys are and how much they had enjoyed them as children, it encouraged them to see what the brand had to offer. While many came to buy sets for their own children, a good number were also captivated by products which appealed directly to them. By 2014, when the film was released, LEGO IDEAS and LEGO *Star Wars* especially were tapping heavily into nostalgia and had been for years. Not only was there a host of great offerings immediately available, but the aftermarket was also full of recently retired models for new fans to collect retroactively. Had the LEGO Group not invested in pursuing the adult fan market when they did and therefore not had the processes in place to manufacture big models, the company would have missed this once-in-a-generation opportunity to capture new fans. Thanks to the relentless push of LEGO Creator Expert and its passionate designers a decade earlier, the company was ready, and everything truly was awesome.

TOP IDEAS set 21110 Research Institute generated an outsized media response when it was released in 2014. After selling out almost immediately, additional copies had to be produced.

ABOVE Movie-accurate accessories, often using special prints on existing parts, are created for licensed characters, such as the *Ghostbusters* team.

Epilogue

I have been granted remarkable access to the inner workings of the LEGO Group for this book. Over six months of interviews with more than sixty past and present employees who generously took time to speak with me, I was privileged to get many insights into how the LEGO Group brings products to life. While I went into this process well aware that there would be plenty of exciting revelations, nothing prepared me for just how much I didn't know, despite having built with bricks for over thirty-five years and followed the company closely for nearly a decade. It was a privilege and an honour to be allowed a peek behind Billund's curtain.

Since beginning this process, I have been asked many times which revelation was the most surprising, or how writing this book changed my experience of the LEGO® hobby. Over time, my answers expanded and grew as I spoke with more company insiders and learned more stories. Upon reaching the end, I found that responding to such enquiries could be distilled down to three observations.

First and foremost, learning so much about the LEGO Group product-development methodology has enriched the experience of building and collecting immensely for me. Now, when assembling sets, I notice parts which must have come from platforms; marvel at how many sorting machines it must have taken to pack all those bags; look for ejector-pin marks or injection points; wonder at how complicated that dual-coloured alien head must have been to mould; count new elements to posit how many frames a theme had that year; appreciate subtle angle changes within building instruction manuals, which make them easier to comprehend; ponder which other options for sets didn't make it onto shelves; imagine which ideas might be working their way through the development funnel, and so much more. Being able to see that additional layer on top of the already enjoyable building experience has been an unexpected delight.

Second, the process by which sets reach shelves is more rigorous and comprehensive than I had ever imagined. I have now been exposed to the sheer volume of ideas that are processed on a regular basis and have seen how the few that rise to the top and make it to shelves have been extensively tested to a degree I could not have imagined. Nothing the LEGO Group does or produces happens by accident; everything is vetted, tested, refined and thought through. Popular culture is an unruly, ever-changing beast with many flash-in-the-pan trends, but the LEGO Group never loses sight of its commitment to quality and sustainable production. I deeply admire that focus on delivering the best play experience and am certain it is part of why I have loved this brand for nearly four decades.

Finally, there is the matter of ethics. In addition to talking with LEGO employees, I also interviewed a variety of personnel from companies that are licensees of the LEGO Group. Space constraints did not allow me to tell these stories but, without exception, every single one of them described the rigorous process for acquiring a licence from the LEGO Group to produce, for example, minifigure plushies or Emmet costumes. Up and down the product chain, anybody who makes anything that goes into a product with the LEGO logo on it must prove, beyond a shadow of a doubt, that their supply chain is ethical. From the stuffing going into a LEGO® NINJAGO® pillow to the paper used for the price tag on a wooden minifigure, every aspect is held to the highest standards. The LEGO Group does not brag about this practice, but I would like to laud the company here for it. I can honestly say I am even more delighted to be a fan after having written this book than I was before.

Too many people contributed to *The Secret Life of* LEGO *Bricks* for me to properly thank them all here. I will be forever grateful to the numerous designers, marketers, external partners, mould engineers, coaches and others who took time out of their busy schedules to speak with me for this book. There are, however, three folks in particular to whom I, and anyone who enjoyed *The Secret Life of* LEGO *Bricks*, owe a great debt. Simon Beecroft from AMEET was my constant companion through the process of writing, and especially editing, this book. He provided invaluable insight, guidance and encouragement through what turned out to be a much bigger process than either of us initially imagined. Randi K. Sørensen, Senior Editor at LEGO Publishing, shepherded the manuscript through the extensive vetting process at the LEGO Group, on top of setting up every single one of the more than sixty interviews. She contacted people, followed up with questions and served as the bridge between me and the LEGO Group. Without her passion for this project, *The Secret Life of* LEGO *Bricks* would never have happened. Last, but emphatically not least, is my friend Signe Wiese, one of the LEGO Group Corporate Historians. Despite her already full schedule, Signe spent countless hours researching facts for me, helping me navigate the digital archive and approving literally thousands of requests for images and information. Her and the other Corporate Historians' unsurpassed knowledge of the LEGO Group and its history were an asset, without which *The Secret Life of* LEGO *Bricks* would not have been possible. To all of these folks, as well as many others at the LEGO Group, Unbound and AMEET, I am forever grateful.

The LEGO Group has an incredible story thus far and I can't wait to read the sequel to this title thirty years from now, to learn about the amazing innovations that will happen between now and then. Thanks for reading, and play well!

A Note on Colour

Each chapter is themed with a specific, relevant LEGO® colour:

Chapter 1: Seeing the System
Bright red, used for the very first LEGO® bricks, is still widely used today.

Chapter 2: Rolling Along
Earth green is a keynote colour in the popular trains set 10194 Emerald Night.

Chapter 3: Populating the LEGO® World
Bright yellow is, of course, the colour of the minifigure face.

Chapter 4: Past, Present and Future
A variety of grey hues has helped define the LEGO® Castle play theme.

Chapter 5: Monorails and Rollercoasters
Blue is a hallmark of the classic era of LEGO® Space.

Chapter 6: Everyday Life
Bright blue is the signature colour of LEGO® City (and its precursors).

Chapter 7: Building at the Highest Level
Black is a classic LEGO® Technic colour that helped to define this advanced building system.

Chapter 8: New Worlds
The colour Brick Yellow was introduced in the era of BIONICLE® and LEGO® Star Wars™.

Chapter 9: Playing with Story
In the era of LEGO® Harry Potter™, the new colour sand green defined the turrets of Hogwarts™ Castle.

Chapter 10: Big Bangs
Bright green, widely used throughout many play themes, will always be keenly associated with LEGO® NINJAGO® – and, particularly, Lloyd, the Green Ninja.

Chapter 11: Everything is Awesome
Dark red was a brand-new colour first used on Modular Buildings in the LEGO® Creator Expert theme.

A Note on Sources

In writing *The Secret Life of* LEGO® *Bricks* I relied heavily on first-hand accounts from employees, both past and present, of the LEGO Group. The company gave me remarkable access to its personnel, who graciously granted me more than sixty interviews over a six-month period. This included:

Tim Ainley
Henrik Andersen
Steen Sig Andersen
Tommy Andreasen
Jamie Berard
Connie Bork
Alexandre Boudon
Adam Corbally
Rosario Costa
Henk van der Does
Steffen Duus
Christian Faber
Allan James Faulkner
Jan Hatting
Henriette S. Jensen
Markus Kossmann
Jens Kronvold
Olav Krøigaard
Erik Legernes
Rasmus Buck Løgstrup
Bjarke Lykke Madsen
Tore Magelund Harmark-Alexandersen
Yoel Mazur
Philip J. McCormick

Kenneth Melbye Wedel
Carsten Michaelsen
Sine Klitgaard Møller
Jesper C. Nielsen
Klaus Elias Nielsen
Jette Orduna
Kim Pagel
Niels Milan Pedersen
Helle Rasmussen
Holger Roslev
Jan Ryaa
Henrik Rubin Saaby
Gabriel Sas
Ronny Scherer
Morten Skrydstrup
Daniel Sri Sudarsono
Scott Selkirk Neillands
Jørn Kristian Thomsen
Bjarne Tveskov
Signe Weise
Tara Wike
Andrew Woodman

Thanks too to the following LEGO licensees interviewed:

Shenandoah Bauer
Anna Kathryn Chase
Jacob Eberhard
Esmeralda Gonzales
Jennifer Gracia

Whithney Hatfield
Ketty S. Nielsen
Tina F. Pedersen
Erica Roberts
Katrine Vinther Troelsen

Acknowledgements

Thanks to the following people at the LEGO Group for their support for the project:

Ana Albouy
Yun Mi Antorini
Tormod Askildsen
Søren Borup
Antica Bracanov
Camilla Broström
Mel Caddick
Johnny Castrup
Sanne Dollerup
Pieter Hannes Lammens
Paul Hansford
Stuart Harris
Hasan Jensen
Karina Møller Juhl
Rok Zgalin Kobe

Nina Koopmann
LEGO AFOL Engagement
Martin Leighton Lindhardt
Jacob McQuillan
Hanne Mørk Hede
Jordan Paxton
Robin James Pearson
Christopher Terrance Perron
Laura Perron
Mike Psiaki
Justin Ramsden
Randi K. Sørensen
LEGO Corporate Communications
Jme Wheeler

Special thanks to the AFOL advisory panel:

Andrew Barnick
William Bonhomme
AnneMarie Brown
Andrew Bulthaupt
Ben Davies
Suzanne Eaton
David Fennell
Alice Finch
Lluis Gibert
Tim Johnson
Tuomas Kukkonen
Emma Park
Francesco Spreafico
Bostjan Svetlicic

Index

'AFC promise', 173
AFOLs (Adult Fans of LEGO), 46-8, 51
Airport Shuttle, 124-5, 127
Ancient Serpenteen Tribes, 276
Andersen, Henrik, 26, 33, 158, 198, 212
Andersen, Steen Sig, 289-91, 304
Andreasen, Tommy, 271
Animal Building System Platform, 234
Aquabase Invasion, 242-3
Aquanauts, 240
Arctic Rescue Unit, 178
Ashton, Matthew, 67
Asterix the Gaul, 95, 254
axles, 30-2, 170-5, 179-80, 186, 234

Bach, Eric, 172-3, 175-6, 197
Back to the Future, 312
Backhoe Grader, 179
ball joints, 201-2, 208, 214-5, 225, 252, 261, 266
Band Booster, 240
Barcode Multi-set, 184
Baron von Baron, 113
'bars', 64
baseplates, 12, 89, 100-2, 126, 291, 302-4
    road baseplates, 134, 140-2, 144-5, 147, 154
    3D baseplates, 107, 109
Beecroft, Simon, 1, 315
Berard, Jamie, 50, 128, 284, 290-2, 300, 307
'big bang', 268-9, 277, 282-3
Big Bang Theory, The, 313
Big Race Day, 131
bill of materials (BOM) lists, 249
Black Monarch's Castle, 103, 106
Black Seas Barracuda, 102
Blacktron, 107, 240
blasters, 218
Blaze Brigade, 153

Boneheads of Voodoo Island, 208, 214
brick proportions, 14, 17
Bucket Wheel Excavator, 197
Bugatti Chiron, 197
Building Bonanza, 287-8, 290
Building Crane, 162-3
Building Instruction teams, 249

Cactus Girl, 70
Café Corner, 291-2, 294-7
Camouflaged Outpost, 106
Captain Redbeard, 99
Car Chassis, 175
cars, early, 32-3
Central Precinct HQ, 151
Chamber of Secrets, 229
'cheese slope', 191, 286, 297
Children's Bedroom, 61
Christiansen, Godtfred Kirk, 7-12, 14, 16-19, 21-2, 24-5, 32-4, 64
Christmas sets, 305
Circus Clown, 68
City Corner, 160
City Harbour, 164
CLAAS XERION 5000 TRAC VC, 193
'clutch power', 14, 16, 22, 24-5, 64, 233, 294
colour palette, 270, 272-3, 316
computer-aided design, 131, 173
connector pairs, 24-5
Construction, 186, 190, 205, 208, 214-15, 219, 223-5, 235, 261, 266
Control Centre II, 181
Corbally, Adam, 220, 231
Costa, Rosario, 58, 81
Cowboy, 68
Creative Play Lab (CPL), 245
cross blocks, 180, 188
Curved Gear Rack, 197
Cyber Strikers, 208

Cybots, 201-2

Detective's Office, 299
Dideriksen, Erling, 124, 127, 137-9, 154, 180
Diesel Freight Train, 44
Disney World EPCOT Center, 118-19
Doctor Who, 313
Dolls Kitchen, 61
Dune Blaster, 181

Easy Builder System (EBT), 49, 51, 53
Eiffel Tower, 47
El Dorado Fortress, 101
Electronic Train, 37
element coaches, 21-5, 48, 51, 249
Element Committee, 20-2
element library, 19, 49, 51, 217
Emerald Night, 28, 52-3
Erling bricks, 134, 138-40
ethics, 315
Europa, 96, 98, 103
Exxon Gas Station, 144

Faber, Christian, 201-3, 214
Face Clinger, 261
Fairground Mixer, 303-4
Fantasy Era, 113
Ferris Wheel, 301
Fire Breathing Fortress, 109
Fire Station, 144-5
Fire Temple, 262-3
Fire Truck, 157, 159
Flatfoot Thomsen, 110, 112
Flintstones, 313
flyers, 276-8
Forestmen, 107, 109
formal federations, 107
Formula 1, 172
Fort Legoredo, 110-11, 240

4×4 Off-Roader, 187, 217
'frames', 34
Frederiksen, Jens Kronvold, 300
Freight Steam Train, 44
friction snaps, 176
Friends, 313
Front End, 244–5, 253, 258, 261, 263–4, 277, 279
Frozen, 306
Futuron, 107, 120, 127

Galidor, 204–5, 215
Gas N' Wash Express, 149
gearboxes, 194–6
gears, 117, 168, 170–5, 179, 215, 271
Genesis, 203–5, 215
Ghostbusters, 312–13
Giant Trolls, 239
Giant Truck, 210
Grand Carousel, 302–5
Great Hall, 310
Green Grocer, 297
guns, 99

hairpieces, 233
Harmark-Alexandersen, Tore Magelund, 273
Hatting, Jan, 23
Hazmat Guy, 71
headlights, 134, 137–8, 154, 180, 191
Heim, Robert, 128
High Speed Passenger Train, 48, 57
hinges, 34, 63–4, 66–7, 88, 91, 135–6, 154, 157, 159, 200, 204, 209, 212, 216, 222, 224–5, 227, 232, 234–5
Hobby Sets, 137, 172, 176
Hogwarts Castle, 222, 226–7
Hogwarts Express, 46–7, 227–8
Homemaker, 61–2, 65–7, 76, 78
horses, 92, 94–5

Hot Dog Man, 70

'illegal connections', 25
Inter-City Passenger Train, 40

Johnny Thunder, 113, 254
jousting, 88–9, 91
jumper plates, 66, 293–4
Jurassic Park, 234

King Solomon's Mines, 110
King's Castle, 95
Knight's Joust, 91
'knobs', 12
Knudsen, Jens Nygaard, 66, 73, 75, 82–3, 91–2, 95, 110, 118–20, 124, 127
Krentz, Daniel August, 88–9, 91–2, 95, 110
Kristiansen, Kjeld Kirk, 32–3, 85, 87, 113, 173, 185
Kristiansen, Ole Kirk, 2, 9, 135
Krøigaard, Olav, 188

lamppost, ornate, 295
Lasgaard, Christian, 30
Launch and Load Seaport, 149–50
Legernes, Erik, 276
LEGO Adventurers, 110–11, 113, 156, 254
LEGO Alien Conquest, 244–7, 254, 260–1, 312
LEGO Alpha Team, 80, 258, 261
LEGO Aqua Raiders, 202, 239, 242–3, 254–5, 288
LEGO Aquazone, 3, 63, 213, 238, 240
LEGO Arctic Action, 177
LEGO Atlantis, 252, 254–7, 260, 268–9
LEGO *Avatar*, 229–30
LEGO Basic, 74, 287, 295
LEGO Batman, 229–30, 232, 258, 283
LEGO Belville, 77–9, 81, 83, 190, 222, 226–7, 295, 305–6

LEGO BIONICLE, 185–7, 189–91, 199–201, 204–5, 214–15, 219, 223–4, 232, 234–5, 238–9, 249, 253, 258, 268
LEGO Castle, 21, 40, 45, 76–7, 89–92, 95–100, 103, 106–11, 113, 117–18, 142, 144, 153–4, 162, 165, 177, 209, 223–4, 226–7, 234, 236, 238–41, 253–4, 261, 295
LEGO Cinematic Universe, 285
LEGO City, 47–8, 51, 54, 57, 71, 132, 135, 154, 157–65, 219, 260–1, 270, 290, 292, 305
LEGO Creator, 287–9, 290, 294–7, 306
LEGO Creator Expert, 52–4, 57, 131, 281, 284, 296–9, 301–2, 305, 308, 313
LEGO Creator 3-in-1, 289, 291, 301, 307
LEGO CUUSOO, 311–12
LEGO DC Universe Super Heroes, 219
LEGO Designer, 287
LEGO Dino 2010, 234–5, 238, 255
LEGO Disney Princess, 270
LEGO Divers, 154, 156
'LEGO DNA', 215
LEGO Dragon Masters, 108–9
LEGO DUPLO, 74, 78
LEGO Education, 53
LEGO Elves, 82
LEGO Exo-Force, 202, 222, 232–4, 238, 253, 277, 288
LEGO Exploriens, 202
LEGO Extreme Team, 156, 164
LEGO Fabuland, 74, 79
LEGO Family, 65
LEGO Fantastic Beasts, 261
LEGO Farm, 165
LEGO 4+, 156, 160
LEGO FreeStyle, 287–8, 295
LEGO Friends, 59, 79, 81–3, 131, 270
LEGO Futura, 7, 20, 202
LEGO Galaxy Squad, 260

Index | 325

LEGO Harry Potter, 46-7, 113, 222, 226-9, 232, 234, 236, 238-9
LEGO Hero Factory, 219
LEGO Hidden Side, 283
LEGO Ice Planet, 177, 295
LEGO IDEAS, 312-13
LEGO Indiana Jones, 113, 229-30, 240
LEGO Jack Stone, 156
LEGO Juniors, 160
LEGO Knights' Kingdom, 80, 222-6, 232, 234, 238
LEGO Legends of Chima, 193, 218-19, 263, 266, 270, 272-9
LEGO Life on Mars, 232
LEGO Mars Mission, 239
LEGO MINDSTORMS, 46, 181, 185-7, 189
LEGO Minifigures, 59, 67-71, 73, 75-6
LEGO Model Team, 46, 190, 211, 213
LEGO Monkie Kid, 283
LEGO MOVIE, THE, 113, 149, 152, 212, 282-3, 313
LEGO Nautica, 148-51, 154
LEGO NEXO KNIGHTS, 280-3
LEGO NINJAGO, 165, 235, 252, 255, 258-71, 274-80, 282-3, 288, 315
LEGO Paradisa, 78-9
LEGO Pharaoh's Quest, 113
LEGO Pirates, 96-103, 106-9, 113, 153, 223, 238, 295
LEGO Power Miners, 71, 202, 244-6, 248-9, 253-4
LEGO Rock Raiders, 202, 239
LEGO Scala, 78-80, 83, 226
LEGO Space, 21, 40, 45, 76-7, 79, 89-91, 95-6, 107, 117-22, 124, 127, 129-30, 135, 142-3, 153-4, 177, 180, 202, 207, 209, 213, 223, 232, 238, 240, 244, 246, 249, 260, 295
LEGO Space Police, 107, 244-5, 247, 249, 253

LEGO SpongeBob SquarePants, 229-30, 232, 240
LEGO Sports, 67
LEGO Star Wars, 47, 67, 127, 140, 157, 165, 170, 199-201, 205-9, 211-19, 225-6, 232, 239, 261, 278, 297, 300, 313
LEGO Super Heroes, 231, 239
LEGO System in Play, 6, 8, 10-11, 14, 34, 46, 87, 137, 140
LEGO Technic, 7, 17, 21, 40, 45-6, 48, 74, 76-9, 88, 108, 138, 166-97, 203-4, 208, 211, 213, 215, 217, 225, 234, 240, 301
LEGO The Hobbit, 71
LEGO The Lord of the Rings, 94
LEGO Town, 10, 21, 45, 48, 76, 78, 89, 91, 95, 117-18, 124-7, 130, 133-45, 147-9, 151, 153-7, 160-2, 177, 180, 216, 223, 240, 276, 292
LEGO Train, 29, 34, 36-7, 40, 44-6, 172, 213
LEGO UFO, 207, 209
LEGO Unitron, 129
LEGO Vikings, 88, 234-40, 261
LEGO Western, 95, 98, 103, 109-13, 240
LEGO Winter Village, 57, 305-7, 313
LEGO World City, 48, 135, 157-9
LEGOLAND Town, see LEGO Town
lightsabers, 17, 205, 207
Lion Knights, 240
Lion Leader Laval, 272
Lone Ranger, 113
Lord Business, 283
Lord Vladek, 224-5
Lord Voldemort, 229
Lunar Lander, 87

McCormick, Philip, 250, 259
Madsen, Bjarke Lykke, 236
Maersk Train, 54-5
'marbled products', 12
Market Street, 144

Masks of Creation, 215
Mercedes-Benz Unimog 400, 192
Metroliner, 45
Michaelsen, Carsten, 20
Millennium Falcon, 129, 201, 207, 215-17, 297-301
minifigures, 37, 40, 59-83, 154, 173
    faceprints, 83, 99, 254
    hands, 17, 32, 63, 65, 74-5, 82
Mobile Crane, 189
Model Committee, 249
Modular Buildings, 47, 57, 207, 286, 291, 294-5, 297, 299, 302, 305, 310
'modules', 14
Møller, Knud, 31-2, 170
monkeys, 108
Monorail Transport Base, 120, 129
Monorail Transport System, 118-19, 126, 130
monorails, 115-20, 122, 124-7, 129-30
Moon Base Project, 290
Motorbike with Sidecar, 177
mould maintenance, 293
'moulded facial features', 66
My Own Train, 46

Naboo Fighter, 218
Napoleonic Wars, 95
NASA, 313
National Basketball Association (NBA), 67
Native American tepees, 102
Native Americans, 111, 113
New Business Group, 311
Nick Bluetooth, 204
Nielsen, Klaus Elias, 267
Nindroids, 263
Nuremberg Toy Fair (1962), 33

Octan, 149, 152, 154, 162
Orduna, Jetta, 4, 11, 16

Original LEGO Brick Patent, 2–3

packing lines, 308–10
Pagel, Kim, 146, 152
Papert, Seymour, 185
Passenger Train, 51
patents, 2–3, 17–19
Pedersen, Niels Milan, 84, 90–2, 94–5, 110
Petersen, Troels, 9, 14
pirates, 95, 98–102
Placement tool, 270
plastic injection, 14, 18, 292–3
Platform Team, 123
'platforms', 122, 124
playing cards, 269
playmats, 10, 12
Pneumatic Crane, 136
Police Car, 136
Porsche GT3 RS, 193–6
Power Crane, 179
Power Functions, 48, 51–3, 301–3
Professor Quirrell, 229

rack winder, 122
Research Institute, 313
Res-Q, 156, 164
'Robin Hood hat', 106
Robotic Control System (RCX), 185–7
Rock Monsters, 71, 246
Roller Coaster, 130, 304
rollercoasters, 116, 129–31
Romans, 95, 98, 240
Ryaa, Jan, 7, 40, 42–3, 166, 172–6, 197

Saaby, Henrik Rubin, 228
'salt pillars', 66–7, 73–5, 83, 135, 141
Sam Sinister, 113
Santa Fe Super Chief, 47–8, 56
Seatron, 209, 240

'sections', 14
Service Station, 162
Sesame Street, 313
shields, 280–1
Shinkai 6500 Submarine, 311–12
ship sails, 102
ships, 29–30, 87
Siege Tower, 96–7
Simpsons, The, 229–30
Slizer/Throwbot robots, 202–3
Sopwith Camel, 47
Sørensen, Randi K., 2, 315
Space Miners, 240
Space Shuttle, 182–4
Speed Racer, 229
Speedorz, 274–5, 278
'spinjitzu', 269
spinners, 252, 266–9, 271, 274–5, 277–8
Squid Warrior, 255
Statue of Liberty, 47
Steam Engine with Tender, 41
'studs not on top' (SNOT), 139
submarines, 95, 311–12
Super Car, 181
Super Street Sensation, 185

Taj Mahal, 47, 308
Tarzan, 110
Technical Sets, 176
Teenage Mutant Ninja Turtles, 254
Thomsen, Axel, 14, 16–17, 25
Thomsen, Jørn, 56, 112
TIE fighters, 211, 213, 215–16
Toa, 214, 224
Tow Truck, 190–1
Town Plan, 10, 12–14, 29, 34, 37, 40, 65, 87, 133–5, 140–2, 147–8
Town Square, 143
trains, 26–9, 34–58

trees, early, 13
T-Rex, 234
Troll warrior, 241
Tveskov, Bjarne, 19, 114, 121
tyres, 32, 194

Ultimate Concept, 193–5, 197
USS *Constitution*, 137

van der Does, Henk, 132
Verne, Jules, 95, 240
video games, 151
Viking helmets, 237–8
Visorak, 219
Vladek Encounter, 224
Volvo, 193

Wabra, Uwe, 193
Warhammer, 215, 279–80
wheels, 27–32, 194
Wiese, Signe, 1, 315
Wike, Tara, 70
Wild West diorama, 241
windows and doors, 12, 42, 48, 291–2
Winter Village Market, 57
Winter Village Toy Shop, 305–6
Wolfpack, 107, 109
Woodman, Andrew, 193, 195–6
Wright Flyer, 47

'X-factors', 269, 274, 276, 278, 280, 283
X-wing fighters, 211–13, 216

Yellow Castle, 91
Yoda, 217, 297

A Note on the Author

DANIEL KONSTANSKI is the US Editor for *Blocks* magazine and a passionate, lifelong LEGO fan who has researched and written hundreds of articles covering every aspect of the hobby. Daniel has been privileged to tell many stories from within the LEGO Group itself and is considered one of the most knowledgeable and authoritative voices in the fan community on the company and its products.

When he is not tinkering on his latest LEGO project, Daniel works as an environmental engineer and enjoys hiking, rock climbing and bike riding with his wonderful wife and three children on the trails near their home in Delaware, USA. He is a regular on the East Coast LEGO fan convention circuit.